Magic Apples

Reflections to Mull

To Diana

ENJOY!

Lee Steels

November 2011

First published by Dog Ear Publishing
4010 W. 86th Street, Ste H
Indianapolis, IN 46268
www.dogearpublishing.net

ISBN: 978-145750-727-4

This book is printed on acid-free paper.

Printed in the United States of America

Introduction

Why another book of daily reflections when there are plenty already available?

A day spent without the sight or sound of beauty, the contemplation of mystery, or the search of truth or perfection is a poverty-stricken day; and a succession of such days is fatal to human life.

Lewis Mumford

The genesis of *Magic Apples* resulted from a short course in Christianity called Cursillo. I did my Cursillo in 1995 at the table of Saint Nicholas.

Cursillos in Christianity (in Spanish: Cursillos de Cristiandad, short course of Christianity) is a ministry of the Roman Catholic Church. It was founded in Majorca, Spain by a group of laymen in 1944, while they were refining a technique to train pilgrimage leaders.

Cursillo has since been licensed by several mainline Christian denominations, some of which have retained the trademarked "Cursillo" name while others have modified its talks/methods and given it a different name.

The Cursillo focuses on showing Christian lay people how to become effective leaders over the course of a three-day weekend. The weekend includes fifteen talks, some given by priests and some by lay people. The major emphasis of the weekend is to ask participants to take what they have learned back into the world, on what they call the "fourth day".

Wikipedia

Cursillo participants are expected to read as a part of their fourth day. I began to read books about religion including daily readers. Many of these were conservative and lacked a modern stance. It wasn't until I read books by Karen Armstrong, Marcus Borg, and other liberal thinkers, that I saw the need for a daily reader with a broader approach. Not being able to find one I liked, I thought I would have a go at writing one myself. Little did I know it would take 15 years and undergo multiple morphs. Here it is at last, and I hope you find daily mulling a useful, enjoyable and enlightening experience.

Why *Magic Apples?*

Surely the apple is the noblest of fruits.

Henry David Thoreau

Many artists depict the "tree of life" in the Garden of Eden as an apple tree. Since the apple has always been thought to bestow favors on the lucky recipient, it makes good sense that the forbidden fruit would be an apple, even if the Bible doesn't specify what fruit the serpent convinced Eve to eat. Not only does "an apple a day keep the doctor away" but in Wagner's opera *Das Reingold*, the goddess Freia keeps her fellow Gods in eternal youth by giving them golden apples. Just as the body can be kept youthful by daily munching on medicinal fruit, the mind can be renewed by fruitful new thoughts. Mulling new ideas is always beneficial and re-mulling old ones certainly can't hurt. Even a response of "Oh ya … I've heard that old one before" can still produce those magical endorphins—if you let it. Just beginning the day with a focusing thought or chuckle can be one of the most useful strategies to help us lighten up. I hope these daily *Magic Apples* help in some small way to lighten your day and keep you mulling both old and new thoughts.

PS If you need something light or silly, read day 6, 12, 18, 24 or 30 of each month. Every 6th day has been made extra-light, kind of a "Silly Saturday" each week.

Acknowledgements

God gives the nuts, but he doesn't crack them.

German proverb

Many kind folks have helped me in this project. Morning e-mails of the reflections were mulled by a host of friends who returned comments and encouragement. I thank the following ref-readers for their daily devotion and assistance in field-testing the reflections:

Peggy-Ann Budd, Terry and Winnie Burk, Dale Chisholm, Jean Finks, Bob and Gloria Gardner, Jeffrey Heath, Pat Holloway, Mike Lonsdale, Ann Mulvale, Annemarie Quinn and Celia Steels. There are countless others who received apple blossoms in e-mails now and then. There isn't room here for all of you—thanks for your patience and tolerance.

Special thanks to Jeffrey Heath and Mike Lonsdale for their story contributions.

This first American edition owes its existence to the wisdom of a wonderful fellow chorister. It was Jean Finks who suggested that a broader audience would appreciate having these reflections. Thanks Jean for your early editing and your timely suggestion.

The most profuse thanks go to my editor, Annemarie Quinn. Your thorough mulling and gentle correcting are indeed a labor of love, without which this project would never have been completed. For all your hard work and infinite patience, I am truly grateful.

January 1

Focus Thought

Though no one can go back and make a brand new start, anyone can start from now and make a brand new ending.

Carl Bard

It's time to start living the life you've imagined.

Henry James

Start living now. Stop saving the good china for that special occasion. Stop withholding your love until that special person materializes. Every day you are alive is a special occasion. Every minute, every breath, is a gift from God.

Mary Morrissey

Here we are at the yearly watershed of New Year resolutions. Pessimists decide what's wrong with their lives and make vows to break bad habits. Optimists feel good about their lives and make long lists about what they can make even better. Idealists make new plans to save the planet. Workaholics vow to become more efficient. Realists know from past experience that their long lists just get broken, so they spend the day watching football and having one last fling at the food. Why do we do this to ourselves on the first of January every year? Is there a better strategy? The answer is "yes," and you are making a beginning at that better way at this very moment!

Begin each day with some focusing thought, and direct your actions around this central thought. Live the day as if it were January the first—as if it were a new beginning, with renewed energy and opportunity. Live the best possible day you can. Setbacks are temporary. Negative thoughts can be turned around to positive thoughts. Forget all those past hurts, wrongs, and sins. Today is a new day and a new chance to savor art and nature, human relationships, and food—as if they were all going to disappear tomorrow. Tomorrow is a desert island, where today's moments are but fleeting memories. A snowflake disappears while we decide what to do with it.

Once you can savor each day, you can do the same with the hours, minutes, and seconds. Time will stretch out as each moment surrounds and nurtures your spirit. May you seek all your days to follow this pattern—but remember to begin each and every day with some guiding light, and keep that light guiding you throughout your day. Happy New Day—every Day!

Cheer Yourself Up

The best way to cheer yourself up is to try and cheer somebody else up.

Mark Twain

I love the story that came in an e-mail last year. It told of two men in a hospital room. The fellow near the door couldn't see out the window, and he would ask the man in the bed by the window what was happening outside. This man near the window kept up a description of what he could see. Outside their room, it seemed, there were many wonders—like a park with people playing and walking their dogs. One day a parade went by, and the fellow gave a detailed description of the floats. Another day was a field day in the park, and everyone was having such a good time. Then one morning, a terrible thing happened. The man near the window died during the night, and the staff came and removed him. The man near the door was very sad at losing his new friend, but he asked if he could be moved to the window bed. He was moved, but when he looked out the window, all he saw was a brick wall. He told his nurse that this was a shock, since the man who had died had told of many wonders outside this very window. The nurse said that the gentleman in the window bed had actually been blind, and that he was also aware that he was going to die at any time. "I wonder why he told me all these wonders if he knew that?" the disappointed man said.

The nurse thought for a moment and said, "I suspect that he just wanted to cheer you up." This rare person who knew his days were numbered spent the remainder of them cheering up others.

I now understand the passing, several years ago, of a wonderful man in our church. When I went to see Jack in the hospital, he told me the doctors had given him between two and five days to live. Jack also said that he had set up a lottery, and how many hours did I think he would last? Then he laughed. I was shocked. I asked him how he could do this, and Jack told me to lighten up and get in the game—so I did. He died three days later. I don't know who won his lottery, but I know the proceeds went to a good cause. I couldn't believe someone would treat their imminent death with this sense of lightness. Now I understand. Jack was cheering us up and telling us that he wasn't afraid to die. What a way to go!

January 3

Shine On

Shine on you crazy diamond.

Pink Floyd

The most pleasant and useful persons are those who leave the problems of the universe for God to worry about.

Don Marquis

When I was about fifteen, I attended a conference for church youth leaders. Philip Cooper, a man in his early twenties, spoke to us on the first night; shining about him was an aura. I didn't mention this to anyone, in case they'd think I was crazy. I have been very fortunate to be associated in many ways with this man whose light shone so bright. Phil became my mentor, my good friend and eventually, my brother-in-law. Anybody that good had to have a little sister and he sure did! I married his little sister, and we have enjoyed over forty years together.

Many people we meet can change our lives, but the whole trick is to be receptive. It just isn't blind luck reaching out to elevate us. We have to be prepared to listen to people who are so obviously making a difference in the world. Such people are rare gems—shining on and lighting up lives.

Such people turn up at the most unexpected times and places. Paul Potts, a laborer in England, entered a British talent show. He had always wanted to sing opera, but he looked as if he should be sweeping up after the show instead of singing in it. You could tell from the looks of the audience and judges that they had already dismissed him before he began. Then Paul opened his mouth, and out came the sweetest tenor voice. All the faces were transformed as Paul's performance simply shone down upon them. Paul won that talent show and has recorded several CD's.

Be open enough to hear the light when it comes. I use the word "hear," because that's how light often comes to us; we must be listening for it. It is a rare thing when we see an aura, but it's common for gems to be given to us through the word—and they come to us every day. We have to be listening.

> *Jesus bids us shine with a clear, pure light,*
> *Like a little candle burning in the night;*
> *In this world of darkness, we must shine,*
> *You in your small corner, and I in mine.*

Susan B. Warner, 1868

January 4

Procrastination

My advice is, never do tomorrow what you can do today. Procrastination is the thief of time. Collar him!

Charles Dickens

Procrastination is Satan's sharpest, finest tool. Why procrastinate when tomorrow is so uncertain? Reader, take warning … don't delay!

Ted Stubbs

Procrastination is the thief of time.

Edward Young

I recall my father, Allen, saying with great emphasis, "Procrastination is the thief of time." I didn't know what the hell it meant—I thought it had something to do with sex. Fast forward ten years to my early twenties and I had so much to get done, there was no time to procrastinate. You had to GO, GO, GO, full out, to survive. I'm not sure if the famous quote belongs to Charles Dickens or Edward Young. Who cares? The idea of putting things off has always held a certain fascination with everyone. It's only human to diddle when action is the rallying cry. After all, things done in haste often make waste! Slow and steady is the lesson from everyone's favorite fable—Aesop's *The Tortoise and the Hare*. My father obviously had never heard of this tale. Al either was frantically performing several tasks, or he was completely morose—there was no happy medium. It was all or nothing.

When our son Craig was little, he loved to diddle when he had school work to do. He would often read a book when he was supposed to be getting school work done. I would set a timer and tell Craig that he had to get his assignments done before he could read his fantasy books. It worked. Recently, Craig went with me to visit his uncle Judd. When we returned, he told me a problem set was due the next day. Craig pulled an all-nighter, but the problems were submitted before the deadline.

Procrastination is my sin.
It brings me naught but sorrow.
I know that I should stop it.
In fact, I will … tomorrow!

Gloria Pitzer

January 5

Reflection

Reflection noun
1.   something, such as an image, that is reflected
       The dog barked at his own reflection in the mirror.
2.   careful thought or consideration
       After careful reflection, I have decided not to vote for that proposition.
3.   an implied criticism
       It is a reflection on his character that he never wavered in his resolve.

When will my reflections show … who I am inside?

Christina Aguilera

In computer science, reflection is the process by which a computer program can observe and modify its own structure and behavior.

Wiki

One of mother's favorite words was "introspection." Fran would say, "It's important to do some introspection now and then." As the baby of the family, I would nod my head, along with my siblings, all the while having no idea what she meant. Finally, I read an article in the *Reader's Digest* explaining how important it is to look at one's self to make any progress. This self-examination was called introspection and the light bulb upstairs finally lit up—what Fran meant by introspection or self-reflection.

Reflection about oneself is a difficult process. How can you be truly critical of yourself? After all, for most of us, we are our favorite person. We should love ourselves, shouldn't we? Of course we should—and we also should not be too hard on ourselves. How do we set aside our ego to obtain any useful information about ourselves—really good stuff that could allow us to make changes—and become a better person? The article suggested writing down ten words that best described us, showing these words to a friend, and asking if they were an accurate description. If you have a delicate disposition, this process may just be a good way to lose a friend. A better process might be to take an accounting of where you are, where you would like to be, and make a plan to get there. Goal-setting is something most of us do every day. There's no reason it won't work for self-improvement.

One objective of these daily apples is to inspire introspection or self-reflection—and allow us to laugh at ourselves in the process. Happy reflecting!

January 6

The Abuse of Tools

You only need two tools in life … WD-40 and Duct Tape. If it doesn't move and should, use the WD-40. If it shouldn't move and does, use the duct tape.

Red-Green T.V. Show

The expectations of life depend upon diligence; the mechanic that would perfect his work must first sharpen his tools.

Confucius

My father had the greatest tool collection in our neighborhood. Folks would borrow tools and then forget to bring them back. That wasn't a problem. Dad just bought better ones. At one time, we owned two motorized cement-mixers and no less than five half-horsepower motors. We also had the most unique tool bench in history. It was made from a grand piano, from which all the guts had been removed. At one end was a very fancy table saw, and the tools hung handily at the other end. How it came into being is another story. Dad also loved good music, and I often wondered why he didn't incorporate his HiFi into that tool bench. After all, it was originally meant for music.

I learned to use the hammer at an early age. There were two large round telephone poles with a high crossbar at the end of our yard, from which were suspended the longest swings a kid could ever hope for. These were con-structed so well, adults could swing without fear. I imagine Fat Albert would have been no problem for those swings. Getting back to hammering, dad would give me a little pail of nails and tell me to go down and hammer them into those telephone posts. There was a technique to hammering—a wrist action that eventually developed into a power stroke—which could drive a nail into that post with one blow. All male family members learned how to wield hammers, axes, and sledge hammers with great accuracy and power. All of us abused this skill. We would often need to work together and hold larger nails and stakes for each other, and you can guess what would happen. There would be a poorly-placed stroke and a finger or thumb would be hit, resulting in an unbelievable torrent of oaths. It didn't stop there. We had long memories, and payback would eventually be gladly given. Few were the days when one of us didn't have a black finger in this terrible abuse of the family tools.

Much time has passed since we asked the question, "Will you hold this for me, please?"—and we have all forgiven this silly abuse of tools.

January 7

Rings

Nearly all men can stand adversity, but if you want to test a man's character, give him power.

Abraham Lincoln

The weirder you're going to behave, the more normal you should look. It works in reverse, too. When I see a kid with three or four rings in his nose, I know there is absolutely nothing extraordinary about that person.

P.J.O'Rourke

Most of us have at least one ring worn on a finger. (Some modern folks have plenty of rings worn on other body parts, but we needn't get into those.) Rings can represent affection, affiliation and accomplishment. Rings can be a symbol of power, and the huge Super Bowl ring is one such ring. A university or college ring represents power of a different sort — the power of wisdom. Rings in themselves really have little power—or do they?

There are two epic works about rings of power. *The Lord of the Rings* by J. R. R. Tolkien was published in three volumes, as a sequel to *The Hobbit*. This fantasy has become one of the most popular works of twentieth-century literature and was made into a spectacular movie trilogy by Peter Jackson. Somewhat less well known is a nineteenth-century story about the power of a ring. *Der Ring des Nibelungen* is a cycle of four operas by Richard Wagner. Wagner's Ring Cycle has a smaller fan base, but every time these four operas are presented, they are sold out. Why are these fantasies about rings so popular?

These two stories contain all the foibles of human existence: greed, lust, and especially the age-old struggle for power. The ultimate end of both stories is redemption. The good go to a higher place, and the bad are burned up. It's a familiar plot. So why are we so wrapped up in these yarns? I suppose it's in the telling—all the little stories within the main tale. They are a metaphor for our existence. We are born. We live. We die. The story of "Life" would be a drag for sure, if it weren't for all the adventures that complicate and seem to sidetrack our lives. Who would have ever thought that simple tales about something normally worn on your finger could get so convoluted?

January 8

Inspiration

A teacher who is attempting to teach without inspiring the pupil with a desire to learn is hammering on a cold iron.

Horace Mann

The pupil who is never required to do what he cannot do, never does what he can do.

John Stuart Mill

The bad teacher imposes his ideas and his methods on his pupils, and such originality as they may have is lost in the second-rate art of imitation.

Stephen Neill

How many inspired ideas have you had in your life so far? By inspired, I mean an idea or thought that is truly original. Some would argue that we never ever have an original thought; we just rehash the thoughts and ideas already rattling around in our heads. This can't be true or humankind would never have advanced beyond the cave-dwellers. There have to be original thoughts or this advanced technological world we live in would never have come to be. The question becomes: how many original inspired ideas does the average person actually have in their lifetime?

Some folks go through life doing the same old stuff and thinking no new thoughts. Extend this out indefinitely and inspiration never comes. Other folks have lots of new ideas and seem to bubble over—getting carried away at every opportunity. I like what Linus Pauling, the Nobel-prize-winning scientist, has to say about ideas. "The trick is to have lots of ideas … and then, reject the bad ones." Pauling pioneered space-filling models of complex molecules. His inspired ideas and models led to advances in chemistry, biology and medicine. Pauling had more original thoughts than the average of four that most people have in a lifetime.

How do we escape from the uninspired rut? We must be open to new ideas and thoughts. All too often, we are dismissive of anything contrary to our present paradigm. If it doesn't fit our thinking, we should mull it over for a while to see if it has any merit. How do we get introduced to inspired thoughts? The answer is simple. READ, READ, READ—and read new stuff. Be open to new experiences and learn from them. Life-long learners have the best chance to produce inspired thoughts by reading—mulling—and discussing what they read. Happy new experiences—and inspiration!

January 9

Isaac Asimov

All sorts of computer errors are now turning up. You'd be surprised to know the number of doctors who claim they are treating pregnant men.

Science can be introduced to children well or poorly. If poorly, children can be turned away from science; they can develop a lifelong antipathy; they will be in a far worse condition than if they had never been introduced to science at all.

A poor idea well written is more likely to be accepted than a good idea poorly written.
All from Isaac Asimov, 1920 – 1992

Isaac Asimov was a biologist who loved to write. Asimov wrote over 500 books on a variety of topics. Most of them were science-related, but he also wrote plenty of science fiction and even a book of dirty limericks. His prose was easy to read, as were his ideas and how he expressed them. I was fortunate enough to have an extensive conversation with Isaac Asimov about twenty years ago. I was on an environmental committee, and we organized conferences at least once a year. I attempted to get Asimov to speak at our conference. He lived in New England at the time, and I phoned him. He was very easy to talk to over the phone, and two things quickly became evident. He thought of himself as a "regular" guy. He had no ego that I could detect, but he admitted to me that he was a "homebody." He was also afraid to fly. Isn't that a paradox—that one who wrote about spacecraft and loved modern technology so much was also afraid to use it? (He also admitted to me in the conversation that computers worried him greatly!)

An important parenting lesson we can all take from Isaac Asimov is his wise statement about spoiling the educational fun of others. We should never admit to children that we have some aversion to a subject, or that we are "no good" at science, math, or any subject for that matter. Our poor attitude can rub off on the children. Why ruin it for them with our dislikes, biases, or silly notions? Why indeed!

January 10

Magic Apples

"God knows that when you eat of it your eyes will be opened" … so when the woman saw that the tree was good for food, and that it was a delight to the eyes … she took of its fruit and ate; and she also gave some to her husband … and he ate … then the eyes of both were opened …

Genesis 3: 4-7

Those wise ones who see that the consciousness within themselves is the same consciousness within all conscious beings, attain eternal peace.

Katha Upanishad

The fruit in the orchard were arguing about who was the best fruit. The grapes delivered a convincing claim that humans loved them best since they could be made into wine and everyone loved wine. The cherries and blueberries chimed in that they had medicinal properties and should be the top fruit. Peaches, pears and pomegranates all put in their propositions. At the height of the rhetoric, the farmer's wife appeared and settled the argument. She went to the big old tree in the middle of the garden and said: "I don't care what that serpent told Eve, you have the tastiest fruit!" She selected the largest, brightest, rosiest red apple; giving it a good wipe, she went back to the farmhouse, delightedly devouring her delicious prize.

Apples have a storied past. The forbidden fruit was possibly an apple tree. The Bible never states what it was, but many masterpieces depict Eve eating an apple. There are good reasons why apples are considered to have magical properties. "An apple a day keeps the doctor away!" holds some truth. Apples are that good. Period! Thank goodness for John "Johnny Appleseed" Chapman, who went around planting so many of these marvelous trees in early America.

We mentioned in the introduction that Freia, the goddess of youth, supplied the rest of the gods with magic apples, which prevented aging. Perhaps these youth-giving fruit are a metaphor for daily love and affection. Consider these reflections as apples—a tasty tidbit with a bonus—a medicinal function—a wee shot of joy juice—a little thought to mull. Everybody can use a magic apple—every day. Enjoy early!

January 11

Modern Tools

We become what we behold. We shape our tools and then our tools shape us.

Marshall McLuhan

Man is a Tool-using Animal.... Nowhere do you find him without Tools; without Tools he is nothing, with Tools he is all.

Thomas Carlyle

The two words "tools" and "idols" are sometimes mixed up by many folks. When this happens, the miracles of the car, telephone, television, computers, the internet, and the mall make slaves of many confused people. Each of these marvelous tools has the capacity, if used properly, to make our lives so much easier. It is a great misfortune of modern society that we have failed to show our children how to make the most of these tools. When we are surrounded by so many "good" things, we often lack direction in our choices. When conditions became good, the people of the Old Testament started sacrificing to a whole host of idols. This led to their undoing.

Let's examine the first of these modern tools, the car. When Henry Ford mass-produced cars for sale at prices people could afford, the automobile ensured the preeminence of America on the world stage. The family car and its extensions—trucks, tractors, and tanks—have completely changed the world. The automobile promised us more freedom to go quickly wherever we desired. This marvelous tool held great potential to make life so much easier. We should have had more time and leisure thanks to the automobile. With proper planning, this might have happened, but so far here's what has actually occurred. People become slaves to their cars. They sit in traffic jams for hours each day. Tempers flare and road rage results. The average person is overweight and out of shape, since they take the car everywhere. Cyclists and pedestrians in cities are at the mercy of cars. The air in most cities has become toxic thanks to cars. Global warming is due mainly to cars and trucks. Millions of people have been killed in traffic accidents. Tens of millions have been injured, and countless people are suffering ill health as a result of our worship of the automobile.

I have no doubt that most of these deleterious effects of automobiles will be reversed by new technology—and sooner than we think! In the meantime, we can rethink the way we use this outstanding tool.

January 12

Stupidity

Only two things are infinite, the universe and human stupidity, and I'm not sure about the former.

Albert Einstein

To be stupid, selfish, and have good health are three requirements for happiness, though if stupidity is lacking, all is lost.

Gustave Flaubert

Yesterday we mentioned examples of stupidity when it comes to the use of automobiles. We can reduce speed, horsepower, drinking and driving, and the emissions of automobiles—if, as a society, we really recognize the misuse and have any desire to be proactive in this regard. Good luck!

When it comes to human stupidity, the movie *Forest Gump* is one of my favorites. It's basically a feel-good story about an intellectually challenged man who, through a combination of luck and love, accomplishes great things—including making a fortune. He has the mentality, wonder, and understanding of a child, and in many situations he acts like one. He has many delightful sayings; one of the funniest is, "Stupid is as stupid does." The irony is that many of his actions we would consider "stupid" eventually turn to gold. Who are we to judge what is truly stupid?

Another funny movie I love is *Oh Brother Where Art Thou?* As with the first film, this one is about stupidity in people—only lots of them. In *Oh Brother*, there is one sublimely stupid moment in the movie when a gubernatorial candidate gets up on stage and exposes himself as the local Klu Klux Clan leader. He is so dumb, he doesn't even realize what he has done! The folks who should be smart are really quite the opposite, and our three convict heroes all come out looking brilliant when Pappy O'Daniel, the actual governor, grants them a full pardon for their contribution to the musical scene. These boys have some musical intelligence, just as Forrest Gump has great spatial intelligence. There are many types of intelligences, and people who appear slow to us often have some gift in a "different" intelligence.

It seems that there is no accounting for all the stupidity out there today—but after all, who are we to judge what is stupid and what isn't? I love Flaubert's recipe for happiness. If you think too much about something, it may make you sad. If you don't think about things much, you may be happy as a pig in a poke!

January 13

Power of Prayer Miracles

Where there is great love, there are always miracles.

Willa Cather

When I was eleven, I almost died from a bout of pneumonia. I remember walking through some puddles on the way home from school, and the next day I had a terrible cold. A couple of days after that, I don't remember much because I was delirious. I am told they took me to the hospital by ambulance, and for the next week it was touch and go. One lung collapsed, and half of the other was full of fluid. Dr. Little told me later that he was amazed at my recovery. I recall being in an amphitheater full of medical students and Dr. Little telling them about my recovery. He never used the word "miracle", but their faces told me how astounded they were.

What I didn't know at the time was that my dear mother and her friends at St Matthew's Church were praying for my recovery. Mother was suffering from a number of ailments herself, but she wouldn't give in to the notion that her youngest son was going to depart this world. I also remember getting Big Blue, the most amazing model working tractor from my big brother Judd, sent all the way from Vancouver.

Then I recall being prayed over by Canon Trumper, a very witty priest who came often to visit me in the hospital. Canon Trumper was a "big shot" to me, but at the same time, a humble man with a twinkle in his eye, a spring in his step, and a short, white brush cut. He looked "old" but was full of youthful humor and wonderful prayers. He had an aura about him. This light about his face put me in awe of him, and I held his wonderful words close to me after he left the hospital.

I was too young to believe in miracles, but now I have no doubt that I was the recipient of a healing miracle. I understood later why my mother's request had been granted. Within a few years, my mother's weak heart, severe arthritis, and Parkinson's disease had confined her to bed. Because my father had one arm and was in demand at work, mother's care fell mainly to me. I had to learn to balance school work, cooking meals and cleaning the house. Through her illness, mother never said a discouraging word to me. I suppose she knew that it was a miracle that I was around at all to help her through her struggle.

January 14

Cynicism

Cynicism is the intellectual cripple's substitute for intelligence. It is the dishonest businessman's sub writer, for self-respect.

Russell Lynes

The temptation shared by all forms of intelligence: cynicism.

Albert Camus

The pub is a wonderful institution. For the price of a drink, you can have comradeship and warmth, watch several sports at the same time, share any number of stories, and have philosophical conversations. I believe it was Samuel Johnson, the English poet and wit, who came up with his greatest sayings while downing a few jars at the local tavern. One of his most famous is: "The road to hell is paved with the best intentions." It seems a pity parliament couldn't be held in the pub. There is, however, a nasty disease which seems to be creeping more and more into good conversation—a cynicism about all things new—in particular, the failings of the times we are living in. If I were to listen to some of my colleagues, it would seem that nothing is right, and everything is wrong. Some of them seem to be affected by the worst cynicism, and it is quickly spreading to include all things political, educational, medical, and religious. The area most often under attack is new technology. It seems as if nothing works, and nobody is interested in making anything work.

I find this a paradox. In a stage of life when these friends are able relax and enjoy life, they seem to be poisoning their existence with cynicism. You would think, to listen to them, that things are so bad we should all—as my father used to say when he was being cynical—go home and dig a hole, get in, and pull the hole in after ourselves. What a terrible attitude. Little wonder people get depressed when they view everything with a critical filter. Why do it at all?

It is so easy to become a critic and a cynic, but why should we? Life isn't perfect—and people aren't perfect—but there is so much beauty and intelligence that seems to be wasted on the cynics. These folks are toxic and often attract other toxic people. Avoid them.

Go to the pub to celebrate life and revel in it. Life is too short to be cynical.

January 15

Worry

And can any of you by worrying add a single hour to the span of your life?
Matthew 6:27

Quid … me anxius sum? (What … me worry?)
Alfred E. Newman in *Mad* magazine

My favorite magazine when I was a kid was *Mad* magazine. My favorite issue of all time (September, 1961) had the Parthenon on the cover; at the top of the columns, holding up the roof, were strong men like Atlas and Hercules—and at one column was Alfred E. Newman, only he wasn't holding up his section. Alfred had his hands behind his head and a big silly grin on his face. Across the front of the building, in big lettering, were the Latin words *Quid, me anxius sum?* I didn't "get it" at first, but once I did, it seemed brilliant and still is! I wish I had shown that cover to all the worry-warts in my life, especially my mother, Francis. Nothing escaped the attention and worry of Fran. She worried that you weren't coming home, and if you were home, mom was fussing over your wellbeing. We could never convince Fran that sitting there stewing instead of doing was a great energy waster!

Whenever you find yourself in a worrisome situation, there are several forms of positive action available. Prayers are good, especially with a friend. Call a caring person. Encouraging words and prayers often result. I recall waiting at the hospital for our first son to arrive. Several men came and happily left while I waited in silence for hours. I worked myself into a nervous mess, and at last a doctor came in to tell me they would need to operate. I finally took positive action. I prayed hard!!! Within the hour, I was with my wife and new son. Prayer is a wonderful way to calm your fears.

I love the story, "Why Worry?" in a recent e-mail. *You really only have two things to worry about. Either you are healthy or ill. If you are healthy, you have nothing to worry about. If you are ill, you have two things to worry about. Either you will recover or you will die. If you recover, you have nothing to worry about. If you die, you have two things to worry about. Either you will go to heaven or hell. If heaven, you have nothing to worry about. If hell, you will be so busy shaking hands with all your friends, you won't have time to worry! So … why worry?*

Mealtime

Better is a dinner of vegetables where love is than a fatted ox with hatred with it.
Proverbs 15:17

When we were kids, we were told, "Eat what's put in front of you and be thankful." Many foods registered high on my hate list. Spaghetti and macaroni made me think of worms. Potatoes seemed like a dirty veggie to me. Porridge, tapioca and a whole variety of fruit were simply disgusting. I was compelled to eat some of each of these things—until my older brothers discovered a wonderful trick. The dining room table had a small space between a hollow pedestal and the table top. When mother was out in the kitchen, some of the hated stuff would find its way into the space. Father worked shifts, and overtime on the day shift, and was rarely at the table to see our disappearing food act. After a time, the pedestal began to hum, and father very quickly figured it out. We were all punished for being wastrels, and that ended the secret of our improved appetites.

Eventually, I got to like most foods, but there was one thing I didn't like about meals. There were constant arguments about petty family "beefs," and we were allowed to be disagreeable because it was thought to be a good thing to get feelings out in the open. The "last supper" occurred when I was ten years old. All six of us were together. This was rare, and rarer still was the great treat of roast beef and corn on the cob. My big brother Judd reached across in front of me to get a cob of corn and said in his deep voice, "Pardon me."

My father looked at him and said, "I don't think I will!" What followed was hard to swallow. Pent up hostility surfaced and, while I don't recall anything that was said with great anger and bitterness, I remember everyone leaving the table and leaving home in a short time. It seemed to me that a relatively harmless little phrase during a meal had been allowed to grow out of control and end in rancor.

When our boys were small, we also made them eat what was put in front of them. They have grown to like most foods. We had one other rule at the table. We could disagree with each other, but we could never be disagreeable. We would never allow the enjoyment of food to be ruined by petty arguing. Mealtime is family time, and we enjoy and celebrate each other with good grace, peace and thankfulness.

January 17

Flight

The airplane has unveiled for us the true face of the earth.

Antoine de Saint-Exupéry

Both optimists and pessimists contribute to our society. The optimist invents the airplane and the pessimist the parachute.

Gil Stern

There are only two emotions in a plane: boredom and terror.

Orson Welles

If a person from a hundred years ago were here for a day, which technology would astound them the most? Automobiles, television and computers are all amazing, but put our time-traveler near an airport and modern jet planes would confound them. As a kid in the late 1940's, I remember some astonishing planes. We would hear them first and run outside to look at them. The mustang, a fighter with a wonderfully loud engine, had a set of sharp teeth painted on its nose. The loudest plane I ever heard was a B-36. This huge bomber rumbled over. It had six engines and was flying low enough to deafen us. To a kid of seven, it was humongous and fantastic. Then came the jet, and you could see the plane ahead of its sound.

Do you remember your first flight? My wife and I were in our late forties when we had our first flights. It always stupefies me that it takes as long to get to the terminal and jump through all the hoops as it takes for the flight! Most terminals seem designed to slow things down. Two exceptions are Philadelphia, where they have big white rocking chairs, and O'Hare at Chicago, which is an amazing place. The Chicago airport is named after "Butch" O'Hare, and it has a replica of his plane on display. The story of the bravery of the O'Hare family is inspirational. Eddie O'Hare, Butch's father, was an attorney and business partner of the famous gangster Al Capone. Eddie helped run Capone's track operation in Chicago. Eddie was described as being devoted to his son. Eddie bravely decided to become an informant for the IRS, and it was with his help that the government convicted Capone for income tax evasion. Eddie's son became a fighter pilot; in 1942, he saved the carrier *Lexington* by shooting down five enemy bombers. The Medal of Honor citation calls it "one of the most daring single actions in the history of combat aviation." Butch was shot down and killed in 1943, but the bravery of both Butch and his father is truly legendary.

January 18

Feet

Feet, don't fail me now!

Various characters in a variety of situations

The farmyard animals were arguing about who had the best feet. "I have the best feet," said the rooster, "because I can scratch up my food and use my feet for sleeping on a perch."

"No, I have the best feet." said the duck. "Webbed feet allow me to swim better than any of you."

The pig argued that his feet allowed him to root the best. The horse argued for hooves because of the great distance he could run. The cat claimed the best feet because they were multi-purpose—good for fighting, and climbing trees quickly. Then the farmer chimed in, "All of your feet are pretty ugly. We humans have the best all-round feet of all animals, so quit arguing and get back to work!"

The farm animals laughed up a storm. They chorused: "How can you make such a ridiculous claim? Your feet are so weak that you need shoes to support you. Is it that you are so ashamed of them that you have to cover them up with something?" Then they all went off to hunt up some grub, leaving the farmer to consider his poor feet.

The human foot is an engineering miracle consisting of 123 separate bones. It must support at least fifty times its own mass and is subjected to tremendous pressure each time a step is taken. No wonder we all have problems with feet from time to time!

Your feet deserve some pampering:
- Gently massage the arch while slowly stretching your toes up and down;
- The next time you give a back massage, massage the recipient's feet;
- Elevate your feet now and then to get the blood back up the legs—put your feet up on your desk or lie on the floor and rest your feet in an elevated position—this feels particularly good if you are in the bathtub;
- If you suffer from heel spurs, keep a large plastic pop bottle almost full of water in the freezer, and use it to gently roll your arches several times each day—pamper those feet, and they will not fail you!

PS   If your feet really hurt, see November 14 on Plantar Fasciitis.

January 19

Your Name

Proper names are poetry in the raw. Like all poetry they are untranslatable.
W.H. Auden

The name of a man is a numbing blow from which he never recovers.
Marshall McLuhan

My mother named me "Lee Allen" because, I am told, she wanted a simple name that couldn't be shortened. My brothers' names were shortened from Bertrand Russell to Bert, and from Julian Huxley to Judd; my sister Aenone Marion became Noni. Dad named my brothers and sister; he must have been getting some revenge for his middle name which was Marmaduke. For most of my life, I have been called Lee—a nice simple name. Everyone likes to hear their name, unless of course they have a truly dreadful name. Usually, there is no sweeter music than the sound of your name, spoken with affection.

I find it difficult to accept that some people rarely use your name even though they know it. I have heard people greet others with "Hi there," or "Nice to see you," and never use a proper name. I don't understand this. As a teacher, I had to work very hard to learn hundreds of names each year; I made it a point to respectfully use the name the student wanted. I don't have a great memory for names, and I have forgotten many of them, but most of the students from my first class are still with me.

Several famous people have had a phenomenal memory for names. It is said that Napoleon and Henry Ford never forgot a name. I suppose this gave them power over those who couldn't be bothered to remember names.

There are two special ladies I'll never forget, and their great impression was made because of the way they said my name. A lady on our street, Mrs. Mundy, always called me "Lee Allen" with a very musical voice. The other lady was in our choir. Phyllis was from the Caribbean and called me "Mister Lee." One of the other choir members once said, "No Phyllis—he is the choir master—call him Mr. Steels!"

Phyllis replied, "Nope—I'm callin' him Mister Lee—it's island style—Mister Lee, Mister Lee, Mister Lee." I loved that lady!

January 20

Have Fun

Make a joyful noise to the Lord; come before Him with singing.

Endorphins are the feel-good chemicals of the body. They are released in larger quantities when we laugh, sing, and perform aerobic activity. Endorphins are responsible for the "runner's high." Children are happy when they get lots of play, since the fun in good play generally involves the release of endorphins. As we progress to adulthood, we often become more serious about life and forget how to play and have fun.

It seems to me that Psalm 100 is telling us to sing and dance and have fun when we are praising the Lord. Carry this over into living, and we should sing and dance and have fun more often than not. It's unfortunate that many people regard life as deadly serious—and not to be confused with play. "Lighten up" is anathema to good business for many hardworking folks.

When I became a department head, with many teachers and thousands of students in my care, I took great pains to provide an ambiance in which people could feel good and experience a sense of accomplishment and fun. One year, we were having such a good time that fifteen department members missed a grand total of seven days in half a year. Then I got pneumonia and missed a whole week. When I returned on a Monday morning, I found the preparation room where our desks were located locked. There were no staff members around, and the room was in darkness. Normally, at that time, it would be buzzing with activity. I thought, "What is going on? I'm not here for a week, and look what happens." I unlocked the door, turned on the lights, and made my way to my desk at the other end—only it wasn't there! In its place was a chair, and propped up in the chair was the department skeleton, named Beatrice Bones. The skull was missing, and in its place was a sign which read: "HEAD WANTED!" I guess the look on my face must have been priceless, because as my staff quickly materialized out of various hiding places, they were all having quite a laugh, and so was I. My desk was quickly moved back in, and we returned to our normal activity, providing students with the best science education you could ever want, with a true sense of fun thrown in—no extra charge!

Change

In a time of drastic change, it is the learners who inherit the future. The learned find themselves equipped to live in a world which no longer exists.

Eric Hoffer

I have a theory about people and change. I call it the human inertia theory. Unless there is some traumatic event which acts as a redefining moment, most people cannot change the fundamental way they act. Simply said, people do not change. Given a set of circumstances, you can easily predict exactly how a certain person will react. I am referring here to so-called "mature" people who have finished their formal education and are moving along comfortably through life. They are the "learned." Ask yourself some simple questions. Can you predict how a person will vote, what they will eat, or how they will dress? Of course you can. Most people are not adventuresome. They are creatures of habit. If someone always shows up late, they will continue to show up late. People who whine about everything will continue to whine about everything. To paraphrase Newton's first Law of Motion, people like to keep on doing what they are already doing. This resistance to change is called inertia, and we all have it.

This sounds like a pretty damning theory about the human condition, and if it were universal, humankind would be extinct. The operative word in my inertia theory is "most". As Hoffer says, "the learners … inherit the future." Who are Hoffer's learners? They are the people who continue to learn after formal education is over. They are the people who value curiosity over training. They are the people who are always trying new things. They are the people who are not going through life on autopilot. They can be bothersome because they are always asking questions, like why things are done in a certain way. The aforementioned Isaac Newton was one of these adventuresome learners, always approaching problems with the wonder of a child and playing in new ways until he got his answer.

The world changes so quickly these days that we cannot afford to rest on our learning. We shouldn't be too comfortable with ourselves. Inertia can result in early onset dementia. If we don't embrace change, and the new learning that comes with it, we may soon live in an unrecognizable world. We may be one of the Hoffer "learned … in a world which no longer exists."

January 22

Telepathy

It has been proven that spontaneous telepathic transmission is closely linked with the type of relationship between the two connected subjects. They attract a certain type of "love energy," which facilitates the reciprocal transmission of thoughts ... whether you want it or not ...

Mabel Iam

Although we have heard of telepathy, most people don't feel that humans have the ability to send thoughts through space. I feel otherwise. I know there is little scientific evidence to support mind communication through space. The reason I believe in telepathy has more to do with many personal occurrences, which could only be explained by telepathy.

Examine well-documented evidence of telepathy. North American natives have many rituals which emphasize communication with nature and specific animals. I believe that animals read minds. How else do we explain the abrupt but perfect changes in the direction of entire flocks of birds or schools of fish? It has nothing to do with reacting to a signal. I'm sure they are "tuned in" to each other and the collective mind of the flock. Pets know when their humans are coming home or going on a trip. They don't need visual clues. Some animals have been left behind by their owners and have miraculously shown up months later at the new home. Could they be tuned into their masters' minds? Since animals don't have a sophisticated means of communication, they need telepathy or extra sensory perception (ESP) as a means of survival.

My own personal experiences with ESP are numerous. My mother was confined to her bed when I was in my final year of secondary school. When I got home from school, Anne, the lady who helped out, always had a fresh pot of tea ready for me. I asked her how she knew when to make it, because I rarely came home at the same time. Anne replied that my mother would alert her when I had left school. Mother never told how she knew. She just knew.

My most intense telepathic experience involved the death of a good friend. I woke up suddenly in the middle of the night with the deepest feeling of loss. When the phone rang early the next morning, I told the caller that our friend had died just after three in the morning. "How did you know that?" the caller asked. I could truthfully say he told me when he left.

January 23

Music Dogs Like

My music is best understood by children and animals.

Igor Stravinsky

Igor Stravinsky, the Russian composer, was one of the more interesting twentieth-century composers. His *Rite of Spring*, written for the ballet, caused a riot when it was first played in Paris in 1913. At first hearing, its wild, pulsating rhythms and unusual harmonies grate on ears used to hearing the lovely melodies of Mozart or Tchaikovsky. Many people fail to understand it at all and quickly refuse to listen.

We played music as background in our science labs. The music was often the classics: Mozart, Beethoven and Haydn. One day for fun, I put on Stravinsky's *Rite of Spring*, and I was quite surprised when several students and staff who never remarked about the background music asked me what it was. When I told them, "It's Stravinsky," most of them thought it was very cool stuff. When I asked the young students why they liked it, the response was that it was colorful and full of pulsating rhythms. Indeed—it was.

Walt Disney used this pounding music to portray the dinosaurs marching to their deaths in the movie, *Fantasia*. The Disney studios paid for the rights to the music, but Stravinsky claimed that "the paltry sum was reduced to a mere pittance by a dozen crapulous intermediaries." Stravinsky visited the studio in California and was invited to a screening of the movie. When he entered the theatre, he was handed a score for the music.

"I don't need that," said Stravinsky. "I wrote the piece after all."

"Oh ... but it's all changed," was the response.

So the great composer had to suffer through a performance which must have sickened him even more than getting paid "a mere pittance."

Time, however, has shown this modern music to be a model for many composers. Musicians and young people especially love the orchestral color in the music, and concerts of Stravinsky's works for ballet always attract enthusiastic audiences.

This illustrates that most highly original music is ill-understood and hated by the public, even if children and dogs perk up their ears at the neat sounds. Is there a lesson for us in this strange paradox?

January 24

Clowns

A clown is like aspirin, only he works twice as fast.

Groucho Marx

The arrival of a good clown exercises a more beneficial influence upon the health of a town than of twenty asses laden with drugs.

Thomas Sydenham

Everybody loves a funny person—well almost everybody. I have some good friends who like a laugh; but when the blues are upon these people, for whatever reason, they refuse to laugh at the funniest stuff. Pity! The endorphins released when you laugh are better than pain pills! Laughter truly is the best medicine.

I remember when the pneumonia almost did me in when I was eleven; I had to keep curling up in the fetal position with a hot water bottle next to my chest to avoid the pleurisy pain. Our parish priest, Cannon Trumper, would visit; he always had a funny story. I remember one of his funniest stories. *It was a very cold winter, and three starving little birds sat on a wire, shivering from the cold. Along came the milkman to make his deliveries, and his big old horse committed a social error on the road, right in front of the little birds. Off the wagon went, and the little birds sat, until finally one of them flew down, had his fill, and flew back up. "Cheep cheep cheep," he said, and immediately he fell off the wire … dead! The two remaining birds sat for a while, but finally one gave in and had his fill. He flew back up and began to sing. Down he went … dead! The last wee bird held out for as long as he could. Then he flew down, had his fill, and flew back up. He began to sing, and he fell off the wire … dead.* At this point, Cannon Trumper looked very seriously at me and asked, "Do you know the moral of that story?"

"No" I answered, thinking some profound biblical lesson was coming.

The dear priest replied: *"NEVER SING WHEN YOU ARE FULL OF SHIT!"*

We have all been in gatherings where everyone is telling jokes. Here are a few ways to ensure everyone gets their endorphin fix.

- Never say, "We've all heard that old story." Some of us may not have heard it, and I love the same story—told by different people.
- Never ever finish someone else's story for them or deliver the punch line before they are finished; this is simply thoughtless, rude and cruel.
- Listen! Folks who are thinking of their next story miss the fun.

January 25

What is a Chair?

We tend not to choose the unknown, which might be a shock or a disappointment or simply a little difficult to cope with. And yet it is the unknown with all its disappointments and surprises that is the most enriching.

Anne Morrow Lindbergh

What is the truth about an object such as a chair? I recall our philosophy professor asking us how we knew that the wooden chair he was holding in front of him existed. I often wondered why he chose a chair instead of a person, or the building itself. The topic was scarier than we thought; when we left that class, we were uncertain if anything existed at all. If you have trouble proving that what you see exists, how can anyone prove the existence of God or Satan? Truth is very illusive and often surprising when it is finally found—if it can ever be found.

Now for a really big surprise about that wooden chair the professor held up. Science tells us that chair is 99.999 % nothing. If you could eliminate all the space between molecules, atoms and sub-atomic particles, the chair would disappear from human sight. There are places in the universe where gravity is so great that all that space between the particles of matter is eliminated. Such a place is called a black hole; matter is so compressed that a speck of black hole stuff would weigh more than the earth. This means that you and I are merely nothing on an astronomical scale. So much for the eighty million brain cells holding all that information. It is nothing! Why do we see a chair if it's mostly nothing? Why do we recognize it as a chair and call it a chair if we are mostly nothing?

Suppose that chair the professor held up gets sat upon by some rather large person and gets broken. Chances are that the chair won't be fixed. It gets into the refuse bin and is incinerated. Now what has happened to the chair? Its billions of molecules have combined with the oxygen of the air to produce mostly carbon dioxide and water vapor. All those molecules go into the atmosphere and are spread all over the earth. In fact, this happens with everything that is decomposed. As you have been reading this, you've probably breathed in a molecule that was once a part of Gandhi, Jesus Christ or Abraham. Is it much of a surprise that things are seldom what they seem, the truth is elusive, and mysteries do indeed abound?

January 26

Great Teachers

An understanding heart is everything as a teacher, and cannot be esteemed highly enough. One looks back with appreciation to the brilliant teachers, but with gratitude to those who touched our human feeling. The curriculum is so much necessary raw material, but warmth is the vital element for the growing plant and for the soul of the child.

Carl Jung

Our grade nine history teacher would regale us with many sports stories, but not much about history. Then just before the exam, he would write a number of "important" pages on the board, and we would know what to study. He must have had the smartest students in his classes, because we always beat the kids in the other classes. We loved history class!

In grade ten, we had a very different teacher, Mr. Slack. He was kind of funny looking, with one eye that looked off to the side. He was no athlete, but he also told us stories. These stories were real history tales. He was very good at telling them. Long before the exam, Mr. Slack told us that we should be reading, and he gave us a huge list of books. We received no list of pages to study in the textbook as we had in grade nine. I wasn't very well prepared.

I clearly recall the day the exams were handed back for us to correct. Mr. Slack had us all move to the sides of the room, and he placed the exams on the desks and told us to find our exam and sit in that seat. I found mine in the third seat of the first row and the mark was embarrassingly bad. My two buddies were in the first two seats. We had all failed and were the three "worst" students in the class! Mr. Slack called the first row the "stupid" row, and he spent the rest of the term patiently showing us how to get involved with history. He loaned us books. He showed us what to look for and what was important. He gave the three of us "stupids" the tools to become self-reliant. His lessons were on how to learn. I learned how to make summaries on index cards and many neat tricks for learning information. I wasn't too pleased at the time, because we really had to work hard. Mr. Slack just wouldn't accept slackers! His methods must have worked, because all three of us "stupids" doubled our earlier marks. More importantly, we did well in history after that. All three of us went to college, and we all became successful teachers. Thank you Mr. Slack— wherever you are!

January 27

Stories

There is no greater agony than bearing an untold story inside you.

Maya Angelou

The universe is made of stories, not atoms.

Muriel Rukeyser

A good writer is basically a story teller, not a scholar or a redeemer of mankind.

Isaac Bashevis Singer

It's a damned good story. If you have any comments, write them on the back of a check.

Erle Stanley Gardner

"Tell me the stories of Jesus I love to hear" is a melodic children's hymn I can remember singing in church. Actually, the stories of the Old Testament are more colorful to a kid. Noah and the ark, and Jonah living in the whale never ceased to amaze me; but the one that was an unbelievable miracle was the story of the fiery furnace in Babylon. King Nebuchadnezzar of Babylon decreed that everyone should worship his huge gold statue. Three of the Israelites refused, and Nebuchadnezzar threatened to throw these boys into a fiery furnace. Shadrach, Meshach and Abednego said: "Throw us in. We're not afraid. Our God will save us." Nebuchadnezzar was so enraged that he had the furnace cranked up to seven times as hot, and the boys were thrown in, fully clothed and bound. It was so hot that the handlers were burned up throwing our heroes into the fire. Shadrach, Meshach and Abednego were unharmed and even danced around inside the furnace. The king was so amazed that he called them out, gave them a big promotion, and declared that everyone should worship their God! I love that story and can picture them dancing around and singing: "Great balls of fire!"

When I was a kid, I remember a huge bonfire we had in the back field. All the kids were watching this blaze when Bob Gay, who had wooden legs, came down with a bucket. (Bob had had his legs taken off by a train several years before.) He was always doing crazy things, and he loved to cackle like a chicken while doing them. This was one of the craziest! He dumped a bucket of bullets in the fire and yelled "Run!" which we all did. The bullets started going off, but miracle of miracles, no one was hit—not even Bob, who was the last one to make it to safety. Some fire that was!

January 28

Angels

Angels have no philosophy but love.

Terri Guillemets

The reason angels can fly is because they take themselves lightly.

G.K. Chesterton

Angels are like diamonds. They can't be made, you have to find them. Each one is unique.

Jaclyn Smith

A friend is always good to have, but a lover's kiss is better than angels raining down on me.

Dave Matthews

Be an angel to someone else whenever you can, as a way of thanking God for the help your angel has given you.

Eileen Elias Freeman

The last quote is from *The Angels' Little Instruction Book*. This lovingly written wee book has lots of good information about how to be an angel. We know all about the work of angels from the Bible. The angel Gabriel brought revelation to the prophets, and in the book of Luke, appeared to both Zacharias and Mary. Gabriel foretold of the birth of John the Baptist, and the birth of Christ (The Annunciation.) Gabriel was a busy angel since many Muslims believe that Gabriel also revealed the Quran to the prophet Mohammed. Earth-shaking knowledge was first foretold by an angel. Today, many folks feel they have been touched by angels, and these angels may come in many different forms, each one unique as Jaclyn Smith tells us.

I would advise against spending the rest of your days combing the earth for angels. They are difficult to expose. Rather, look for subtle ways you can be an angel to someone. This person need not ever find out that they were the beneficiary of your largess or altruism. You are that beneficiary since you attained the Kingdom by touching others.

I get a good laugh from what Rodney Dangerfield said about angels. (I think Henny Youngman, Red Skeleton and Hal Roach all said it as well.)

My wife is an angel ... always up in the air harping over something.

January 29

Planning vs. Spontaneity

The course of life is unpredictable ... no one can write his autobiography in advance.

Abraham Joshua Heschel

Children are unpredictable. You never know what inconsistency they're going to catch you in next.

Franklin P. Jones

You can either take action, or you can hang back and hope for a miracle. Miracles are great, but they are so unpredictable.

Peter F. Drucker

When it comes to planning, our family seemed to be divided in half. My two brothers, Judd and Bert, liked to be fairly spontaneous, whereas my sister Noni and I had daily planners and preferred to have things nailed down well ahead of time. As you can imagine, planning any kind of event with the whole family would be a circus. The old spontaneous vs. ordered or planned seemed to come up often. We actually weren't that bad, as each of us had enough flexibility to accommodate the others. Nothing was ever "etched in stone" as it has to be with some folks.

Some folks have routines predictable almost to the minute. Daily meals and activities must happen at specific times, or upset occurs. No flexibility is allowed. More common today, however, is quite the opposite. Some families have catch as catch can—which is often fast food and hurry here, there and everywhere, in total multitasking confusion. The happy medium seems to be somewhere between these two extremes. A good friend has a sign which reads, "God Bless our home—clean enough to be healthy—and messy enough to be happy!" Similarly, we need to plan our activities with some built-in flexibility, which allows for spontaneity when it's called for.

I remember a bus trip in Europe in which a large family was always ten minutes late, and everyone had to wait for them. When we were in Venice, a gondola ride was part of the package. The tour director emphasized that we would leave on time. The family was late and missed the gondola. They also managed to get separated and missed the afternoon's activities. When they all arrived back at the hotel separately, they held a loud party and talked as if they hadn't seen each other in years. Now that is spontaneity!

January 30

Parties

Life itself is a party: you join after it's started and you leave before it's finished.
Elsa Maxwell

When people sing together, community is created. Together we rejoice, we celebrate, we mourn and we comfort each other. Through music, we reach each others' hearts and souls. Music allows us to find a connection.
Peter Yarrow

Whether a party can have much success without a woman present I must ask others to decide, but one thing is certain, no party is any fun unless seasoned with folly.
Desiderius Erasmus

Some of the best parties we have are those in which we can both talk and sing. I watch some folks, and there are those who just love to talk. And they do—you know who I mean—just blah, blah, blah without much listening. But when we go to sing, they either clam up or drag somebody off to a corner to keep up their personal barrage of words. Blessed are those who love to talk, for they shall be known as motor-mouths. Now don't get me wrong— I just love a good motor-mouth, but only if they are truly funny. I recall one party where we all got really happy quickly except for our son, Anthony. He began a monologue which went on for quite some time. I don't remember what it was about, but he had us rolling on the floor with laughter. It was just about the funniest thing I had ever heard. Now that is certainly allowed and welcomed. A funny person holding forth can be the life of the party.

My favorite parties include singing and dancing. The good feelings from both those activities last for days for me. All the endorphins from heavy breathing are good for you, and you certainly don't feel any pain when you are having such a good time. I am in awe of folks who can sit down to a piano and play practically anything. The head of the physical education department at our first school could play any song, and we would all gather around the piano to sing anything requested. Some of those songs were so silly that an observer might think we were nuts, but we didn't have a care in the world, being so silly. We just "let 'er rip" and had more fun than you can ever ask or imagine! Party on!

January 31

Return to Love

Cruel persecution and intolerance are not accidents, but grow out of the very essence of religion, namely, its absolute claims.

Morris Raphael Cohen

In the matter of religion, people eagerly fasten their eyes on the difference between their own creed and yours; whilst the charm of the study is in finding the agreements and identities in all the religions of humanity.

Ralph Waldo Emerson

One of the most outrageous news stories I recall was: "Teacher jailed over a bear's name." A British teacher in Sudan allowed her students to name a teddy bear after the Prophet Mohammed. A class of seven year olds had chosen the name, and the teacher didn't realize this was a blasphemy under Shariah law. The school was forced to close because of protests and fear of reprisals by groups of Islamic fundamentalist men. Eventually, after a few days in jail, the teacher was deported back to England.

If the Prophet Mohammed were alive today, he would have been shocked by the behaviors of Islamic fundamentalists. The same is true for all the great prophets and teachers who became initiates of religions. They were all more interested in their people than in ruling them. Their philosophies were very similar. The "Golden Rule" that we should treat others as we want to be treated is the basic rule of most major religions. However, every religion seems to go off the rails with the notion that theirs is the only true religion. Historically, loving each other becomes bogged down in rules and rituals, administrators, and magnificent edifices. So many new and improved versions of the "same" religion abound and each one states that they have the "best" form. A return to rule rigor often results in "fundamentalists" who say, "if you're not with us, you're against us."

Why was Jesus Christ crucified? The simple answer is that he was anti-religious. Jesus' philosophy wasn't based on rules but on a love of God, others and self. I suppose when many folks read today's news, they will decide that anti-religious isn't so bad an answer. This is a pity because as someone once wisely said, "If you don't stand for something, you'll fall for anything!" A return to love may be the only answer to the grace and the peace we all desire.

February 1

What's in a WORD?

If you take care of the small things, the big things take care of themselves.

My friends are my estate. Forgive me then the avarice to hoard them!

Not knowing when the dawn will come, I open every door.

The soul should always stand ajar, ready to welcome the ecstatic experience.

I know nothing in the world that has as much power as a word. Sometimes I write one, and I look at it, until it begins to shine.

All from Emily Dickinson   1830 – 1886

Emily Dickinson has given us many splendid words which do indeed shine with her innate goodness. I wonder what she was truly like as a person—what would it have been like to be a confidant of Emily Dickinson?

There is a neat question some interviewers ask their guests. "If you could have lunch with anybody in history, who would it be?" Many of us think of the obvious: Jesus Christ, Mohammed, Buddha or the Dalai Lama, or some other great leader. Their wisdom is so well documented that I wonder how they could add anything new to our knowledge over lunch. I would love to have lunch with a great composer to ask where all those treasured compositions really come from. I don't understand how the human brain could ever invent such perfection from simple scales and rhythms. Great wordsmiths such as Shakespeare, Milton or Winston Churchill would be very interesting. Emily Dickinson, whose words we see above, would be my ideal of a lunch companion. The conversation might go something like this, I imagine.

"Emily, I am in awe of the way you use words. How are you able to select the perfect word so often?"

"Lee, I simply pay attention. The people around me—and these people may be friends in books,—will invariably give me the word when I need it."

"Does this word come to you right away, Emily?"

"Not always—I sometimes wait for years for the word to come, but eventually it does. Then I have such a wonderful, ecstatic feeling." Amen!

February 2

Sharing Leadership

A leader is someone who steps back from the entire system and tries to build a more collaborative, more innovative system that will work over the long term.

Robert Reich

I worked at a cereal factory in the early 60's. We could look out the rear windows of the factory and see people walking from the parking lot to the rear entrance. Many of the men would look out the windows about 20 minutes before the change in shifts to watch the girls coming to work the next shift. I recall a tall man in a sharp dark brown suit walking that walk; only it was more like a strut. The men would say, "Get away from the windows boys—here comes you know who!" They were in awe of this man, who was the "big boss" of the Company. Today he would be called the CEO. He was a legend around the factory but was rarely seen, except for that strut across the lot at any time of the day. He could be called the invisible leader.

There are as many different leadership styles as leaders. I worked for folks who like to control everything. No detail is left untouched, and the leader's stamp is on everything. This is fine as long as the system is working well, but it's lousy when things begin to go downhill. This style may work in small groups or athletic teams, but it doesn't produce long-lasting results. Bringing out the best in people won't work if everything is controlled.

In highly effective departments, people work as teams for projects and administration. If everyone knows how things work and has input into the planning, there is less to worry about, because each person knows the details. Everybody takes ownership and feels important to the success of the project. On the other hand, no one is exempt from "grunt" work. Time for play and relaxing together are also keys to team-building.

Many families operate with these same principles of collaboration and ownership. Everybody feels as if they are part of a team, and no one is adverse to "rolling up their sleeves and pitching in." No problems are too difficult when everyone pulls together. The adage, "The family that prays together stays together," is true. These families also plan together, play together and celebrate their successes together—as a family unit.

February 3

Sermons

A woman can say more in a sigh than a man can say in a sermon.

Arnold Houtain

If you haven't struck oil in 10 minutes, stop drilling.

Old saying

One filled with joy preaches without preaching.

Mother Theresa

I figure I have listened to over two thousand sermons. How many of them do I actually remember? Few, I'm afraid! I can only quote a few lines that have stayed with me. "And so on and so forth …" I remember one preacher saying. I guess he said it a thousand times, so I remembered that. I can recall sermons when the whole back row of the choir would fall asleep. I guess they were all visual learners. It's not that I haven't heard any good sermons. Some of them have been absolutely brilliant, and I have been blessed to hear many outstanding preachers. So why is it that I don't remember any of them? Maybe I have a bad memory.

I feel the best words from a holy person aren't words at all, but deeds. Mother Theresa said it best, and it bears repeating. "One filled with joy preaches without preaching." My goodness! I just remembered something from a sermon. I believe it was Father Mark who preached "**JOY**!!!" What he was saying was you have to have the proper order …"**J**esus … **O**thers and then **Y**ourself." Now I don't feel so bad about my memory. However, what was it Father Mark was talking about? I'm just kidding.

A southern Baptist preacher was preaching to his congregation on the evils of drink: "Now let's take all that demon whiskey and dump it in the river!" he shouted.

"Alleluia!" came back the response.

"Now let's take all that bourbon and dump it in the river, and after that we'll take all the wine and dump it in the river!"

After the sermon, the choir director announced: "We'll now sing hymn 351: *Let's all Gather at the River.*"

PS A huge THANKS to all the clergy for their many inspirational sermons.

February 4

More Miracles

The miracle, or the power, that elevates the few is to be found in their industry, application, and perseverance under the prompting of a brave, determined spirit.

Mark Twain

When our choir took part in the Billy Graham crusade back in the 90's, we had preparatory workshops. One memorable session was a motivational talk by Mike "Pinball" Clemens, who at the time was a running back for the Argos Football team. I'll never forget the energy and enthusiasm of this rather small man who was a powerhouse of a player. Pinball would run the ball as if it were his last carry, bouncing off tacklers twice his size. In his talk, he told of his struggles making his school team. "They told me, 'You are too small to play football,' but I knew I could shine, and I did!" said Clemens with a huge smile. At every level Pinball tried, he was told that he was too small; and every time, he knew he could shine. That a person the size of Mike Clemens could play football seemed like a miracle.

I'm no Pinball Clemens, but I have been blessed in a number of ways. As a little kid, I liked to sing, and the earliest memory I have of performing is going around our street singing, "When yer heart goes bumpity bump … it's lub lub lub!" Then I got sick. I had a condition called bronchiectasis, and my mother and sister had to pound mucous out of me every day. When I was eleven, a bout of pneumonia almost ended my life, and I have large amounts of scar tissue in my bronchi and trachea as a result of this and several subsequent bouts of pneumonia. Our doctor told my mother that it would be a good thing for my breathing if I took singing lessons. Thus began my career as a reasonable baritone. I still need to "clear the pipes" every morning and I suffer from attacks of "frogs" from the blockages in my trachea. A sports therapist once asked me, "How do you run or play racquetball when you have trouble moving air out of your lungs?" The answer is simple. It has very little to do with me other than determination and faith. Every time I perform, I call on the Holy Spirit to grant me the grace to breathe and not croak.

PS I love the line sung by the major-general in Gilbert & Sullivan's *Gondoliers*: "I know the croaking chorus from *The Frogs* of Aristophanes."

February 5

Live Life

Men are apt to mistake the strength of their feeling for the strength of their argument. The heated mind resents the chill touch and relentless scrutiny of logic.

We look forward to the time when the power to love will replace the love of power. Then will our world know the blessings of peace.

Be happy with what you have and are, be generous with both, and you won't have to hunt for happiness.

All from William Gladstone, 1809 – 1898

Fat heads often get in the way of true bliss. When we think we have all the answers, we may be on our way to a shocking change. When things are going really well, we have probably forgotten something. If we think our lifestyle or way of doing things is the best way, we may be on autopilot instead of really living life.

During the winter in sunny Florida, it amazes me how many retired folks are doing new things. There are no fat heads to get in the way. They have the usual fun—happy hour—rooting for their sports teams—getting together just to chew the fat. The more fat I hear chewed, the more I think that this is a whole new world, and these new friends just fill it up with activities. They bike ride, power walk, kayak, sew quilts, bowl, and line dance to name a few. They do aerobics in the pool. They play all kinds of games day and night. There is an endless list of new things to try, but everyone seems to have the attitude that, "If I don't get it done today, that's OK—I can do it tomorrow." The main thing is that they all have fun doing new things—like kids! Everyone is welcome to try anything. I've noticed a number of folks in wheelchairs who are very active. Our new friend Andy runs the computer clubs, arranged a car rally and goes out to photograph unusual birds—all from his wheelchair. He is certainly not on autopilot or just existing! These folks enjoy living life to the fullest while sharing the fun with all those around them. Their motto seems to be: "Every day is a new day in which you can try something new."

February 6

Volkswagens Part 1

If all of the cars in the United States were placed end to end, it would probably be Labor Day weekend.

Jack Handley

Every one of us is, even from his mother's womb, a master craftsman of idols.

John Calvin

The first year Volkswagens were imported into North America was 1953. There were about 350 V.W. Beetles, and my big brother Judd had one. The rear window had a little bar down the center. The rear tail lights were tiny. There was a one gallon spare gas tank and a lever to switch over when the main tank ran out, which happened often when I drove it. I eventually got to drive the Beetle most of the time when Judd bought the "Banana", a yellow 58 Meteor with a Thunderbird V-8. The V.W. adventures began. Since there was no gas gauge, I would forget that I was on the spare one gallon tank; I think I hold some kind of record for running out of gas. The car was light. In fact, you could grab the front bumper and lift the front of the car off the ground to show folks how strong you were. They were impressed, unless they knew the engine was in the rear.

The car would do 76 mph, foot to the floor! Other Beetles would only do 75 mph, so you could pass all the newer ones. Celia and I were driving on a four-lane freeway, passing all the other Beetles and waving to them in derision. Suddenly there was a mighty "Bang" and the car slowed to 50 mph. All the V.W. drivers we had passed caught up, thumbing their noses at us. I was understandably mad and wondered what had happened. Celia chimed in, "You know … just before the big bang, I crossed my legs."

"What the hell does that have to do with the car slowing down?" I asked.

"I think I kicked the keys," she replied. The ignition keys hung low in the middle of the dash. Suddenly, it dawned on me what had happened. The car had shut off for a second and backfired. I pulled off the road and opened up the "hood" in the rear. Sure enough, an ignition wire had blown off when the Beetle backfired. I quickly put it back on and off we went at 76 mph again to thumb our noses right back at those rude Beetle drivers. Hooray!

February 7

Water

Hamlet:	"How long will a man lie in the grave before he rots?"
Grave Digger:	"Well … if he be not rotten before he dies, he'll last you five year, but if he be a tanner, he'll last you nine year."
Hamlet:	"Why he more than another?"
Grave Digger:	"Well sir … his hide is so tanned with his trade, it will keep out water a great while … and water is a sure decayer of your hoarsen dead body!"

Conversation between Hamlet and the gravedigger   Shakespeare

I used to tell my science classes that Shakespeare knew his science. There were many scenes where he showed a good grasp of principles. In the above scene, one could claim that Shakespeare knew that water was the universal solvent. Given enough time, water will dissolve practically anything. Think about the three most common commodities we take for granted: air, earth (soil) and water. As long as they are in constant supply we never think of them as valuable. We often "treat them like dirt." As soon as one runs out, however, panic sets in. If we run out of air, we have a few minutes to live. If there is no water, we have a few days. We eventually starve if we don't have soil to grow our food. Ah yes, we can still eat the animals, but soon they will be gone as well. So we must begin giving these three basic substances more respect!

Of the three ubiquitous commodities, water to me is the most fun. You can play with water. I recall a silly scene from childhood. Our next door neighbor, Edith Gay, loved to talk and one hot summer day she held us captive on our veranda. "Blah blah blah"—on and on Edie talked, and we listened because we were taught that it was impolite to interrupt. We didn't notice that my dad, Allen, had snuck up onto the roof of the house with a pail of water. Edie didn't either, and suddenly, down came the whole bucket of water and soaked her. Everybody laughed uproariously—including Edie. She could take a joke. I often wondered how Al got up there with that pail of water. He had one arm, and he would have had to go up the ladder with a full pail of water, carefully walk across the roof, and toss the water with a good aim so that it would all get on Edie. I don't know how he did it, but Al was sure our hero that fine day.

February 8

Endorphins

Laughing is one of the more serious activities of mankind.

Anonymous

Mister Steels … you do too much singin' and dancin'.

Dr. Chan, our physical chemistry professor

There is a great deal of scientific evidence which shows that it is impossible to get an ulcer while you are singing, dancing, aerobic exercising, or laughing. There is probably a whole host of ills that can be cured with these activities. I have seen people change instantly when they hear a good belly-busting joke. Like all good things, be careful to use jokes in appropriate situations. Avoid telling rude jokes at funerals or to someone recovering from a hernia. Don't dance with heel spurs or when your back is "out." Let common sense prevail! It is amazing, however, what a little levity can do for the minor and imagined ailments we fall prey to almost daily. What is the basis of this free medical self-help?

There is a very simple scientific reason why having fun is good medicine. Activities such as singing, dancing, laughing and exercise all release endorphins, natural chemicals in the body that act as painkillers. Endorphins do much more than relieve pain. These natural mind and body drugs stimulate the immune system and raise consciousness to a higher level. You may have heard of the "runner's high." Some of my best thinking is done after a long, hard bike ride. Solutions to problems come like magic. An easy ride can cure a headache, relieve tension and make you feel very much alive. The same applies to running and fast walking, as well as dancing and singing. Many an evening, I dragged myself to choir practice but left buoyed up. Those magic molecules are simply amazing! Be careful, however, not to overdo it. Living on endorphins, like living on nervous energy, can lead to a crash.

My physical chemistry professor used to say, "You are going to fail … you do too much singing and dancing." I guess he had heard about all our partying. He was right. I failed his course. An overdose of anything can lead to trouble—even an overdose of those amazing endorphins.

February 9

A Good Digestive System

A good reliable set of bowels is worth more to a man than any quantity of brains!
Henry Wheeler Shaw

Once upon a time, not that long ago, the parts of the body got into an argument about who should be the boss of the body. The brain argued that since it was the brain that did all the thinking, the brain should be the boss. The heart argued that only the pumping action of the heart supplied the body with all its life-carrying blood. The arms and legs said that without the manual labor done by the arms and legs, man wouldn't be able to make a living. The legs were adamant that since they carried the body everywhere, the legs really should be boss. The eyes maintained that the arms and legs couldn't function without direction from the eyes. The stomach contended that without all the churning, the food would never get to the blood and the body would soon shrivel up and die. Then the bowels applied for the job. The other parts of the body laughed long and hard at this notion that the lowly bowels should be boss of the body. The bowels became angry and closed up! The stomach soon up-chucked. The heart rate elevated. The brain became foggy. The legs wobbled and the eyes crossed. As the body came closer to a shuddering halt, the other parts gave in and made the bowels the boss! In the original version of the story, there is a moral of course about what you need to be in order to be boss. You figure it out.

Isn't it amazing how much we take a well-functioning body part for granted? Just let that part get a little out of whack and life can become miserable. The bowels are perhaps the prime example of this. If the part responsible for waste elimination malfunctions, toxic substances can build up and poison the rest of the body. The disposal of toxins is necessary on so many levels. Toxic thoughts can poison the brain. What is needed is lots of roughage. For the body, roughage is fiber in fruits and vegetables. For the brain, roughage is reading and reflection producing good positive thinking. So fill yourself up with lots of roughage, and you will soon have a state of calm and relaxation in which all the parts of the body work in harmony together.

February 10

Do Some Good

The luxury of doing good surpasses every other personal enjoyment.

John Gay

I believe ... that every human mind feels pleasure in doing good to another.

Thomas Jefferson

There is a sort of gratification in doing good which makes us rejoice in ourselves.

Montaigne

To be doing good is man's most glorious task.

Sophocles

My cousin, Bob Sproule, was a very special person. He lived a full life as a husband, father, teacher, administrator, and producer for his local theatre.

The first recollection I have of Bob was when I was about 9 years old. Mom and dad went on a holiday and left me with my Uncle Ed and Aunt Nelly. The Sproules were lovely folks, but both my cousins were out all day and all night as well. They were in their early 20's and had full social lives. I was bored silly. T.V. hadn't arrived yet, and I sat on their front porch and watched the world go by. Then my cousin Bob came to my rescue.

Bob played the violin, and he was playing in a musical at the local theatre. He asked me if I would like to go, and I jumped at the chance. I found myself in the middle of the first row of the balcony—the best seat in the house—and there in the orchestra, playing the violin, was my cousin Bob. He gave me the biggest smile I had ever seen. I can't remember the musical, but I sure remember that smile.

The last time I saw Bob was a couple of summers ago. It was up in Espanola where he and his lovely wife, Sharon, were very active in the local theatre. They also traveled extensively to help local theatres get started and maintain productions. We had a lovely morning with Bob and Sharon, and I'll never forget his parting words. "Go and do some good." That's what Bob had done all his life. He lives on in the hearts of so many of us.

February 11

Pressure

Courage is grace under pressure.

Ernest Hemingway

This is a catastrophic universe, always; and subject to sudden reversals, upheavals, changes, cataclysms, with joy never anything but the song of substance under pressure forced into new forms and shapes.

Doris Lessing

There is a terrific little self-help book *Don't Sweat the Small Stuff.* It has wonderful stories of grace under pressure. Then after all the inspiring illustrations, the author makes the bold statement that "It's all small stuff!" For many people, problems aren't "small stuff." Whatever it is that's causing the feeling of "pressure" may not feel that small. Difficulties cannot be waved away with a brave front. They remain and resurface to keep up the pressure and the longer this problem hangs about, the more likely we are to become ill. Stories of courage in this self-help book may not relieve the effects of long-term pressure. So as not to be discouraged, what does help?

I love the phrase one of our choir members taught us. Whenever we are about to begin our task, we join our hands together and begin with a prayer: "Still our hearts, Lord, so that we may know we are in your presence." The key point here is that we are together in our task. You need never feel you are battling your demons alone. Giving the problems to God and letting Him work them out through others can result in a peaceful feeling. You know that eventually, everything will work out. We must be receptive to unexpected solutions. God works through others, and if we aren't listening, we may miss the answers we seek.

When I was helping to direct a cabaret show, we initially feared rehearsals because performer's ego sometimes gets in the way. When they don't like something, some talented people can become very difficult. Eventually, we found the solution. We prayed together before the rehearsal. This had a calming effect on the proceedings. We took time out when disagreements arose. We worked together to dispel rancor and to have fun. The problems still came, but so, too, did their resolution. Grace works much better when people work together in love instead of with ego. Maybe that's what the author meant when he said, "It's all small stuff." It can be, with the help of others—collaborating to resolve difficulties.

Volkswagens Part 2

He led his regiment from behind. He found it less exciting!

When everyone is somebody, then no one's anybody!

Gilbert and Sullivan operetta, The Gondoliers

Gilbert and Sullivan wrote some wonderfully witty operettas; I was fortunate to play the tenor lover "Luiz" in *The Gondoliers* in my last year at Western. I sang two duets with the soprano with the sparkling gorgeous eyes. Another soprano lead had a crush on me. Life was good. Then the Duchess decided to make my life miserable. She was great for the part, being wonderfully padded. This splendid thespian latched onto me and made me jump through hoops. I guess she thought I walked funny, so she made me walk up and down the halls with a book on my head. "Stand up straight … no slouching!" she would shout at me. For some reason, she decided I needed remaking, and she was the one to do it. There was an operetta going on apart from the Gilbert and Sullivan, and I was in the middle of it. Things quickly got worse.

The Duchess decided she would come to a party with us. She knew that I drove an old V.W. Beetle, and she boldly stated in the deepest alto voice: "I have never had a ride in a Volkswagen before, so I am coming to the party in your Volkswagen!" What could I do? We got her into the back seat, and I turned the car on, but before we could move, the Duchess intoned from the back seat, "I smell smoke!" We looked around and there she sat, like a giant toad, with smoke billowing up around her. With a huge effort, we managed to extricate her from the back seat, which by now was ready to burst into flames. Once she was out, I took the bench part of the seat and tossed it out onto the road, where it landed upside down. The springs were glowing red but quickly cooled off, and little damage was done.

I realized what had happened. I had recently added water to the battery, which was located under the back seat bench, but I had neglected to put the battery cover back over the battery. When the Duchess flounced down, the springs touched the battery terminals and shorted out the battery, heating up the springs!

We got it all back together, and off we went to the party to continue the operetta.

February 13

Hope

Hope is the thing with feathers that perches in the soul.

Emily Dickenson

Hope smiles on the threshold of the year to come, whispering that it will be happier.

Alfred Lord Tennyson

There is one thing which gives radiance to everything. It is the idea of something around the corner.

G.K. Chesterton

The stories of many scientific discoveries are fascinating studies of serendipity. A serendipitous discovery involves luck or chance. I believe that many of the great discoveries weren't just due to luck, but were the result of belief and hope that almost made the discovery a self-fulfilling prophesy. In other words, the breakthrough favored the person with ample optimism. There are countless stories of serendipity, but one of my favorites is the discovery of the element radium by Marie and Pierre Curie.

The Curies were convinced that there was another element found in pitchblende, the mineral known to contain the previously discovered element, uranium. They figured this other element was very rare and elusive, but they had high hopes that they would be able to isolate this new element. They also knew it would be an onerous task of separation, an almost impossible chemical "experiment." They began meticulously refining mountains of pitchblende and ended up with minuscule amounts of the suspected compound containing the new element. When they completed the final steps and captured their element in a porcelain crucible, they were shocked when they looked into the crucible. There was nothing there. Tons and tons of rock had been reduced, and there was nothing left. Imagine their dissatisfaction when they went to bed that night. Their hopes were dashed! It seemed they had failed!

They couldn't sleep. Pierre got up in the middle of the dark night and wandered down to the lab. He was astounded by a huge glow giving brightness to everything. The glow was coming from the crucible. He roused Marie and they looked into the crucible and realized that they had the element after all. The radium had been absorbed into the walls of the container, and they were able to get a few micrograms out the next day. Their hope and hard work had given the world a new element!

February 14

Love

And now faith, hope, and love abide, these three; and the greatest of these is love.

1 Corinthians 13:13

I kissed my first woman and smoked my first cigarette on the same day. I have never had time for tobacco since.

Arturo Toscanini

For love is strong as death, passion fierce as the grave. Its flashes are flashes of fire, a raging flame. Many waters cannot quench love, neither can floods drown it. If one offered for love all the wealth of his house, it would be utterly scorned.

Song of Solomon 8:6

When yer heart goes bummity bump ... it's love love love.

Old 40's song

Here we are again at the day of the year devoted to romantic love—the day named after the Christian Martyr, Saint Valentine. I've always figured that every day should be devoted to love, just as every day should be Earth Day, and every day should be Thanksgiving Day. Wouldn't it be nice if every day we could treat those we love as very special?

I love the silly Valentine story Gord MacKay told at one of our cabaret shows. A man had never been able to please his wife with any Valentine gift. This year, he thought he would get her a pet to make her happy. He went down to the park to watch people walk their dogs with the idea that he would get some inspiration. Sitting on the next bench was a lady with an unusual looking animal on a leash. "What on earth is that animal?" he inquired.

"It's very rare," said the woman. "It's called a beasle ... a cross between a beaver and a weasel ... and it makes things vanish." Then she pointed at a small stump and said, "Beasle that tree stump." The animal attacked and chewed the stump away to nothing! The man told the woman he had to have the animal as a gift for his wife, and he would give this woman any amount—so they came to an agreement, and the happy fellow got the money from his bank, gave it to the woman, and hurried home with his gift.

When he went in the house to give this new pet to his wife, she asked him, "What the hell is that?"

"It's a beasle, dear," he said, "and I got it just for you."

"A beasle," she said disparagingly—"beasle my ass!"

45

February 15

Mistakes

There are only two mistakes one can make along the road to truth; not going all the way, and not starting.

Buddha

We made too many wrong mistakes.

Yogi Berra

The only man who never makes mistakes is the man who never does anything.

Eleanor Roosevelt

An expert is a man who has made all the mistakes which can be made in a very narrow field.

Niels Bohr

Niels Bohr was one of the more interesting of the "atomic" physicists. Many of his colleagues thought he was a little crazy because of some of the wild things he did, and for what he suggested about atoms. Bohr was somewhat rebellious, out drinking with friends when he wasn't driving his motorcycle or thinking about the hydrogen atom. After the nuclear model of the atom had been proposed by Lord Rutherford, physicists realized the model wouldn't work. The difficulty was that the negative electrons zipping around the positive nucleus should spiral into the oppositely charged nucleus in an instant. In other words, atoms should all collapse! Many scientists figured that Rutherford model must be a huge mistake! Atoms do not collapse under normal conditions.

Niels Bohr thought about this for some time, and then he made a suggestion which eventually shook physics to its very foundations. Bohr suggested that it was a mistake to use the laws of classical physics in regard to atoms. The electron doesn't fall into the nucleus because it can't! The laws of classical physics simply don't apply to atoms. This pronouncement seemed rebellious to many physicists but made others think in very new ways and eventually reinforced the new quantum theory of modern physics.

Speaking of mistakes, my father once told me I was a mistake. He was telling me this to encourage us to have lots of children I suppose. I guess if they had the pill in the 40's you wouldn't be reading this. Oh well, as my brother Bert used to say with great authority: "Always remember. No one is a completely useless mistake. You can always be used as a very bad example!"

February 16

Observation

Don't miss the beautiful colors of the rainbow looking for a pot of gold.

Anonymous

There is a story about a young man who found a coin on the ground one day as he walked along. This is a lucky day he thought as he put the coin in his piggy bank for safekeeping. From that day on, he was constantly looking on the ground for money, and find it he did. In the next twenty years he was lucky enough to fill his piggy bank many times over—and in doing so, he missed many treasures nature has to offer.

We are often caught up in the trivialities of everyday survival, and we forget to observe what is really happening around us. The beautiful colors of the rainbow can be found in people as well as nature. Take an honest look today at those around you. Notice the many shades of color in skin, hair and eyes. Listen to the music in their voices. All our fellow humans are unique. Sit on a bench and watch them. Look at what they are wearing. Look closer at nature, at the birds and plants which surround us. Observe the detail surrounding all of us, which is all but invisible to many people who go through their day on autopilot.

I love the beginning of William Blake's *Auguries of Innocence*:

> *To see the World in a grain of sand,*
> *And a Heaven in a wild flower,*
> *Hold infinity in the palm of your hand,*
> *And Eternity in an hour.*

Are you a student of nature, including human nature, or have you been on automatic pilot missing out on rainbows? Begin today. How many hues will you see today? How many colleagues can you look at today as if for the first time? Go beyond the task of everyday living and working, and explore all the beauty and simple joys of intent observation. Look with keener eyes at the world about you. Infinite delights await you!

February 17

Latin Expressions

Quid me anxius sum	What … me worry?
Seniors priores	Elderly first.
In loco parentis	Children drive their parents crazy.
Varietas delectate	Variety is delightful i.e. the spice of life
Quod Dixie Dixie	What I have said, I have said.

I find Latin gains more appeal as I get older. The "seniors priores" has a wonderful sound and meaning not appreciated until recently. In fact, at one time, I found Latin a terrible bore with little appeal and lots of pain.

We had our first exposure to Latin in grade ten. The Latin teacher—a lovely old gentleman—seemed as old as the language. He had a very soft voice; he was the only teacher who used a microphone in class in order to be heard. I remember having to stand up and say, "Sum es est, sumus estis sunt," and "Terra terrae terrae terram terra," while everybody in class waited and hoped that you would stumble all over it and have to do it again the next day. I got the lowest mark in the room—fifty-eight—and needless to say, I didn't take any more Latin. So why can I remember it all now? And why does it suddenly have appeal? Strange!

Fast forward to grade twelve, when I had what I believed was a calling to the ministry. I can't remember much about the actual calling, but it had something to do with the aura I had seen about my future brother-in-law, Philip Cooper; although he wasn't to be related to me by marriage for another decade. I even went to a seminar at Huron College for teens having a calling to serve God. This was a very serious vision I had for the future, but it all changed very quickly a few months later, thanks in a way to Latin. My guidance counselor pointed out to me that I didn't do that well in languages and that I would have to take Latin and Greek to become a man of the cloth. I remember my guidance counselor saying to me, "Lee … you are lousy in French but excel at math and science. Maybe you should think of teaching science." So I did!

February 18

Volkswagens Part 3

I am a very model of a modern major general. I deal in matters vegetable, animal and mineral.

Major General Stanley in *The Pirates of Penzance*

Oh please … sing it again … only faster!

Kevin Cline as the Pirate king to Major General Stanley

L
ife is often like a Gilbert and Sullivan operetta, going faster until it spins out of control. Just such a scenario happened to me the infamous night of our post-dress rehearsal party.

At that party, I was introduced to a drink called a "Black Russian." I don't recall how much I had, but I don't recall much of anything from that night. I do remember driving Angela and the Duchess back to their residence after the party. Then I drove through the university grounds on my way home. The next thing I remember was sitting with an awful mess about me. I managed to turn the engine off and shakily got out of the car. The Beetle was a mess. I'd hit some brush, and the front fenders were pushed in. The lights were broken. The windshield was cracked. The running boards were torn off, and even the rear taillights had disappeared. I seemed OK. Nothing was broken, but there was blood on my nose. What was I to do? If the university cops caught me, there was a good chance I would be expelled—or worse yet, miss taking part in the two performances of *The Gondoliers* the next day.

Just then some angels arrived. Four guys I didn't know stopped in their big Pontiac. They knew I was in a pickle, and they got some two-by-fours out of their trunk and pried the fenders off the wheels. They attached a rope to the VW and towed me home. Then they left. I never found out who these angels were.

Thank heavens our attitude to drinking and driving has completely changed from the careless, stupid approach we had when I was an "immortal" youth. Media coverage of the heartbreaking carnage caused by drunken drivers has made most people intolerant of drinking and driving today. The concept of the designated driver is simply common sense. We certainly didn't give much thought to it back in the 60s. Zero tolerance is the only acceptable approach today.

February 19

Equilibrium

If all the year were holidays, to play would be as tedious as to work.

William Shakespeare

If everybody's somebody, then no one's anybody!

William Gilbert

Grandma had a wonderful way for obtaining the conduct she wanted from children. If you were too spirited, she would say you were being "heard too much" and you required a dose of what she called "equilibrium-restorer." All of us would then be given a spoonful of cod liver oil. This had to be about the worst-tasting stuff ever invented, but it was a wonder-worker. The very mention of cod liver oil was enough to restore us to our "inside voices." What was totally unfair about Grandma was that she would dish the stuff out if you were too quiet as well. You were "out-of-sorts" and needed the equilibrium-restorer.

I thought I had escaped this no-win situation when I boarded away from home for the first time. Our landlady, Mrs. C, had to be in control, and she corrected us at every turn. If you ate too fast you were "gobbling" your food. If you ate too slowly, you were "playing with your food!" We boarders had a great time drawing each other's sins to Mrs. C's attention, and she dished out liberal doses of correction. It got to be a good game. Not one boarder could ever achieve the perfect balance of eating at the proper pace.

Equilibrium is another word for balance, and the loss of balance in life inevitably leads to problems. We must strive to balance work with play, activity with relaxation, socializing with quiet time by ourselves. The worst case of disequilibrium is addiction. When most of our time is taken up with one activity, we lose perspective. We all know people who are so single-minded that they can only think of one thing all the time. "Get a life" is a common expression directed at obsessed individuals. By "life" we mean balance in our activities.

The importance of equilibrium can be simply illustrated. Suppose you ate nothing but your one favorite food. How long would it remain your favorite? "Variety is the spice of life" is a cliché, but it holds especially true in today's busy world. The best equilibrium-restorer is often a change of routine. Do something to escape the rut today. Take time for yourself. Restore your equilibrium.

February 20

Paradigms

A habit is a shirt made of iron.

Harold Helfer

*O*ne fine sunny day, a man was driving his sports car on winding roads. Suddenly, another convertible wove around a corner right at him. The driver of this weaving car regained control, but as she went by the man, she screamed, "Pig!" to which he yelled back, "Road hog!" The man accelerated around the blind corner and crashed his car into a large pig on the road! The woman had been trying to warn him, but he saw it as an insult from another driver.

This story was told at a seminar about paradigms. A paradigm is an internal set of rules, or a filter, which controls the way we behave. When we drive a car in North America, we drive on the right side, and we stop at stop signs and red lights. Green means go. We never think about these internalized rules. They are automatic. If we go to Britain, however, we must constantly remind ourselves to keep left, and to yield to the traffic in roundabouts. A new set of rules or paradigm takes time to adopt, since our comportment is constantly controlled by the paradigms we have internalized. What we consider to be normal may be totally wrong in a different society. In Amsterdam, after we were almost run down by cyclists several times, someone finally told us that bicycles have the right of way over pedestrians. We must learn to think differently when we travel.

I love the silly story of the fellow from Maine who was visiting Newfoundland. His taxi driver drove through a red light. "You just drove through a red light," said the New Englander. "Don't you know that red means stop?"

The Newfie replied: "Don't worry. It's all right. My brother does it all the time."

Then the driver came to a green light and he stopped.

The Maine man said: "What are you doing? Green means "GO!"

The Newfie replied: "That's true, but my brother might be coming the other way!"

The next time you find yourself doing something without thinking, ask yourself the question: "Do I control my paradigms, or do my paradigms control me?" The answer is in the above quote from Harold Helfer.

February 21

Paradigm Shifts

Flow with whatever is happening and let your mind be free. Stay centered by accepting whatever you are doing. This is the ultimate.

Chuang Tzu

I think young people ought to seek that experience that is going to knock them off center.

James A. Michener

Nicklaus Coppernic, born in Poland in 1473, studied the classics, math, and art in preparation for life in the ministry. He studied canon law and practiced medicine before accepting several administrative positions in the church. Each of these positions gave him rooms in a castle, with access to the towers, from which he observed the motion of the stars and planets in the night sky. Over a period of years, he was able to demonstrate that the earth rotated each day and orbited the sun each year, overturning the established Ptolemaic theory of cosmology. His major work, *De Revolutionibus Orbium Coelestium* was published under his Latinized name: Nicolaus Copernicus. The idea that the earth was not the center of the universe was upsetting—especially to the church, which put humanity at the center of the cosmos. Both Western science and religion were turned totally upside-down by a huge paradigm shift to the Copernican model of the universe.

Paradigms are filters through which we view the world, and directors of how we behave. In the ancient world, the Ten Commandments affected the way the Old Testament people behaved. They used these commandments and the purity laws to live their lives. In the modern age, we are controlled by a very different set of paradigms. Green means "go", and red means "stop." A ringing phone demands that we answer. A sales flyer with over 50 % off means a traffic jam. How the world has changed! Are there subconscious filters that control our actions? Are we doing what we do simply because our paradigms tell us what we should do? Is it possible to say, "I don't want to do that anymore?" Can we actually stop ourselves from answering that ringing phone? Are we able to escape from the subconscious paradigms which can cause us to act impulsively without thought? Just what is the center of our universe? What really counts?

February 22

Paradigm Paralysis

Do not judge, and you will not be judged; do not condemn, and you will not be condemned … forgive and you will be forgiven; give and it will be given to you.

Whatever you do to the least of my brothers, you do unto me.

For all who exalt themselves will be humbled, but all who humble themselves will be exalted.

Teachings of Jesus Christ found in the Gospel of Luke

Paradigm shifts occur more often and faster in our modern technological society than at any moment in history. We find ourselves being controlled by new sets of rules which often involve the tools we have at our disposal. I am constantly delighted at the new toys which are available today. In the past ten years, we have seen digital phones, portable hard drives, flat screen TV, the Blackberry, the iPod, iPhone, iPad, the Kindle reader and HD TV just to name a few. There is practically no part of the human body which cannot be replaced. I'm certain that there will be artificial eyes and ears within my life time and perhaps even brain implants. There is hope for me yet!

Sometimes when a huge paradigm shift occurs, many people are unable to react to the new paradigm, or even to realize what has occurred. People often become even more entrenched in the old paradigm when changes are called for. This is called "paradigm paralysis." We all know people who refuse to accept new ways of doing things. In its worst form, people can actually be so controlled by the old paradigm that they cannot see the new one at all. The business world is full of failures because of paradigm paralysis. A change in the way things are done may doom businesses who continue to use old paradigms.

The teachings of Jesus were radical to the world at that time. People could not accept his new and revolutionary ideas because they did not fit in with their old rules. In a way, we can say that it was paradigm paralysis which resulted in the decision to crucify Jesus. The Pharisees constantly questioned Jesus about why he refused to obey the regulations they taught without question. His teachings, simply based on Love and not regulations, didn't fit in with their old religious paradigm, so they had to get rid of the radical Jesus. I sometimes wonder if some "Christians" still have paradigm paralysis in accepting his love-based teaching.

February 23

Quiet Place

Prayer is when you talk to God; meditation is when you listen to God.
Diana Robinson

In quiet places, reason abounds … in quiet people there is vision and purpose, that many things are revealed to the humble that are hidden from the great.
Adlai Stevenson

Beginning the day with some quiet reflection is something I have valued since I retired. When I was still working, I often worked out, played racquetball or went for a run early in the morning. If I didn't get exercise first thing, chances are I would never get it. Now that I'm retired, I need that early quiet because we get so busy doing stuff together, the quiet time may not be available later in the day. The quiet meditation is a great way to get the day off to a peaceful beginning. When I was at work, I often went for a quiet walk in the woods, and I was lucky enough to have trails through the woods close to where I worked. If you still your heart and mind, you can hear the little voice within.

If you need a quiet place to meditate, try your imagination. If you don't have a quiet room you can use, you can visualize a secret spot or quiet place. If you are stuck inside in a dreary winter, you can imagine this scene. The following is a poetic description of a quiet place someone once gave me.

When I pray or meditate, I go into a forest and sit on a warm rock in the sun or walk by a stream. It's usually late June, and there are birds chirping away here and there, and a few squirrels and chipmunks for local color. There's a light breeze, just enough to ruffle your hair a bit and cool your face, and make the pines whisper a bit above the stream talking to itself. The air is scented with the pine needles that carpet the ground in this stand of trees. The sun shines through the maples on the other side of the stream and dances across the ground and the rock. With your eyes shut, you can lie here and feel the warmth and watch the light playing from behind your eyelids. This is the warmest, most peaceful, most beautiful place in my world, where I can always come to hear and see HIM.

The mind is powerful enough to make a heavenly quiet place like this. Try it!

February 24

Vodka

I never drink water because of the disgusting things that fish do in it.

W. C. Fields

I have a punishing workout regimen. Every day I do 3 minutes on a treadmill, then I lie down, drink a glass of vodka and smoke a cigarette.

Anthony Hopkins

Money, like vodka, turns a person into an eccentric.

Anton Chekhov

The relationship between a Russian and a bottle of vodka is almost mystical.

Richard Owen

We were enjoying happy hour today when my neighbor told this funny story. We were talking about vodka at the time. Brian told me about injecting a watermelon with a quart of vodka and then rolling the watermelon around for a day or so. When sliced up, the melon disappears very quickly—a party favorite. On one occasion, they didn't realize their cocker spaniel was following folks around and chewing on the discarded watermelon rinds. Brian said both he and the dog got loaded, and the next day, he found that the only thing worse than a vodka hangover is a dog with a vodka hangover. It was pitiful, he remarked. We laughed at this story of another vodka victim.

Vodka is a favorite of those wishing to hide the fact they have been drinking, because you apparently can't smell it on the drinker's breath. I remember graduation day. I came home early because my son wanted me to take him for a haircut. He was sleeping in the mid-afternoon! When I woke him, I suspected he had been into the booze, but you couldn't smell the demon drink. The barber had a good time cutting his hair, as his head wouldn't stay upright. I didn't say anything because the poor guy was probably suffering from a vodka hangover for the first time, and I remembered my first and last vodka hangover.

At a Friday after-school party, the principal and I had an extended conversation in front of a punchbowl that kept emptying; each time our host refilled it, the color changed. That's about all I remember; when I woke up the next day, I had the worst headache in my life. I found out on Monday that the punch was half vodka. It was the last time I ever got loaded on a drink the Russians love so much.

February 25

Insects

Small bugs have smaller bugs to bite 'em ... and so on ad infinitem.

Old saying

When nuclear winter devastates the planet, the survivors will be the insects.

Biology text

If you do not let my people go, I will send swarms of flies on you and your officials, on your people and into your houses. The houses of the Egyptians will be full of flies, and even the ground where they are.

Exodus 8:21

About a week ago, our RV Park neighbor, across the road, was walking along looking very glum. "What's the trouble Lynn?" I asked. His unit was parked under a tree infested with tiny ants, and these ants were using the roof for a parade ground, and coming through the vents in droves. Lynn had tried three different sprays and had coated the roof with repellant, but these tiny ants wouldn't give up. Later in the day he moved his unit to a new site, and the park crew came and trimmed and sprayed the tree. Lynn moved back two days later, but the same thing happened. Those tiny insects were bound to bug Lynn, and he gave up and moved out again. The site is now vacant. The insects won!

I remember the second night of our honeymoon. We were pulling a small tag-a-long tent trailer. We set up camp and the mosquitoes were so bad we couldn't sit out. The next day, I remember a large truck coming through the campground, blasting everything including us with huge clouds of DDT—the bad stuff Rachel Carson wrote about in her book *Silent Spring*. DDT was eventually banned after a huge battle with the chemical companies. The white clouds got rid of the insect pests, so we didn't mind DDT at that time.

I've often wondered why God created so many different species of insects. Of what value are mosquitoes or flies, other than to "bug" us? The answer is found in the connection between organisms within ecosystems. Without these insects, many song birds wouldn't have food. Everything in the food chain munches on something else. Many pesky creatures help break down dead organisms. Without these munchers, the earth would be piled up with at least 20 feet of dead leaves. So everything, including these insect "pests", is connected—even if we have to battle the insects at times.

February 26

Think

Nothing so conclusively proves a man's ability to lead others as what he does from day to day to lead himself.

It is better to aim at perfection and miss it than to aim at imperfection and hit it.

both from Thomas John Watson

My brother Bert worked for the International Business Machines Corporation, IBM, a company once known as "Big Blue." Bert worked in Poughkeepsie, New York; Raleigh, North Carolina; Tallahassee, Florida; and finally in Toronto. The company moved employees around so much that the letters "IBM" were said by the employees to mean "I've **B**een **M**oved!" In Bert's case it was certainly true. After a time, Bert couldn't take the constant moves, so he retired from IBM at the ripe old age of forty-eight years old.

IBM was brought to the zenith of computing by Thomas John Watson. He originally worked for National Cash Register at Dayton, Ohio and was general sales manager at the time he left with a felony conviction based on his part in NCR's conspiracy to control the used cash register market. He joined the Computing Tabulating Recording Company in 1914 and made president the next year. Within a decade, the company took on the name International Business Machines. Watson developed IBM's effective management style and turned it into one of the most effective selling organizations yet seen. Watson was called "the world's greatest salesman" when he died in 1956. He had placards saying "THINK" placed in all offices. This word was on the most conspicuous wall of every room in every IBM building. Each employee carried a THINK notebook in which to record inspirations. The company stationery, matches, scratch pads, all bore the inscription, THINK. A monthly magazine called *Think* was distributed to the employees. Is it any wonder, then, that the laptop computer marketed by IBM is known as the "ThinkPad"? Now—I think—you know the reason why.

Post Script: "What goes up must eventually come down." IBM is no exception. Its stock has suffered several dynamic reversals. I wonder if those "THINK" signs are still up on the walls of IBM offices.

February 27

Vegetables

Better a dinner of vegetables where love is than a fatted ox and hatred with it.

Proverbs 15:17   (recall this quote from January 16 Mealtime)

Carrots are divine ... a dozen costs you but a dime ... its magic!

Bugs Bunny in Loony Tunes

A society can be measured by the way it treats its animals.

George Bernard Shaw ... noted vegetarian

All the vegetables in the garden were arguing about who was the best veggie. The carrots, always first to toot their horn, claimed that they were full of vitamins and allowed man to see well at night. The celery stalks put in their oar because they were nice and crunchy but had very few calories, so man would stay slim eating celery. The potatoes claimed the crown because they could be done in so many ways, two of man's favorites being fish and chips and a bag of crunchy potato chips. The other veggies had a good laugh of derision, claiming that potatoes weren't true veggies at all, but lowlife roots called tubers! Turnips, parsnips and rutabagas all put in their two cents but were similarly dismissed by the others. Garlic, peppers and various other smelly plants each tried to claim that man put them all over everything, so they should be the champs. Then the tomatoes applied for the job. The tomatoes claimed that they should be the best because they are in almost every Italian dish including spaghetti and the ubiquitous pizza. The veggies laughed tomatoes to scorn for their ignorance of the fact that, since they were full of seeds, they weren't true veggies at all but fruit!

There is an advertisement on TV lately in which a diner at a high-class restaurant gets a bop on the noggin when he leaves his veggies on his plate. We are always being told by nutritionists to eat our vegetables and fruit. This makes more and more sense all the time. This new era of overweight people may be from too much meat. The most amazing fact I remember from the John Robbins book, *Diet from a new America,* was that you could feed thirty people from the undeveloped world with the amount of money spent on meat by one North American. Is it time to reconsider what we eat?

Belief in Yourself

Crede quod habes, et habes

Latin (Believe you have it and you have it.)

My father always told me that I was a carbuncle (boil) on the behind of humanity.
Peter Ustinov in the movie *Topkapi*

The way we act is a product of our thoughts, both conscious and unconscious. Our self-image and our perception of our capabilities and our limitations are formed over a long period of time. We are conditioned, both by ourselves and others, to believe we have certain levels of talent, intelligence and abilities. What we think about ourselves is often what we become. Our perception of what we can and cannot do may be wrong.

We have often heard the old expression, "You can't teach old dogs new tricks." While this may be true for dogs, it can be wrong about people. People are resistant to change. Inertia comes naturally to us all. There are many people, however, who are very different than they were ten years ago. Wouldn't it be a drag if people were entirely predictable? I am often pleased to meet former students and to discover that they are very successful and happy. They may have done poorly in school, but how well one does in academics is only one predictor of success. What students do in extra-curricular activities is often a better predictor, and as we have seen, attitude is everything. Attitudes can and do change. People change. Both Albert Einstein, the father of modern physics, and Winston Churchill, the savior of the English-speaking peoples, were mediocre students in their early schooling. They are famous dyslexics. Thank goodness they refused to let poor marks keep them down. They believed they could do it, and they did it!

In the movie *Topkapi*, Peter Ustinov plays an awkward, bumbling motor-moron. (A motor-moron is a person who in eating an ice cream cone, gets more on himself than in himself.) Is it any wonder he is a bumbler? He tells us his father constantly put him down. A beautiful woman in the film keeps telling him, "You can do it, big boy!" He eventually performs a feat of great strength, a feat all motor-morons would cheer lustily. Keep believing you have it, and you will have it—in time!

February 29

A Paradox

A paradox, a paradox, a most ingenious paradox!

Gilbert & Sullivan,   *The Pirates of Penzance*

I have found the PARADOX that if I love until it hurts, then there is no hurt, but only more love.

Mother Theresa

The PARADOX of education is precisely this … that as one begins to become conscious one begins to examine the society in which he is being educated.

James Baldwin

Don't you feel sad for someone born on this day? When they are finally old enough to drink, they are really only a little child of five! Gilbert and Sullivan used this ingenious paradox in their operetta, *The Pirates of Penzance*—my favorite G&S, since it contains so many paradoxes. The pirates are all "pansies", and the police are all scared of their own shadows. When they eventually have to do battle, about the best they can do is to hide from each other! The pirate king sings a wonderful recitative, in which he reveals that the lover cannot have his freedom but has to stay as one of his pirates; although he is 21 years old, he was born on February the 29th, so he is only "five and a little bit over."

Life is full of paradoxes. When you have the strength of youth, you often lack the knowledge of how best to put this power into play. Then, when you are old and wise, the spirit is willing but the flesh is weak. It's the ultimate paradox of life, I suppose! Happy are those who are young and wise—or old and strong. Hey—we could write an opera about that, couldn't we?

I love the silly story that came in an e-mail last week. Two fellows graduated from Psychiatry and Proctology at the same time. They decided to practice together so they hung up a sign saying "Doctor Jones and Doctor Smith—NUTS and BUTTS"—Quite a pair of Docs!

Have a great February 29th! It won't return for four years, and thank goodness for that, when you have to read silly stuff like this.

March 1

Ludwig

Music should strike fire from the heart of man, and bring tears from the eyes of woman.

Music is the mediator between the spiritual and the sensual life.

What you are, you are by accident of birth; what I am, I am by myself. There are and will be a thousand princes; there is only one Beethoven.

Music is a higher revelation than all wisdom and philosophy.

All from Ludwig van Beethoven 1770-1827

I was listening to Beethoven's "Eroica" Symphony, and it suddenly struck me what a revolutionary piece of music this symphony is. He originally dedicated his 3rd Symphony to Napoleon, but when Beethoven heard that Napoleon had made himself emperor, he tore up the dedication page and wrote a new one "to the memory of a great man." Ludwig could not tolerate ego in others. He once refused to bow as the King passed by.

The 3rd Symphony ushered in a new era in music. It contained unusual harmonies and passages which were pure discord to ears used to the cultured tones of Mozart and Haydn. One commentator was heard to say: "It sounds like Beethoven is shaking his fist at the sky!" Beethoven had to struggle over his compositions. The music didn't flow out of him as it had flowed out of Mozart and Haydn. Ludwig constantly revised his compositions until they sounded right in his mind. This relentless struggle for perfection is evident in the music, yet his music always sounds powerful and inevitable. Add to this struggle the fact that he couldn't hear the results, and it's a miracle what he achieved. To my ears, Beethoven's music has no equal. I never grow tired of the power and glory in the Master's symphonies, concerti, sonatas and chamber music. I have listened to his 7th Symphony hundreds of times!

Beethoven is my greatest hero. He overcame his deafness to give us glorious music that will last forever. Each year, more Beethoven is scheduled in concerts than any other composer. There are few vacant seats when the Master's music is performed.

March 2

Morph

The moment we indulge our affections, the earth is metamorphosed, there is no winter and no night; all tragedies, all ennui vanish, all duties even.

Ralph Waldo Emerson

The story of Americans is the story of arrested metamorphoses. Those who achieve success come to a halt and accept themselves as they are. Those who fail become resigned and accept themselves as they are.

Harold Rosenberg

The more a man can forget, the greater the number of metamorphoses which his life can undergo, the more he can remember the more divine his life becomes.

Soren Kierkegaard

Although it hasn't shown up in many dictionaries, the word "morph" has been used as a common short form for metamorphosis. In science, the change from caterpillar to butterfly is known as metamorphosis. To morph, then, means to change. I love to use new words that are in vogue. There is a computer game called "word morph," in which you type in a word and the computer changes one letter to give a whole new bunch of words and their meanings. To morph has connotations of neat or unusual transformation.

The month of March could be called the month of morphing. Changes begin to happen around us. Birds return from the south. In many mid-northern climes, buds begin to burst open, and crocuses and daffodils poke up. It's the beginning of a great awakening—a resurrection when the earth shakes off the last vestiges of bleak winter, and morphs—or unfolds into all the hues and greenery of spring. When you think about it, the morphing of our surroundings each spring is a miraculous change from shapeless sod, almost dead, into a riot of color and life. The mere thought of the new season of growth makes me want to sing an old Gilbert and Sullivan refrain:

The flowers that bloom in the spring, tra-la, breathe promise of merry sunshine ... As we merrily laugh and we sing, tra-la, we welcome the hope that they bring, tra-la, of a season of roses and wine ...

We can indulge our affections—we can morph as well. Alleluias!

March 3

The Planet

We don't inherit the Earth from our ancestors ... we borrow it from our children.
Unknown Source

Don't blow it. Good planets are hard to find.
Time Magazine

What is the use of a house if you haven't a tolerable planet to put it on?
Henry David Thoreau

A young family lived in the inner core of a big city. The children accepted the sights and sounds of a poor neighborhood. For the first five years of their life, they had never been outside their own little community. What they watched on television was a mixture of bad news, sitcoms and violence. Their world was very small. Then one weekend, their parents took them camping for the very first time. They went on nature walks, had a campfire and made some friends. When it came time to go home, the children refused. "Why can't we stay here?" they pleaded, "for this is like heaven. There's no meanness or bullies. There are no piles of garbage or boarded-up buildings. It is so peaceful and beautiful here. We don't want to go back to that messy and yucky place ... please, please, please may we stay?"

One of the more startling facts about a forest is that there are no lasting piles of garbage—no dumps—left by the inhabitants of the woods. However, the forest may be teaming with more life than any city. Why is it that nature leaves no lasting piles other than the garbage humankind creates? How is it that other organisms can get by without leaving trash?

Humans believe that everything on Earth is for our use. Once we have used something, we throw it away. All other organisms recycle everything. Everything, including the bodies of organisms, is reused repeatedly, and life is renewed. Recycling is nature's way of restoring the earth.

If humankind is to survive, we need to change our attitude. Our children and future generations deserve at least as much of the planet as we have. We must ask of every action we take: "Can I borrow this for now, or will someone in the future do without as a result of this action?" Good stewardship is taking care of something borrowed. Will we leave the planet a better place for our children and grandchildren? It all depends upon whether we are capable of changing our attitude!

March 4

Talent

Everyone has talent; what is rare is the courage to follow the talent to the dark place where it leads.

Erica Jong

Use what talents you possess; the woods would be very silent if no birds sang there except those that sang best.

Henry van Dyke

No one can arrive from being talented alone. God gives talent; work transforms talent into genius.

Anna Pavlova

We just finished our talent show at our RV Park. There was a variety of talent on display. I was singing a serious song, and they put me second, which is a good position to be, since you don't have to think about your song all through the show. I was a part of later acts, but when you are up with others in a quartet or chorus, it's less intimidating than doing a solo. The only problem with my spot in the show was that I had to follow Lacie, the rat terrier, who was the most amazingly talented dog I had ever seen. Lacie did everything from walking a tightrope to standing on the pointy end of a tiny football—and I had to follow this dog act. I think it was W.C. Fields who said: "Never get on stage after a kid or animal act." Anyway, I got up and did my solo thing, and enjoyed myself; and I hope and trust that some people were moved by my singing. I always feel that singing has to come from the heart, and the wonderful words and thoughts of the composer of the song must be made clear and immediate to the listener. Too often, I hear terrifically talented artists who draw all the attention to their rendition and very little to the meaning of the song. This happens often at sports events when a famous pop star butchers the national anthem, adding a raft of notes never written by the composer.

The true talent is often in the genius of the lyrics and melody, and this is what we performers always need to remember. We are the vessel through which the real meaning and message are delivered, and to my way of thinking, that's where genuine talent shines—in the delivery of the composer's intention!

March 5

Wow

Treat people as if they were what they ought to be and you help them to become what they are capable of being.

Goethe

I will speak ill of no man, and speak all the good I know of everybody.

Benjamin Franklin

If you have zest and enthusiasm you attract zest and enthusiasm. Life does give back in kind.

Norman Vincent Peal

Tuesday morning in our Florida RV Park is announcement time. Most of the Riverside RVers gather for coffee, and Dieter and Heather tell us all about the upcoming events. This morning they introduced a lady who had been in the park about a month. She told about being in many RV parks—but none like Riverside, where everything seems so well organized. She had many superlatives for the office staff, the activities and the general demeanor in the campground. The phrase she used over and over was: "We went back to our unit and we said, 'Wow!'" It is no accident that the park gets five stars in every category.

Rewind to twenty-five years ago. We used to go to football games to see the Buffalo Bills. After the game, we often ate at an Italian restaurant owned and run by the family of Ilio DiPaolo, who was a famous good guy wrestler on TV when I was a kid. Ilio's restaurant was a happy place. The food was excellent and the staff courteous, friendly and attentive. Ilio often came around to make small talk. The restaurant has been a gem in Buffalo for almost fifty years. When Ilio was killed in a car accident, the celebration of his life was also worthy of a "wow."

What do these two happy places have in common? The person in charge is truly interested in people and knows how to organize and maintain a welcoming ambiance. An enthusiastic atmosphere surrounds you as you enter these positive places. Everyone gets caught up in the "wow," and pessimists, whiners, and negative folks are simply ignored. If they don't get listened to, they soon give up their nonsense. Courtesy is contagious! So is "wow."

March 6

Smoking

To cease smoking is the easiest thing I ever did. I ought to know because I've done it a thousand times.

Attributed to Mark Twain

I thought I couldn't afford to take her out and smoke as well. So I gave up cigarettes. Then I took her out and one day I looked at her and thought: "Oh well," and I went back to smoking again, and that was better.

Benny Hill

A thousand Americans stop smoking every day ... by dying.

Unknown

There's something luxurious about having a girl light your cigarette. In fact, I got married once on account of that.

Harold Robbins

We were having a good chat this afternoon about our days of smoking. It seems that all of us remember smoking whether we liked it or not. Second-hand smoke was a way of life a generation ago. Everybody lived with somebody who filled the house with smoke. I remember my father, Allen, lighting up and then coughing and hacking. It was painful to watch Al smoke his thirteen cigarettes a day. My wife, Celia, never smoked directly, but her house was constantly full of smoke. Joyce, her mother, would light one off another, and then forget where she had left the last one, so she would light another. It wasn't unusual to have two cigarettes and a cigar or two blazing away in the Cooper household. I was guilty as well!

Vacation was no better; we would pile into our car and Joyce would always have a cigarette going, while Celia's father Gil and I smoked our pipes or cigars. Celia would have to turn the quarter vent in Big Red, our '68 Ford Galaxy, towards her and hold her nose six inches from the vent in order to breathe! Some car trip it was for Celia, but that's the way it was in the day of smokers and smoking.

Now, everything has changed. Once the health epidemics of emphysema, lung cancer and other various health woes were connected to tobacco, it was soon stupid to keep up with the filthy habit; and so, along with most of my friends, I managed to stop. It seemed rather silly to stand on the front porch in freezing weather to burn up hard-earned dollars in smoke—only to ruin your health—so we all quit.

March 7

Faith

Science is not only compatible with spirituality; it is a profound source of spirituality.

Carl Sagan

Faith is the bird that sings when the dawn is still dark.

Rabindranath Tagore

Daughter, your faith has made you well; go in peace.

Luke 8:48 Jesus tells the woman who touched his robe that her faith has cured her.

In faith there is enough light for those who want to believe and enough shadows to blind those who don't.

Blaise Pascal

We live in an age when people put their faith in a large number of modern institutions which, in one way or another, can let you down. I am constantly amazed by the number of people who tell me about all the investments they have and how well they are doing. There never seems to be anybody who will tell you how much they have lost. One investor used to tell me that you should put your faith in gold and gold stocks because in the long run, gold always goes up. This person put his money into gold in the mid 1980's, and sad to tell, the company eventually went belly up. He lost everything. Another investor owned several millions worth of Nortel stock when it was at a high. I noticed that the Nortel CEO had unloaded his shares, so I suggested to this person that they should liquidate their stock. I was told to have faith in this wonderful corporation. Within two years, the stock value sank to less than a dollar!

Another institution we put our faith in is modern medicine. Mail-order drugs have become a huge industry. There seems to be no end of miracle cures out there. The promotions say, "Satisfaction guaranteed or your money refunded." There are many honest folks who endorse these marvelous mail-order miracles. What people don't know is that even if the cure doesn't work, only 12 % of the people ever send in for a refund.

I like what our preacher told us last week about faith. "You don't put your faith in the minister, in people with authority, or in present-day institutions. They can all let you down! You know where you should put your faith."

March 8

Beauty

Everything has beauty, but not everyone sees it.

Confucius

Beauty ... when you look into a woman's eyes and see what is in her heart.

Nate Dircks

Beauty ... in projection and perceiving ... is 99.9% attitude.

Grey Livingston

It amazes me how often people miss out on the most beautiful delights of the world because they have no time to pause—or because they are on autopilot, and fail to perceive the beauty around them. When the kids were small, we taught them a system for telling everyone to look for beauty in a particular direction. Whether we were driving, biking or hiking, we would alert the others by saying, "alert at two o'clock." Since twelve o'clock is straight ahead and six o'clock is directly behind, we should all look slightly to the right. If you saw a worthy object to your left, you would say, "alert at nine o'clock."

The *Washington Post* conducted an experiment about priorities and perception. They had a world-famous violinist, Joshua Bell, play beautiful music on a Stradivarius in a Metro station for an hour. Although twenty people threw money without stopping, only six people stopped to listen for a while. Several children wanted to stop and listen, but their parents forced them on. At the end, there was no applause since everyone had moved along.

The *Washington Post* asked: *"How do we perceive beauty? Do we stop to appreciate it? Do we recognize talent in an unexpected context? One possible conclusion reached from this experiment could be: If we do not have a moment to stop and listen to one of the best musicians in the world playing some of the finest music ever written, with one of the most beautiful instruments — **How many other things are we missing?**"*

March 9

Reflection

In quiet places, reason abounds.

Adlei Stevenson

Be still and know that I am God.

The Psalms

One of the teachers in our department was always in a hurry. He would rush here and there. If you could ever slow him down long enough to talk, he always seemed out of breath and resented an intrusion into his time. His to-do list was always longer than everyone else's, and he constantly let us know that he was busier than the rest of us slackers. One of the other fellows, who always had time for anyone, said to me one day, "Why the hell is he always in such a hurry? He's going to hurry himself into an early grave! Can't he learn to relax like the rest of us?" Wise words indeed!

We all know that an active life will keep the blood moving and probably extend our life. This is true—to an extent. The real secret probably lies in a balance between activity and relaxation. Some people find themselves overwhelmed by the hustle of modern life. Get up and gobble breakfast (if at all.) Rush to the bus or drive like a maniac. Do some work while eating lunch. Go to the club and work out. Pick up groceries on the mad rush home. Get going to that evening meeting. Get ready for tomorrow. Stop! Please let me off! If you find yourself in this type of rush, you won't rust out—you will burn out! You need some quality quiet time. In the midst of turmoil, there must be calm. Learn to shut out the rush and turn off your racing thoughts. Here are a few ways to achieve quiet or calm.

Begin each day with some quiet, focusing thought or prayer. Think about this during the day, and let all your body molecules relax each time you ponder this great thought or prayer.

Close your door and turn out the lights. Breathe slowly and deeply and concentrate on sustaining totally relaxed breathing. Quiet your mind.

Find a "magic spot" where you can go to relax and ponder the big questions of life or just be quiet. This could be an inner sanctum at home, a church chapel, a prayer garden or a place in the woods. A chair somewhere and a good imagination, prayer or a mantra will also work. Let every molecule just relax and bask in the quiet.

March 10

Empty the Trash

Forgive and forget. Sour grapes make for a lousy wine.

Anonymous

Forgiving and being forgiven are two names for the same thing. The important thing is that a discord has been resolved.

C.S. Lewis

Thomas Keene, in his book on paradigms, suggests a good reason why the Swiss are no longer the top-selling watchmakers in the world. Apparently, the quartz movement was invented in Switzerland but was ignored by watchmakers, who all believed that to make a good watch, one needed at least a 17-jewel movement. The Swiss were at that time the greatest watchmakers in the world. Twenty-five years later they were no longer on top. What happened? It seems that the Japanese watchmakers adapted the Swiss quartz movement and based their new watches on the invention the Swiss had rejected. How could the Swiss watchmakers have made such a mistake when the quartz movement was their invention?

Have you ever reacted poorly in a situation, or failed to react at all, and then later wondered why this happened to you? Have you ever wondered, "How could I have been so dumb?" or, "How could I have failed to see that?" Sure you have. We all have! The reason we miss what later becomes obvious is the same reason the Swiss watchmakers missed the obvious advantages of the quartz movement. The human mind stores up vast amounts of information and is conditioned by this information to react in certain ways when new data are presented. It is paradigm paralysis, and we aren't even aware that it is happening to us. The Swiss were so conditioned to think in terms of jeweled movements, they failed to see the value of the new movement. We often make poor decisions based on past knowledge we forget is even there. Our subconscious can influence how we react without our knowing why.

Is there a way to reduce the influence of our past experiences? Of course there must be, or nothing new would ever be invented. We would be no better than insects if we simply operated on stored instinct. To reduce old ways of thinking, we must begin to forgive old wrongs, hurts and sins, including our own. It takes courage to forgive the past and begin anew, but it must be done. Empty the trash now, and begin to see with new, unbiased eyes.

March 11

The Kingdom

The "kingdom of Heaven" is a condition of the heart ... not something that comes "upon the earth" or "after death."

Friedrich Nietzsche

I am surrounded by priests who repeat incessantly that their kingdom is not of this world, and yet they lay their hands on everything they can get.

Napoleon Bonaparte

My mind's my kingdom.

Francis Quarles

...Thy Kingdom come ...

The Lord's Prayer

Once Jesus was asked by the Pharisees when the kingdom of God was coming and he answered ... "in fact, the kingdom of God is among you."

Luke 17:20

"Kingdom" is a much-used word in the gospels. Jesus uses the phrase "kingdom of God" and "kingdom of heaven" many times in his parables. According to Matthew, Jesus often begins stories with one of these phrases. What exactly did Jesus mean by the word "kingdom?" The word has connotations of a ruler and his or her subjects. A kingdom implies a "king" and conjures up visions of Camelot or some ideal place where everything is orderly—and justice, peace, and plenty are standard fare. This is far from what Jesus was teaching in his sermons and stories. Perhaps the word "kingdom" could be replaced by the phrase "spiritual utopia of LOVE."

There is huge irony in the fact that Friedrich Nietzsche seems to be the closest to what Christ actually meant. Nietzsche also said that "God is dead," and many thought that the famous philosopher was an ardent atheist. From the quote above, it seems that Nietzsche is saying that love is the way to the kingdom. The disposition to give oneself to others elevates one to a spiritual Camelot, with heavenly feelings of ecstasy—the kingdom.

If we can love everyone with the same love and light shown in the gospel stories, the kingdom of God—the kingdom of heaven—is indeed among us.

March 12

Bicycles

When I was a kid I used to pray every night for a new bicycle. Then I realized that the Lord doesn't work that way, so I stole one and asked for forgiveness.
Emo Philips

The bicycle, the bicycle surely, should always be the vehicle of novelists and poets.
Christopher Morley

It would not be at all strange if history came to the conclusion that the perfection of the bicycle was the greatest incident of the nineteenth century.
Author Unknown

Our RV Park has a large population of bicycles. Today on my two-mile circuit around the park, I counted the number of bikes and the types. Almost every unit has at least two bikes, and they come in all sizes and shapes—just like people. I am surprised by the number of old balloon-tire bikes, some of which must be fifty years old. They even have snazzy white-wall tires! Many of these are so ancient, you must peddle backward to apply the brakes. If you stand up on the pedals—with the pressure applied backwards—you can stop on a dime! My big brother Judd had a balloon-tire bike. I was surprised he would ride his bike at all after an accident he had as a kid. He was riding down the sidewalk, and a car backed out in front of him. Judd went in the car window, and without the safety glass they have today, he was cut all over the shoulder and needed several hundred stitches.

The most spectacular spill I had was on a hill down to the railway tracks. If the man came out of his shack with his "S T O P" sign, you had to apply the brakes or risk running into a train—or worse—having it run into you. This almost happened one day as I zoomed down the hill. Out came the man. Up went the "S T O P" sign. I stood on my brakes and the damn chain broke! I kept going with NO BRAKES! There was a car already stopped for the train, so I ran into the back bumper of that well-positioned car and flew over the roof, landing on the hood! Amazingly, there was no major damage to me or the car. If you have to choose between a car and a train—take the car.

March 13

Leaping

That's one small step for man; one giant leap for mankind.

Neil Armstrong

The most dangerous thing in the world is to try to leap a chasm in two jumps.

David Lloyd George

Sometimes you just have to take the leap and build your wings on the way down.

Kobi Yamada

Life leaps like a geyser for those willing to drill through the rock of inertia.

Alexis Carrel

About the only exercise some folks get is leaping to conclusions and jumping all over other people. As Henry Miller suggests, all growth comes from taking a chance and leaping in the dark. What we often need are catalysts to make that leap. Luckily, catalysts are all around us. Parents, teachers and good friends will give assistance when we want to spread our wings and make a leap that seems too far for our present capabilities. On the other hand, there are only five fingers—and some overused and dangerous expressions like, "Don't you think you've bitten off more than you can chew?" and, "Look before you leap!" If we never took any chances, we would all still be in caves, or in the garden. Maybe that wouldn't be so bad for some people, but I happen to love the unknown around the corner rather than the comfort of the same old routine. Doing the same old think quickly leads to boredom. We need lots of leaping to overcome inertia and keep us young!

Getting on the stage in front of others is a huge leap for most people. One of the best examples of taking a chance is my good friend Ted. We used to do a cabaret show at our church, and Ted had never been on the stage. He has a great sense of humor, and I knew if I could just get to him once, he would be fine. So, encouraged by his wife, Jane, and the rest of us, Ted joined in the show. Now he anchors the bass section in the choir, gets up in all the shows, and will perform as he probably never thought possible when he "did me a favor" many years ago by getting up on the stage when he really wasn't comfortable with it. There is no such thing as a "natural." It took an initial leap for all the great actors. What barrier are you going to leap today?

March 14

Listen

The first duty of love is to listen.

Paul Tillich

Listen, or thy tongue will keep thee deaf.

Native Proverb

You talk too much. You worry me to death. You talk too much. You even worry my pets!

From a 50's Song

No one really listens to anyone else. Try it for a while and you'll soon see why.

Mignon McLaughlin

My dear Aunt Dorothy was a lady of few words. When she spoke, everyone listened. She hated small talk, but would always have something of import to say when she did speak. My brother Judd phoned up Aunt Dot one time, just to blather, and she said to him: "State your business." Judd got off the phone quickly and told us what Dot had said, and we all had a good laugh. At different times, Dot said the same thing to all of us. I recall a time when Dot drove into the big city to do some shopping with my sister Noni and a friend. When Dot returned from the expedition, she looked a little bedraggled, and she said to me, "That's the last shopping trip I'll ever go on." My sister told me that the friend had talked all the way in and back, and nobody else could get in a word. They had to sit and listen while this person rattled on and on. That would not have pleased my aunt, but she was too polite to make it an issue.

I love what the Native Proverb is telling us. If we don't listen to what others are telling us, we will never learn anything from anybody through the art of conversation. I often wonder why some people never figure this out. Maybe nobody has ever told them to stifle themselves like that nasty old sitcom character, Archie Bunker, who would talk nonsense all the time, and then tell his wife, Edith, to stifle herself. Archie never listened to anybody, and he definitely should have been the one to stifle. I have often wished that we all had a large round "off" switch on our nose, and this could just be turned off when we talk too much. The art of good listening is important to personal growth. Let us try today to listen carefully and minimize our own words.

March 15

Listening

As regards anything besides these, my son, take a warning: To the making of many books there is no end, and much devotion to them is wearisome to the flesh.

Ecclesiastes 12:12

Tell me the stories of Jesus I love to hear; things I would ask him to tell me if he were here: scenes by the wayside, tales of the sea, stories of Jesus, tell them to me.

William H. Parker

When it comes to listening to others, there are several topics which can raise emotions to a high level. Religion may be the most difficult to discuss, because it strikes at the core of a person's beliefs and value system. Some well-meaning folks knock on your door with the intention of converting you to their way of thinking about God and His "chosen" people. Since the person visited is not one of the chosen, these folks feel they are doing God's work by trying to make you "see the light." I always welcome them, and I agree to have a discussion with them—as long as I get equal time. They can tell me what they want for five minutes, and then I get five minutes to explain my views. This can go back and forth for as long as they like. They must agree to listen to what I am saying to them. Most of them are secure enough as a team to accept my offer.

Then I get out over five different Bibles and piles of reference books about religion. I have these bookmarked with index cards for quick reference. The point I make over and over again is simply this. If you use any literal translation of the Bible, you will find yourself in difficulty, particularly if you take the lines out of context. To me the Bible stories are stories. I feel very strongly that the Bible should be studied as a metaphor. What language did God use? Every Bible translation is open to differing interpretation. What we should be asking is: "What is this passage trying to tell us? How best can we live our lives with the lesson this story tells us? What lesson about Love was illustrated?"

I like what some churches say after the Bible readings: "Hear what the Spirit is saying to the Church."

March 16

T.E.A.M.

Coming together is a beginning.
Keeping together is progress.
Working together is success.

Henry Ford

We are most effective as a team when we compliment each other without embarrassment and disagree without fear.

Unknown

A boat doesn't go forward if each one is rowing their own way.

Swahili proverb

There is no I in Teamwork.

Unknown

We must all hang together, or assuredly, we shall all hang separately.

Benjamin Franklin

Teamwork: Simply stated, it is less me and more we.

Unknown

This morning at coffee hour, somebody presented us with an acronym which was new to us. Oh boy—another bloody bunch of letters to forget. Actually, this one was useful: T.E.A.M. "Together, Everyone Achieves More."

This catchy acronym reminded us of a story in *The Last Lecture* by Randy Pausch. As a kid, Randy dreamed of being in the NFL. In his first practice, the coach ran all the kids through drills with no footballs. When asked where the balls were, the coach replied, "We're working on what the other twenty-one guys are doing." He meant the guys without the football.

I am also reminded of a little something my dear wife said to me when we first met. "You had better behave yourself. See these five fingers? Individually they may not be much—but rolled into a fist, they become a weapon terrible to behold."

Somebody once described a committee as six folks with a dozen arms and twelve legs—but no brains. This can be true—especially if each member has a separate agenda. Teamwork is one of the most valuable skills we can ever teach children—and it's never too late to learn!

March 17

Libraries and Librarians

My two favorite things in life are libraries and bicycles. They both move people forward without wasting anything. The perfect day: riding a bike to the library.

Peter Golkin

Outside of a dog, a book is a man's best friend. Inside of a dog, it's too dark to read.

Groucho Marx

You go into the restaurants of a town and you see people with hungry stomachs, but you go into the library of the same town and you will see hungry brains feasting upon their favorites. There are all too few libraries, and far too many restaurants. People should eat less and think more.

Matthew Adams

My first encounter with the library wasn't a happy event. In the ninth grade, we were trouped down to the library and informed how to use it by an ancient, wrinkled lady who told us—at least five times—that if we found any of the library books at home, we were to bring them to her. I had a copy of the complete novels of H.G. Wells at home. It was a large, heavy volume with an old, frayed yellow cover, but I loved that book. One of my brothers had taken it out years before and not returned it. In the intervening years, I had read it from cover to cover several times. Yet it did have "Property of the Library" stamped in several places, so I dutifully took it back and presented it to the librarian. She didn't even smile as she made disparaging comments about my ancestry before revoking my library privileges for the next week. I was punished for the sin of my brothers. Out of spite, I never used the school library much after that.

Today, everything has changed. I love libraries and librarians. I have several library cards and constantly have large numbers of items out—and more on hold. The Internet and computers have made it easy to reserve ahead, and so for me, the library is an often-visited place. The librarians have changed since high school days. They are the friendliest people in the world and will do anything to be helpful. Have you thanked a librarian this week?

March 18

Baseball

So I'm ugly. I never saw anyone hit with his face.

The game's isn't over until it's over. You can observe a lot just by watching.

You should always go to other people's funerals; otherwise, they won't come to yours.

When you come to a fork in the road, take it.

Baseball is ninety percent mental. The other half is physical.

If people don't want to come out to the ballpark, how are you going to stop them?
    All from the Yankee catcher Yogi Berra — 15 straight seasons as an all-star

Some people find the game of baseball to be incredibly boring—and it is—for them. Perhaps they don't know what to "observe by watching," as Yogi tells us. There is a huge mental battle going on between the pitcher and the batter. If you are lucky enough to sit where you can see the pitches, the game becomes very interesting. Sitting behind home plate or watching on a large screen TV gives you the best perspective. It's then that you realize what Yogi was getting at when he said, "Baseball is ninety percent mental." I love watching baseball, and it's certainly fun to be at the game. We were at a Blue Jay—Red Sox spring training game, and the first thing that struck me was how many people never watch the game. They are eating, drinking, talking or traipsing down to get something more to eat or drink. Oh well, I guess as long as they are having fun—but why pay all that good money for tickets and parking if you aren't going to watch the game? For a while, it looked as if the game that evening would be canceled. The players had a dispute with the league over their coaches not getting paid to go to exhibition games in Japan. I told Ted that the game would start an hour late, and it did. I am very good at reading baseball minds and on many occasions have correctly predicted what would happen on the next pitch. It's all a matter of tuning into the conceptual game. The next time you watch a baseball game, try and tune into the mental battle going on.

March 19

Bonuses

I gotta tell ya, with our $2.4 billion in profits last year, they gave me a great big bonus. Really, it's almost obscene.

Lee Iacocca

The most unfair thing about life is the way it ends. I mean, life is tough. It takes up a lot of your time. What do you get at the end of it? A Death! What's that, a bonus? I think the life cycle is all backwards. You should die first... get it out of the way. Then you live in an old age home. You get kicked out when you're too young, you get a gold watch, you go to work. You work forty years until you're young enough to enjoy your retirement. You do drugs, alcohol, you party, you get ready for high school. You go to grade school, you become a kid, you play, you have no responsibilities, you become a little baby, you go back into the womb, you spend your last nine months floating ... and you finish off as an orgasm.

George Carlin

How many people ever receive a monetary BONUS? And I wonder—what on earth is the bonus for? Whoever invented the idea of bonuses should be taken out and given the ultimate bonus described by George Carlin. Nobody gives you the lottery for raising your children properly. Nobody gives you a monetary bonus for doing a great job of teaching, nursing, doctoring or janitorial work. The end product—people satisfied you did your best for them—is thanks enough. So why do financial institutions and large companies feel they need to give bonuses?

We had an acquaintance who was a bank executive, and this person said to us one Christmas: "I must have done a lousy job this year. My bonus was only 50 thousand." Hell—that is more than either of us ever made in a full year of teaching, back in the last century.

I read where over 100,000 brokers on Wall Street averaged bonuses of almost a half million each, several years ago. Do the math. No wonder we have economic woes, when companies give 50 billion extra dollars to people who already make huge salaries. It is simply obscene—the word President Obama used as he exposed the greed of large company executives at the trough. Let's hope the government can put a definite end to the concept of corporate bonuses. These days, most executives should be paying back their huge salaries for lack of performance.

March 20

Time

How long a minute is, depends on which side of the bathroom door you're on.

Zall's Second Law

Time wastes our bodies and our wits, but we waste time, so we are quits.

Author Unknown

Time is the fire in which we burn.

Delmore Schwartz

I was always amazed how students would complain that there was never enough time to do everything expected of them. These same students would sit around and make small talk when they were given class time to apply the day's lessons to practical problems. I would get their attention; look them in the eye and say, "Time flies by, sixty seconds to the minute … never to return." If they still didn't get it, I would take them aside and explain how precious time really is, and how they were wasting the one valuable commodity you can never get back. Many would eventually understand and would use the time given to them. Good for them!

Some people are always telling me how busy they are. These same folks talk on the phone for hours or spend the evening watching sitcoms on TV. Unbelievable! There is no accounting for wasted time, is there?

How fast time passes is a function of how much you have to do and how well you handle having lots to do. When you have no choice, you do what you have to do. I know it sounds trite, but it's true and worth repeating. You do what you have to do to survive. In my third year of university, I was on my own financially, and I had to work the night shift from 11 p.m. to 7 a.m. for the first three months of the term. I survived on 3-5 hours of sleep each day, snatched whenever I could get it. I quickly learned how to successfully balance work and studies with little sleep. If you are so fortunate as to require less sleep, it's like a gift of extra hours each day to work and play. (Naps don't count.)

We all have the same amount of time, twenty-four hours each and every day—and it still flies by at sixty seconds to the minute, never to return. If you have a time problem—don't worry. Be happy. Call in some less-busy friends to help get stuff done.

March 21

Droughts

Definitions of drought: Dryness; want of rain or of water; especially, such dryness of the weather as affects the earth, and prevents the growth of plants; aridity.

The world is a drought when out of love.

Brandon Boyd

To meet an old friend in a distant country is like the delight of rain after a long drought.

Chinese Proverb

We often experience a winter drought here in southwestern Florida. It may rain once in a month, and everything gets dry as dust. The brush is ready to blaze, and the little lakes that pretty up our parks are almost empty. One night we were driving along the road to our park, and somebody ahead of us threw a lit cigarette out their car window. I couldn't believe it. We could have a brush fire that would burn down many homes, and some cretin throws out a lit cigarette. Unbelievable!

The radio stations talk about ways of preserving water and call water a precious commodity. This is getting to be truer every day. Clean water has always been a valuable but often unappreciated resource. I am reading a novel, *Pillars of the Earth*, by Ken Follett; it amazes me how brutal life was a thousand years ago. Droughts were common, and water, food and shelter were commodities NOT to be taken for granted.

Many of these very commodities—clean air, water and soil—are becoming scarcer, and we need to conserve them for future generations. Our grandchildren are going to have unimaginable droughts, unless we change our disposition to these resources. As the first quote suggests, it all begins with a genuine love for our fellow passengers on planet Earth. We are all in the same boat. Hopefully, our actions today can prevent droughts tomorrow. Is it time for an attitude adjustment?

March 22

The Villages

The trouble with retirement is that you never get a day off.

Abe Lemons

Retirement: It's nice to get out of the rat race, but you have to learn to get along with less cheese.

Gene Perret

Retirement: World's longest coffee break.

Author Unknown

We visited good friends who are staying in a retirement community in central Florida. The "VILLAGES" are a huge planned community of over 75 000 folks. It is an amazing accomplishment for a number of reasons. The founders put much effort into ensuring beautiful, happy surroundings. Everywhere you go, it is almost disgusting to see so many old farts having such a good time. Don't these old people know they shouldn't be playing so many games and having so much fun? This place seems like a giant candy store full of kids who all have sweet teeth—retirement as it should be. You can do as many activities as you like or just vegetate if that suits your fancy—although the numerous community pools weren't full of folks as one might expect.

There are over 40 golf courses in the villages and tens of thousands of fancy golf carts that constantly zoom to and fro. Everybody seems to own a unique golf cart. The place holds the Guinness record for the longest line-up of carts. We even saw people playing bingo in their carts and going to the drive-in movies in their carts. That doesn't make much sense to me, as you can't make out very easily in a golf cart.

The number one activity in the Villages isn't golf! It's "Pickle Ball!" This game is a combination of tennis, racquetball and badminton. It's played on a small court, with a hollow holey ball hit with a paddle about twice the size of a ping pong paddle. We had a go at the pickle ball, and it is fast, furious and—like so much of this wonderful place—designed for fun.

March 23

Soul in Music Performance

Music is the divine way to tell beautiful, poetic things to the heart.

The art of interpretation is not to play what is written.

The heart of the melody can never be put down on paper.

All from cellist Pablo Casals

We were on a Caribbean cruise, and as always, we were impressed by how well performers are able to do flawless routines aboard a ship rocking from side to side. Amazing is the word that always comes to mind. I can't walk down the hall to the room without bouncing off the walls, and these artists sing and dance up a storm, as if they were on dry land. The performances are usually entertaining, and everywhere you go on the ship, there are talented musicians performing for your pleasure.

On this cruise, there were three lady pianists who played in the central foyer twice each day. All of these talented performers had flawless technique, but as I listened throughout the first two days, it suddenly dawned on me what Pablo Casals meant when he said, "The heart of the melody can never be put down on paper." Although all three ladies were excellent pianists, one of the three had real soul to her playing. Her name was Monika, and she came from Poland. I requested several of my favorites—Beethoven, Bach, Mozart and Rachmaninoff—and she gave very moving performances from memory! Then I asked for Chopin's *Fantasy Impromptu*, and the performance brought tears to my eyes. Monika played with such poetry and soul that the real heart of Chopin's great melody shone through her. More than just notes on a page—there was a world of love and yearning in this music as it came from Chopin's creativity as a composer through Monika's talent as a poetic performer.

It is a great pity to me that people seldom listen to these wonderful private performances. People seem to go for the "big" productions with the doctored sound of amplifiers, speakers and a techie at the back making everything sound really good and loud. The true heart and soul of music can often be found in the salon or the free concerts given at various places at noon. I have been treated to amazing performances by looking for them in unexpected places. True heart in music doesn't require a huge price tag.

March 24

Beer

Not all chemicals are bad. Without chemicals such as hydrogen and oxygen, for example, there would be no way to make water, a vital ingredient in beer.

Dave Barry

You can't be a Real Country unless you have a beer and an airline. It helps if you have a football team or some nuclear weapons, but at the very least, you need a beer.

Frank Zappa

24 hours in a day, 24 beers in a case. Coincidence?

Stephen Wright

Beer, beer glorious beer... fill yerself right up to here!

Old beer-drinking song

I have a friend who jokingly calls beer "piss." He comes by his dislike for beer honestly. His father calls beer "horse piss." Pity! My old truism, "If you don't like something, that's too bad for you," applies. It's one less thing you have to enjoy. Luckily there are plenty of other drinks to enjoy, and when it comes right down to it, it's fine to dislike something. "Chacun a son goût," as the French say.

I wasn't that crazy about beer when I first tried it. It tasted very bitter and I spat it out. My brother Bert insisted that it was an acquired taste, whatever that meant. I recall the first instance where the beer really tasted quite good and kept getting better. The occasion was Bert's first wedding. After the rehearsal, the men got together to drink beer. I think I was 18 at the time, and drinking age was 21. I can't remember how much I drank, but the next morning, I was supposed to help Bert's best man, Ross, with his dry cleaning deliveries. I was still happy, but very thirsty, so I drank a half dozen Cokes and sang songs from *H.M.S. Pinafore* as we delivered dry cleaning in a rural area. At one point Ross yelled at me to slide open the delivery van door on my side. He quickly braked to a stop, reached around behind his seat, aimed a .22 rifle across in front of me and fired a shot. "What the hell are you doing, Ross?" I yelled in surprise.

"Just shooting a ground hog," Ross replied, as if it were an everyday routine. See what funny things happen when you drink beer?

March 25

Physics

Our son Craig did a science fair project in grade seven using the potato cannon invented by his uncle Bert. This device consisted of soup cans arranged so that you could shoot a potato or a tennis ball up into the air 100 to 300 feet, depending on a number of factors. Craig looked through the grade 11 physics text and decided to measure the acceleration due to gravity. We took the cannon to the football field and had great fun timing tennis balls shot straight up from the cannon. We used trigonometry to calculate the height of the shots, and Craig had to learn the physics to determine a value for the gravity constant, "g." He read the material in the text, and I showed him where he could find the information and formulas he needed. His calculated value was 25 percent too low, but he came up with a good explanation involving air resistance to account for his low value. It was outstanding science, particularly for an elementary student.

Craig wrote up his experiment and entered it in the science fair. It didn't win anything. It rated a "C" from his science teacher. The winners were works of art, which were beautifully laid out but of questionable "science" value. Craig's had the best science in it but wasn't understood by the judges. The physics probably escaped them. The "C" was disappointing, but I pointed out that we had fun doing the experiments, and that he learned a great deal of valuable information about physics. Five years later, the science fair project really paid off. None of the students whose pretty projects had won prizes really understood physics the way Craig understood physics. Craig scored a 93 in physics in his senior year of high school, and he did it on his own. Hooray!

Mercury

"The time has come," the Walrus said, "To talk of many things: Of shoes - and ships - and sealing-wax - Of cabbages - and kings - And why the sea is boiling hot - And whether pigs have wings."

If you don't know where you are going, any road will get you there.

It's a poor sort of memory that only works backwards.

All from Lewis Carroll, pen name of Charles Lutwidge Dodgson

Don't you just love the MAD HATTER from Lewis Carroll's *Alice in Wonderland?* He is crazy sly, in a controlling way. Where did the term "mad as a hatter" came from? Here is the scientific explanation. People who worked in hat factories often lost their minds. They became crazy—or mad, as it was called in the old days. The reason they became mad was mercury poisoning. Mercury, a liquid at room temperature, was used to stiffen the bands of hats. Mercury vaporizes slowly, and some of the vapor was absorbed through the skin of these hat factory workers. Mercury accumulates in the body, and long-term exposure results in mercury poisoning. Symptoms include skittishness and unusual behavior—madness, if you will. So the Mad Hatter came by his name honestly.

Mercury poisoning is an insidious disorder that often shows up decades after the initial exposure in the environment. In Japan, cats around Minamata Bay began to terrorize neighborhoods. Children were born with defects, and eventually, older people became victims of early onset dementia. These disorders were finally traced to mercury poisoning. The mercury was dumped into the bay from several industries, and the fish absorbed the mercury. People and cats eating the fish became poisoned over a period of many years.

When we were teaching chemistry, we did numerous experiments that produced mercury vapor. We studied the mercury—a silvery liquid—and lost much of it on the floor, where it eventually vaporized. Maybe that explains why old chemistry teachers are all a little crazy. They were in those labs for decades with the mercury vapor. Now you know why these reflections are sometimes off the wall. I taught chemistry for over 25 years!

March 27

Airports

It can hardly be a coincidence that no language on Earth has ever produced the phrase, 'as pretty as an airport.' Airports are ugly. Some are very ugly. Some attain a degree of ugliness that can only be the result of a special effort.

Douglas Adams

I did not fully understand the dread term 'terminal illness' until I saw Heathrow for myself.

Dennis Potter

The devil himself had probably redesigned Hell in the light of information he had gained from observing airport layouts.

Anthony Price

The comment on Heathrow Airport certainly fits the last time we were there. The luggage agent made an error; our luggage, which should have been transferred to our plane to Istanbul, ended up on the baggage claim at Heathrow. When we arrived in the terminal, there was a huge mob of travelers waiting to claim luggage and go through immigration. We had one hour to accomplish this impossible task and to travel to another terminal to catch our plane. This should never have occurred. The agent had made the fatal mistake and doomed us to the Hell of Heathrow. There were two line-ups, one for "Euro" citizens and one for "other." We were relegated to a giant unmoving mob of "other," while the travelers who were members of the European Union zipped through with no line-ups! Our travel advisor took us under his wing; with much haranguing and threatening, he circumvented the mob and got us to the next plane on time. I still don't know how he did it.

We smartened up on the next trip to London. We flew into Gatwick, a much smaller terminal. This time we were at the mercy of more incompetent folks. The van driver deposited us at the wrong hotel; on the return trip, the bus driver got lost. The airline was closing its check-in desk an hour before the plane was to take off, which would have stranded 16 of us, had my buddy Wayne not sprinted from the bus through the terminal to the desk. Why do terminals have to be so impersonal and so poorly designed? It's a paradox that we often spend more time in the terminals than on the flight itself. Madness!

March 28

Remain a Kid

Happiness is a butterfly, which, when pursued, is always just beyond your grasp, but which, if you will sit down quietly, may alight upon you.

Nathaniel Hawthorne

All our dreams can come true ... if we have the courage to pursue them.

Walt Disney

The pursuit of truth and beauty is a sphere of activity in which we are permitted to remain children all our lives.

Albert Einstein

We have all heard the phrases, "Grow up!" and "Stop being so childish!" I hear these more often than some, since I'm just a big kid in lots of ways. I love cartoons. *Looney Tunes, The Simpsons,* and *Sesame Street* always make me laugh. I remember one time going to an after-school party; the kids in the house were watching cartoons, so I sat down and did all the voices. Soon they were trying to imitate the Tasmanian Devil and Foghorn T. Leghorn. Don't disparage cartoon-watching. This may be the only exposure some kids get to good music!

There are countless times in the stories of the Bible where the disciples ask Jesus what they need to do in order to get into heaven. They didn't have cartoons back then, but Jesus tells the disciples: "Truly I tell you, unless you change and become like children, you will never enter the kingdom of heaven." Now what do you suppose He meant by that? I figure Jesus was encouraging all of us to love each other with unconditional love, to accept each other at face value with no stereotyping, and finally, to have a childlike sense of wonder at all the beauty in the world. He was also obviously thinking of the innocence of very young children. They haven't learned how to do all the "grown-up" things that get us into so much trouble.

Another famous Bible passage states, "but when I became an adult, I put away childish ways." That doesn't mean we can't live life with a child's wonder. It means we should conduct our lives in a mature manner—not as silly, selfish children. We can still love, laugh and play like kids. That is certainly allowed.

March 29

The Golden Rule

Something we will examine in our daily time together is a great thought as it appears in a variety of cultures, languages or religions. Today we will take a look at the "Golden Rule" as it appears in a variety of religions.

What you do not want done to yourself, do not unto others.
The Golden Rule ... Confucian version

What is hateful to you, do not to your fellow men.
The Golden Rule ... The Talmud, Judaism

Hurt not others in ways that you yourself would find hurtful.
The Golden Rule ... Buddha

Love thy neighbor as thyself.
The Golden Rule ... Christian version

Do nothing to others which would cause you pain if done to you.
The Golden Rule ... Hindu version

No one is a believer until he desires for his brother that which he desires himself.
The Golden Rule ... Islam version

Regard your neighbor's gain as your own gain and your neighbor's loss as your own loss.
The Golden Rule ... Taoist version

I made this list into a large poster and put it up in my physics lab. One student told me they all said the same thing. I asked what that was, and she said, "Do unto others as you would have them do unto you." Another student pointed out that most of them are stated in a negative fashion, as "DO NOT..." I must confess to a dislike of negative statements. How many times have you gone to a facility and seen a long list of "NO this, and NO that"? The power of the thought is really in its positive statement.

How about a new version?

"Treat everybody as you would like to be treated ... on your birthday."

March 30

The Telephone

The bathtub was invented in 1850 and the telephone in 1875. In other words, if you had been living in 1850, you could have sat in the bathtub for 25 years without having to answer the phone.

Bill DeWitt

I like my new telephone, my computer works just fine, my calculator is perfect, but Lord, I miss my mind!

Author Unknown

I'd rather sit down and write a letter than call someone up. I hate the telephone.

Henry Miller

A woman is a person who reaches for a chair when she answers the telephone.

Milton Wright

Cell phones are the latest invention in rudeness.

D.H. Mondfleur

I love the *Far Side* cartoon showing a large snake, a python, at home in his reclining chair. He is in the middle of dinner—a fat suckling pig—and has swallowed only half of the piggy. The pig's rump is sticking out of the snake's mouth, when suddenly, the phone rings. All the snake can say is an imagined "DRAT!!!" Forgiving the cartoonist for showing a poor piggy being swallowed, I enlarged that cartoon and stuck it up beside the science preparation room phone. I figure teachers often need a laugh—particularly when talking to parents on the phone.

How many of you can ignore a ringing phone? I always do if we are at the supper table. I know people who cannot refuse to answer the phone. I guess they feel each call is so important that they may miss winning the Irish sweepstakes if they don't answer. When I leave the phone ringing at our home, some people actually want to answer it! I usually say, "Let it ring. They will call back if it's important enough."

Have you ever been in the middle of a transaction at a store when the phone rings? The sales clerk answers and then completely ignores you while talking to the caller. I have even had sales clerks turn their backs on me when they answered the phone. I might be tempted to phone such a sales clerk and complete my sale over my cell phone, which could be hilarious—except for one thing: it's usually in my wife's purse or in the car.

March 31

Arthur C. Clarke

Any sufficiently advanced technology is indistinguishable from magic.

As our own species is in the process of proving, one cannot have superior science and inferior morals. The combination is unstable and self-destroying.

I'm sure the universe is full of intelligent life. It's just been too intelligent to come here.

The intelligence of the planet is constant, and the population is growing.

all from Arthur C. Clarke, 1917 – 2008

Arthur Charles Clarke was born in England, on 16 December 1917. As a young man, he enjoyed stargazing and reading old American science fiction magazines, which were used as ballast in freighters returning from the U.S.A. to England. He was a radar specialist with the Royal Air Force during World War II and contributed to the system that allowed the R.A.F.'s success in the Battle of Britain. He eventually became a prolific writer of science fiction. You may have seen the film *2001: A Space Odyssey*, based on one of Clarke's science fiction novels. I've always enjoyed his novels. They seem to me to be entirely within the realm of the possible. He had an imaginative intelligence and several of his ideas have actually played a huge role in today's technology.

Clarke's most important scientific contribution may be his idea that geostationary satellites would be ideal telecommunications relays. He described this concept in a paper titled, "Extra-Terrestrial Relays—Can Rocket Stations Give Worldwide Radio Coverage?" The geostationary orbit is now sometimes known as the Clarke Orbit or the Clarke Belt, in his honor. The satellite orbits in the direction of the Earth's rotation, at an altitude of approximately 35,786 km (22,240 miles) aboveground. This geosynchronous altitude produces an orbital period exactly equal to the Earth's period of rotation. All the satellites that we use for television are in geosynchronous orbit around the Earth and stay above the same spot on the Earth. Next time you watch satellite television, thank Arthur.

When he died in March of 2008, his chosen epitaph was: "He never grew up; but he never stopped growing."

April 1

Baseball 2

Take me out to the ball game. Take me out to the park.
Buy me some peanuts and Cracker Jack, I don't care if I never get back.
For it's root, root, root for the home team, if they don't win it's a shame.
For it's one, two, three strikes yer out at the old ball game.

Old Baseball song

An opener is not like any other game. There's that little extra excitement, a faster beating of the heart. You have that anxiety to get off to a good start, for yourself and for the team. You know that when you win the first one, you can't lose 'em all.

Early Wynn

The baseball season usually begins around the first of April. The home opener used to be a good excuse to take a day off school or work and go and welcome back the boys of spring. I never did this, but I knew guys who did. I often wondered what all the hoopla was about. There are eighty home games left to go and root, root, root. I remember the first Blue Jays home opener at Exhibition Stadium in 1977. It was freezing, and it actually snowed. Doug Ault became an instant hero, hitting two home runs. I wasn't there, but I saw a replay of the game on television. In fact, I have never been to a Blue Jays home opener.

The only home opener we attended was in Chicago. Four of us were in Chicago in early April 2005 to see Wagner's Ring Cycle. On a whim, Allan Smith and I went down on a Monday afternoon to the White Sox stadium to see if we could get into the home opener. We were lucky. We got tickets behind home plate. What a fantastic show! A humongous American flag, held by hundreds of people, covered the entire outfield, and jets buzzed over the stadium the moment the anthem finished. The folks at Cellular Field certainly understood how to put on a "really big shoe!" The White Sox beat Cleveland 1-0 in an hour and 47 minute-long pitchers' battle. I said to Allan, "The White Sox will win it all this year." Guess what? They did!

April 2

Teaching

I touch the future. I teach.

Christa McAuliffe

Good teachers are worth their weight in gold. When I was a kid, many teachers used fear as the motivator—fear of the strap—fear of failure. It never worked with me. Then I experienced a great teacher, Miss Bradford, who cared for her students. She found out what your strengths were and built on them. She celebrated your successes and made you feel special. She instilled a love of learning and gave you self-reliance. She changed our lives for the better. I repaid Miss Bradford by becoming a teacher myself. What a wonderful legacy Miss Bradford left.

Ron Clark was an elementary school teacher in North Carolina, but after watching a program about a New York City school that had difficulty attracting qualified teachers, he decided to head to New York with the goal of teaching in one of its toughest schools. Clark eventually landed a job doing just that—in Harlem. He asked if he could teach a class of fifth-graders who had been performing at a second-grade level. The school's administrators wanted to give him the gifted class, but Clark insisted on the under-performing students. In one school year, Clark's fifth-grade class outperformed the gifted class. Clark became Disney's teacher of the year, a best-selling author, and an Oprah guest. A Business Week article shares Clark's thoughts on how managers can use his techniques to motivate their own teams.

If I were to distil Ron Clark's tips into two rules they would be:

1. Operate with love and not fear as a motivator—love for learning and the process of learning together;

2. Develop self-reliance in your students.

If people learn how to learn, and they have a love for learning, it becomes a life-long journey of pleasure in accomplishment.

Go and hug a good teacher today. They make less money in a life-time than many professional athletes make in a year—but "they touch the future" as Christa McAuliffe said.

April 3

Faces

Family faces are magic mirrors. Looking at people who belong to us, we see the past, present and future. We make discoveries about ourselves.

Gail Lumet Buckley

Nature gives you the face you have at twenty. Life shapes the face you have at thirty. But at fifty you get the face you deserve.

Coco Chanel

Strangers are exciting, their mystery never ends, but there's nothing like looking at your own history in the faces of your friends.

Ani DiFranco

We have all heard the old expression "Put on a Happy Face!" If we have all heard the expression, why are so many folks so serious about everything? Here at the RV Park most folks are very content and smile most of the time, except maybe during the church service. Why should it be that way? I like to "let er rip" in lots of songs, and I feel the wild performance put on by the singing and dancing James Brown in the *Blues Brothers* movie is how a religious celebration should be done at times. There is a time for a prayer face, a time for a peaceful face, and a time for a happy face—all in the same service.

When I was teaching I would walk around the halls greeting students and teachers with a smile. I was often asked by a few staff: "What the hell are you smiling about??? … this is a serious business!!!" Some teachers would even tell me that they had two faces—a "teacher" face and a "home" face. I guess it worked for them, but I couldn't do it.

One of our principals used to tell us: "A teacher is a teacher all the time!" If I am going to set an example for folks because it's an expectation of being a teacher, it is this. Learning can be loads of fun. If it's going to put lines on your face, they might as well be laugh lines!

Today when you are out and about, try the following. Put on a happy face and greet strangers with enthusiasm. People all have their burdens, and if you can forget about your own and spread good cheer, pretty soon you will feel much better and you will probably have made somebody's day. Ignore the whiners and grouches. If nobody listens to them, they will eventually give up. You don't have to get carried away, but make your "happy face" a habit.

April 4

Boredom

The chief product of an automated society is a widespread and deepening sense of boredom.

C. Northcote Parkinson

Your true traveler finds boredom rather agreeable than painful. It is the symbol of his liberty ... his excessive freedom. He accepts his boredom, when it comes, not merely philosophically, but almost with pleasure.

Aldous Huxley

I have difficulty with this quote from Huxley. There is no way for me to tolerate boredom "with pleasure." My sister Noni and I attended hundreds of concerts, and we sometimes found the odd one to be brutally boring. We would glance at each other and instantly know, without saying it, that we were leaving at the next interval. When this happens, I can sometimes survive without pain by attempting to nap, pray or meditate. Even surrounded by tedious sound, I have the ability to attain a meditative state and escape momentarily from the mundane world.

The worst example of being trapped was in a production of *Carmen*. This is normally a wonderful opera with robust melodies, but in this instance, the tenor sounded worse than awful. To us, he was emulating the shrieks of a wounded bull moose. Every time this note-butcher opened his mouth, Noni and I physically cringed. I looked around and only a few folks were having the same reaction. This upholds my notion that about 75% of the populace has tin ears for really good singing. Sure enough, when the intermission finally came, some of the audience joined us in the rush out the doors to the nearest tavern where we could have a good laugh about the worst "singing" we had ever heard. I wonder how many of the audience who stayed were as bored as we but felt, as Huxley states, that a person should "accept boredom, when it comes, not merely philosophically, but almost with pleasure." The next time you find yourself in a painfully boring situation, make every attempt to escape to pleasure. Life is too short to accept boredom stoically.

April 5

The Internet

I'm a great believer in particularly being alert to changes that change something, anything, by an order of magnitude, and nothing operates with the factors of 10 as profoundly as the Internet.

Andrew Grove

The Internet is becoming the town square for the global village of tomorrow.

Bill Gates

Give a person a fish, and you feed them for a day; teach that person to use the Internet, and they won't bother you for weeks.

Author Unknown

The Internet is the first thing that humanity has built that humanity doesn't understand, the largest experiment in anarchy that we have ever had.

Eric Schmidt

The Internet is so big, so powerful and pointless that for some people it is a complete substitute for life.

Andrew Brown

A number of "F" words come to mind when I think of the Internet. I know what you are probably thinking, and over the past few months I have been totally frustrated trying to send anybody anything. When I try to send an e-mail, one program signs me out. On another, my home server rejects e-mails from contacts as spam. My latest e-mail account seems to work well, so I say "hallelujah"—until the next electronic glitch springs up when I am least expecting it! So often, the words frustration, frantic, and feared apply to the beastly invention we know as the Internet.

For now it's working again, and it's fast. When it works, the word frustration instantly morphs to fantastic. There was a message in my inbox asking if we were okay, because the daily reflection hadn't shown up as usual. Within minutes, several e-mails flew back and forth, including the missing day's reflection; for this person, everything was back to normal. When the computer and the Internet behave, I must admit to loving this technology. Where else can you find out so much so fast?

April 6

Playing Cards

Life consists not in holding good cards but in playing those you hold well.

Josh Billings

A deck of cards is built like the purest of hierarchies, with every card a master to those below it, a lackey to those above it.

Ely Culbertson

There are no friends at cards or world politics.

Finley Peter Dunne

The bizarre world of cards is a world of pure power politics where rewards and punishments are meted out immediately.

Ely Culbertson

We play cribbage almost every day. Today was a dandy. I won by one point—for last card. We keep track of "championships"; at the end of the year it's amazing how close we are. Our boys love to play cards when they come home. We have played cribbage, euchre, go fish, rummy, hearts, crazy eights, rumoli, poker and plenty of games with rude names. The game of bridge plays a major role in our social life, and it's not unusual to play several times each week. Some of you folks reading this will probably say to yourselves: "What a colossal waste of time!" I would argue with you all night about your great loss, but I'm probably busy having fun at a card game.

Celia's father, Gilbert, was in a long-term chronic care facility for the last five years of his life. We would go up to the hospital to see Gil and play several games of cribbage. His wonderful sense of humor found its way into those games, and he never lost his cribbage-playing skills.

Playing cards teaches social skills, etiquette, and higher intellectual skills involving math and memorization. Psychologists have shown that children who are taught card games are further ahead in all these skills. They have also shown that elderly people who play bridge retain their faculties much longer than those who never play. Celia's Aunt Florence still drives her friends to bridge each week—at the wonderful age of 98. You are never too old to learn!

April 7

Reading

Good children's literature appeals not only to the child in the adult, but to the adult in the child.

A library is a hospital for the mind.   *People die, but books never die.*

If you can read this, thank a teacher.   *Beware of the man of one book.*

All Anonymous

Our pastor made the following statement in today's sermon. "Children today don't get the reading we did. They aren't exposed to the classics. If it isn't on a screen of 17 inches or larger, they aren't interested." He also commented on all the fantastic teaching occurring in the schools in spite of a lack of reading in so many "modern" children. I always look around at people during a sermon, and I could see loads of people nodding their heads in agreement to his comments on the trend away from books to the screen. Think about this for a moment. Is it true? Perhaps it is—to a degree.

I taught for over thirty years, and my impression is that students are better informed today than ever before. Moreover, they can find needed information very quickly and thoroughly from a variety of media, from the library to the Internet. Most of them are equally adept at these resources. My wife, a grade 3-4 teacher, tells me that young children are reading more than ever—from Harry Potter to non-fiction material in libraries and the Internet.

After the church service, I met a young fellow at coffee hour. We got talking about the sermon, and he also disagreed. Pretty soon we were quoting Shakespeare at each other and lines from films. William was about 30 years old, and it was obvious that he was a walking contradiction to the notion that young people don't read. Perhaps it has to do with your environment when you are young. If you are surrounded by good resources and role models, you have a better chance to be an avid reader. If everybody in your household sits and watches TV, you may do the same. Take those kids and grandkids to the library a couple of times each week. Teach them how to access the library catalogue on the Internet. Reading is a lifelong pleasure!

April 8

Showering

I like American women. They do things Russian women never think of ... like showering.

Yakov Smirnoff, Russian comedian

Everyone who has ever taken a shower has an idea. It's the person who gets out, dries off and then goes and does something about it that makes a difference.

Nolan Bushnell

I was taking my morning shower here in the RV Park when a thought struck me. What a great luxurious shower these park showers give. Then I thought back to our homestead. There was no shower. We took baths. My father had done time-motion studies and could take a bath in one gallon of water in three minutes! He could never sell the rest of us on his method. I loved a good soak and still do. I'll take books, food and drink, and the portable stereo into the bathroom and spend a couple of heavenly hours in the tub. When I had my hip replacement, the tub was verboten for three months, and I dearly missed the long hot soak.

Like my father, I have a Mister Clean Body Three Minute Wash—only it applies to showers—not baths. You turn on the water for 30 seconds and get wet. Turn the water off and soap your hair. Turn the water back on and rinse your hair. Turn the water back off. Soap your hair again and the rest of your body—finally, a quick rinse. So you have only had the water on for three minutes total and have used about three gallons.

I could never convince our sons to conserve water. They love long hot showers the way I love a long hot bath. I remember Craig would get out of bed, and the first thing he would do was to have a long luxurious shower. One time we had the family and guests for dinner, and Craig had gone upstairs for a nap. Before we sat down to dinner, I woke Craig from his nap. After a few minutes, someone asked, "What's that noise?" It was the shower going full blast, so I went up to the bathroom and asked Craig why he was showering.

"Isn't it morning?" he asked. When I told him it was dinnertime, and we were all at the table waiting for him, he began to laugh. When I went down and told the family what happened, we all had a good laugh. That must have been a really good nap!

April 9

Appearances

Appearances are deceiving.

Old Saying

Never judge a book by its cover.

Another Old Saying

There are several forms of the element carbon. A hunk of coal is a loose arrangement of carbon atoms. Under pressure, the carbon can arrange into layers, to form the slippery form of carbon known as graphite. Under extreme pressure, the carbon atoms arrange themselves into an orderly, three-dimensional crystalline structure known as diamond. These different forms of one element are known as allotropes. They are all composed of carbon atoms, but the internal arrangement makes all the difference in the world. People are like that, in a way. They all look similar—a head with two ears, two eyes, a nose and mouth; and a body with two arms, two legs, a chest and abdomen. Society has notions of what makes people attractive, but the real worth of a person radiates from the inside. You could say, as with allotropes, that the internal make-up is what counts.

We had a memorable vacation in Newfoundland a few years back. We were in the pub of the largest hotel in Western Newfoundland, enjoying a local Newfie band. They were very good; the accordion player, a short, interesting-looking fellow, was jumping around and having the time of his life. I commented to a local at another table that the fellow with the squeeze box was sure enjoying himself. The local told me: "He should be having fun … he owns the joint!"

The next day we were in Gross Mourne National Park, and we took a short boat tour to view the inland fiords. I did a quick calculation and figured out that these boat tours were grossing about ten thousand dollars each day for some wise entrepreneur. I asked the skipper: "Who owns all these tour boats?"

He replied, "Do you know the wee fellow that owns the hotel back in town? Well, he owns all these boats as well. Not only the hotel and the boats, but he owns the entire Cummins diesel franchise for all of Newfoundland. The boss is one smart cookie!" That wee fellow, dancing around, having fun with his accordion was one of the smartest—and richest—men in all of Newfoundland. The true worth of a person is found inside, and appearances can indeed be deceiving!

April 10

Happiness

Happiness is never stopping to think if you are.

Palmer Sondreal

Most people would rather be certain they're miserable, than risk being happy.

Robert Anthony

If only we'd stop trying to be happy we could have a pretty good time.

Edith Wharton

I used to ask my students what they wanted to be when they finished school. A surprising number of them would tell me that they wanted to be "happy." In fact, for many students this seemed to be the one ideal they wanted more than anything—to be happy. Then I would put a damper on their youthful fantasy by telling them that there is no such commodity as happiness. This generated lots of good arguments—but in the end, they would begin to agree with me that, as an aim, the pure pursuit of happiness is a lousy goal. It is never an end in itself but rather a byproduct of more worthwhile pursuits. Nothing gives people more pleasure and happiness than real accomplishment one can see.

We have a friend, Bill, who retired from teaching and is seriously into art. He loves to paint people, and he often shows me his work in progress and requests my opinion. He then revises until he is happy with the results. What a sense of fulfillment an artist must feel. I taught all my life, and felt a sense of achievement at what I thought I had given to students. I could not, however, point to something and say, "I did that."

When I retired, we decided to build a cabana in the backyard. We designed and built a miniature house, complete with electricity and insulation. The number of problems we solved during the design and construction was amazing. Five years later, it hasn't moved an inch and has needed zero maintenance. We look at our creation, and I suppose we could say, "Oh boy—this little house gives us happiness every sunny summer day—and we built this together."

April 11

Trees

Keep a green tree in your heart and perhaps a singing bird will come.
Chinese proverb

I like trees because they seem more resigned to the way they have to live than other things do.
Willa Cather

When I was at our School Board, we would order thousands of trees from the Ministry of Natural Resources and hold tree-planting sessions all over the county. We planted trees at the Board office farm and at many schools. There would be leftover trees, and we planted them at cottages and on my brother Judd's property. We planted eight trees on the front lawn of Aunt Dot's "Gingerbread House," and we gave them the names of family members.

Why do we plant so many trees? That's easy. Planting a tree is the MOST ENVIRONMENTALLY FRIENDLY act you can do. Trees remove carbon dioxide gas from the atmosphere, combating a main cause of global warming.

Be sure to name your trees and give them follow-up TLC including water, tree food and a hug! The planet will LOVE you right back for caring.

TREES

I think that I shall never see
a poem as lovely as a tree.
A tree whose hungry mouth is prest
against the sweet earth's flowing breast.
A tree that looks at God all day,
and lifts her leafy arms to pray;
A tree that may in summer wear
a nest of robins in her hair;
Upon whose bosom snow has lain;
who intimately lives with rain.
Poems are made by fools like me
but only God can make a tree.
Joyce Kilmer

April 12

Attitude

It is our attitude, more than anything else, which will affect a successful outcome.

William James

There are no menial jobs, only menial attitudes.

William J. Bennett

Each spring the zoo animals gathered for a ritual celebration for surviving the winter. It was their custom to elect one of the wisest among them, who would give a speech to inspire every single member of the zoo to live together in harmony during the year. All members had a write-in vote, and the top three vote-getters had a preliminary contest to see who got the ultimate honor. When the votes were tallied, the "winners" were the lion, the gorilla and the human. All the other animals agreed these were wise choices, except for the wart hog. "You have chosen for the wrong reasons," said the hog. "You picked the lion because he's the so-called 'king of the beasts', the gorilla because he's the strongest and the human because you want to please your keeper. If you had thought about this, you would have picked an animal with some smarts instead of making it a popularity contest."

"And who do you suppose that is?" all the animals cried out in unison.

"Me!" replied the wart hog.

All the other animals laughed loud and long and made snide remarks, but to amuse the insistent wart hog, they permitted him to enter the preliminary round, thinking, "This pig will make a fool of himself!"

As it turned out, the hog easily beat the other three. That year, the inspirational pep-talk was the best ever, which of course would never have happened, had the hog not been a glutton for punishment—a glutton, however, with some attitude!

As it sometimes happens in life, it's who you know and not what you are that wins the prize. True talent may initially be overlooked. If this happens to you, keep doing what you do best, honing and broadening your skills. There will eventually be some opportunity for true talent to shine. Actions speak louder than words—and the results may come as a surprise to the uninitiated.

Most folks look down their noses at the funny-looking animal called the pig. What they fail to realize is that the lowly hog is one of the "rocket-scientists" of the animal world, with a large intelligence and nose to match. It's our poor attitude that dooms these amazing animals to the pigpen.

Shepherd

The Lord is my shepherd; I shall not be in want.
He makes me lie down in green pastures and leads me beside still waters.
He revives my soul and guides me along right pathways for his name's sake.
Though I walk through the valley of the shadow of death, I shall fear no evil;
For you are with me; your rod and your staff, they comfort me.
You spread a table before me in the presence of those who trouble me;
You have anointed my head with oil, and my cup is running over.
Surely your goodness and mercy shall follow me all the days of my life,
And I will dwell in the house of the Lord forever.

Good arguments can be made that the 23rd Psalm is the most powerful passage in the Bible. It is for me one of the greatest messages ever written. Full of beauty, simplicity, optimism and comfort, it says many things to many people. It tells us that no matter what happens—no matter how bad things get at times—everything will eventually work out.

Through these reflections, we often consider the rewards of being still and having a quiet meditative place. There it is in the Psalm's second line. We will be revived if we take the opportunity to quiet our minds and seek the beauty of a quiet place—where nothing can dull our light.

We might sometimes question why we can be optimistic about things eventually working out. The psalmist tells us why. We all go through troubled times, but no matter how dark things get, we are never alone. We only need to give our troubles to the Lord and trust in Him.

I love the final thought of the psalm. If we allow the Shepherd to look after us, we will be in a wonderful place. We will experience the "house of the Lord", which for me means a Heavenly place—a paradise here on Earth. To exist in this kingdom, surrounded by LOVE, is awesome.

April 14

Spelling

A man occupied with public or other important business cannot, and need not, attend to spelling.

Napoleon Bonaparte

It's a damn poor mind that can think of only one way to spell a word!

Andrew Jackson

I don't give a damn for a man that can only spell a word one way.

Mark Twain

A kiss can be a comma, a question mark or an exclamation point.
That's the basic spelling that every woman ought to know.

Mistinguette

I remember those awful spelling bees our second grade teacher ran almost every day. She would line up the girls on one side of the room and the boys on the opposite side. The girls always got to go first, and last day's champion could ask any boy to spell a word from the list. If you got it wrong you had to sit down. The last one standing was the champion of the day. I never knew who was champ because by the time the bee ended, I was fast asleep at my desk. Perhaps that had something to do with the fact that I was the only student to fail the second grade! I was a sickly little kid, but I had street smarts, so I figured out very quickly that you got to sit down early if you were the lousiest speller. I have always been a great believer in the rules, "Never ever stand when you can sit," and "Never stay awake when you can nap!" So what if I spent a little extra time sitting and napping my way through the second and third grades? Who wants to hurry their way out of school, just to go to work? It never made any sense to me.

Now I no longer need to worry about spelling. We have a wonderful device called a spelling checker!

I have a spelling checker, It came with my PC
It plainly marks for my revue Mistakes I cannot sea
I've run this poem threw it ... I'm sure your please to no,
It's letter perfect in it's weigh
My checker tolled me sew

Anonymous

April 15

Wiki

What really matters is that there is so much faith and love and kindliness which we can share with and provoke in others and that by cleanly, simple, generous living we approach perfection in the highest and most lovely of all arts. ... But you, I think, have always comprehended this.

James Branch Cabell

Today's quote comes from a "wiki" web site, Wikiquote, which has over 15 000 pages of quotes. "Wiki" is a technology for creating collaborative websites. You have probably looked something up online and been given a long list of web pages to visit. Often the Wikipedia page is either the first page or very close to it. I use the Wikipedia several times each day. So the question of the day is, what is the "Wikipedia", and where did it come from? In its own words, "**Wikipedia** is a free, multilingual, open content encyclopedia project operated by the non-profit Wikimedia Foundation. Its name is a portmanteau of the words *wiki* (a technology for creating collaborative websites) and *encyclopedia*. Launched in January 2001 by Jimmy Wales and Larry Sanger, it is the largest, fastest-growing and most popular general reference work currently available on the Internet."

If you have never used this free web encyclopedia, try looking up some information you are very familiar with. Are the articles in Wikipedia accurate? Are they presented in an understandable fashion? Are the articles well-written? The amazing fact is this: all the entries are written by volunteers, and anybody can edit or add information to any entry. Given this fact, it astounds me that all these "wiki" resources are as good as they are. I constantly cross-reference before using any of the information and am amazed at the general quality and accuracy of Wikipedia. I realize it probably has loads of "warts", but I like it!

If you made it this far in this reflection, consider this: here is a valuable resource, even if you need to check its accuracy. It's FREE, and you can use any of the information, anytime you want. The neatest point about "wiki" sites is that they are a collaborative effort, in which people like you and I have shared their knowledge with others without expecting any return. I suppose this makes this resource a giant global conversation, all written down and constantly edited—every day.

April 16

Expectations

"Blessed is the man who expects nothing, for he shall never be disappointed" was the ninth beatitude.

Alexander Pope

Expect nothing, live frugally on surprise.

Alice Walker

Expecting the world to treat you fairly because you are a good person is a little like expecting the bull not to attack you because you are a vegetarian.

Dennis Wholey

Never idealize others. They will never live up to your expectations.

Leo Buscaglia

The best things in life are unexpected ... because there were no expectations.

Eli Khamarov

Most of us live with great expectations. When I was walking our dogs, Chewy and Mozart, Mo saw a deliveryman. Thinking he was going to get a cookie from this fellow, Mo began to bark and pull persistently. He expected the man had cookies in his bag like our mailman. Dogs are funny. Whenever I go to the front closet, they get excited. They anticipate we are going for our walk which is a highlight of their day. These two dogs live with great expectations, especially around meal time.

We are no different than dogs when it comes to great expectations. We expect our athletic heroes to perform perfectly. We expect to be able to find exactly what we want when we go shopping. We expect our meals when we are hungry, and for many, there always have to be potatoes on the plate. We assume our cars will start, our TVs and computers will function properly, and our family and friends will act in certain ways. How silly we are! These expectations can result in disappointment at any time. Unlike the dogs, however, we can choose to be flexible and accepting of disappointments or letdowns.

The next time your expectations aren't met, perhaps you expected too much. If you always expect perfection, prepare for frustration. It's a wonderful world, but it has its imperfections. "Get over it!" is something a good friend always proclaims when things don't work out exactly as anticipated.

April 17

Flowers

Earth laughs in flowers.

Ralph Waldo Emerson

I'd rather have roses on my table than diamonds on my neck.

Emma Goldman

The violets in the mountains have broken the rocks.

Tennessee Williams

The flower is the poetry of reproduction. It is an example of the eternal seductiveness of life.

Jean Giraudoux

Flowers really do intoxicate me.

Vita Sackville-West

Bread feeds the body, indeed, but flowers feed also the soul.

The Koran

Winter puts everything to sleep. The grass is brown. The trees are barren. The flower beds are ugly. Then slowly, the renewal begins. Crocuses poke up their wee heads. Long green leaves frantically push up with the promise of daffodils and tulips. Trees awaken with signs of the glory to come—beginning with a faint yellow, soon transforming to a lush green canopy. Dead grass isn't dead after all and darkens up to a thick cushiony carpet.

Spring is such a miraculous time of year. There are daily reminders of the rebirth of our beloved flowers. All the different shades of green are complimented by the return of the colorful bulbs and perennials. As the spring bulbs fade for another year, we can replace them with a variety of annuals to let the beauty continue through the fall.

Our town maintains hanging baskets, container plants and beds of annuals to keep the flower show going all summer. The earth truly does *laugh in flowers.*

April 18

Eureka

It's not that I'm so smart; it's just that I stay with problems longer.

Albert Einstein

Believe it is possible to solve your problem. Tremendous things happen to the believer. So believe the answer will come. It will.

Norman Vincent Peale

For every failure, there's an alternative course of action. You just have to find it. When you come to a roadblock, take a detour.

Mary Kay Ash

There lived a king in ancient Greece who gave the state goldsmith a bar of gold to make the king a new crown. Being a suspicious sort of person, the king carefully weighed the gold bar before and the crown after it had been delivered. The weight was the same. The king still suspected that the goldsmith had somehow cheated him by substituting a baser metal for some of the gold, but how could he prove it? The king gave the crown to his state scientist, Archimedes, with the instruction to find out if the crown was pure gold. The king also told Archimedes not to mark the crown in any way, and to report back the correct solution in one week, or the scientist would be executed in the public square.

Poor Archimedes! He couldn't solve this problem, so he began to worry. Being a wee bit corpulent, his clothes got soaked with perspiration. He decided to take a bath. In those days, you had to go to the public bath in downtown Athens, so off he went. The attendant decided to play a trick on poor Archimedes, so he filled the tub too full. Archimedes took off his clothes and got into the tub, which immediately overflowed. He suddenly realized the answer to his problem and jumped out of the tub. Legend has it that he ran home naked to his lab yelling, "Eureka!" which in Greek means, "I have it." He immersed the crown in water and measured the water displaced. He calculated the density of the crown, and it was less than the density of pure gold—proving the goldsmith had cheated. Archimedes kept his head, and the goldsmith lost his.

There is a lesson in this story. Let "impossible" problems stew away subconsciously in your brain. Eventually, the answer may come serendipitously. The trick is to be prepared for the solution when it eventually presents itself! In the meantime—take a bath!

April 19

Touch

Don't make art for other artists or for 'intellectuals', make art for people ... and if you can touch just one person in a lifetime and make a difference ... you have succeeded.
Ray Conniff

Some men know that a light touch of the tongue, running from a woman's toes to her ears, lingering in the softest way possible in various places in between, given often enough and sincerely enough, would add immeasurably to world peace.
Marianne Williamson in *A Return to Love*

Let us touch the dying, the poor, the lonely and the unwanted according to the graces we have received and let us not be ashamed or slow to do the humble work.
Mother Teresa

Love is like a beautiful flower which I may not touch, but whose fragrance makes the garden a place of delight just the same.
Helen Keller

Then suddenly a woman ... came up behind and touched the fringe of his cloak ... and instantly the woman was made well.
Matthew 9:20-22

And when he laid his hands on her, immediately she stood up straight ...
Luke 13:13

"I am touched" is an expression we often use when an act of kindness is extended to us. The word "touch" can mean physical contact, like the gentle touch of a parent with a new-born infant, the holding of hands, or the squeeze we share in an affectionate hug. It can be very physical, as in a massage or the laying on of hands in a healing ceremony. When spouses argue, a gentle holding of hands can dispel disagreeableness. Touches can have a healing effect. Many miracles in the Bible came with a mere touch.

Prayer is often responsible for healing without physical touching. You can be touched and touch someone without direct contact. The connectedness of humanity doesn't require us to be in the same place at the same time to give or receive the healing touch. You have probably experienced a feeling that someone somewhere is holding you in their hands. This someone may be living or dead—or spiritual—an angel or a deity. We need to reach out daily and touch lives—and we are touched, held and uplifted in return.

April 20

Judgment Day

In a moment, in the twinkling of an eye, at the last trump: for the trumpet shall sound, and the dead shall be raised incorruptible, and we shall be changed.

1st Corinthians 15:52 (King James Bible)

Then I saw a great white throne and him who was seated on it. Earth and sky fled from his presence, and there was no place for them. And I saw the dead, great and small, standing before the throne, and books were opened. Another book was opened, which is the book of life. The dead were judged according to what they had done as recorded in the books.

Revelation 20:11-12 (New International version)

Whenever the afterlife is emphasized, the most invariable result is that it turns Christianity into a religion of requirement. Emphasizing the afterlife focuses our attention on the next world rather than on transformation in this world.

Marcus J. Borg

Many masterpieces portray Judgment Day. Michelangelo's spectacular painting of the Judgment Day comes to mind. The work covers the entire wall behind the altar of the Sistine Chapel. It took four years to complete. *The Last Judgment* is a depiction of the second coming of Christ and the apocalypse. The souls of humans rise and descend to their fates, as judged by Christ, surrounded by his saints. Musical masterpieces also portray the final judgment. In Handel's *Messiah*, the bass aria, *The Trumpet Shall Sound*, goes on long enough to raise the dead. After listening to this aria, I found myself picturing a humongous line of over ten billion souls ready to be judged. I also wondered what would happen to all those billions of basically good humans who have never heard of Jesus Christ. Would they have any chance on Judgment Day?

I went to see Bob, our Lutheran pastor friend in the trailer behind us in the RV park. I asked him what he thought of Judgment Day. Bob's response initially struck me as funny, but then I realized he was saying the same thing as Marcus Borg in the above quote. "Lee," Bob said, "judgment day was an invention of the Church to keep the flock in order." Thank goodness for that. I've always hated line-ups!

April 21

Bloodshed

A pint of sweat saves a gallon of blood.

George S. Patton

The tree of liberty must be refreshed from time to time with the blood of patriots and tyrants. It is its natural manure.

Thomas Jefferson

God and Country are an unbeatable team; they break all records for oppression and bloodshed.

Luis Bunuel

People will quickly go to war when their country calls. In all wars, both sides are fighting for what they believe is "right." Back in the sixties, young people refused to go to Viet Nam. They protested about being called to go to a country that nobody knew much about, to fight against communists who were spreading their evil influence among the gentle people in the south of this far-off land. In the end, nobody "won" that war. You could have predicted the result, because there had been a war going on for over 50 years in "Indo-China", and the resilient inhabitants had managed to embarrass several major powers by never giving up in spite of all the bloodshed.

We have now lived over 60 years without a major world war. The nuclear bombs and the Holocaust were horrific; they are a deterrent against ever allowing a repeat. Watching films from the world wars gives us the sense that war truly is hell. Human history since the time of Napoleon seems to have been a series of major battles for the right to be considered the world's "top" nation. War has become more horrible as science developed the ability to destroy humankind many times over. In spite of the confrontations in the Middle East, we might say that, since the end of the Second World War, we have lived through an era of relative peace. Perhaps it is time we began to fight wars against injustice, poverty, hunger and disease. Many people believe we are also in a battle to save the planet for future generations. Science and technology have given us the tools to accomplish a peaceful and equitable world. Do our national leaders have the will to say, "No more bloodshed"? Is a lasting peace possible when 5% of the world's people possess 90% of the world's wealth?

April 22

Earth Day

Nature is a labyrinth in which the very haste you move with will make you lose your way.
Francis Bacon

Let us a little permit nature to take her own way; she better understands her own affairs than we.
Michel Eyquem de Montaigne

Be such a man, and live such a life, that if every man were such as you, and every life a life like yours, this earth would be God's Paradise.
Phillips Brooks

We have probed the earth, excavated it, burned it, ripped things from it, and buried things in it ... That does not fit my definition of a good tenant. If we were here on a month-to-month basis, we would have been evicted long ago.
Rose Elizabeth Bird

The Earth has a skin and that skin has diseases, one of those diseases is man.
Friedrich Wilhelm Nietzsche

Today has been celebrated as "Earth Day" since 1970. I have always thought that like so many celebrations, we should extend the party infinitely. Every day should be Earth Day! I humbly submit for your kind consideration three changes you can make to hug the planet:

A: If you idle your car for more than 15 seconds, TURN IT OFF. This includes diesel engines. Some folks mistakenly think that it takes gas to start the car up. It takes the same amount of gas as 15 seconds of running;
B: Leave the car at home and walk or RIDE A BIKE or use public transit;
C: Purchase a PUSH MOWER for your grass. They are inexpensive, easy to push—and you get a better workout—and no fumes, noise or gas to waste!

Somebody sent me this lovely prose this morning. Enjoy your Earth Day. Remember to hug the planet.

Nature is ever at work building and pulling down, creating and destroying, keeping everything whirling and flowing, allowing no rest but in rhythmical motion, chasing everything in endless song out of one beautiful form into another.
John Muir, Naturalist and explorer

Art

At the deepest level, the creative process and the healing process arise from a single source. When you are an artist, you are a healer; a wordless trust of the same mystery is the foundation of your work and its integrity.

Rachel Naomi Remen

It's on the strength of observation and reflection that one finds a way. So we must dig and delve unceasingly.

Claude Monet

A good painter has two main objects to paint, man and the intention of his soul. The former is easy, the latter hard as he has to represent it by the attitude and movement of the limbs.

Leonardo da Vinci

I tell you, the more I think, the more I feel that there is nothing more truly artistic than to love people. The only time I feel alive is when I'm painting.

Both from Vincent van Gogh

America received a shock in 1961. The Russians launched the first orbiting spacecraft with the astronaut, Yuri Gagarin. The USSR had also launched the first satellite, Sputnik, in 1957. American technology found itself behind in the space race. One result of this shock was a shake-up of the education system. Mathematics and science became foci for secondary school students. New, more difficult courses resulted, and students were required to take more mathematics in order to graduate. In many boards of education, fewer arts courses were required. In our board, students could graduate with one arts course, which could include family studies. Art and music courses had fewer students each year, as more students selected math and science courses. America eventually beat the Russians to the moon—but was it worth the cost?

There are worlds of pleasure waiting in great music and art. You don't need to draw pictures or play an instrument to enjoy them. Far too many folks never experience truly great art. They never develop the "eyes and ears" to enjoy many of the world's remarkable art treasures.

There is another important reason "you've got to have art." Medicine is discovering that art and music can enhance intelligence and HEAL the body and mind. That's for another day. Listen to some Mozart and look at some Renoir today. You will feel all the better for it.

April 24

A Nice Challenge

Golf appeals to the idiot in us and the child. Just how childlike golf players become is proven by their frequent inability to count past five.

John Updike

Golf is so popular simply because it is the best game in the world at which to be bad.

A.A. Milne

Golf is like an 18-year-old girl with big boobs. You know it's wrong but you can't keep away from her.

Val Doonican

Golf is a lot of walking, broken up by disappointment and bad arithmetic.

Author Unknown

I am acknowledged as a definite duffer—hitting bad golf shots often. For this reason, we go to the driving range to launch balls out into a green field populated by thousands of previous bad shots—and the odd majestic one. Having a definite lack of "jock" genes, I just have one rule for hitting the wee white dimpled globe—SEE BALL: HIT BALL. On some drives, the ball goes up and up and away in a perfect arch—but more often than not, the damnable thing seems to have a mind of its own and goes curving off to the right of left—or ignominiously plowing through the grass in what's known as a "worm-burner." I usually finish my bucket of range balls first, since I refuse to over-analyze everything. Then I get to watch the other folks and some of them can really launch the balls.

I was sitting behind one chap who took lots of time with each shot, and he had a compact swing which resulted in a good drive almost every time. I complimented him on his swing, and he replied, "Well … I take a lot of time to think about the 23 things I need to remember before I swing."

I told him: "It must work … your drives are very consistent … unlike mine. I must be challenged!"

He looked at me and said: "Well that's what golf is after all … a nice challenge."

"A nice challenge" could be anything we struggle with. If it were easy, would we bother doing it? Keep working at whatever challenges you. Good work usually overcomes adversity—and always develops character.

April 25

Center of Everything

There seems no plan because it's all plan. There seems no center because it's all center.
C. S. Lewis

I think young people ought to seek that experience that is going to knock them off center.
James A. Michener

There are many fundamental questions every human asks sooner or later. "Where did everything come from?" is probably the most-asked question, causing heated debate with no definitive answer. Our planet could just be an atom in some giant's fingernail for all we know. There is an amazing race going on in science at present to prove the existence of the "GOD" particle. Will its ultimate discovery give the final answer to the question?

Here's an interesting question with storied answers. "Is humanity the center of everything?" Until the 1500's, the Earth was the center of everything. This seemed obvious, until Copernicus proposed his model. (See February 21)

Recall that Copernicus studied the classics, math and art in Krakow, in preparation for life in the ministry. Then, over a period of years, he was able to demonstrate that the earth orbited the sun each year. Copernicus, a Catholic cleric, dedicated his work to Pope Paul III! The idea that the earth was not the center of the universe eventually upset the Church, especially when Galileo Galilei championed it. The Inquisition convicted Galileo of heresy for "following the position of Copernicus, which is contrary to the true sense and authority of Holy Scripture." He was placed under house arrest for the rest of his life. In 1992, Pope John Paul II finally expressed regret for how Galileo had been treated and issued a pardon.

Copernicus put the sun at the center of the universe. Oops! Modern astronomy tells us that our sun is an "ordinary star" in one arm of the Milky Way Galaxy, and as Carl Sagan said, "There are billions and billions of galaxies!"

We aren't even close to the center. What a letdown!

116

April 26

Time Management

Time is an equal opportunity employer. Each human being has exactly the same num-
ber of hours and minutes every day. Rich people can't buy more hours. Scientists can't
invent new minutes. And you can't save time to spend it on another day. Even so, time
is amazingly fair and forgiving. No matter how much time you've wasted in the past,
you still have an entire tomorrow.

Denis Waitely

Time pressure can have powerful effects on the body. Our brain regards clocks, dead-
lines, and interrupted schedules as a threat, and calls up the "fight or flight" stress
response. The incessant struggle to do more and more in less and less time also makes
us more likely to respond with toxic anger to anyone or anything slowing us down.

From the Healthy Mind, *Healthy Body Handbook* by David S. Sobel M.D.

I know people who are totally busy. They will use that word, "busy", whenever they engage in conversation—as if they are the only folks who lead a busy life. If you try and set up some social activity, they don't have time to fit it in. It must be very stressful to have such time pressure controlling your life. I have one simple question of these folks. If you died later today, would the world still go on without you tomorrow?

Some people feel the need to fill every minute with productive activity. Why? What is wrong with watching T.V., reading a book, or playing cards? None of these could be considered very productive, and I suppose that could make for guilty feelings. Well—I say, down with guilt! Up with relaxation!

There are many good books written about time management, so I don't need to conduct a mini-course here. What you need to do if time pressure concerns you is to find some quiet time, meditate and pray—and then set your priorities.

Here's a wee Internet poem to help you get started.

Hands interlinked,
Walking slowly down the street.
Every moment savored and true,
Why can't I spend more time with you?

Author Unknown

April 27

Driving

It takes 8,460 bolts to assemble an automobile, and one nut to scatter it all over the road.

Author Unknown

The best car safety device is a rear-view mirror with a cop in it.

Dudley Moore

Everybody thinks they are the best driver in the world.

Author Unknown

It amazes me that people drive their cars without thinking about the great responsibility that goes with driving. You have over a ton of projectile traveling at high speed, mere seconds from disaster at any moment. Most people seem to drive as if accidents could never happen. Young people in particular drive as if they were immortal. What is it about driving that causes so many minds to turn to mush?

I saw on the news the other day the incredible wreckage when a loaded dump truck traveling at high speed went out of control and reduced dozens of cars to junk. Looking at the crushed cars, it was hard to believe that no one was killed! It seems to me that driving a huge vehicle should be a huge responsibility. We drive a truck and fifth wheel with a mass of over ten tons. We leave an envelope of space around us and extra room for stopping. We drive at the speed limit—in good conditions—so other drivers won't lose their patience behind us. In spite of the extra care, close calls still happen. Some drivers pass us and pull in too close in front of us, reducing our stopping space. Others get in the passing lane and stay there, driving so slowly that others are forced to pass these lane-hogs on the inside.

About twenty years ago, we were driving a rented motor home on a busy I-71 in Ohio when I noticed a car cutting in and out as he drove up behind us. I figured that he might cut in front of us, so I took my foot off the gas just in time for him to lose complete control. He did two and a half complete circles right in front of us while I stood on the brakes. He ended up backwards with his front bumper two feet from ours. All the cars around us braked to a stop. There were NO COLLISIONS! Anthony said to me: "Dad ... how did you stop so fast???" To this day, I still have no idea how we came through unscathed. It seemed a miracle!

April 28

The Bicycle 2

Every time I see an adult on a bicycle, I no longer despair for the future of the human race.

H.G. Wells

Bicycling is a big part of the future. There is something wrong with a society that drives a car to work out in a gym.

Bill Nye ... the "science guy"

Yesterday we reflected on driving. Consider an alternative—the bicycle.

A few years ago, I could barely walk and was even having trouble standing up. I didn't know at the time, but there was no cartilage remaining in my right hip, and both knees were letting me know of their existence. The surprising fact is, I could still get on my bike and cycle for over an hour. When we went camping, the only way I could get around was on my bike. Now why do you suppose this is? It's very simple. Your weight is off your joints and on your backside. Having a well-padded derrière really helps you on a bike. If you don't own a bike, think about getting one. Ride it around your neighborhood and on the trails. Ride it to the library and on short excursions. Your body will love you for it. The planet will love you for it! And it's easier that you think!

P.J. O'Rourke's Problem with Bikes

O'Rourke's sometimes amusing, sometimes mean-spirited campaign against the bicycle is well documented. Here is a summary of his problems with bikes—odd how many of them are the very reasons so many of us ride.

The Principle Arguments That May be Marshaled against Bicycles:
1. Bicycles are childish.
2. Bicycles are undignified.
3. Bicycles are unsafe.
4. Bicycles are un-American.
5. I don't like the kind of people who ride bicycles.
6. Bicycles are unfair.
7. Bicycles are good exercise.

April 29

Walking

Happiness is a state of activity.

Aristotle

All truly great thoughts are conceived while walking.

Friedrich Nietzsche

One step at a time is good walking.

Chinese Proverb

I can remember walking as a child. It was not customary to say you were fatigued. It was customary to complete the goal of the expedition.

Katherine Hepburn

Yesterday we extolled the virtues of bike riding. There are plenty of excuses for not riding a bike—as we saw at the end of the reflection. There is one activity, however, that most people can do, and it's free! I'm talkin' 'bout walkin', of course. There are more books written about the virtues of walking than any other form of exercise. There is even a *Complete Idiot's Guide* to walking. Give me a break! How difficult is it? For me with my bad knees and funny way of walking, it can be a challenge. A person confined to a wheelchair would give anything for the luxury of a good walk. Yet how many folks who are fully capable actually do much decent walking? Very few! This is a great pity, since walking is a wonderful way to control your weight and keep healthy.

Our neighbors walk together for a good half hour twice each day. If the weather is lousy, they walk in the local mall. Another couple we know walk down to the mall or to the local coffee shop most mornings. It is no accident that all four of these people are in good shape and have plenty of energy. They all stay at a proper body weight and are very healthy. I know they do other good routines like weightlifting and yoga, but I'm sure they would tell you that the walking keeps them youthful!

Walking is so good for you, many songs have been written about it. Fill your iPod with these and get moving!

I'm Walkin' to New Orleans   *Walk Hand in Hand with Me*
Love Walked In   *Walk Right In*
Walking the Dog   *The Baby Elephant Walk*
The Stroll   *Walk the Talk*

April 30

Enough

If you can't explain it simply, you don't understand it well enough.

Albert Einstein

You have played enough; you have eaten and drunk enough. Now it is time for you to depart.

Horace

He who knows that enough is enough will have enough.

Lao Tzu

Our care should not be to have lived long as to have lived enough.

Lucius Annaeus Seneca

I am constantly amazed by the moderation shown by my wife. I have no recollection of Celia ever drinking too much, eating too much or doing too much shopping. One of the greatest compliments one could ever give a person is to say that it doesn't take much to make them happy. That describes my partner and best friend of over forty years. Celia always seems to have enough, and if I ask her what she wants for her birthday or Christmas, she always tells me she has everything she wants. She is easily pleased. I don't feel that I need to jump through a whole pile of hoops to keep her happy. What a lucky fellow!

On the other hand, I always "get carried away," to quote Aunt Dorothy. I do love my food and drink, and if it weren't for Celia's attention to healthy cuisine and gentle reminders of moderation, I would be perfectly round. I have little control, and if a little of anything is good, I just can't get enough. I have always been that way—a collector. It's in my blood, as my father, Allen, loved collecting. Al collected tools and records. I figure at one time we had more half-horse electric motors than the whole population of the city. That may be an exaggeration, but Al definitely had the largest collection of Enrico Caruso records. So my father could never get enough of a good thing, and I am the same way. I just love to collect my favorite stuff.

I don't collect stamps or coins, but I probably have the largest collections of Beethoven Symphonies, old running shoes and pigs—of anyone you know. And guess what—it's never enough!

May 1

Forgetting

Every composer knows the anguish and despair occasioned by forgetting ideas which one had no time to write down.

Hector Berlioz

Even philosophers will praise war as ennobling mankind, forgetting the Greek who said: "War is bad in that it begets more evil than it kills."

Immanuel Kant

A man who pays his bills on time is soon forgotten.

Oscar Wilde

The 21st century may be remembered as the "Century of Forgetfulness." All our friends, both young and old, constantly complain about how forgetful they have become. "I go to the fridge, open the door and then stand there wondering why I went to the fridge in the first place," is a common problem. Other folks tell me they drive somewhere; yet when they arrive at their destination they have no idea of how they got there. Scary!

My worst forgetfulness occurs when I wake up and then quickly go back to sleep. People phone me in the middle of my nap. I'll answer, and we have a conversation, and then I go back to sleep after the call. Later, when I wake up for good, I have no idea what the call was about—if I even remember the call. The worse scenario is to wake up in the middle of the night with some great idea for a reflection. If I don't get up and write it down, it's certain to be gone in the morning!

I also suffer from a slow memory. I'll see somebody I know, but their name momentarily escapes me. I remember their name about ten seconds after I need it. If I watch *Jeopardy* on television, I get many of the answers about five seconds after the contestants push their button.

I think I've finally figured out why these bouts of forgetting occur. There's so much stuff crammed in there, the least little distraction seems to seize up the memory molecules. Forgetting is a defensive mechanism to prevent overload. It's like opening the fridge to get a beer—and there it is—gone!

May 2

Showing Off

Telling lies and showing off to get attention are mistakes I made that I don't want my kids to make.

Jane Fonda

Showing off is the fool's idea of glory.

Bruce Lee

It is no use to keep private information which you can't show off.

Mark Twain

My father was a very powerful man. He had strong arms and shoulders from construction work he did in the late 1920's. Then the Depression came, and there was no construction work. Allen eventually got a job at the cereal factory. He was the rice picker machine man; it was his job to poke at a large mass of cooked rice using a chrome rod, weighing 25 to 30 pounds, as the clumps were broken up by the metal prongs of the machine. You were supposed to use both hands to hold the chrome bar. Dad was so strong that he would stir the rice using his mighty right hand on the rod, and hold a cigarette with the other hand. Unfortunately, the rod slipped that fateful day; Al tried to grab it as it fell into the machine. The prongs of the rice picker machine trapped his arm before the machine stopped. It took two hours to dismantle the machine, and the men told me that Al smoked a pack of cigarettes and told stories as they took the machine apart.

At the hospital, the doctors decided there was too much damage done to dad's hand, so they amputated his arm just below the elbow. This traumatic accident happened about five years before I was born, but I remember hearing several stories about the event. My brother Judd tells me that he was two at the time; when Al came home from the hospital, Judd told him, "You're not my dad!" It was a natural thing for a little boy to say, but it must have been a shock. As the safety commercials say on TV—one second of inattention and a life is changed forever.

When Al was in the hospital after his accident, Aunt Dorothy went to see him. She is reputed to have said to dad, "Al … you can lay there and feel sorry for yourself for losing your right hand … or you can learn to write with your left hand. Here's a pen!"

May 3

The Test

All life is but a continual test.

William Shakespeare

If I'd known there was going to be a test, I would have been sick today!

Bart Simpson

When I went to work at the cereal factory in the late 1950's, there were people who said to me, "The only reason you got a cushy job is because your dad is a big cheese supervisor there." While it was true that my father was the Supervisor of Sanitation, he told me to apply for a job but not to mention his name. (I found out later the men called him "Mr. Clean" and "Stainless Steels.") I was to get the job on my own merits and not because my father worked there.

On the day I applied, they told me there were no jobs available for summer students, so I should apply elsewhere if I wanted work. I saw a worker I recognized, and he gave me an important tip. "Come back early every Friday morning and bug them." Sure enough, one Friday morning they told me to get a uniform and be ready for work before 7 a.m. on Monday morning. I was to report to the sanitation office.

The foreman took us four rookies over to the mill, and told us to "clean all the crap out from under the mill; it's been there since the war, so be careful!" The space under the mill was about three feet high and filthy. There was no end of rusty metal and rotted wood under there—and it was hot and full of spider webs! The first guy quit at noon. On Tuesday morning only two of us showed up, with aching backs, to go under the mill. Wednesday morning I was left by myself to complete the dirty task. I had no sooner gone under the mill when I heard: "Come on out. I've got a new job for you!" Hallelujah—those were the best words I heard all summer.

From then on, the jobs were comparatively easy. I became the main assistant janitor to the permanent janitors. They told me that they gave rookies the mill job as a test—and very few made it past two days. Thank heavens I came back for the third day! For that persistence, I earned the name, "Stainless Steels Junior."

May 4

Flames

Life is a flame that is always burning itself out, but it catches fire again every time a child is born.

George Bernard Shaw

You lack the courage to be consumed in flames and to become ashes: so you will never become new, and never young again!

Friedrich Wilhelm Nietzsche

The spread of civilization may be likened to a fire; First, a feeble spark, next a flickering flame, then a mighty blaze.

Nikola Tesla

Have you ever wished you could "do it all over again?" Knowing what you do now, life would be so much easier, and you would have a better chance of avoiding all those mistakes and doing it "right." What a silly notion. The only way to get your youth back, according to Gounod's opera *Faust*, is to sell your soul to the devil. How does that work? In the opera, Satan restores Faust to a youth with his brain chock full of wisdom; but when he dies, the devil is there to drag his soul down to hell to spend the remainder of eternity in pain and agony. If you could have your youth back, or become a famous person, would you exchange your soul? Probably not!

There is an alternative. According to Nietzsche, we can reinvent ourselves. To do this requires the old self to be consumed in flames and become ashes. Imagine how difficult this is. We have previously said that there is terrific inertia to any change in human behavior. How do we get rid of old habits? How do we dump all that baggage? Nietzsche never tells us how. He simply says that the old self must go up in flames! Is it at all possible?

Here's a way to begin. Suppose you had no restrictions limiting what you could accomplish. Make a list of all the things you would like to accomplish, starting now—a "bucket list" of things you would like to do before you kick the bucket. Then begin on one thing you can achieve, and go from there with gusto. The satisfaction and resulting energy will recharge your batteries and make you young again—physically and spiritually!

Are you doing the same things you were doing five years ago? If you live by the adage, "Try something new each and every year," you should be doing lots of new things and reinventing yourself. Maybe you are. Hooray and hallelujah! Or, is it time for a recharge?

May 5

Reinventing Yourself

The only real voyage of discovery consists not in seeking new landscapes but in having new eyes.

Marcel Proust

Since God made us to be originals, why stoop to be a copy?

Billy Graham

Discoveries are often made not by following instructions, but by going off the main road, by trying the untried.

Frank Tyger

The most powerful weapon on earth is the human soul on fire.

Ferdinand Foch

Have you decided on one thing you would like to do to recharge your batteries? Can you do this yourself or do you need help? Help is a click of the remote away! There are many programs on television about people remaking themselves. Several PBS documentaries show people trying to achieve what they previously thought impossible. One follows ten average people of all ages and shapes in training to run the Boston marathon. Eight of them did just that—with help! Help is also a click of the mouse away. There are so many resources on the Internet, you can find almost anything. Just keep surfing your topic or area. It's surprising where it will lead.

Here's a short list of new things being done by some of the folks I know:

Bill is taking art classes and has several canvasses under his belt;

Cliff is designing and making beautiful pens;

Judy has become a travel agent for a cruise company;

Pat has taken a pile of old car parts and built a restored Morgan;

Phil returned to school to become an Anglican priest;

Marie took workshops to become a horticultural judge.

Now here's the point of all this. These folks are "RETIRED." You are never too old to learn or to reinvent yourself!

May 6

Dazzling Moments

One's performance is often heightened by the brilliance and generosity of other actors.
Cyril Cusack

The aged love what is practical while impetuous youth longs only for what is dazzling.
Petrarch

When science, art, literature, and philosophy are simply the manifestation of personality they are on a level where glorious and dazzling achievements are possible, which can make a man's name live for thousands of years.
Denis Diderot

If you can't dazzle them with brilliance, baffle them with bull.

W. C. Fields

One of our old high school cheers went something like this:

Razzle, Dazzle, sis-boom-bah!
Come on Spartans ... eat 'em raw!

This seemed to work for our basketball and football teams. After the fans worked themselves into frenzy with the cheer, a player would score an incredibly long basket—or some wide receiver would make a one-handed catch that simply dazzled us—and the cheer would go on and on—over and over. Do you remember those school days—and the Razzle-Dazzle?

Today, no one cheers when we are on the golf course, and although there may be many lousy shots, there are dazzling moments. One of my buddies, Ron, hits majestic arching drives which stop dead when they hit the green. Dazzling! We all sink the odd 20 foot putt—watching the ball curl slowly into the hole. Dazzling! In one game, I remember chipping a ball into the hole from over 30 yards—twice in the same round. Another dazzling moment! All these moments are greeted politely but quietly so as not to disturb other golfers.

I feel that life itself is an evenly lived time with the odd dazzling moment, and when they come—and everyone is dazzled—we should savor, celebrate and replay those moments as often as we please.

May 7

Reinventing Yourself 2

The only real voyage of discovery consists not in seeking new landscapes but in having new eyes.

Marcel Proust

Discoveries are often made not by following instructions, but by going off the main road, by trying the untried.

Frank Tyger

The most powerful weapon on earth is the human soul on fire.

Ferdinand Foch

Sometimes, people are forced to reinvent themselves out of an accident rather than by intention. We all wish to make a better person out of our "old" self now and then. "If I could only …" is something we have all said when we find ourselves making the same old mistakes or doing the same old boring routines we can't seem to escape. Consider what happens to a person when they are forced to reinvent themselves because of an accident or change in health. We heard the sad story one Saturday morning, at the coffee klatch, of a woman who without warning suddenly went totally blind. Imagine a change in your health so dramatic as to completely change all your routines!

I can only imagine the trauma and lifestyle changes my father had to endure when he lost his arm in a factory accident in the 1930's before I was born. Since he lost his right arm, he learned how to do everything left-handed. He not only learned how to do everything well, he had the attitude that he could be better with one hand that most men are with two! He succeeded at this so well that he was promoted to foreman and shift supervisor in short order. Al's shift was always known as the one that got things done. Al had indeed overcome his handicap in so many ways. We knew at home that there was nothing dad couldn't do—and in spite of severe "phantom pain" in his missing hand, Al seldom complained or felt sorry for himself.

The downside of all Al's success was how obsessive he became about his job, especially in his capacity as environmental supervisor. You could almost say Al became the great eradicator of molds and fungi—everywhere! However, that's a story for another day.

May 8

Work

Zeal: a certain nervous disorder affecting the young and inexperienced.

Ambrose Bierce

When I was elevated to head custodian of the fourth floor of the factory, the foreman gave me a long list of jobs that needed doing. One of the first jobs was to vacuum the dust from the top of the fluorescent fixtures. I became a whirlwind and finished the job in a couple of days. When I went back to get another job, the foreman seemed surprised that I was done. At the break in the afternoon, the other custodians gave me proper hell, telling me: "What are you doing up there, Stainless Junior? The last time we dusted and replaced the bulbs, it took three weeks. Slow down, or you will ruin it for the permanent men! Be careful from now on, or we'll take a round out of you." From then on, before attacking any job, I asked the men how long it should take. Before long, I became "one of the boys," and I was forgiven for initially working too fast.

The roll room was on the fourth floor. After the corn was cooked in huge stainless steel cookers, conveyor belts carried it to the roll room where rolls squeezed the cooked corn into the corn flakes everybody knows so well. The noise from these huge rolls was deafening. The men had to wear ear plugs. One day I was dusting the electrical boxes in a small room off the roll room; suddenly, all the rolls began to slow down and stop. The conveyor belts, however, kept going, and cooked corn began to pile up all around the fourth floor. Men in white shirts materialized out of nowhere, shouting instructions to each other, while the workers stood watching and smiling. One of the supervisors asked me: "Did you touch that box on the wall?"

"Not me!" I replied. It was morning break time, so I went down to the canteen where I was welcomed like a hero by some of the workers.

"Way to go, Stainless Junior ... that mess will take the bosses the rest of the day to clean up! We won't have to do anything for the rest of this shift."

"Don't we have to help clean up the mess?" I inquired.

"It's not in our job description," was the answer. As management cleaned up and we played euchre the rest of the morning, I learned how the union "worked."

May 9

Leonard Bernstein

Inspiration is wonderful when it happens, but the writer must develop an approach for the rest of the time ... The wait is simply too long.

This will be our reply to violence: to make music more intensely, more beautifully, more devotedly than ever before.

To achieve great things, two things are needed; a plan, and not quite enough time.

All from Leonard Bernstein, 1918-1990,
American musicologist, composer, conductor and educator

We just returned from a symphony concert. There was a rare program featuring the music of American composer, Leonard Bernstein. I use the word "rare" since symphony concerts with American composers don't happen very often. American composers like Copland, Gershwin and Charles Ives are seldom performed in the concert hall, in contrast to Mozart, Tchaikovsky and Beethoven. As much as I love the Germanic and Russian composers, there is a wonderful sense of "letting loose" in American music. I suppose it's the influence of jazz that gives a terrific sparkle and energy to the music of American composers and especially to Leonard "Lenny" Bernstein, a composer of both symphonies and Broadway musicals. The greatest praise I can give to Lenny is:

He could communicate his great sense of wonder!

Here is a brief list of the wonders he gave to music lovers:
- One of the greatest musicals ever written: "West Side Story", with beautiful melodies and driving dance music;
- Generations of people learning about music from his televised "young peoples' concerts" from 1958 to 1972;
- Many definitive recordings with the New York Philharmonic and Vienna Symphony Orchestras. There is always emotion in a Bernstein performance.

Upbeat, jazzy, immersed in all aspects of music—these only begin to describe Lenny Bernstein, an amazing American musicologist.

May 10

Showing Off 2

I will not show off!!!
Bart Simpson

When I became the sanitary engineer on the fourth floor at the factory during the summer of 1964, I met a number of characters who razzed me because I was a summer student. The regular men loved to put you to the test because you were going to an institute of "higher learning" which they, as factory workers, had never experienced. If a regular could put one over on a student, it earned him bragging rights in the canteen; the student who was "so smart" would be the butt of derision. One chap who looked after a corn cooker had intense blue eyes and a Machiavellian mind for devising ways to trick me. He also had big strong arms from moving the 58 pound cooker lid off and on the corn cooker drum. He rolled up his sleeves to show off his biceps and flexed them in front of me as I swept around. He would say, "You may be tall, Stainless, but you summer students are a bunch of weaklings!" What I never told him was that I lifted weights, and my special talent was a one-handed clean and jerk of over 60 pounds. One day, Mister Biceps was razzing me and daring me to lift the 58 pound cooker lid up over my head. He claimed I'd never be able to do it, and he took the lid and put it over his head—using both hands. "Try that, Stainless … a buck says you can't do it!" So I grabbed the cooker lid and put it up over my head easily—with ONE hand! Old Blue Eyes couldn't believe it. I became an instant celebrity around the factory. Regulars would come up to the fourth floor to watch Stainless Junior clean and jerk the cooker lid over his head with one hand.

What I didn't realize was that Old Blue Eyes was making bets on the side because nobody believed a skinny university guy was that strong. I may have been strong, but I wasn't very smart! One day as I hoisted up the cooker lid for the boys, there was a nasty crunch. I ended up on the floor in terrible pain, with my back "out." The regulars saved my skin by telling the foreman that I had slipped on the floor when I was mopping up. They also took me to a chiropractor, where a week of adjustments allowed me to stand up straight again. That act of showing off cost me years of lower back pain, adjustments and millions of pelvic tilts. I suppose you could say the apple doesn't fall very far from the tree.

May 11

Recording

Making records is like making sausages ... the end result is palatable but you don't want to see how it's done.

Bill Flannigan

My workout buddy Mike and I listen to music as we pump the morning iron. We listen to quite a variety of music, from Beethoven to Jazz to the Beatles. We can feel it as much as hear it—and the low notes are particularly good. One morning we were listening to Beethoven's symphonies, which I had downloaded from an online store, and we were both remarking at the quality of the sound and the performance. It sometimes seemed as if the woodwinds, horns and timpanist were right in the room with us. Amazing!

The whole process of reproducing a performance of 60 or more players on your home stereo and getting the sound right is miraculous. Consider the many steps that resulted in our enjoyment. (I am omitting many small steps!)

Beethoven had to imagine the symphony in his mind (he was deaf!);
He wrote the notes down for all the instruments using musical notation;
Somebody published a score and all the parts for the musicians;
The musicians learned the parts and a conductor imposed his will upon them to play his vision of the piece;
A recording engineer put the performance "in the digital can;"
The record company produced and manufactured the recording;
The performance was licensed for sale at the online store;
I bought the "album" and downloaded it to my computer;
I burned a CD of the performance, and we played the CD in the stereo!

Ludwig must have been listening in the place in heaven reserved for the immortal composers and shaking his head in absolute awe!

May 12

Battle of the Bands

Madam, you have between your legs an instrument capable of giving pleasure to thousands ... and all you can do is scratch it.

Brass bands are all very well in their place ... outdoors and several miles away.

Try everything once except folk dancing and incest.

There are two golden rules for an orchestra: start together and finish together. The public doesn't give a damn what goes on in between.

All from Sir Thomas Beecham ... famous British conductor

My workout buddy Mike has made great progress in our morning workouts. He has reshaped both his body and his ears! We have been listening to a new set of Beethoven's symphonies, and we both agree that the performances are ear-opening. We previously liked the 1962 Berlin Philharmonic set under Herbert von Karajan. The power and glory of Beethoven shines through Karajan's muscular and well-recorded CD's. This new set is by the Tonhalle Orchestra of Zurich under David Zinman. You have probably never heard of either of them. Mike says the name of the orchestra makes you think that it consists of three fiddles and a banjo. Zurich, Switzerland is a smallish city of 350 000 folks. You would not expect a city the size of Buffalo, New York, to have a world-class orchestra. You would be wrong!

The sound on these recordings is amazing. It has body and presence. All the instruments shine through. The horns have an edge. The timpani and woodwinds sound like they are in the room, and the overall string sound has a wonderful bloom. The performances are lively with a clarity which must come from the excellent acoustic of the "Tonhalle." Mike and I keep saying, "There's something we haven't heard before!"

These recordings make the last three full-price sets from major orchestras in capital cities sound dull by comparison. Like the older Karajan set, the set is a bargain price. If Sir Thomas Beecham were alive today, he probably would have said, "A most distressing spectacle, ladies and gentlemen ... miracle performances for a mere pittance!"

May 13

Recording 2

It's not how loud you make it … it's how you make it loud.

Anon

I turn the good parts up and the bad parts down.

Jim Dickinson, recording engineer

Classical musicians do this all the time. They want perfection. So they piece things together. Glenn Gould said that with a recording he wanted to make perfect versions of pieces.

John Abercrombie

I have been fascinated with recordings ever since I was a kid, and I am constantly amazed and delighted at all the changes recordings have undergone in the last half century. My father had an extensive collection of 78 rpm records. Many of them were only playable on one side, and they were easily damaged. They sounded pretty good sixty years ago, but now they seem lifeless and scratchy. Al had all of Enrico Caruso's opera arias, and they sounded as if Caruso sang into a hose and out of his nose. The old recordings have been enhanced by engineers, but they still sound awful by today's standards.

When the record was replaced by the compact disc, the "clicks" and "pops" disappeared into an absolutely silent background. I could hear all sorts of stuff on the early CDs—pages turning, musicians groaning and taking a big breath before blowing. On one recording of Beethoven's 9th, I can hear the conductor admonishing the musicians. On many CDs recorded in the church of St Martin-in-the-Fields in London, England, I can hear the deep drone of the trucks in the streets of London. Isn't it wonderful what a silent background will reveal?!

I don't even need to go out of the house to find new music anymore. I simply go to the iTunes store or emusic.com and download to my computer. Then I plug in my iPod, and it sucks in all the new recordings. My iPod holds the equivalent of over a thousand albums, and I can play it through headphones or any stereo system. Actually, the computer will also play the music through the system. My laptop has half my collection stored on its hard drive, and a simple wire connects it to any stereo. How do iPods and computers sound? Amazing!

May 14

Opera

I don't mind what language an opera is sung in so long as it is a language I don't understand.

Sir Edward Appleton

One can't judge Wagner's opera Lohengrin after a first hearing, and I certainly don't intend to hear it a second time.

Gioacchino Rossini

Opera is where a guy gets stabbed in the back, and instead of dying, he sings.

Anon

In opera there is too much singing.

Claude Debussy

We just returned from a performance of Rossini's *Barber of Seville*. That's the opera where Bugs Bunny is the barber and sings, "Welcome to my shop, let me cut yer mop ... yer so NEXT!!!"

I took our son Craig to the opera and he remembered the words to the whole aria that Bugs sang in the cartoon version. It was Craig's first opera at the new Four Seasons Centre, and it was a dandy performance. In Rossini's operas, you are sure to hear plenty of notes and at least six loud singers, each singing a different story, all at once. Most of his operas have funny stories, and the hilarity is enhanced by the many fast songs known as patter. Craig loved the production and was amazed by all the basses, who gave outstanding performances. I was wowed by the mezzo-soprano, who negotiated all the notes with the agility of a gymnast and produced huge high notes that made my head ring. Sitting in the third row, with the soprano a mere 20 feet away, gives you a great "rush"—of adrenalin.

This performance of *The Barber* was outstanding—the set, lighting, costumes, orchestral playing, staging, acting and singing all came together to make every minute a delight. When all these elements are really well done, opera cannot be beat as an art medium. In a great performance, it doesn't matter how ridiculous the storyline or text—you suspend your disbelief in order to immerse yourself in the visual, orchestral and vocal vibes that wash over you. This may only occur in half the operas—but when it happens, your body molecules keep up the good vibes for some time. Mine are still vibrating!

May 15

Rusting Out

Few minds wear out ... more RUST out.

Bovee

The human body rusts out before it wears out.

Jim Fix (runner)

I think it was Mel Brooks who said that you've got to keep all the body parts moving because the opposite is death. When a cast is removed from a limb, the limb is smaller and weaker because of the immobilization. If you are forced to spend extra time in bed, the whole body becomes lethargic. This atrophy can affect the brain as well. You need to keep the blood flowing through those gray cells and make them do some good thinking or the brain will get rusty. Students and teachers know how difficult it can be to get cranked up again after the summer holidays. Holidays are good to recharge the batteries, but a permanent holiday can really rust the brain and body out quickly. You have to have some purpose to your daily routine. I've listed a few ways of adjusting to keep the brain and body in motion:

Run, walk, ride a bike ... move your arms ... wiggle your nose and your toes ... but keep that blood moving ... good alone or in company;

Party actively ... with games ... cards ... scrabble ... Balderdash ... singing ... dancing ... silly stuff with lots of laughing;

Watch T.V. actively. It's easy to ride a stationary bike or walk on a treadmill while you watch T.V. I often do stretching or light weightlifting while I watch my favorite sports programs.

To remain sharp requires constant active honing and some imagination to prevent whatever you are doing from becoming tedious. There are many different ways of embellishing routines to avoid stagnation. Always ask, "Is there an active way of doing this so that I can keep the body and brain from rusting out?" And—oh yes—don't become obsessed with your computer! Opps—guilty as charged!!!

May 16

Waiting

How much of human life is lost in waiting?

Ralph Waldo Emerson

People count up the faults of those who keep them waiting.

Proverb

A sure way to irritate people and to put evil thoughts into their heads is to keep them waiting a long time.

Friedrich Nietzsche

I went to the fracture clinic at the hospital today to get shot. When I arrived early, a huge mob of hobbled folk was already waiting. I counted over forty with the usual collection of crutches, casts and canes you always see at the clinic. All the seats in the waiting room were taken, so more than a dozen were standing in the main hall. As I looked around, there wasn't one smile on the lot of them. I took my number "72" out of the dispenser and went back into the hall to stand and wait. I struck up some conversations and said some funny stuff, but laughs were difficult to come by. I finally got some laughs when I acted like a traffic light to get the wheelchairs, carts and pushed beds through the waiting mob. Some people thought this was cute, but others weren't having any of it. Then an official-looking man announced that we were blocking a "fire lane" and we had to move. Most folks went into another room down the hall, but I went into the clinic waiting room and sat in a space on the floor. Thus began a three-hour wait to get injected with nasty needles; during those three hours, I made some observations about people who wait.

Most folks just sit and look unhappy—only a few folks actually look around at others—and talking to someone next to you seems almost impolite.

At the start I was the only one reading a book, but by the end of the wait there were two prepared folks who had brought their own books to read.

I discovered that the person beside me was born and raised in Boston, so when I related a funny experience I had at Fenway Park in Boston, several folks around us actually laughed quietly. One chap said to me, "You wouldn't do that in Yankee Stadium … the fans would kill you!" Then others started telling their stories of sporting events, and guess what? It was soon time to get shot!

May 17

Sporting Events

A puck is a hard rubber disc that hockey players strike when they can't hit one another.
Jimmy Cannon.

How would you like a job where, every time you make a mistake, a big red light goes on and 18,000 people boo?
Jacques Plante   (famous goalie for the Montreal Canadiens)

I went to a fight the other night and a hockey game broke out.
Rodney Dangerfield.

Son, when you are participating in sporting events, it's not whether you win or lose ... it's how drunk you get.
Homer Simpson to his son Bart

I love going to a sporting event. You never know what's going to happen. It is real life—not played out to a script—unless it's wrestling or has been fixed by crooks. You can yell and whistle and eat and drink and look at a load of people dressed like a bunch of kids with silly hats and numbers on their backs. It's usually loads of fun.

I have good recall for some of the more memorable games I have attended. I was in Boston for a science conference, and I played hooky one night and went down to the Boston Garden to see if I could get into the Bruins hockey game. I got a ticket for $ 35, and once inside, I decided to get a beer. The server asked me for I.D. I had to fumble around for my driver's license, and he didn't even look at it. So I'm standing there in the midst of a mob going to their seats, and I realize I have lost my bloody ticket. How the hell can I get to my seat if I don't know where it is? Some local Bostonian noticed my perplexed look and asked what was troubling me. So I told him, "I've lost my damn ticket and I don't know where I'm sitting!"

He laughed and replied, "Try looking at the bottom of your beer glass!" Sure enough—the ticket was stuck to the bottom of the glass by moisture. I guess I had put the ticket on the counter when I was getting my I.D. and the server had put the beer glass on top of it.

Talk about going from agony to ecstasy in a minute. It's a good thing the natives were friendly—especially when I ended up cheering for the visiting team.

May 18

Boredom

If you knew what you were doing, you'd probably be bored.

Fresco's Law

Life is never boring but some people choose to be bored. The concept of boredom entails an inability to use up present moments in a personally fulfilling way. Boredom is a choice; something you visit upon yourself, and it is another of those self-defeating items that you can eliminate from your life.

Wayne Dyer

We were working the Altruists' bingo one day, and I had the exciting task of providing the payouts for the runners. I sat there in the back of the bingo hall and doled out the loot when a bingo was called. Sometimes it would be fifteen minutes between payouts, and I didn't have a book or anything with me so it was dragging—every minute felt like an hour—boring! Celia came by and knew by the look on my face that I wasn't thrilled. She handed me a piece of paper and told me to work on a reflection. When I looked down at the paper, she had already written the word "boredom" at the top. At bingo that afternoon, I managed to fill that page with ideas for reflections, and soon the bingo was over. Hooray!

The first year I taught, I was required to teach botany to a class of "failures." One older kid used to lie with his head on his hands, and one day he blurted out, "This stuff is boring!" I must have looked shocked, and I didn't know how to react.

Then one of the other kids came to my defense and astounded me by saying, "Don't take it personally, Sir. Larry is bored with everything. This stuff is actually pretty good." Some of the other kids also said they liked the botany. One of them told Larry that it was his own fault that he was bored. There I was, a rookie teacher, and kids were sticking up for me. I was quite amazed by this.

Our class in second year college had an award system for the lecturers. One of our professors won our LEAD prize as the most boring lecturer. During one lecture, the prof suffered a brain cramp and stood for the longest time, his arm outstretched and pointing a finger at us. It seemed an eternity—as if he were frozen. Somebody at the back of the class whispered, "Hey … he looks like he's going to fart!"

May 19

Invisible World

The sky is filled with stars, invisible by day.

Henry Wadsworth Longfellow

Vision is the art of seeing what is invisible to others.

Jonathan Swift

Ninety-nine percent of who you are is invisible and untouchable.

Buckminster Fuller

We live in a sea of invisible particles. This can be a good thing or a bad thing, depending on the type of particle. The good guys are mostly molecules. The bad guys can be ions, quanta and the odd molecule and atom. There are also tiny particles that are visible only if you have really good vision. All of these particles affect your disposition and your health, so it's important that you understand all those "beasties" and "beauties" around you, and how they affect you. Then you can make some simple changes to reduce the nasty particles in your vicinity. Let's have a look at what some of these invisible particles are.

The air you breathe is normally a solution of 21% oxygen and 78% nitrogen. The last 1 % is a number of trace gases, of which carbon dioxide at 0.04 % is one of the most important. The real "good" gas here is the oxygen. You need the oxygen to power your metabolic processes. Without the oxygen in the air, you would suffocate in a few minutes. The nitrogen is largely ignored by your body, but can become very important in plants and car engines.

Air also contains water vapor in varying amounts. The relative humidity can vary from a very dry 0 % found in Death Valley, California, to 100 % found in air saturated with invisible water vapor. Clouds may form and rain may fall when air becomes saturated with water vapor. The bottom line with water vapor is simple. Dry air is unhealthy. You can increase the water vapor in your house in several ways. Besides having a good humidifier, plenty of house plants will increase the water vapor and remove toxins from the air.

Congratulations on getting through the science lesson. Reward yourself with a drink of pure clean water. Give your plants a drink while you are at it, but not too much!

May 20

Beneficial Illness

I enjoy convalescence. It is the part that makes the illness worthwhile.

George Bernard Shaw

I reckon being ill as one of the great pleasures of life, provided one is not too ill and is not obliged to work until one is better.

Samuel Butler

There was a little boy who loved stories, especially stories about animals who acted like humans. Some of his favorites were "Paddy the Beaver", "Sammy Jay", and "Ratty"; but his best-loved was "Buster Bear's Twins". He loved the way his older sister and mother used their voices for the different animal characters in the books. One day he wasn't feeling well, so he stayed home from school. Much to his delight, his mother read him his favorite book that day. He discovered that being sick wasn't so bad, since he kept warm, received special food, and best of all, heard his precious stories. He missed so much school that he fell far behind all his friends. This didn't worry him much, since being at home with mother was so much better than yucky school. In fourth grade, this all changed. The teacher was kind and gentle and made everyone feel special. His health changed for the better, and he blossomed, developing a love of school.

History has stories of many famous people who effected great changes from their bedrooms. Rene Descartes, the French philosopher and mathematician, spent much of his life in the comfort of the covers. He and many others discovered that everything gets delivered to you when you are ill. Why give up this luxury?

The eminent American psychologist, Dr. Murray Banks, said**: "Never ever give a person any extra care, attention or love when they are sick!"** This sounds like an uncaring attitude, but think about what may happen. At worst, we may be making the person into a full-blown hypochondriac. At best, we may be encouraging someone to think illness is rather a good thing and should be milked for all it's worth! This is a bad attitude, but you may know someone who is like this. We should be sympathetic without pampering the convalescent.

Granny had a nasty approach. She would say, "You don't look sick to me. If you want to stay home, I'll give you something to be sick about!" Thank heavens she wasn't there much when I stayed home!

May 21

Gratitude

Saying thank you is more than good manners. It is good spirituality.

Alfred Painter

Gratefulness is the key to a happy life.

David Steindl-Rast

Let us rise up and be thankful, for if we didn't learn a lot today, at least we learned a little, and if we didn't learn a little, at least we didn't get sick, and if we got sick, at least we didn't die; so, let us all be thankful.

Buddha

Oh how sharper that the serpent's tooth it is to have a thankless child.

King Lear in Shakespeare's play by the same name

The first thing we do when we get up in the morning is to say, "Thanks for another day." We are truly grateful for all the blessings of this life and often wonder why we merit the riches bestowed upon us. We often take for granted the abundance and variety of good food, clean air, water and living space missing from the daily living of 90 percent of the world's people. In one hospital in Africa, 200 000 people were treated in one year on a budget of $ 40,000. Do the math. That's 25 cents each! How would you like to get treated there? "You've had your two bits' worth of treatment ... out you go!"

I wasn't always very thankful for all the bounty. I remember being resentful when I was a kid that we never had a car or went on holidays. A few of our friends and neighbors would jump in their cars every weekend to go to their cottages. We never learned to say "Thanks" for any blessings, because we were never taught how many we really had. I suppose that's one important thing we should all be teaching our children and grandchildren—how to be thankful for what we have, and not to be envious of those we "think" have more. The quote, "Gratefulness is the key to a happy life," is very true if you think about it.

I like what Walt Kelly, the inventor of the cartoon, *POGO*, has to say about ingratitude in the young. The three bratty bat boys are giving Mother Grackle a hard time as she is trying to tell them the important facts of life—so she finally informs them, in a twisted Shakespearian misquote from King Lear (found above), **"If you don't stop being sharper nor a serpent's tooth ... you ain't gonna be a spank-less child!"**

May 22

Invisible Ions

Ionization was shown to reduce transmission of the Newcastle Disease Virus in an experiment with chickens.

Wikipedia

A negative ion generator has been shown to reduce depression and fight asthma.

Advertisement for Air Ionizers

There must be a pile of positive ions in the air this morning. These weights are heavier than they were last time we worked out!

Mike Lonsdale

Have you ever received a shock when you touched a doorknob or another person? Of course you have. You have probably taken off a sweater in the dark and seen little miniature lightning bolts jumping around. We are surrounded by invisible charged particles called ions. There are negatively charged particles called "anions" and positively charged ions called "cations." Whenever there is the rubbing called friction, equal numbers of both kinds of ions are formed. When you walk across a carpet, you can get all charged up, especially if the air is dry. These excess charges can escape en masse from a point—such as your finger when you touch metal, or someone who has less charge than you or even the opposite charge. The air itself can become charged when dust particles carry charged ions. The water molecules in invisible water vapor all get together and stick to charged dust particles to form little droplets of water. At ground level, this is fog or mist. Higher up, clouds are formed from the water droplets.

That's enough science lessons for now. What does it mean to us in our everyday living? There is some evidence that excess positive ions in the air can make you feel lethargic. Next time you feel the heaviness upon you, blame it all on those damn cations. You can purchase an ion generator which produces negative ions, the so-called "feel good" ions. These quickly combine with dust and fall to the floor. Maybe that's a good thing, as the dust may be causing allergic reactions and even breathing problems. No extensive studies have been done to see if there are health benefits to ion generators. Yet how else could we explain why those workout weights seem so heavy some days and so light on others? It just has to be those ions!

May 23

Good Vibrations

A composer is a guy who goes around forcing his will on unsuspecting air molecules, often with the assistance of unsuspecting musicians.

Frank Zappa   1940 – 1993

Frank Zappa was considered weird, or at least unusual, by loads of folks. If you read *The Real Frank Zappa Book*, you will soon find out how far from the norm Frank's thinking could get. The interesting point about Frank is that some of his thoughts had real substance—indeed, genius. His definition of "composer" shows brilliant mental manipulation and a scientific understanding of the invisible molecules surrounding us.

You may remember a popular science demonstration from the ninth grade. A ringing bell or buzzer is put under a bell jar, and the air is pumped out, leaving a vacuum. The ringing can no longer be heard, proving that air or some medium is required for sound to travel. You can still see the bell, so light doesn't need any medium. Why does sound need a medium? The explanation is rather neat!

Sound begins with vibration. The clapper on the bell vibrates; this causes the air molecules to vibrate, although you cannot see them. This vibration is passed through the air by a molecular chain gang, reaches your ears and causes the eardrum to vibrate. The inner ear changes the vibration to nerve impulses that are sent to your brain, and you perceive the sound. When the air around the bell is removed, the molecular chain gang cannot do its work, so you cannot hear the vibration, even if you can still see it.

Both the composer and the conductor are making the air molecules vibrate in a certain way by causing the musicians play the notes in a specific way. So in effect, they are forcing their will on the players, and on their instruments, and on the air molecules, and on your brain! Simple isn't it? The interesting point of all this is how different people will listen to the same performance and then violently disagree about whether they like it or not. Just as beauty is in the eye of the beholder, so music is in the ear of the beholder. Seeing and hearing are really in the brain of the beholder and actually depend on the experience and understanding of that brain! Frank really understood all this—and now you understand it as well—don't you?

May 24

Sporting Events 2

The pitcher boo ... the catcher ... boo ... the ompire ... he ess no good
... but I go me back der every day to see de short-him-stop.

From a poem on baseball by Wilson MacDonald

A hot dog at the ball game beats roast beef at the Ritz.

Humphrey Bogart

Boston is a highly cultivated city. There are plenty of beloved institutions in this historic town—the Red Sox, the Patriots, the Celtics and the Bruins, to name a few. We were at Fenway Park one very hot day in July, and we had tickets in the center field bleachers, about 430 feet from home plate. As we walked down to our seats just as the game was about to begin, I screamed at the top of my lungs, "Hit the ball here, Devo!" Devon White, the athletic center fielder was leading off for the Blue Jays against the Red Sox. Guess what? On the first pitch, Devo smacked the ball right at us and a fan a few rows down caught the lead-off home run. Some fans began yelling at me, but of course they were all very polite things like "Send that ugly Canuck back to his igloo!" and "Somebody give that loudmouth a facelift ... he's so ugly!" That's half the fun of being at the game—the good-natured razzing that goes on constantly, especially if you aren't cheering for the home team. If they don't win, it's a shame after all.

There are always leather-lunged fans that can produce more sound than a whole opera chorus. Listen to a game on the radio or TV and you can hear the constant barrage of encouragement and insults hurled at anyone. The most famous hecklers in the history of the game were two brothers in the city of brotherly love, Philadelphia. One sat on the first base line and the other was opposite on the third base line. They would pick on some poor devil from the opposing team and give it to him in stereo all game. The worst razzing was when they didn't like one of their own players. They would razz him terribly until he was traded—or had a nervous breakdown! Of course, I never say mean or nasty things to anybody at the baseball game. They are liable to throw something at you—like a bat or some such.

May 25

Disasters

There are two big forces at work, external and internal. We have very little control over external forces such as tornadoes, earthquakes, floods, disasters, illness and pain. What really matters is the internal force. How do I respond to those disasters?

Leo Buscaglia

Sorrows and disasters are like the clouds that flit across the sky; they cannot injure the blue depths of space. Your duty is just to strive on from this very moment. Do not vacillate or postpone. Who knows when death knocks? Maybe, he may knock this very night, this very moment; therefore, do not delay. Do you postpone for tomorrow the dinner of this day! Feed the spirit as scrupulously as you now feed the body.

Sri Sathya Sai Baba

Every year we hold our collective breath as hurricane season approaches. We can still see the scars of Charlie and Katrina in the Southern States. Earthquakes bury people in piles of rubble almost every year. Each spring brings floods as swollen rivers overflow their banks. We all feel sorrow and helplessness when these terrible events occur, and there seems to be no end to calamity at times. I frequently read the following question in the newspaper: "How can God allow this to happen?" It's a natural question for people to ask. I once heard a clergyman respond: "I'm afraid I just don't have a good answer to that question."

I have an answer to the question. I believe that God does NOT directly interfere in human affairs. God does not dole out good things to some and bad things to others. We shouldn't blame God for disasters. All events happen by chance. If I sincerely believe this, then do I believe in miracles and the power of prayer? If God doesn't directly interfere in the world, why bother to ask God for anything? Is there any sense in praying? Absolutely! Can miracles really happen? Yes! I believe that when we desire a certain outcome and we pray for it, it has a greater chance of happening. When large numbers of people are praying, there is even a greater chance for a good result. Why? If we believe in and work for a good result, God incarnate in all of us can work miracles through our LOVE. Love can heal. Love can cure. Prayers can be answered. Miracles can happen.

May 26

Bike Month

Biking on the streets ... are mad-eyed couriers, spidery-legged racers and baby-toting moms and dads. Some cyclists sit upright, some lean into the wind; some wear helmets and others spurn them; some resent any red light that impedes them and some are scared witless in traffic. There are earnest commuters with trousers tucked into their socks, kids who cycle to school and weekend pleasure riders.

Leslie Scrivner

Today is the beginning of *BIKE MONTH* in some North American cities. I have preached the biking gospel twice this year already, so you may be thinking, "Oh no—not his cycling nonsense again." Yes indeed—when the price of gas is going out of sight, consider the bike! It is one of the three earth-friendly strategies for saving the planet from green-house gases. Plant a tree, trade the power mower for a push mower, and drive the gas-guzzler less by riding a bicycle. Not only will the planet and all its passengers benefit, you will be healthier and more physically fit for all these activities.

Biking in most big cities, however, is hazardous to your health. Once when I biked to work, a transit bus brushed me. Luckily, I fell into the grassy median and not under the wheels. Another time, we were standing with our bikes waiting for a light to change when an 18-wheeler came around the corner. The rear wheels would have run over us had we not seen them coming and jumped out of the way. Craig used to bike to university. He told me that motorists in SUV's and trucks, which are plentiful, have a disregard for cyclists, so he had to be particularly vigilant. This disregard is a huge barrier to most people, and until many more bike lanes and paths are created, bike-riding will remain hazardous.

What we need is a paradigm shift to provide cyclists with safe routes. The City of Chicago is a model cycling scene with over 2000 miles of bikeways. The membership dues for the 6100 members of the Chicagoland Bicycle Federation, and the 3 million dollar city budget, provide for a fast-growing number of cyclists. Hopefully, events like Bike Month will allow more people to be introduced to the intelligence and fun of cycling. I continue to be pleased at the number of bike lanes being painted onto the roads. Now—if only I could find a safe route downtown to my favorite record shop!

May 27

Names

Boredom is a vital problem for the moralist, since at least half the sins of mankind are caused by the fear of it.

Do not fear to be eccentric in opinion, for every opinion now accepted was once eccentric.

If there were in the world today any large number of people who desired their own happiness more than they desired the unhappiness of others, we could have a paradise in a few years.

It has been said that man is a rational animal. All my life I have been searching for evidence which could support this.

Most people would die sooner than think; in fact, they do so.

All from Bertrand Arthur William Russell (1872 – 1970)

During the Great Depression, my father Allen was unemployed for a time. He read voraciously and kept index cards of every book he borrowed from the library. Two of the writers who were popular at the time were Julian Huxley and Bertrand Russell. Al liked their ideas and named his first two sons after them.

My oldest brother, Judd, was named after Sir Julian Sorell Huxley (1887-1975), an English evolutionary biologist, humanist and internationalist. Huxley was a proponent of natural selection and a leading figure in the mid-twentieth century evolutionary synthesis. He was Secretary of the Zoological Society of London (1935-1942), the first Director of UNESCO, and a founding member of the World Wildlife Fund.

My brother Bert was named after Bertrand Russell, whose philosophy can be found in the quotes above. Russell, an atheist, was eccentric—but interesting nevertheless. In 1950, Russell was awarded the Nobel Prize in Literature, "in recognition of his varied and significant writings in which he champions humanitarian ideals and freedom of thought".

You may be wondering why I have a simple common name, Lee Allen. Well—I was an accident, so dad didn't have a favorite writer picked out. Mother said, "I'm naming this one!" and she did—thank heavens for that!

May 28

Jazz

I never heard of a jazz musician who retired. You love what you do, so what are you going to do? Play for the walls?

Nat Adderley

Jazz does not belong to one race or culture, but is a gift that America has given the world.

Ahmad Alaadeen

New Orleans is the only place I know of where you ask a little kid what he wants to be and instead of saying "I want to be a policeman," or "I want to be a fireman," he says, "I want to be a musician".

Alan Jaffe

During our last workout, Mike and I were listening to Wynton Marsalis, the famous trumpeter. We were listening to his jazz album, *Think of One*, which was recorded 25 years ago. The amazing fact is that Wynton Marsalis won Grammys that year, both in jazz for *Think of One*, and in classical for his recording of *Haydn's Trumpet Concerto*. Both albums illustrate a mastery of trumpet playing which borders on the miraculous. If you get a chance to listen to either of these albums—I mean really listen to the playing—your jaw should drop at the sound Marsalis gets from a trumpet— amazing, astounding—absolutely perfect!

So why is it then that most jazz aficionados I know would much rather listen to Miles Davis than Wynton Marsalis? The answer is central to the question of what jazz really is, or what separates a perfect performance from true inspiration. Great jazz has to have some sense that it is being extemporized— that there are surprises and maybe some wandering about. Every note "in its place" doesn't necessarily mean good. There may be no soul—no discovery going on. You have a sense with Miles Davis that the genius is in the exploration which continually happens. The genius certainly isn't in the perfection.

Here's an analogy from stand-up comics. Would you rather see Bob Hope or George Carlin? Nobody could deliver a punch line like Bob. George is all over the place—making up stuff as he goes. I suppose it's a matter of taste, but when it comes to extemporaneous brilliance, I figure performers like Miles Davis and George Carlin are simply in a class of their own.

May 29

Extempore

Forget your perfect offering. There is a crack in everything. That's how the light gets in.

Leonard Cohen

The art of extemporization or improvisation seems to have become a thing of the past in our high-tech world. This is a great pity, as our over-engineered and controlled lives can lack the true excitement that accompanies extempore action. You can probably come up with tons of examples, but here are a few. Classical composers like Mozart and Beethoven were great at improvising and included cadenzas in their works, which allowed the soloist to improvise on their own. Today soloists use "perfect" cadenzas written by somebody else. Like music, football can also be predictable when set plays are done over and over again to perfection—in an often-boring fashion. The only time improvisation may occur is when a player fumbles or intercepts the ball. I just love it when that happens—finally, some excitement! An exception to the usually predictable NFL play-calling occurred in Super Bowl XLIV. New Orleans surprised everyone, including Indianapolis, when they tried a short kick-off to begin the second half. It worked, and they kept the ball out of the hands of the powerful Indy offence. Like big sports events, awards shows, too, are often painfully predictable. The "great" actors stand and read from the teleprompter—boring!!! Billy Crystal is about the only host who could improvise. Please Billy—come back!

Consider the way you go through the day. Do you do the same old stuff over and over? Do you hear the same old small talk, complaints and whining repeatedly? Do you eat the same old food all the time? Do you watch the same old TV programs? Do you listen to the same old music?

Or are you more like the Leonard Cohen song—not worrying when everything isn't perfection, and allowing good stuff to happen extempore and accepting it, warts and all, high-tech perfection be damned?

I loved a show on Canadian TV called *Ad Lib*. The actors, Paul Soles, Ward Cornell and Beverley Eynon, were given a topic and had to invent an extemporaneous play on the spot. It was hilarious. You never knew what to expect, other than a bunch of imperfections, but hey—it's an imperfect world. Get used to that, and you'll never be disappointed.

May 30

Motorsport

The track is my canvas. My car is my pencil.

Graham Hill

I think I've proved that, in equal cars, if I want someone to stay behind me ... well, I think he stays behind ... Finishing second means you are the first person to lose.

Gilles Villeneuve

Aerodynamics is for those who cannot manufacture good engines.

Enzo Ferrari

Have you ever been to a car race? Stock car races and drag races don't count. I'm talking about loud, sleek, shiny, powerful cars driven by world champions. I haven't been to a car race in almost 40 years, but there was a time when we would go to see the races—and other delights. The cars had wonderful names like Ferrari, Lotus and Porsche. The drivers had even more wonderful names like Sterling Moss, Olivier Gendebien, and Ludwig Heimrath. The parades were delightful—especially the girl parade.

You may be saying to yourself, "People who go to car races or horse races need their heads read!" Well—you haven't felt the power of 500 horses roaring around a track on death's edge or the scream of a Formula 1 racer revving at 12,000 rpm. You don't just hear it—you feel it, as it makes your whole body resonate. When the Shelby Cobra first appeared at the track, the earth literally shook. You could hear it thundering for miles—all the way around the racetrack. It was simply stunning—and so were our ears—stunned!

The "filler" races came first. Most people used them to satisfy their thirst and their eyeballs. A regular parade of delights would constantly move about in the crowd, just to be seen. Of course I would watch the lesser races, especially the Formula V's, which were a Volkswagen chassis without the body. These would buzz around the track at over 100 mph. My workout buddy Mike raced one; he is one of the best drivers I know, and his alertness comes from racing Formula V's.

We used to have an expression for people who drove very fast. We would ask, "Who the hell do you think you are ... Sterling Moss?"

May 31

The Hockey Game

American professional athletes are bilingual; they speak English and profanity.

Gordie Howe

By the age of 18, the average American has witnessed 200,000 acts of violence on television, most of them occurring during Game 1 of the NHL playoff series.

Steve Rushkin

The greatest hockey player who ever lived: Bobby Orr, and I love him.

Donald Cherry ... he who must wear LOUD jackets

I was lucky enough to attend the Boston Bruins' last game of hockey in the old Boston Garden. The Buffalo Sabres were the visiting team. I had a seat three rows behind the goalie, and the view was spectacular. I cheered for the Sabres, much to the protestations of all the hometown fans around me. They were good-natured about my rooting for the Sabres and razzed me continuously, but I gave back as much as I got. Nobody hit me with anything or poured beer on me. I was used to cheering for the Toronto Argonauts at Ivor Wynne stadium, home of Toronto's CFL archrivals in Hamilton, and I would be struck by umbrellas, programs and beer. The Hamilton fans stopped short of a challenge to fight, since I was bigger than most of them. The Boston fans were much more refined and imaginative in their razzing.

The Boston game itself was very exciting. Boston was outplayed, and it looked like the Sabres would win, until the last minute of the game. Boston pulled their goalie for an extra attacker, and in that frenzied last minute of play, they managed to tie the game. I never did see the puck go behind the goalie ten feet in front of me, but the fans around me went absolutely nuts.

Then came the ten-minute overtime, and with eight seconds remaining, a Boston rookie scored his first goal to win the game for the Bruins. The whole place went crazy, and I really got a ribbing. The next day, the National Hockey League went on strike. I had seen the historic last game played in the old Boston Garden without even realizing it!

June 1

Ecclesiastes

For in much Wisdom is much vexation, and those who increase knowledge increase sorrow.
There is nothing better for mortals than to eat and drink, and find enjoyment in their toil...

(repeated five times)

This also is vanity and a chasing after wind.

(repeated many times)

There is a time for everything ... a time to be born and a time to die ...
A time for joy and a time for sorrow ...

(part of a famous passage often read at funerals)

Ecclesiastes is one of my favorite books in the Bible. It is full of wisdom about how to live, but at first reading, it seems to be contradictory. Initially, the book emphasizes that everything in life is futile. It doesn't matter what you do, you'll end up as dust. All your hard labor and everything you collect, including wisdom, amount to nothing as you become older. Then you die. What an absolute downer life seems to be. All is vanity and like chasing the wind. Well folks, that may be the way of the world "under the sun," but that's not what God really wants for us. As you read the book, you begin to realize that the author hints at a better way. Yes, everything in this world under the sun may be futile, but we are to Love God and rise above the world to bask in God's grace. God wants us to enjoy our food and drink and toil and relationships, and the author keeps telling us this—repeatedly.

So there is a stark contrast—a huge contradiction—which says that everything is futile on one hand—and on the other, everything is wine and dine and enjoy. Why does the author, a wisdom teacher, go back and forth between these two poles? I think it's because the author wants us to realize the huge difference one piece of wisdom makes—that God is the author of our enjoyment—and without God in our lives, all is fruitless. With God in our lives, everything is meaningful and gives enjoyment. The author never states this plainly. It's for us to comprehend. That's why I like it. It's similar to much of the truth in life. You have to reach for the lesson and draw your own conclusions. It's OK to reach.

June 2

Motorsport 2

Why did I take up racing? I was too lazy to work and too chicken to steal.
Kyle Petty, stock car driver

The first time I fired up a car, felt the engine shudder and the wheel come to life in my hands, I was hooked. I still get it every time I get into a race car.
Mario Andretti, F1 and Indy driver

You do things, you f**k people, it's racing.
Niki Lauda, F1 driver

It doesn't matter if you're in a wheelchair or have healthy legs. If you have the will to do something, you can get it done. I race the same as anyone else does; I just don't use my feet. And, I never give up.
Evan Evans, the first paraplegic competitor to win a racing title

My big brother Judd was driving his racy red 1962 Volvo P 544 to the car races. Keith and I were along for the usual feast of sights and sounds. The Volvo P 544 looked like a miniature '48 Ford. Some folks thought it was a Volkswagen with modifications; but it would do about 40 mph faster than a VW, and we loved to leave them in the dust!

On the trip to the park the traffic was terrible—an endless parade. People wanted to arrive early to get a good position and quench their thirst. As we inched along, my brother announced that he had to pee. Keith and I chimed in unison, "No way are we getting out of this line—they will never let us back in!" Judd insisted, so I opened my door and ran around to the driver's side, and made Judd switch drivers. Instead of going over to the bushes along the side, Judd decided to make use of an old construction hard hat he had on the back window ledge. It was the proper color after all—yellow. He was almost finished when the line began to move quickly. I let the clutch out too fast. The P 544 took off like a shot—and so did the yellow hard hat. Judd's jeans were soaked.

When we arrived at the park, he got a blanket out of the trunk and wrapped it around himself to walk about. Judd was able to laugh heartily at himself, particularly after we had enough joy-juice to dampen our inhibitions.

June 3

Conductors

Someone commented to Rudolph Bing, manager of the Metropolitan Opera, that George Szell was his own worst enemy. "Not while I'm alive, he isn't!"

Bing retorted.

After I die, I shall return to earth as a gatekeeper of a bordello and I won't let any of you in.

Arturo Toscanini to the NBC Orchestra

We cannot expect you to be with us all the time, but perhaps you could be good enough to keep in touch now and again.

Sir Thomas Beecham to a musician during a rehearsal

The first great conductor I saw was George Szell doing Beethoven's 8th with the Cleveland Orchestra. The ensemble discipline was amazing. Over 65 musicians were exactly at the same millisecond together. Every violin bow was in the same place on the instrument of every player. The sound was precise and powerful. The orchestra was simply a giant metronome. How did Szell build his Cleveland Orchestra into the best Beethoven ensemble in America? Simple—IRON DISCIPLINE! You could say that conductors have to be the ultimate control freaks to get what they want.

There is a story about a conductor of the Chicago Symphony. He had a very small, almost imperceptible, beat. One day, as a joke during rehearsal, one of the bass players took out a telescope to watch the beat. The maestro quickly wrote something on a piece of paper and held it up for the bass player to view through his telescope. The note said "You're fired!" and he was! No nonsense was tolerated—but the sound of the symphony was good! The recordings are still benchmarks. I guess it's the results which count. There were conductors who could get good results without being severe. Sir Thomas Beecham used good humor to get what he wanted. Bruno Walter never raised his voice other than to say "Gentlemen … please!" Today, the rigid disciplinarian conductors are mostly gone, replaced by dynamic, talented musicians who don't seem to need to berate the players to get them to play well.

June 4

Choice

We choose our joys and sorrows long before we experience them.

Kahil Gibran

We often hear the expression: "We all have choices to make." One of my friends, commenting on a terrible accident in which a moment of distraction cost three lives, asked, "Is being distracted a choice?" We can easily be distracted and forget what we are doing. This very interesting question can have two answers, depending on the distraction. I was walking into church one day, when a bee stung me on my tongue and I almost fell down the stairs to the basement. That sudden distraction could have resulted in a terrible accident. I certainly didn't make a choice about getting stung by a bee. You can probably think back to unexpected distractions that may have given you a close call. I feel that some types of distractions don't involve choice. I think what my friend was asking about, however, was a general state that some folks get into—like living on autopilot. There was an interesting exercise about longevity in a magazine, with a series of questions asking how distracted you are when you are driving. Here are some of the questions:
DO YOU:
Read or look at maps when you drive? Comb your hair or put on make-up?
Talk on your cell phone? Reach for things on the passenger seat?
Turn around to look at people in the back seat, or reach for anything in the back seat? Talk to passengers incessantly? Listen to loud music?

For each of these distractions which you definitely CHOOSE to do at times while you drive, you are to subtract three years off your life. I don't how the author came up with this formula, but it is interesting. (If you are guilty of them all, maybe you are dead already—and you are just too distracted to notice.)

My friend actually answered her own question about distraction being a choice. She commented: "Our attitude is a choice. We should be living in the moment—being fully aware and attentive to the 'NOW!'"

June 5

Chance

I returned, and saw under the sun, that the race is not to the swift, nor the battle to the strong, neither yet bread to the wise, nor yet riches to men of understanding, nor yet favour to men of skill; but time and chance happeneth to them all.

Ecclesiastes 9:11 (King James Version)

Chance favors only the prepared mind.

Louis Pasteur

There is no such thing as no chance.

Henry Ford

"There is not a chance in hell of that happening!" is a phrase I have heard some folks use. For them it is what we call a self-fulfilling prophecy, which they make not happen by their attitude and actions. Now this saying is undeniably true about winning millions in the lottery, but when it involves everyday stuff, there are many times when you can "take a chance" and make things happen that others have given no chance.

Our preparation room at our new high school was poorly designed. It had an entrance at one end. There was a small office at the other end that terminated in a wall of concrete blocks. On the other side was a hall, and there should have been a door designed and built in. Our department asked the Principal to requisition a door, and his response was, "Not a chance."

I can't remember exactly how it happened, but we were at the school for some event one weekend—it may have been a basketball tournament, since we all coached basketball—and my assistant head said to me: "Let's go and take out the concrete blocks and make ourselves a door." When the Prince eventually discovered what we had done, I really got hell for it.

While he berated me for our "crazy" actions, I kept saying, "Yes Al... I know." Inwardly, I was laughing—and secretly, I was very proud of my boys who took a chance to improve our work environment. We all know that it is often much easier to get forgiveness than permission.

How many times have you said, "The answer is so simple ... now why didn't I think of that?" Chances are it may have entered your head, but your subconscious dismissed it because learning filters said, "Not possible." This is something we all need to escape—inhibition. I like Henry Ford's statement, which uses the word "no" twice but really is telling us to say "yes" to taking a chance.

June 6

Basketball

Enjoy the journey, enjoy every moment, and quit worrying about winning and losing.
Matt Biondi

When I taught high school during the sixties, the head of the Physical Education department was an enthusiastic fellow who was always joking. One day, Ron said to me: "Steels ... a big tall fellow like you ought to be good at basketball. I need somebody to coach the senior team."

I figured he was joking, and I joked right back, "Yeah sure, Ron, but I'll need several assistants who really know what they are doing." He twisted my arm enough that I became the senior basketball coach of a bunch of losers. They'd hardly won a game in several years. How on earth could I ever help these guys when I couldn't play the game myself? I didn't know the first thing about basketball, let alone winning. What was I to do?

Ron gave me some coaching books to read and sent me to a coaches' clinic. I worked hard at getting the proper drills and formulating a plan. I figured the game was all about passing, shooting and rebounding, so I selected sequences of drills to improve the kids in these three areas. For rebounding, I had them jump back and forth over a bench, and I gradually moved the bench up until they could jump ten times over two benches. The players hated it, but I eventually had the best rebounding team in the league. We would always get two or three shots at the basket.

The season consisted of eight games, and we actually won three games that first year thanks to the players who were willing to work. My three strategies paid off because of their hard work. Once they saw that working hard in practice produced results, their intensity took a quantum leap.

Ron was so pleased with the results that he bought jackets for the whole team—including myself. The main lesson from all of this is simple. Hard work can overcome a lack of talent—and this isn't just true for games of sport!

June 7

Honesty

Honesty is the first chapter in the book of wisdom.

Thomas Jefferson

Honesty pays, but it doesn't seem to pay enough to suit some people.

Kin Hubbard

Several times in the past year, stories of deceptive politicians have made the news, as always. Some of these stories severely tax our patience with elected officials. When one of them tells us, "I have never knowingly done anything wrong in my life," it is difficult to trust anyone. It's even tougher when an individual who should have been trustworthy bilks some elderly person out of life savings. I find it hard to understand how anybody can treat others this way. How can somebody look another person in the eye and devastate that person by stealing a large portion of their life savings? Yet we hear about this happening more often these days. It is becoming commonplace through Internet fraud and identity theft. Houses are mortgaged without the owner's knowledge. There seems to be no end of the bogus schemes dishonest people can conceive. The credit card companies write off billions in fraudulent purchases every year. "What is the world coming to?" is a question that comes to mind. Deceit seems to be a way of life for so many people these days—or does it?

I would guess that the percentage of people who lead dishonest lives has actually decreased! When I was a kid, our neighborhood was replete with thieves. Anything that could be stolen was. I recall one kid who had an unbelievable stamp collection. He boasted to me that he had stolen most of these stamps. I wasn't very careful with this thief. He relieved me of my collections of plane and car cards by "borrowing" them, and then suddenly moving. I've always been gullible. Oh well—I guess he needed them more than I did. There have always been dishonest folks—and there probably always will be.

Little wonder Shakespeare said, "To be honest, as this world goes, is to be one man picked out of ten thousand."

June 8

Terrorism

With a small fraction of the hundreds of billions of dollars spent on the Iraq war, the US and Australia could ensure every starving, sunken-eyed child on the planet could be well fed, have clean water and sanitation and a local school to go to.
Bob Brown

Terrorism isn't insanity. It grows out of social conditions that are well known: poverty, social oppression, dictatorship, and a void of meaning in the lives of ordinary people.
Deepak Chopra

Some images are burned forever into the brain. I'll never forget the airliners crashing into the World Trade Center, or the towers collapsing into huge clouds of dust. Perhaps even more shocking were the tiny black specks hurling down from the burning towers—people jumping from the upper floors to avoid being burned to death. These are images you want to bury in your brain and hope you never see again. I'm certain, however, that we will see other horrific acts of terrorism in our lifetime. The gruesome images will come back to haunt us repeatedly.

The reaction to 9/11 began a "war on terrorism" which changed forever the way we travel and do international business. Our border restrictions were tightened up. Security in airports has become so intense that you must remove your shoes and submit wireless devices to thorough scrutiny. Hundreds of suspected "terrorists" were rounded up and incarcerated in Guantanamo Bay prison without trials. The news reports in the years after 9/11 fixed international terrorism in the minds of all Americans. There was paranoia—a fear that you could be the victim of a terrorist attack at any moment. Fortunately, the fear mongers seem to have relaxed—until the next episode occurs.

I feel Brown and Chopra get to the very source of terrorism—the social injustice experienced by so many depressed people in the world. The world's poor wonder why a small handful of people should control most of the world's wealth while the majority must do without adequate food, clean water and health care. We should change the war on terror to the war on poverty and social oppression!

June 9

The Violin

I am not handsome, but when women hear me play my violin, they come crawling to my feet.

Niccolò Paganini

A table, a chair, a bowl of fruit and a violin; what else does a man need to be happy?

Albert Einstein

When I was about twelve, we went to a movie in which a violinist played while some building burned. I don't know what the movie was about, but I do remember that it was Jascha Heifetz fiddling—and my, how he could play! A violin is an instrument that, poorly played, grates on your nerves—but played really well, is a spiritual experience—for me anyway. I have been told that the violin is the most difficult instrument to play, for several reasons. The left arm is placed in an extremely awkward, almost painful position. The player needs excellent pitch to know where the fingers go on the fingerboard, since there are no frets as in a guitar. If the fingers are off a little, the notes can sound truly awful. The bow has to be in fine control because the four strings are so close together. The damnable instrument mimics a cat-fight when you first try to play.

I began taking lessons from a big sweaty fellow who came around to the school each week. We rented his fiddles, and bought his books, and scratched away making awful grating sounds for two years. I figure I was the worst—but we all played together, so nobody knew. The results somehow pleased my mother, and she bought me a "Collin-Mezin" violin set for about two hundred dollars. I changed teachers, and the new fellow was a chain-smoker. He would take my violin from me when I arrived and play on it for about three cigarettes' worth, dropping the ashes down the s-hole of my fiddle. Finally, he would sadly shake his head and give it to me to have a go. He would then play loudly on his own fiddle to drown me out. I got the feeling he didn't like my playing—but he loved my Collin-Mezin. He once told me that it was better than any of the violins in his symphony—but it was "wasted" on me. He sure got that right!

PS Today, a Collin-Mezin from the 1950's will fetch up to over ten grand! That was a good violin—even if I never realized it!

June 10

Energy

If we did all the things that we are capable of doing, we would literally astound ourselves.

Thomas Edison

And what is a man without energy? Nothing ... nothing at all.

Mark Twain

Do you remember the things you were worrying about a year ago? How did they work out? Didn't you waste a lot of fruitless energy on account of most of them? Didn't most of them turn out all right after all?

Dale Carnegie

Energy and persistence alter all things.

Benjamin Franklin

Our dogs sleep an average of 18 hours a day. They are laid out in La-la land as I write this. Why do they sleep so much? I suppose it's because they can. They have the luxury of having slaves—us. We provide them with everything. They don't work, perform or get into T.V.—so why not hunker down and have a lovely nap? Why not indeed? Why work when you can relax? Why stand when you can sit? Why sit when you can lie down? Why remain awake when you can nap? These dogs aren't so dumb after all.

There is one magic four-letter word that will instantly give dogs a huge shot of energy. You can say the word or spell it, and they leap up ready to rock and roll. That word is W – A – L – K, and it has worked its magic every time on every dog that has ever owned us. Dogs see the world with their noses and the word "walk" means a cornucopia of interesting smells is soon coming their way.

Are all dogs as lazy and dozy as ours? Yes—unless they are working dogs. Huskies can pull sleds for hours. Seeing-eye dogs can perform all day for a blind person. Police dogs can remain alert when they are on the job. Bloodhounds can follow a scent for hours, all the while pulling like mad on the leash. Dogs are no different than people. If they have a sense of purpose, they won't sleep. They remain fired with enthusiasm for the task, with boundless energy.

Humans have a four-letter magic word to fire them up—to give them energy and persistence in all things. That word is L – O – V – E and everything is possible when you apply it to anything you do.

June 11

Singing

Produce the tone in your backside and float the tone on your breath, which is always well-supported by the diaphragm and projected to every corner of the room. It should make your head ring!

Mrs. Knapp … my first vocal teacher

When I was a little kid, I went around our street singing songs for Mrs. Gay and other neighbors, who would then reward us with cookies or candy. I grew up singing all those Sunday school songs like "Ezekiel Saw a Wheel A-Rollin' " and "We are Climbin' Jacob's Ladder." As most singers with no vocal training, I sang with gusto, from the heart. I still do! There was no consideration of the "art" of singing or vocal production. When I eventually began to sing heavier stuff, the way you sang depended on the recording you had listened to. You could also mimic good singers in the choir. Now, the only way to be successful as a mimic was to have an accurate ear; and even that barely allows you to scratch the surface of vocal production.

When I took my first vocal lessons from Mrs. Knapp in London, I was amazed at the size of her diaphragm. She had me place my hands on each side of the bottom of her lungs (at her sides!), and she took a breath. My hands moved out several inches. The same thing didn't happen when I tried it on myself. I had to learn how to expand and control each breath. The whole key to good singing, according to Mrs. Knapp, was to float the vocal line on this controlled breath, which originated in the middle of your gluteus maximus (your backside.) The tone made your head ring if you did it properly. It all had to be projected to the far corners of any room, and that depended on keeping the sound "on the diaphragm." I have had several vocal teachers and all their methods differed. The art of good singing is quite complex, but the actual sound must appear effortless! This takes great coordination, concentration and good luck!

After all the preparations which go into good singing, about 75% of the audience doesn't have the ears to discern an outstanding performance from lousy singing. In other words, most people don't have much idea about what is good or bad when listening to a song. You only need hear the way the national anthem is butchered before most major league games to realize this. Everybody cheers like crazy anyway. Maybe they are glad it's over!

June 12

Hellions

The thorn from the bush one has planted, nourished and pruned pricks most deeply and draws more blood.

Maya Angelou

Oh how sharper than a serpent's tooth it is to have a thankless child.

Shakespeare … in King Lear

Dear Lord, thank You for this microwave bounty, even though we don't deserve it. I mean … our kids are uncontrollable hellions! Pardon my French … but they act like savages! Did You see them at the picnic? Oh, of course You did … You're everywhere, You're omnivorous. Oh Lord! Why did You spite me with this family?

Homer Simpson

How is it possible that God-fearing folks can sometimes raise "hellions"? As a kid, I remember a family—the mother and father were the loveliest people you could ever meet. You were always welcome at their house. They worked very hard at our church and were pillars of parenthood. Their oldest son had a heart defect and spent much of his life in bed. That didn't stop him from excelling in his studies or being a model of how a teen should behave. This delightful couple also had a younger son. He was good-looking and full of beans. He was a delightful hellion with a genius for devious behavior. All the girls were in love with him, and he had the world by the tail. I often wondered how the two brothers could be so different.

Thinking back to our own family, I heard stories of times when my two older brothers could be considered hellions. I remember a story about Judd and Bert discovering a cache of liquor in an unlocked car and pouring the booze all over the car. Somebody squealed on them, and dad had to pay for this careless person's illegal liquor cache. It was during prohibition in the States, and this person may have been a smuggler!

In spite of rebellious behavior when they were kids, my brothers both turned out just fine, thank you. I figure the peer group pressure of the neighborhood we lived in was a major influence in their transgressions. Several older boys ended up incarcerated—the ultimate punishment for hellions. Fortunately, most of them had grown up, moved, or been put away by the time I came along.

164

June 13

Gambling

Quit while you're ahead. All the best gamblers do.

Baltasar Gracian

The roulette table pays nobody except him that keeps it. Nevertheless, a passion for gambling is common, though a passion for keeping roulette tables is unknown.

George Bernard Shaw

The urge to gamble is so universal and its practice so pleasurable that I assume it must be evil.

Heywood Campbell Broun

Gambling: The sure way of getting nothing for something.

Wilson Mizner

At the RV Park in Florida, Alberta Rick persuaded me to play Texas Hold'em with the gang. I had lousy luck and was the first one out each time. I couldn't get anything good—and when I had something decent, somebody else had a better hand. Oh well—I had an evening of fun, even if I lost the twenty dollars. That's not bad for an evening's entertainment, and somebody went home really happy. When it comes to gambling, I dislike throwing away hard-earned money. I will go to the casino on a cruise ship and feed twenty bucks into a poker machine. I try and get an hour of play, but on most occasions I end up leaving my deposit with the casino. I think of it as entertainment and don't worry about losing in the end.

There has been the rare win. I once played a nickel machine in Las Vegas for three hours and won over fifty dollars. I also won enough on a Caribbean cruise to buy a new watch. The only time we played in the Brantford Casino, I won enough to buy our group a very classy lunch.

The best gambling story I recall is the time Aunt Dorothy and I bet a dollar each on a 65-to-1 long-shot horse to "show" at the trots. There was a pileup, and our sulky—dead last at the time—avoided the mess and finished third, winning us a good pot. Aunt Dot had picked the horse "because it had a good Irish name!"

Always remember: bingo, casinos and horse races are set up with the odds in their favor, and we need to keep saying to ourselves, "The more we play, the more we'll lose."

June 14

Basketball 2

If the NBA were on channel 5 and a bunch of frogs making love was on 4, I'd watch the frogs even if they were coming in fuzzy.

Bobby Knight

In my second year of coaching the senior basketball team at Blakelock, Ron Zeigel, the P.E. head, gave me a winning team. Three juniors advanced to the senior level and the boys had talent, led by Jim Brown, athlete extraordinary. Jim could fly ten feet through the air to lay the ball up—and he looked like a ballet dancer as he scored. Our two guards, Jim and Rick, would come to school early to practice their long set shots. They quickly became the two best guards in the league. We won our first six games by lopsided scores. We thrashed White Oaks by tripling the score on them—twice. This was particularly pleasing to me because the White Oaks coach had played for the Harlem Globetrotters at one time! I couldn't play the game of basketball, but my team had talent.

Then we got to play a home and home series with the previous year's champs, the Oakville-Trafalgar Red Devils, led by their brilliant coach. We played the first game at their tiny gym at the oldest High School in Oakville. The Devils outscored us by ten in the first half. Our set shots weren't going in, and my boys told me that our basket was "dead"—a term that means the rim is poor and the balls just won't go through. Just before the beginning of the second half, my manager told me that while we were in the dressing room to talk over our strategy, the Devil manager had opened the curtains at the end of the gym. No wonder the set shots didn't work. Jim and Rick had a poor view of the rim with the curtains closed. I went to the referee before the second half began and told him what the Devils had done. He asked their coach if this was true and he had to admit it. For this gross infraction, the ref gave the Devils two technical fouls, and Jimmy Brown sunk both shots to bring us within eight points. The second half was unbelievable. I'll tell you about it another day.

PS: I met the White Oaks coach about 25 years later at some teacher function, and I said to him: "Hey ... we used to coach against each other back the sixties. I was the T.A. Blakelock senior coach."

He replied: "Yeah ... I remember that ... we used to thrash you guys!"

166

June 15

The Violin 2

I occasionally play works by contemporary composers and for two reasons. First to discourage the composer from writing any more and secondly to remind myself how much I appreciate Beethoven.

If I don't practice one day, I know it; two days, the critics know it; three days, the public knows it.

There is no top. There are always further heights to reach.

All from Jascha Heifetz ... famous fiddler

I attempted to play the violin for about five years but eventually gave it up as a lost cause. So, before my third year of teaching, the Principal invited me into his office and told me he had heard that I played the violin. I was surprised that he somehow knew this, as I was certain I'd never mentioned it to anyone. He then introduced me to the music head, Peter Hughes, who turned out to be an extremely fine fellow with a great sense of humor. Peter told me that the string teacher was going on a sabbatical leave, and they needed somebody to teach the two string classes in the fall—some tenth graders with one year of music, and a class of ninth graders who would be new to music. I had never touched a viola, cello or string bass in my life, but somehow I was supposed to teach students how to play them!

I don't remember saying "yes" to either Peter or the Prince, but I had both classes come the fall. The tenth graders were in need of loads of help, but they were good kids and worked pretty hard to improve. The ninth graders were another story all together. A few of them took to their instruments and were playing better than the tenth graders in a very short time. I couldn't believe how good they were. I worked to remain ahead, but one of my rookies soon produced a better violin sound than the teacher!

One day, an inspector showed up from the Ministry of Education. He observed me for about ten minutes and then asked if he could take over the class. What could I say? The first thing he did was to get one of the bass players to "get over on the proper side of that instrument!" The kid had been hiding behind a post, playing the bass left-handed—a definite no-no—even if he was my best bass player. Oh well—the inspector told me that I was doing a good job, and that the kids liked me. Some of them actually became decent string players—in spite of me.

June 16

Copies

We are all born originals ... why is it so many of us die copies?

Edward Young

Every kind of imitation speaks; the person that imitates is inferior to him whom he imitates, as the copy is to the original.

Robert South

The only good copies are those which make us see the absurdity of bad originals.

François, Duc de La Rochefoucauld

Chester F. Carlson was born in Seattle, Washington in 1906. Due to his father's ill health, Chet grew up poor. Early in life he made Edison his hero, realizing that a successful invention was a route to wealth. After college, he ended up doing patent filings, like Einstein. There were never enough carbon copies of patent information, so he experimented with a way to produce inexpensive copies of documents. Carlson was able to duplicate an image in 1938 by a process he then called electro photography. After the war, the Haloid Corporation licensed his inventions and called it xerography. In 1950, the first Xerox copier was sold, and the copies have been streaming out at ever-increasing rates ever since.

When I first taught, we had a machine called the "ditto" machine. If you wanted to give your class copies of something, you wrote or typed out a ditto, and you included any drawings on the same ditto. Then you would put the master in the ditto machine and crank out copies. You were very lucky to get 100 copies from your ditto. The machine used methyl hydrate, which smelled good to me. The kids liked the smell as well and would sniff new ditto copies with little sighs of pleasure. Then somebody found out that long-term exposure to methyl hydrate was hazardous to your health, and that ended that. The stencil replaced the ditto, and eventually the "Xerox" copier replaced both. The copy machines were initially frustrating but quickly improved so much that thousands of exams could be programmed into the copier and out they would come, fully collated and stapled. Chester Carlson's invention streamlined the teaching profession in a way he never imagined.

Nowadays, a hundred dollar printer produces color copies and decent photos with a simple click of your mouse. Technology is amazing; however, it is thanks to the enquiring minds of people like Carlson that we can marvel at such convenience in our day-to-day tasks.

June 17

Dreams

A child on a farm sees a plane fly overhead and dreams of a faraway place. A traveler on the plane sees the farmhouse and dreams of home.

Carl Burns

Man is flying too fast for a world that is round. Soon he will catch up with himself in a great rear-end collision and Man will never know that what hit him from behind was Man.

James Thurber

I have seen the science I worshiped, and the aircraft I loved, destroying the civilization I expected them to serve.

Charles Augustus Lindbergh

It will free man from the remaining chains, the chains of gravity which still tie him to this planet.

Wernher Magnus Maximilian von Braun

D o you dream? If you do, of what do you dream? When I was a kid I dreamed of a big house with luxurious rooms. Then I dreamed of fancy cars and driving fast. Finally, I dreamed of flying—either with wings or in a fighter plane. I don't have dreams much anymore—other than the odd fantasy—but if I do dream on the rare occasion, it's still about flying.

What is it about flying that strikes our fancy so much? Watching the birds zoom about in the sky, one can't help being envious of our feathered friends. I love stretching out horizontal in the Florida sun, watching hawks do lazy circles in the bright blue sky. Here in southwest Florida there are large numbers of hawks and buzzards circling about. What a sight!

Speaking of sights—the most awesome flight display can be seen a couple of hours east of our winter home in Florida. The launch of the space shuttle from Cape Canaveral is awe-inspiring. The noise is stupendous. The sight of the huge machine inching up so slowly at first and then accelerating to over ten miles covered in each second is a tribute to human engineering. The space program owes a substantial debt to a German rocket scientist, Wernher von Braun. He experienced many failures during the war but, fortunately for America, he came over after the war and applied all his experience to the Apollo space program. Those phenomenal Saturn V rockets, which blasted the Apollo missions to the moon, were the results of the dreams of von Braun and an amazing core of rocket scientists.

June 18

Basketball 3

When it's played the way is spozed to be played, basketball happens in the air; flying, floating, elevated above the floor, levitating the way oppressed peoples of this earth imagine ... in their dreams.

John Edgar Wideman

There we were in the Red Devils' gym, losing by ten points to start the second half. Then the referee found out about the "curtain trick" that the Devils' coach pulled on us. Jimmy Brown sank the two technical foul shots we were awarded, so we began our quest for a perfect season only eight points behind. Our high school senior team, the Tabbies, had never had a winning basketball season. The Red Devils had won the league every year for what seemed like centuries. It would be an understatement to say that a win for us would be a huge upset. That would mean that the final game of the season could result in a perfect season for us for the first time ever. The Devils' coach had his guys playing a very tenacious defense to try to keep the lead. I began to feel very sick in the second half, but the game meant too much for me to let the boys know I wasn't feeling well at all.

Our set shots began to go in. We caught up and tied the game. Jimmy Brown was playing the game of his life, and believe me, it was the most exciting performance I had ever seen. With about ten seconds left and the score tied, Jimmy dribbled into the Devil end and began to shoot one of his famous set shots. The Devil defender slapped Jimmy on the arm, but the whistle didn't blow. I jumped to my feet and yelled "foul" as loud as I could. Two things happened simultaneously. The ref blew his whistle and I yelled so loud that I spit my false tooth half way across the gym floor. I quickly sprinted out, retrieved my tooth and returned to the bench—the kids all asking: "What are you doing, coach?" Other than my players, nobody, including the ref, had seen me. The referee gave the Devil player a foul. Jimmy Brown made the shot and we won the game. Unbelievable—spitting out my false tooth and getting it back in about two seconds without the ref noticing! He could have given us a technical if he'd been watching my silly performance!

POSTSCIRPT: I had pneumonia and missed the next two weeks. Ron Zeigel, the department head, coached for me. Our Tabbies beat the Devils, again by one point, to register the first perfect season in the annals of our school's senior basketball history.

June 19

Chance 2

If you have a dream, give it a chance to happen.

Richard M. DeVos

A man has cause for regrets only when he sows and no one reaps.

Charles Goodyear

I love the story about how Charles Goodyear discovered the vulcanization of rubber. Rubber, before Goodyear's discovery, was a sticky substance which became soft and gooey at higher temperatures. Without vulcanization, rubber flip-flops would melt off your feet on a hot day. Tires on cars wouldn't last a mile before melting all over the road at the high temperatures caused by rolling friction with the surface.

Goodyear's life was filled with grief and tragedy. Half his children died in infancy. He was in and out of debtor's prison all his life. When he died, his family was over $ 200,000 in debt. He never made any money from what was perhaps one of the top ten technological discoveries of all time.

Charles used the kitchen stove for many experiments; according to the story, some sulfur accidentally spilled into a vat of hot rubber he was cooking up. Instead of discarding the mess, Goodyear played around with the failed batch and eventually realized that the sulfur somehow prevented the rubber from going gooey at higher temperatures. He had serendipitously invented the process of vulcanization. I like the story, even if it may only be partially true.

There are good lessons to be taken away from Goodyear's tragic but inspiring life. Never give up on your dream. Charles had to pawn his valuables to continue his experiments. He spent time in jail for not paying his bills. He always kept trying against all odds. Although Charles died a pauper, one of his sons was infected with his father's persistence and became a very successful inventor. His son indeed reaped what the father had sown.

The next time you get a smooth ride from the tires on your car—say "Thanks Charles—for NOT throwing out the batch of ruined rubber on the hot stove!"

June 20

Satchel Paige

Avoid fried foods ... they angry up the blood and produce a heaviness which is not a good thing.

If your stomach disputes you, lie down and pacify it with cool thoughts.

Keep the juices flowing by jangling around gently as you move.

Go very light on the vices, such as carrying on in society ... the social ramble ain't restful.

Never look back ...you never know what might be catchin' up on you!

All from Leroy "Satchel" Paige, 1906 – 1982

Satchel Paige had to be one of the funniest men who ever lived. He was also one of the greatest athletes who ever threw a baseball. He pitched for many years in the Negro Leagues, and his statistics were unbelievable. He compiled 64 scoreless innings, 21 wins in a row and a record of 33-4 in 1933. He also had amazing stamina and would pitch both games of a double header, winning both games. He always wanted to pitch in the major leagues, and his dream came true when he was 43 years old, pitching for the Cleveland Indians. A scout had reported: "I have no idea what he was throwin' ... cus whatever it wus ... it wus too fast to see." Satchel became the oldest rookie ever to play in the major leagues. In 179 major league games, he never made an error.

Perhaps his greatest claim to fame is being the oldest player in major league history, pitching in 3 innings for the Kansas City Athletics when he was 60 years old. Somebody asked him how old he was, because his birthday was in dispute, and Satchel answered: "Age is a question of mind over matter. If you don't mind, it doesn't matter."

June 21

The Rome Report

When in Rome, do as the Romans do!

An old saying

Oh Rome! My country! City of my soul!

Lord Byron

All roads lead to Rome ... Rome was not built in a day

both from Jean de la Fontaine

See the wild waste of all-devouring years! How Rome her own sad sepulcher appears, with nodding arches, broken temples spread!

Alexander Pope

W e arrived in Rome on a Friday, and the trip into the city from the Leonardo da Vinci airport was harried! There seemed to be close shaves every minute on the busy roads. Tiny cars and scooters zoomed in and out with wild abandon, as if it were their last day on earth. The show was only beginning. After we arrived at our convenient downtown hotel, we hired a car and driver for a few hours and took a quick overview of all the sights. The driver agreed that the scooter drivers were crazy and seemed to have a death wish. They would cut in and out, drive between cars and on the wrong side of the road at times. When you were walking, you had to be extra vigilant, as the scooters would go anywhere, at any speed, at any time. They seemed to be completely out of control—and this in the city of Rome, the center of the Church with the greatest control in the world.

Rome is a fascinating city of contrasts—you could say a huge paradox of control opposite its complete lack of control, ancient against modern, civilization versus crudeness, art up against ugliness, religious opposed to secular—and all packaged very expensively for the multitudes of visitors whose mouths continually drop at the Roman excesses.

The architecture is simply incredible. The time and effort that went into building the religious edifices—St. Peter's, St. Paul's and the Pantheon—boggles the mind. Opposite this amazing ancient architecture are some of the most elaborate works of graffiti seen anywhere in Europe.

So the Eternal City is a fascinating place for sure; the one thing immediately evident is the fact that amid all the old ruins, statues, and tributes to bygone eras, today's Rome is alive with an almost reckless energy.

June 22

Pride in Workmanship

Pride makes us do things well. It is love that makes us do them to perfection.

Author Unknown

One summer when I was about thirteen, the summer holiday began to drag as never before. I had lots of energy but nothing to spend it on. My father Allen sensed this, and he hired me to work around the house. I was to follow in my brothers footsteps and excavate the basement. Grandfather Anthony was five and a half feet tall, and he had made the basement with a six-foot ceiling. All the boys in our family were Murphy's Law incarnate, as we all turned out over six feet. So every summer I had watched my older brothers bent over double, shoveling out clay. Forms were constructed and concrete was poured. Now it was my turn.

What a taskmaster Al was. He niggled over everything. Measurements had to be done to the nearest millimeter, and he kept repeating, "Are you sure those forms are strong enough? Don't you think you should put in more supports? Concrete is awfully heavy stuff!" I kept assuring him that the forms would take a direct hit from an A-bomb, and would he please lay off! He finally did, and I finished the forms with no more of my father's form fanaticism. They were ready for the "awfully heavy stuff." The big day arrived. The Ready-mix truck thundered up. The delivery trough went into the window. Dad's eyes lit up. (He was "crazy over concrete," my brothers told me.) The wet concrete poured into my forms. As they filled up with the oozing gray glop, there was a loud crack, and the bottom of one of my forms moved out as if it had a mind of its own. Lucky for me the form stopped moving after a few inches. The stuff was so heavy that it would have taken a battalion to get it upright again. To this day, that extension of the basement wall remains at an obscene angle for the world to see.

When we create something to last for a long time, we must lavish all the care and love on its creation that we can muster. Imperfections last as a monument to our flawed or careless creativity. My father put passion into perfect sidewalks, walls and curbs. They were almost works of art, if concrete could ever be considered artful. Luckily, my crooked wall was out of sight in the basement. He never said anything to me about it. I guess he didn't have to— but I sure learned that concrete is "awfully heavy stuff!"

174

June 23

Being Alive

He who joyfully marches to music in rank and file has already earned my contempt. He has been given a brain by mistake, since for him the spinal cord would fully suffice.

Albert Einstein

Keep your dreams alive. Understand to achieve anything requires faith and belief in yourself, vision, hard work, determination, and dedication. Remember all things are possible for those who believe.

Gail Devers

Have you heard the expression, "I'm running around like a chicken with its head cut off"? I have never seen a chicken running around with its head missing, but I am told that it happens. Apparently, the autonomous nervous system can make the limbs move without nerve impulses from the brain. Insects have pseudo brains called ganglia in various areas and can live without their heads for some time. Some reptiles can also survive without their heads. The point here is that thought is NOT required for the body to march. Indeed, some people say they manage to go through the day without having to think at all. Maybe we have ganglia in our backsides, which can allow us to not have to think much about anything!

Albert Einstein hated war. He was a pacifist. As the above sentence illustrates, he figured that people who glorify war are severely deficient in brains if they have a brain at all. It is a supreme irony that it was Einstein who convinced President Roosevelt that the Nazi scientists were experimenting with nuclear fission and that America must mount a supreme effort to be the first to build an "atomic" bomb.

The lesson to be learned from Einstein's words and deeds is that we must think about what we really believe in. We must also be aware of what is happening in the world and take a stand when it is called for. This is the essence of being alive as a human being in this world. At times we cannot march to the popular drum beat. We must take a stand, because as some wise person has said, "If we don't stand for something—we'll fall for anything!"

June 24

Motorsport 3

Auto racing is boring except when a car is going at least 172 miles per hour upside down.

Dave Barry

An actor is a puppet, manipulated by a dozen other people. Auto racing has dignity. But you need the same absolute concentration. You have to reach inside yourself and bring forth a lot of broken glass.

Steve McQueen

If everything seems under control, you're just not going fast enough.

Mario Andretti

The car races in the 60's became so popular that it became hell to get there and bedlam once you arrived—just like out on the track. My brother Judd bought himself a Mercury truck. We could cart a ton of good stuff to the races. I borrowed a 30 foot scaffold and we loaded it and a couple of cases of beer into the back, with a tent and blankets and loads of food. Off we went on a Friday night. I thought it would be neat to ride in the truck bed, so I got under a couple of blankets. I don't know how fast Judd was driving, but I fell asleep. I suddenly woke up as one of the blankets blew off and drifted back and forth behind us like a giant manta ray. Nobody behind us got caught up in the blanket, but by the time I got Judd's attention, the blanket had long disappeared.

We set up the scaffolding and had the best seats in the park. There we were on a very hot Saturday race day; thirty feet up on the scaffold with our case of beer, when the damn thing suddenly lurched back about two feet. We looked down, and there was some huge drunken madman trying to climb up the back of our tower. He was determined to tip us over, and the crowd began to cheer. A thirty foot jump is no fun. What were we to do? Almost simultaneously, we began to pour our beers down upon his head. The crowd went wild and began to shake up their drinks and spray the big guy. It was a waste of good suds, but we were saved. He quickly climbed back down and disappeared. Thank God— I mean—he was at least 400 pounds!

Funny things happen in threes. At the end of the day, Keith went nuts and with lit-up eyes, he managed to collect over 20 cases of empty beer bottles in record time. He seemed to move faster that the cars on the track. What a performance!

June 25

George Carlin

Have you ever noticed that anybody driving slower than you is an idiot, and anyone going faster than you is a maniac?

Just think ... people seem to read the Bible a whole lot more as they get older; then it dawns on me ... they're cramming for their final exam.

If God had intended us not to masturbate he would've made our arms shorter.

Not only do I not know what's going on, I wouldn't know what to do about it if I did.

The very existence of flame-throwers proves that sometime, somewhere, someone said to themselves, You know, I want to set those people over there on fire, but I'm just not close enough to get the job done.

George Carlin was one of my favorite funny men. Many folks considered Carlin to be ill-mannered, insensitive and irreligious. When you examine the essence of his wit, however, you will discover a brilliant mind which had a terrific impact on our overuse of language. George's lists of redundancies are wonderful. They, along with many of his "rants," can be found in his book *Brain Droppings*. This has to be one of the most caustically critical books ever written. His "George Carlin Book Club" lists get funnier every time I read them. My brother Bert and I used to read them to each other any time we needed a laugh, and we would laugh so hard we would cry. My dear sister Noni always said that swearing is a sign of a weak vocabulary, and Noni lived up to this credo by rarely using a bad word—yet she loved George Carlin, and would go to see his show when he came to town.

Carlin reinvented the "rant", and some of them were masterpieces. You may have read the "The paradox of modern times", which is attributed to George Carlin and circulates around a few times each year by e-mail. Unfortunately, it's just a hoax. If you go to Carlin's website, he called the paradox prose "sappy shit" that he would never write! George Carlin—a modern day Solomon—or a carping critic? He is worth a read, just to get you thinking about what you really value—even if you can't tolerate his atheistic acerbity.

June 26

Embellish

to embellish ,
1. To make more beautiful and attractive; to decorate.
2. To make something sound or look better or more acceptable than it is in reality ... to distort.   *to embellish a story, the truth*

The great enemy of the truth is very often not the lie ... deliberate, contrived and dishonest ... but the myth ... persistent, persuasive and unrealistic.

John F. Kennedy

A Historian, to convey the truth, must lie. Often he must enlarge the truth by diameters, otherwise his reader would not be able to see it.

Mark Twain

History is more or less bunk.

Henry Ford

History is a set of lies agreed upon.

Napoleon Bonaparte

When telling a story, humans are prone to embellishment. Jokes, tales, family stories, and history are all stretched by storytellers, and there are two great truisms about this stretching or embellishment. The first is: the longer the time between the actual event and its telling, the greater the likelihood untruthful extras will creep in. The second is: the more often the tale is told, the more embellished it becomes.

This is how myths are created. When we are suspicious about the truth of some fantastic event, our suspicions are probably correct. The original event was exaggerated by much retelling over long periods of time. Before the printing press was invented, stories were passed on by word of mouth in song and verse. Wandering minstrels and court jesters passed on fantastic fables. All these tales picked up embellishments as they went along.

In the library, books are divided into fiction and non-fiction. Many of the books in the non-fiction section—biography, history and even the self-help section—are regarded as the truth, but are they really? They are often one person's view of some person, event or subject and may contain distortions. History, as Henry Ford noted, is "more or less bunk." Is anything free of embellishment?

June 27

Return From the War

Life forms illogical patterns. It is haphazard and full of beauties which I try to catch as they fly by, for who knows whether any of them will ever return.

Dame Margot Fonteyn

I shall return.

Douglas MacArthur

When I was about three-and-a-half years old, a great event occurred in my life. My aunt Dorothy returned from the war. First, let me tell you a little about Aunt Dot—the family matriarch. Dorothy Melrose Knight was born on the family farm, the youngest of three daughters of my grandfather, Andrew Joseph Knight, and my grandmother, Ellen Francis Foster. Grandfather died of a ruptured appendix in 1920, leaving Grandma Ellen and the three girls to look after the farm. Aunt Mary was 16, my mother Francis was 11 and Dorothy was seven. With their father gone, they had to look after the farm together. The girls certainly learned self-reliance. My mother married in 1927 and Aunt Mary married in 1930. Dorothy found a different sort of love in nursing, and she never married. She received her RN in the 30's in Chicago, and went to war in the 40's as a nurse in an operating tent in Europe.

When Dorothy returned from the war in the summer of 1945, it was quite an event for our family. Mom had built up her sister as a wonderful hero. I had seen the graduation picture of Dot, and she was a very beautiful lady. On this great occasion of her return, mother bought me a little sailor outfit and told me not to get dirty. Then I was sent out to play so the house could be cleaned up. I figured as long as I had on a sailor outfit, I might as well take my toy boat down to the front creek to sail it. I was having fun, when along came Richard Mundy—a normally pleasant chap from down the street. When he saw my cute little sailor outfit, something must have snapped—he pushed me into the creek. I went home, soaking wet, bawling my eyes out. Mother quickly made everything right just in time for Aunt Dorothy's arrival, and what a time we had. She was a true hero to us.

June 28

The Agony and the Ecstasy

I have always believed, and I still believe, that whatever good or bad fortune may come our way we can always give it meaning and transform it into something of value.
Hermann Hesse

*T*he *Agony and the Ecstasy* is a 1965 film directed by Carol Reed, starring Charlton Heston as Michelangelo and Rex Harrison as Pope Julius II. The movie tells the story of Michelangelo painting the ceiling of the Sistine Chapel in the Vatican. Several reversals of fortune occur before the famous painter is finally convinced to complete one of the greatest masterpieces in the history of art. Both Michelangelo and the Pope go through agonizing moments, eventually leading to the ecstasy when the great fresco is completed. Reversals of fortune can occur quickly, as we know too well.

When Celia was pregnant for the second time, she was so large that I suspected there could be more than one baby. We even picked out names—Craig and Christopher—if they were boys. Sure enough, on the great day, which came a month too early, the nurse brought me two babies—twin boys. The second one had problems breathing, but the nurse reassured me that this was common, and that his lungs would soon expand properly and not to worry. Everything was under control.

I went home, ecstatic about having twins, and informed everyone about our new sons. The ecstasy was short-lived when the hospital phoned to tell me to come back immediately. When I arrived, I was told that Christopher had died. I was devastated. I agonized over my inaction. Should I have insisted on tests which could have shown Celia was carrying twins? Should I have asked the doctor to transfer Christopher to Sick Children's Hospital? Why did I go home when I should have been there at the hospital? At the end of the day, no amount of agonizing would have returned our son.

After arranging a private funeral, we focused our energy on our four pound, six ounce miracle. Craig initially struggled, being a month premature. Ultimately, he thrived, and was a delightful baby, and grew up into a wonderful son. I often mull how Christopher would have developed—but what is the sense in that? Why wonder what may have been, when we should simply enjoy the joy-filled gift we have been given?

June 29

The Report Card

We have met the enemy, and he is us!

Walt Kelly ... in Pogo

In the middle of difficulty lies opportunity.

Albert Einstein

Self-reliance is like a flashlight; no matter how dark it gets, it will help you find your way.

Author Unknown

The second year college student was devastated by his lousy report card. Although he had done well in four of the courses, he had failed the physical chemistry. It served him right. The phys-chem professor had told him that he did "too much singing and dancing" and that he was going to fail. The failure of the car brakes making him an hour late to the exam didn't help. The unhappy student's first reaction was to blame everybody but himself. When he eventually came to his senses and thought about it, he had nobody to blame but himself. He had relied too much on the brains of his friend, Keith, to help him on the weekly problems set. Keith had suggested that they should do the problems on their own, and compare answers later. All the singing and dancing skills in the world didn't help with the phys-chem problems!

The student decided to take a rest from all the heavy science, and for the next year he took Psychology, Philosophy, Shakespeare plays, European History, French Literature and Economics. A wonderful thing happened. An unknown world opened up in these courses. The previous failure turned into a great opportunity, as new and exciting ways of thinking opened up.

The following year he returned to the sciences and scored some of his highest marks. The big difference was the self-reliance he developed after his initial failure, which turned out, after all, to be one of the best things that had ever happened to him.

Walt Kelly's wonderful but absolutely true notion that we are our own worst enemy is close to the top of the all-time cartoon quote list. How then can we escape from ourselves? Besides the lessons of failure, how do we improve? Surprise—we are often our own best teacher—if we do some meditation, and mull it over a little.

June 30

The End

Due to the lack of experienced trumpeters, the end of the world has been postponed for three weeks.

Anon

Don't wake me for the end of the world unless it has very good special effects.

Roger Zelazny

I laugh every time I see a cartoon showing a zealot with a long beard holding a sign which states "THE END IS AT HAND!" There don't seem to be as many zealots these days and no bumper stickers making the dire prediction. One group of fanatics predicted the end of the world in 1925 and again in 1957. They kept asking folks if they were "ready." We are all witnesses that it never happened—but it did! One of our family friends firmly believed the prediction and for her it turned out to be true. She died in 1957. The sect actually predicted the end a number of times.

The second half of the 20th Century could be called the "Time of the End of the World Worry", as the world was the push of a button away from nuclear Armageddon. The U.S.A. and the U.S.S.R. could mutually annihilate each other many times over. Many folks, including my father built themselves bomb shelters. Al put in a concrete slab 3 feet thick as a driveway, and then I had to excavate the dirt from under this concrete. I'm sure it would have survived a direct hit from an atomic bomb, but in two years the road salt had eaten the top inch off the concrete! Numerous movies showed the horror of nuclear war, and the best was *Doctor Strangelove or How I Stopped Worrying and Learned to Love the Bomb*. The worst case scenario happens when a mad American general launches the B-52's at Russia as a pre-emptive strike. THE END unfolds to the song, "We'll meet again ... don't know where ... don't know when". Hilarious!

Speaking of "don't know when," I know people who believe that everything is determined ahead of time—predestination—and "when your number is up ... it's up." I don't think so. I figure that it has to be chance. Who is handing out the numbers in the first place? Why would Methuselah be given over 900 years and Mozart only 35? Besides, I forgot to take a number when I came in anyway.

July 1

Excess Meter

Moderation is a fatal thing. Nothing succeeds like excess.

Oscar Wilde

The road to excess leads to the palace of wisdom.

William Blake

If music be the food of love, play on. Give me excess of it ...

With eager feeding, food doth choke the feeder.

Both from William Shakespeare

In our workout this morning, Mike and I were both commenting on our current ailments. Mike had trouble getting to sleep last night, and I have a big toe on my left foot which feels like it's broken. I don't know what causes insomnia, but I do know why my big toe is complaining. I just returned from a trip to Vancouver, and I got carried away with the "enjoy your food and drink" advice from Ecclesiastes. Every time I pig out, my big toe tells me. It's almost like a meter that goes into the red when I enjoy food and drink to excess. My toe is a built-in "excess meter."

Many ailments are built-in excess meters. Tennis elbow, writer's cramp and carpal tunnel syndrome are three common ailments that probably result from excess repetition of a movement. Sitting for too long in front of the computer or text-messaging with the same finger can result in pain. The wisdom of the body is at work. The body seems to be saying, "If you are going to get carried away doing the same thing, I'll soon put a stop to it!" If your livelihood depends on that repetitive motion, it can be disastrous for you. Athletes and musicians are especially prone to injury when they perform the same motion to excess. Many have been forced to change their professions when a repetitive motion injury resists treatment.

Our son, Craig, majored in string bass. He became an excellent musician and played several gigs in a jazz trio. To his dismay, Craig couldn't play for very long without severe pain in his left hand. When he went to a repetitive strain practitioner, he was told that his hand is missing a muscle and that he would never be able to play for more than an hour without experiencing pain. Sometimes the excess meter seems to be telling us, "Life is not fair ... but get over it and get on with something different."

July 2

Depression

If depression is creeping up and must be faced, learn something about the nature of the beast: You may escape without a mauling.

Dr. R. W. Shepherd

If I had not been already been meditating, I would certainly have had to start. I've treated my own depression for many years with exercise and meditation, and I've found that to be a tremendous help.

Judy Collins

It's a recession when your neighbor loses his job; it's a depression when you lose yours.

Harry S. Truman

Several members of our family suffered from bipolar syndrome—commonly called manic-depression. A person who is bipolar goes through periods of "highs" and "lows", and the depression often comes in the winter when the sunlight is at a minimum. The medical profession has done studies relating depression to the lack of vitamin D. This may be true, but many people often suffer clinical depression after surgery, especially heart surgery. Depression may accompany childbirth. The fact is that most people at some time in their lives will suffer from depression, and it can be debilitating for those people.

Folks who don't suffer depression are at a loss when they need to be consoling. You can see a broken arm or some physical impediment, but mental suffering seems invisible. "Why don't they snap out of it," or "Get a life," are mean-spirited comments from some folks who don't care to understand invisible suffering. These comments aren't helpful.

I recall my big brother going into the psychiatric ward at our local hospital. Judd had been seeing a psychiatrist about fifty years ago but had reached a watershed. I arrived in his room for a visit, and Judd was concerned for my wellbeing. "Watch out Lee," he warned, "there is a crazy woman around who will reach into your pants and grab your penis ... and she won't let go!" Damn—I must have missed her. Judd came out of the hospital in much better shape. He also remained depression-free for a long time. I asked him why.

Judd told me: "We would have group sessions—like in the movie, *One Flew over the Cuckoo's Nest*—and when I heard the stories of the rest of these folks, I suddenly realized that I was all right ... I wasn't so crazy after all. I mean ... these people were *really* nuts!"

July 3

Naps

I take a two-hour nap ... from one o'clock to four.
Yogi Berra

I don't generally feel anything until noon, then it's time for my nap.
Oliver Wendell Holmes

No day is so bad it can't be fixed with a nap.
Carrie P. Snow

Think what a better world it would be if we all, the whole world, had cookies and milk about three o'clock every afternoon and then lay down on our blankets for a nap.
Barbara Jordan

When I retired, a good friend gave me a neat book: *The Art of Napping*. I should have written that book, as I have been a napper for as long as I can remember. I suppose I should have been born in a Mediterranean country where a nap or siesta after lunch is mandatory. As enjoyable as a good cat-nap is, there are those who treat nappers with disdain—turning up their noses while self-righteously proclaiming: "I never nap!" These principled folks don't know what they are missing by thumbing their noses at naps. Why do many folks frown on catching a nap? Snoozing has been found to be beneficial. Twenty minutes can help freshen your mind, elevate your mood and increase your alertness. Nodding off may benefit the heart. In a study of adults in Greece, researchers found that men who napped at least three times a week had a 37 percent lower risk of heart-related death. This research proves my perception that napping is good for you. To back up my point that naps are beneficial, here's a short list of famous nappers: Albert Einstein, Winston Churchill, Thomas Edison, Napoleon Bonaparte, Johannes Brahms, John F. Kennedy, Eleanor Roosevelt, Ronald Reagan, Leonardo Da Vinci, John D. Rockefeller and Gene Autry.

When I was teaching, I would sometimes sneak a twenty minute nap after lunch. There was a small office off the prep room which was hidden and quiet. If nobody was around to catch me napping, I would use this office and nap with my head on somebody's desk. One afternoon, I awoke to the din of a loud class. I went into the noisy class prepared to deliver a reprimand, and guess what? It was my class—and I was five minutes late!

July 4

Battle of the Sexes

Women are never disarmed by compliments. Men always are. That is the difference between the two sexes.

Oscar Wilde

The same passions in man and woman nonetheless differ in tempo; hence man and woman do not cease misunderstanding one another.

Friedrich Wilhelm Nietzsche

A man loses his sense of direction after four drinks; a woman loses hers after four kisses.

Henry Louis Mencken

One of my theories is that men love with their eyes; women love with their ears.

Zsa Zsa Gabor

At a recent class reunion I heard the comment: "Of 18 of my friends who married, 17 ended in divorce." Someone responded: "Of the past eight weddings I attended, only one has lasted." It made me wonder where the notion of long-term commitment has gone. I also found myself wondering how the children of these failed unions are faring. Contrast those short partnerships with the 42nd, 52nd, and 60th anniversaries we celebrated at our last Family Campers and RVers camping weekend. Why did these folks have good staying power?

Although good luck is certainly a factor, the couples we know who are still united after all these years, have overcome crises together to emerge with an even stronger union. Strong families work together, play together and pray together. There is also room for individual growth. Everyone contributes their strengths. No one controls everything. The family and support groups are true democracy in action.

July 4th is the day for huge hugs as we celebrate Independence Day. For families, this should also be a reminder that we depend on each other for support. Independence is good, but no one is an island unto themselves.

July 5

The Spiral Staircase

Life is a series of experiences, each one of which makes us bigger, even though sometimes it is hard to realize this. For the world was built to develop character, and we must learn that the setbacks and griefs which we endure help us in our marching onward.

Henry Ford

How would you like to spend three years working on a thesis for your doctorate, only to be told by the examining officer that the topic was inappropriate and that he wouldn't read it? Do such injustices actually occur? Apparently they do. Just such a setback was handed to Karen Armstrong, the talented and prolific British author of more than five classic books on religion, including a magnificent volume entitled *The History of God.* Karen's life story, as described in her autobiography, *The Spiral Staircase,* seems to be one setback after another after another.

Karen was "called by God" and went into a nunnery when she was seventeen. The molding and contemplation didn't work for her; after seven years she left the convent, having lost her faith in the process. This was the first of a number of rejections, and Karen had years of psychiatric therapy which didn't seem to help. Finally, she was diagnosed as having epilepsy; once she found this out, she was finally able to rise above all these setbacks to become the well-researched author of several books on religion. These insightful books have quickly become classics in the genre. The unbelievable fact about Karen's epilepsy is that, although she has all the classic symptoms of the disease, none of the medical practitioners in the convent ever diagnosed it—and her psychiatrist missed it as well. Maybe it's a good thing. Without all the adversity, she might not have developed the strength to become what she is!

Speaking of psychiatry, do you know the difference between "neurotic" and "psychotic?"

A neurotic builds castles in the air. The psychotic lives in them!

(The psychiatrist collects rent from both.)

July 6

Looney Tunes

Bugs (reading) ... "Tasmanian Devil ... eats cats, rats, dogs, hogs etc. but it don't say nothin' about rabbits."

Tas (pointing a fat finger) ... "and especially rabbits!"

"Welcome to my shop ... let me cut your mop ... you're so next."

Bugs Bunny in "Rabbit of Seville"

"Be wary wary quiet ... we is huntin' wabbits."

Elmer Fudd

"I say, I say boy ... I am not a chicken ... now that there is a chicken."

Foghorn T. Leghorn to Henry Chicken Hawk ...

"You're not a chicken ... you're a schnook!"

Henry's response

One of the cultural delights when I was a kid was the cartoon. We didn't get to see many of them. On Saturday, for a dime, you could go to a double feature. There was usually *News of the World*, a serial that continued every week, and a cartoon—five items for a dime! Now it's 100 times that expensive to watch some advertisements and one feature—and no cartoon!!! What a rip.

One of the bonuses of having kids was to delight in the Bugs Bunny cartoons on T.V. I used to love all the voices—done to great effect by Mel Blanc. Where else can you be destroyed repeatedly and still return for more punishment? Where else can the same old lines like, "What's up Doc?" be laughed at so many times? The *Looney Tunes* of Bugs and friends were brilliant; we loved to watch them over and over and we still know all the lines. I quoted a line from "The Rabbit of Seville" recently to my son Craig, and he came back at me with the entire song.

A huge bonus was the music of Rossini or Wagner that accompanied the cartoon. We remember Elmer Fudd playing Brunhilda and singing "Kill the Wabbit, kill the Wabbit," to the strains of Wagner's "Ride of the Valkyries".

If you have never laughed at Yosemite Sam riding a camel and Foghorn T. Leghorn looking after Henry Chicken Hawk, or watched the Tasmanian Devil trying to eat Bugs Bunny, you haven't—I say—you haven't lived, you varmint! So haste ye down to your local library, where they are all available on DVD!

July 7

Failing Yourself

By Failing to prepare … you are preparing to Fail.

Ben Franklin

A mighty fortress is our God, A bulwark never failing.

Martin Luther

If you're not failing every now and again, it's a sign you're not doing anything very innovative.

Woody Allen

An essential aspect of creativity is not being afraid to fail.

Edwin Land

This is the date, as I recall, that summer school used to begin. You usually had a week after the end of June before you had to go to summer school. Each year from 10th to 12th grade, I managed to fail French and had to go to summer school to make it up. You had to take two courses, so I usually did the English Literature over because there was new stuff. So how, you ask, did I manage to fail French for three years straight? Simple—I didn't do the work. I got Charlie Cunningham (a great teacher) at summer school—and there was this girl at summer school. Failure sometimes has its rewards!

Much later, as a teacher, I would begin the year with a pep talk, and one of the things I said with great emphasis was: "I have taught thousands of students and I have yet to fail anybody!"

Then I would pause and wait, and eventually somebody would say, "Yes, we know … they failed themselves." It's true. We tend to blame everybody else for our failures, but most of the time, we fail ourselves. There is nothing wrong with failure. The process can be a great teacher. You also have to realize that if you aren't failing some of the time, you probably aren't doing anything worthwhile.

When I was a choir director, we tried some pieces that were perhaps too difficult for us. The odd time, the performance "failed." I used to tell the choir not to worry, "God accepts the offering … warts and all!" If you never try anything new and challenging, you simply won't grow. It's easy to do the same old stuff over and over.

With this in mind, in spite of my dismal record in the French language, I selected "French Philosophers" as a third year course at college. Would you believe, I actually earned an "A" in the course—and although I still can't speak the language, I sure enjoyed Voltaire and Racine!

July 8

Exercise

It's easier to maintain your health than to regain it.

We don't stop exercising because we grow old, we grow old because we stop exercising.

So I've broadened the fitness concept to make it one of moderation and balance.
All from Dr. Kenneth Cooper ... fitness guru

We recently joined a fitness club here in Port Charlotte. I am a firm believer that exercise should be done with a partner or a group. There is a better chance to make it a habit if we have someone to encourage us. My neighbor and good friend, Mike Lonsdale, comes over at 6:45 a.m. three times a week to work out for an hour. For seven months of the year, we exercise together and enjoy a variety of music during our workouts. We rarely miss a session from May to November. Celia and I head to Florida in mid-November and Mike and Nan go a little further to Naples, where Mike does the machine routine at a club early every morning. Mike is disciplined when it comes to staying in shape, and it shows—no arthritis, hypertension, diabetes or other late-developing health issues. Mike is my hero when it comes to exercising. He enjoys exercise, keeps fit, looks terrific and enjoys excellent health. I am not quite up to his level—but I'm working at it.

Our new club has an excellent atmosphere, with posted quotes, including the ones above from Kenneth Cooper. The owner of the club, William gave us a personal training session when we began, and what he emphasized certainly made good sense to us:

Warm up with stretching exercises including lots of deep breathing;

Use the elliptical trainer or rowing machine after your stretching for a complete body workout—gradually increase the level of difficulty;

Learn to use the machines properly and change your workout often to prevent your muscles getting used to the same old routine.

PS   You could apply that last tenet to anything you do in life. Avoid the same old-same old. Keep doing new things!

July 9

Splendid Isolation

Isolation is a dream killer.

Barbara Sher

Isolation is the sum total of wretchedness to a man.

Thomas Carlyle

If you want to end your isolation, you must be honest about what you want at a core level and decide to go after it.

Martha Beck

For so long in my marriage and afterwards I'd been in isolation oblivious to everything but my darkest hedonism and darkest hours.

Courtney Love … diary extract

There was an essay in the newspaper this morning written by a lady who had moved across the continent from a city with eternal summer and sunshine to a city where winter took its toll, six months of the year. Friends asked her "Why?" and she initially responded that her husband's job had required the move. What happened in the new city was totally unexpected. People were welcoming and friendly. People would stop to chat with her when she walked her dog. On one occasion, a neighbor cut her grass. On another, her sidewalk was shoveled out after a heavy snow. On both these occasions, her neighbors actually apologized for their good deeds, saying: "We thought you weren't home!" Over time, the move turned into a blessing rather than a trial.

In her previous neighborhood, people kept to themselves in splendid isolation—putting in alarms and walls to keep out intruders. People thought that survival required you to put on a coat of armor each day and to eschew any involvement with the folks around you. Part of this armor meant never looking a stranger in the eye, as that might be interpreted as an invitation. It was better to remain in one's own world—isolated from the evil machinations of the loony fringe "out there."

We all have a choice to make about our neighbors and those we meet. We can choose to treat them as we would like to be treated, and do some good whenever we have the opportunity—or we can choose isolation. What will we do today?

July 10

Wagner's Cottage

Is Wagner a human being at all? Is he not rather a disease? He contaminates everything he touches … he has made music sick. I postulate this viewpoint: Wagner's art is diseased.

Friedrich Nietzsche

Wagner has lovely moments but awful quarters of an hour.

Gioacchino Rossini

I have been told that Wagner's music is better than it sounds.

Mark Twain

We were in Lucerne, Switzerland about fifteen years ago. It was a bus tour of cities in Europe; about half the bus was Australians, and there was one lady from New Zealand. The interesting thing was that these folks didn't speak to each other. The Aussies thought she was prudish, and she thought the Aussies were rude and crude. I managed to get along with the lot of them by ignoring insults and treating all with lightness. Everyone has their story to tell, and all these people were interesting. I found out that the lady from New Zealand (whose name escapes me) loved opera and could talk about Wagner for hours, so when we arrived in Lucerne, I suggested to her that we visit Wagner's summer home which was now a museum.

We discovered that this villa was in Tribschen, a suburb of Lucerne, and that we could get there on the public transit trolley. I tried to buy tickets to the trolley from a machine with no luck; so we just got on at the back door of the tram and hoped nobody asked for our ticket. Nobody did ask, so we got a free ride to Tribschen and back.

When we got to the lovely villa on Lake Lucerne, the grounds were gorgeous, the setting was idyllic and the museum was stuffed with great memorabilia—but I couldn't enjoy a minute of the visit. I suddenly discovered I was without our expensive camera. I must have left it on the trolley, so I fretted about it the whole time, and the artifacts meant nothing to me. I'm afraid I ruined the visit for my New Zealand friend as well. When we returned to the hotel, there was the camera sitting on the bed. The lesson I learned was to focus on where your camera is before you go off to explore. Hey—maybe I could write an opera about my silly performance that day! In opera, it doesn't matter what it's about—as long as it's sung!

July 11

The Unknown

A ship in port is safe, but that's not what ships are built for. Sail out to sea and do new things.

We tend not to choose the unknown, which might be a shock or a disappointment or simply a little difficult to cope with. And yet it is the unknown with all its disappointments and surprises that is the most enriching.

Anne Morrow Lindbergh

Twenty years from now you will be more disappointed by the things that you didn't do than by the ones you did do. So throw off the bowlines. Sail away from the safe harbor. Catch the trade winds in your sails. Explore. Dream. Discover.

Mark Twain

The pessimist complains about the wind; the optimist expects it to change; the realist adjusts the sails.

William Arthur Ward

I read with sadness this morning about an avalanche in the Himalayas ending the climb and the lives of over ten mountain climbers. They had made it to the top of the second highest mountain in the world and were on their way down the mountain when disaster struck. These climbers court disaster every second of their climb; yet they ascend the mountain knowing that they are looking death directly in the face. Most of us don't understand what makes folks climb mountains. We can't comprehend why some people risk everything for a moment of glory. The majority prefer the safe and known path to the unknown trail where we might fail. Why risk everything for something with an unknown outcome? Pause for a moment and consider the number of times you have taken a risk which changed your life for the better. I'll wager that every person I've met has faced the unknown many times. Marriage, changing jobs, and moving are all risky business. Each day, in fact, is a new adventure for many of our fellow-travelers. The question is: is every day a new adventure for us? Do we have something fresh to engage us today? If not—maybe it's time to "adjust the sails" and risk something new and unknown. We need to "sail out to sea and do new things."

July 12

Pigs

And the unclean spirits came out (of the demoniac) and entered the swine; and the herd, numbering about two thousand, rushed down the steep bank into the sea, and were drowned in the sea.

Mark 5:13 ... also in Luke 33 ... my least favorite story in the Bible

The bloodhound has the intelligence of a rock whereas the pig is the rocket scientist of animals.

From the video "Pigs Might Fly"

I understand the inventor of the bagpipes was inspired when he saw a man carrying an indignant, asthmatic pig under his arm. Unfortunately, the manmade sound never equaled the purity of the sound achieved by the pig.

Alfred Hitchcock

I like pigs. Dogs look up to us. Cats look down on us. Pigs treat us as equals.

Winston Churchill

I like pigs. I collect them. I even have a large copper pig weather vane up on my roof. It was my retirement gift, and that very evening, after the party, the family came home and had its own pig-mounting party—up on the roof. People have asked me why I like pigs so much, and to tell you the truth, I guess it's a collection of pig-tales just like the pig collection itself.

When I was teaching, I had a video called *Pigs Might Fly*, showing unbelievable feats of pigs. They are the most intelligent of animals. As Churchill said, "Pigs treat us as equals." Then I read a book by John Robbins called *Diet for a New America*, which points out the terrible treatment of animals in factory farms. If you read this book, you will understand why I avoid eating pork and veal. A society which treats animals the way veal calves, pigs and chickens are treated is cruel and brutal.

Our pig collecting began in earnest when I saw the huge inflatable pig at a Pink Floyd rock concert. This humongous hog was part of the set for the album "Animals", which makes much of the sound pigs make. We have been collecting ever since—and our house, fifth wheel and yards are replete with pigs—pigs—pigs everywhere—and they all have names. Wherever we go, we bring back a pig. Other folks return from their travels with piggies for us. They get a place of honor and a name—the pigs, that is!

July 13

National Parks

Some national parks have long waiting lists for camping reservations. When you wait a year to sleep next to a tree, something is wrong.

George Carlin

The fire is the main comfort of the camp, whether in summer or winter, and is about as ample at one season as at another. It is as well for cheerfulness as for warmth and dryness.

Henry David Thoreau

When we bought our second camper, a Nimrod tent trailer, we decided to cross America and visit as many National Parks as possible. What follows is a list of the parks we camped in. At that time, you could purchase, for 25 dollars, a Golden Eagle Passport which allowed you entrance to the parks. This has been replaced with: *America the Beautiful – National Parks and Federal Recreational Lands Pass – Annual Pass.*

A LIFETIME pass is available for seniors and for disabled persons.

Rocky Mountain in Colorado: We drove up to the top of the mountains, where beautiful meadows with delightful wild flowers welcomed us. There were patches of snow even in July, and we made snow balls to throw at each other. One could spend the summer here and only scratch the surface.

Black Canyon of the Gunnison in Colorado: We were unaware of this narrow canyon until we reached the edge. A deep and craggy gash opened in the earth before us and took our breath away.

Zion in Utah: Steep walls in various colors rose up on both sides. We discovered a shallow creek which rushed over smooth stones. You could slip down this natural water slide for hundreds of feet.

Grand Canyon in Arizona: We visited the North Rim where tame birds ate out of our hands. The colors and shades of this spectacular wonder change as the day goes by. One could spend a lifetime exploring. We have returned many times to both rims, and marveled at the variety of breathtaking beauty. Absolutely and unbelievably spectacular!

These parks should be on your bucket list of places to see while you can. If you cannot drive, search your local library and internet for video tours.

July 14

Food

With eager feeding, food doth choke the feeder.

William Shakespeare

We live for, by and through the stomach.

Anon

A favorite four-letter word in the English language is "food." As we take a stroll in the early evening, wonderful summer BBQ smells make our mouths water, even if we have already eaten. While most of the animals on earth eat for survival, the human animal derives great pleasure from the thrice-daily feast—or perhaps we should say "should derive", since in the age of fast food many folks on autopilot have reverted to wolfing without enjoyment. Our attitude towards eating can make a huge difference in our lives and our health. It is helpful to know something about the origin of food and what happens once we consume our grub.

Food contains stored chemical energy. This energy originates in sunlight or artificial sources and is fixed in green plants in a process known as photosynthesis. Only plants containing chlorophyll are able to make food. The bottom of the food chain must be photosynthetic plants, so if all the chlorophyll on earth suddenly went on strike, all life on earth would soon end. All animals rely on the energy fixed in their chow by green plants. When we eat, our digestive system breaks complex molecules into simpler ones; our circulatory system delivers these simpler molecules to our cells where the energy is extracted. Our level of energy, our health and our sense of wellbeing depend on these processes and especially on the food we consume. So much for the science lesson; how can we help this internal system to perform at its best? Here are a few tips to extract the greatest pleasure from our sustenance:

Make each meal a great pleasure—pleasurable conversation—relaxing music—concentration on savoring the taste of the food—and eating slowly;

Avoid overeating, and avoid eating while watching T.V.—pay proper respect to the good stuff which allows you to continue living;

Snack on natural foods, such as fruit and raw vegetables—they are easier to digest and release energy quickly.

Bon appétit!

July 15

Construction

The shortest distance between two points is under construction.

Leo Aikman

The whole difference between construction and creation is exactly this: that a thing constructed can only be loved after it is constructed; but a thing created is loved before it exists.

Charles Dickens

Our family has contracting and construction in our genes. Both my grandfather and father built houses. Although I helped my dad with deconstruction and concrete work some summers, I never really considered building things as a vocation. I loved to take things apart but erecting edifices didn't hold much appeal at that time.

There is one commonality in engineering and construction—problem-solving. We certainly learned this several years ago when we decided to build a cabana, a fancy shed, in the backyard. We designed it from foundation to roof, so that it would look like a little house but be totally maintenance-free. We also wanted to recycle mirror doors and French doors from our house. We drew up several plans and settled on a design with a full front porch, mirrored back wall, vinyl siding and vinyl soffits, shutters and trim. A solid foundation was provided by nine sona tubes four feet long, filled with concrete. We notched them at the top so that a wood base of two-by-eights would be anchored into the concrete pillars. This was but one of many solutions we came up with in fabricating our wee house. When it was finished after about six weeks, we could say we designed and built it and solved many problems along the way. To this day, the cabana hasn't moved an inch and hasn't required any painting or upkeep. It serves as a practical storage area for all the outside furniture during the winter and as a change room, bar and music room in the summer.

Problem-solving in any endeavor always requires one important reminder to get the best solution. Let the conundrum and resolutions simmer in your brain for some time before deciding on the solution. It also is important to get help. Two heads are certainly better than one when it comes to designing most things—as long as you are patient with each other and allow enough time for good fermentation to occur.

July 16

National Parks 2

Even in a time of elephantine vanity and greed, one never has to look far to see the campfires of gentle people.

Garrison Keillor

How hard to realize that every camp of men or beast has this glorious starry firmament for a roof! In such places standing alone on the mountain-top it is easy to realize that whatever special nests we make ... leaves and moss like the marmots and birds, or tents or piled stone ... we all dwell in a house of one room.

John Muir

Yosemite Valley, to me, is always a sunrise, a glitter of green and golden wonder in a vast edifice of stone and space.

Ansel Adams

The national park is the best idea America ever had.

James Bryce

In 1971, we took a camping trip across America in which we tried to visit as many National Parks as possible. At that time, there were no reservations. Campsites were allotted on a first come basis. We camped within an hour or two of the park and arrived by mid-morning. We spent glorious moments in breath-taking vistas only found in the national parks.

In the July 13 reflection, we described four parks. Here are the highlights of three more national parks.

Yosemite in California: There were waterfalls over a thousand feet high. One waterfall could actually be climbed to a safe height, and loads of folks climbed up the slippery rock to prove they could climb higher than others.

Sequoia in California: There was a huge tree, General Sherman, whose trunk was so large that it took thirty-five people to encompass it. It's estimated that 40 houses could have been built from the wood from this thousand-year-old giant Sequoia.

Yellowstone in Wyoming: This was our favorite. There was a huge variety of sights: beautiful meadows, bubbling cauldrons, Grand Canyon with waterfall, and bison, bears and moose. "Old Faithful" is a spectacular old geyser. We have returned several times to Yellowstone and hope to return again.

July 17

Eleanor Roosevelt

Learn from the mistakes of others. You can't live long enough to make them all yourself.

Beautiful young people are accidents of nature, but beautiful old people are works of art.

Great minds discuss ideas; Average minds discuss events; Small minds discuss people.

Do whatever comes your way as well as you can. Think as little as possible about yourself and as much as possible about other people and other things that are interesting. Put a good deal of thought into happiness that you are able to give.

Remember always that you have not only the right to be an individual; you have an obligation to be one.

I once had a rose named after me and I was very flattered. But I was not pleased to read the description in the catalogue: no good in a bed, but fine up against a wall.

All from Eleanor Roosevelt   1884 – 1962

The year I was born, there was a special couple in the White House. Franklin D. Roosevelt was a larger-than-life president, in spite of having leg paralysis. He conducted his presidency with élan. I have this wonderful image of F.D.R. sitting in his wheelchair—his cigarette smoking away at the end of a long holder—throwing his poker-chips out on the table. (Roosevelt loved poker and found that it took his mind off the war.) His wife, Eleanor, was a strong woman; arguably the most admired first lady ever to serve in the White House. Eleanor Roosevelt left a legacy of wise sayings. They could be considered as modern proverbs. It is little wonder that Eleanor received 48 honorary degrees.

PS   When Gallup released their final list of people from the 20th century who were "most admired", the only couple to make the top ten were Franklin and Eleanor Roosevelt, who were numbers 6 and 9 respectively.

July 18

Cake

You know you are getting old when the candles cost more than the cake.

Bob Hope

A bad review is like baking a cake with all the best ingredients and having someone sit on it.

Danielle Steel

All the world is birthday cake, so take a piece, but not too much.

George Harrison

Nothing seems to please a fly so much as to be taken for a currant, and if it can be baked in a cake and palmed off on the unwary, it dies happy.

Mark Twain

You can't have your cake and eat it too.

Old Expression

I wonder what *"You can't have your cake and eat it too."* really means. Does it literally mean you cannot possess something and enjoy it at the same time? Does it mean you have to live with the consequences of your actions? Or is the meaning simply the same for any food which is devoured? Once it slips down your esophagus, it's impossible to restore it to its original form. Who knows for sure? (As of this writing, there is no answer to this question on Wiki.) It can be argued that, except for food and drink, everything can be had and enjoyed continually. All the people you know, the places you go, and the art and nature surrounding us can be savored repeatedly. You certainly can have all these good things and continually "eat" of them. It would be silly not to. It is obvious that what is true for cake and whatever we stuff down our gullets, cannot be true for everything else—and thank goodness for that.

From the scientific view, the meaning is fundamental. If you do anything—perform any action—you make a change in the world that goes on to affect everything. The consequences may be startling, according to Chaos Theory. It's sometimes called the "butterfly effect." The fluttering of butterfly's wings in Costa Rica may eventually affect the weather in Georgia. I find that interesting—but hard to swallow.

I prefer what George Carlin has to say about cake. *What's the use of a cake you can't eat?*

July 19

BO

I was an engineer by trade. Our group was responsible for manufacture, assembly and testing of all kinds of complex equipment. Some designs were first-off, unique approaches which had never been tried before. Needless to say, we ran into all kinds of problems and we settled into a routine where three or four of us would get together and brainstorm. Each of us had different strengths (and weaknesses) but each contributed in their own way. It was amazing the number of great solutions we came up with. Often, we had to let things ferment for a little while before the answer would percolate down.

Mike Lonsdale

I consider the 70s to be the youth of old age. So all you women out there who are afraid of getting older, just keep your orgasms in place, eat a lot of vegetables, take exercise, and you'll be fine.

Betty Dodson

I know what you are thinking after seeing the title of this reflection. In this case, however, "BO" is a "brain orgasm." So what, pray tell, is a BO? It's simply the terrific high you get from either having a huge burden removed, or from coming up with the solution to a complex problem. This wonderful feeling could be called a brain orgasm—or BO—since it involves thinking and not physical activity. Why are these ecstatic feelings of well-being so important? How do you consistently get them?

Let's switch for a moment to a world-famous cardiovascular surgeon, Dr Michael DeBakey, who pioneered such now-common procedures as bypass surgery and invented a host of devices to help heart patients. He was still going to work and performing surgery in his early nineties. DeBakey isn't the first person who worked into his nineties. Many scientists, doctors and attorneys seem to keep working! (America's oldest active mayor, Dorothy Geeben, died recently. She was 102 years old.) Have you ever wondered why some people never retire? Some suggest that they have "nothing better to do." I believe that the commonality among these working fiends is simply the brain orgasms they experience daily from having such challenging and rewarding careers. Hooray for these wonderful BO addicts!

July 20

Trucks

All those trucks and barges that carry our goods to port are vital connections to the only force which can balance our trade deficit: export. We must keep doing what we do best if we are going to get America out of the red.

Jo Ann Emerson

There is more credit and satisfaction in being a first-rate truck driver than a tenth-rate executive.

B.C. Forbes

We were returning from a dinner party the other night when the traffic slowed to a standstill. As we inched along, we suddenly realized we were surrounded by trucks. Everywhere you looked there were these huge monsters; Celia keep remarking about the size of them, and how many axles they had, and how big the tires were. I felt as if we were in a valley of transports, and it brought back memories of the collision we had with a monstrous eighteen wheeler.

We were driving our '68 Ford Hardtop, "Big Red," in Los Angeles late one evening. I watched in horror as this huge truck bumper came over at us and ripped my driver's side from one end to the other like a can-opener. Lucky for us, no one was injured; Big Red was a mess, but drivable. The trucker apologized. He calmly said that he had been on the road for too long, had missed us in his mirrors, and that his company would repair our car, which they did.

I have great admiration for the drivers of big rigs. Most of them have excellent driving skills and remain calm in spite of the antics of crazy car drivers. They sit patiently through traffic messes because they know that there is no sense letting it get to you. They endure hours of waiting at the border to ensure that all our stuff gets delivered to us. Many truck drivers are very educated people. Rolling down the highway in an eighteen wheeler holds a fascination frantic for lots of smart people.

Next time you pass a truck, give the driver a friendly wave—and remember to respect the hard-working, hard-driving people who bring you all your stuff!

July 21

Barber Shop

I must to the barber's, monsieur; for methinks I am marvelous hairy about the face, and I am such a tender ass, if my hair do but tickle me, I must scratch.

William Shakespeare, *A Midsummer Night's Dream*

Hey you!   Welcome to my shop, Let me cut yer mop ...
Don't look so perplexed ... Yerrrrrrrrrrr so next!!!
How about a nice, close shave? Teach your whiskers to behave
Lots of lather, lots of soap ... Please hold still, don't be a dope.
Now we're ready for the scraping ...There's no use to try escaping.
Yell and scream and rant and rave ... It's no use, you need a shave! There, you're nice and clean !!!
Although your face looks like it might have gone through a ma-chine.

Bugs Bunny to Elmer Fudd in "Rabbit of Seville"   Google it!

I have gone to the same barber for over twenty-five years. Claudio is an Italian gentleman with marvelous hands, and he takes great pride in lowering your ears and making you young again. He always says, "She's a gonna lova you tonight," when he finishes. The barbershop is much different from the ladies' beauty salon. Great philosophical discussions occur about any topic, and there is much wisdom and common sense dispensed, because barbers like Claudio have "heard it all" and can talk about anything from the Buffalo Bills to the lousy markets.

Speaking of markets, there was a number-one business seller some years back called *The Wealthy Barber.* The book discussed everything about investing from a common sense point of view. You may wonder how a barber would know so much about so much but consider this. The barber probably averages ten to twenty conversations a day, six days a week, and fifty weeks a year. So Claudio has taken part in over one hundred thousand conversations in the last twenty-five years. A barber who is really good at "picking brains" can become conversant in practically anything!

There are many movies with famous scenes in barber shops. Many of these are horrifically violent. The funniest, however, remains: "The Rabbit of Seville" with Bugs Bunny and Elmer Fudd. If you Google the title, you will get an extensive Wikipedia entry and the full cartoon itself, which is classic!

July 22

Crisis in Bar Harbor

When written in Chinese, the word "crisis" is composed of two characters… one represents danger, and the other represents opportunity.
Children are the world's most valuable resource and its best hope for the future.

Both from John F. Kennedy

When Anthony was four and Craig was two, we went on a camping trip to the East Coast. The camping was excellent and the weather held until we arrived in Bar Harbor, Maine. That evening, we were having fun playing garbage-can basketball with the littlest campers in our campground. I had a half-size bouncy ball, and the toddlers were trying to shoot the ball into the cans. Anthony was racking up the points, but Craig was completely out of sorts. He wouldn't share the ball and was as contrary as I had ever seen him. He was sent to bed early.

Just after dark it began to rain, and there was no letup. About two in the morning, Craig began to cry and arch his back. He couldn't get comfortable and quickly got worse. We threw on some clothes and drove to the hospital in Bar Harbor. Fortunately, the emergency department wasn't busy, and the doctor on call examined Craig quickly. He said the word "flu" and prescribed aspirin. I argued with him that there was more to it than simple flu, and the nurse agreed. She suggested phoning Doctor Green, a new pediatrician at the hospital. She was a strong lady and won the old GP over. I don't know what she said to Dr. Green, but he was there in ten minutes and quickly examined Craig. I could tell by his look it was more than the flu.

"Your son is showing all the symptoms of spinal meningitis," he said, "and I am going to take a chance that it is bacterial meningitis and administer antibiotic. If it is viral, we are probably too late. If it is bacterial, the next 24 hours are critical. He has a 50/50 chance of deafness, brain damage or worse. You will need to sit with him with this round stick and keep him from convulsing. Are up for it?"

I was scared skinny, but Craig came through the crisis unharmed. Two weeks later we went home, having made many new friends in the hospital and community. They gave everything to ensure the best care of our little boy. They say timing is everything. It sure was for us in Bar Harbor that summer.

July 23

Inner Cities

All cities are mad: but the madness is gallant. All cities are beautiful: but the beauty is grim.

Christopher Morley

No city should be too large for a man to walk out of in a morning.

Cyril Connolly

Cities are the abyss of the human species.

Jean-Jacques Rousseau

From the quotes about cities, one can conclude that poets didn't hold cities in very high regard. We can certainly understand that aversion in the very core of cities like London, Rome and Los Angeles. The air and din are toxic. The average life expectancy of folks who live in the inner core of big cities is over ten years less than those who live in towns or the country. Have you driven in the core of a big city lately? The traffic is terrible. Gridlock is common. In Rome, bicycles are only evident on Sunday. The problem is too many cars, all spewing toxic vapors. I have a simple plan to change the inner core of cities with one piece of legislation.

Ban the internal combustion engine from the inner core.

I can hear the uproar already. How do we get around? How do trucks make deliveries? How do you cut your grass? It's all very simple. There would be lots of bicycles and push mowers and small silent electric cars much like golf carts. There would still be public transit, but it would be electric. Buses and delivery trucks could be powered by fuel cells which produce water vapor. They are also quiet! Without the noise and exhaust of cars, trucks and buses, the health of people living and working in the city would improve dramatically. The extra cost of transit would be offset by the lower cost of health care. The greatest advantage to this model would be the transformation from a car-centered to a people-centered paradigm. The din would change from the cacophony of cars and trucks to the sounds of people enjoying themselves in a transformed atmosphere. You can make this happen by having a friendly chat with your city council members and encouraging this model. Letters to the editor and Internet blogs are also useful.

July 24

ℬingo

We love the bingo. You tell them the people on Social Security will sit at home in a rocker and die if they don't have bingo.

Barbara Thompson

I think the Irish woman was freed from slavery by bingo. They can go out now, dressed up, with their handbags and have a drink and play bingo. And they deserve it.

John B. Keane

When one old woman yells 'bingo' a whole bunch of her friends whisper 'fuck.'

George Carlin

It's amazing how much the game of bingo has changed since I was a kid. I remember my first and only game of competitive bingo. We sat at picnic tables and used hard corn kernels on actual cardboard cards. The lady beside me noticed that I had a bingo. I won a large blanket, and took it home to mother. I have never played since. I figure you may as well exit a winner at least once. Since then, the number of cards has expanded, and there are even computers which multiply the cards you play. I have seen women playing 15 cards at a time—all the while smoking, eating and carrying on a conversation. These bingo-playing pros are the ultimate multitask magicians!

Lots of funny things happen in the hall at each session, but my friend Ted had the best story, one that kept us all laughing for a very long time. When two or more people have bingos on the same number, the pot is split. One day, no fewer than 12 people yelled "bingo" for a 25 dollar pot. Ted went to pay an old regular, who looked like somebody's grandmother, her two dollar prize, and she quietly said to him, "I come in here every F—-ing day and that's my first F—-ing bingo all year... and 12 other F—-ing people have the same F—-ing bingo." Ted's jaw dropped.

A funny bingo story is the old joke about the three buddies who hear that the world is about to end. They don't know what to do, and then one of them suggests that they should pray. None of them have been to church, however, so they don't know how to pray. Then one of them says that he lives next door to a Catholic church, and he has heard them in there praying. They get on their knees and fold their hands, and this fellow reverently begins the prayer ... "Under the B ... five."

July 25

Trails

May your trails be crooked, winding, lonesome, dangerous, leading to the most amazing view. May your mountains rise into and above the clouds.

Edward Abbey

It's fun to be a little bit different in the world, to make a few new trails of your own.

Dennis Weaver

There's a long, long trail a-winding into the land of my dreams.

Stoddard King

When I was a kid, our street was sandwiched between the front woods and the back woods, and both had creeks running through them. Exploring those woods and creeks was a delightful pastime, and there were well-established paths through the woods. As we got older, it was great to leave those trails and blaze one of your own to a secret spot in the woods where nobody seemed to have been. What a feeling to imagine that nobody had ever discovered this spot in the woods.

Trails have always been important in our family. In all the camping we have done, we have tried to walk or bike the trails in the parks. Whenever we took trips, we would always stop at signs indicating there was a trail to some point of interest. Celia and I were on a trip out West and stopped at just such a sign in Wisconsin. We hiked up through dense brush to what should have been a panoramic view of the surrounding countryside. When we finally arrived at the top, there was one snag. The lookout might have been great when it was built, but over the years, thick foliage had grown all around, and the view was completely obscured. It was really a trail to nowhere, thanks to those fast-growing trees! As we trekked back down, we jokingly vowed to take a chain-saw with us on all future treks.

Trails.com is a great website with the top 100 trails in America as voted by hikers. For a yearly fee of fifty dollars, you get access to thousands of trail maps and topographical maps that you can download. For enthusiastic hikers, the site has a wealth of useful information.

Happy trails to you, until we meet again.

Dale Evans

July 26

Bears

The grizzly is a symbol of what is right with the world.

Charles Jonkel, American Bear Biologist

Is that a bear out there? If that's a bear out there ... well you better leave ... cus I've got a gun!

A fellow camper in Yosemite Park in the middle of the night as a bear wandered about the campground

Bears are made of the same dust as we, and breathe the same winds and drink of the same waters. A bear's days are warmed by the same sun, his dwellings are overdomed by the same blue sky ...

John Muir

If we can learn to live with bears ... then maybe we can also find ways to use the finite resources of our continent and still maintain some of the diversity and natural beauty that were here when Columbus arrived.

Stephen Herrero

On our 1971 trip to the national parks, we had many memorable encounters with bears. In Sequoia, the wardens warned us not to leave any food out. In the middle of one dark night, we could hear heavy breathing outside our tent-trailer, so we made sure our miniature Schnauzer, Koko, was very quiet while the bear wandered about. The next morning we awoke to find the dog missing. We looked everywhere for Koko and finally went to the ranger office to report her lost. The ranger assured us that bears are afraid of dogs and don't eat them. It seemed to us that the wee dog would make a tasty morsel for a large bear, and we kept searching with no success. We went back to the trailer to reorganize a search party, and we could just hear some muffled cries coming from one end under the trailer. We loosened the canvas and found Koko trapped between the canvas and the bottom of the bed. She must have slipped down there during the night. What a relief!

In Lake Louise, a bear walked boldly up the road at lunchtime, and Celia and her mom and dad dashed madly into the car, "Big Red", with their sandwiches. I was laughing so hard, I never made it to the car. Meanwhile, the bear spied another meal up the road; he sat in the middle of a large picnic table and ate all the goodies while the campers remained quietly in their car, watching the big black bear enjoy their lunch.

July 27

ꟿusic 3

In music one must think with the heart and feel with the brain.

George Szell

I always felt rock and roll was very, very wholesome music.

Aretha Franklin

You have to get past the idea that music has to be one thing. To be alive in America is to hear all kinds of music constantly: radio, records, churches, cats on the street, everywhere music. And with records, the whole history of music is open to everyone who wants to hear it.

Jerry Garcia

I think music in itself is healing. It's an explosive expression of humanity. It's something we are all touched by. No matter what culture we're from, everyone loves music.

Billy Joel

On a recent trip to Ireland, we discovered an unusual radio station—LYRIC Radio—playing every kind of music—well, almost every kind. Hard rock, heavy metal and rap were absent. There was an eclectic mix of classical, opera, jazz, pop and even some country and western. The announcers always had interesting things to say about each piece, and the station added greatly to the enjoyment of our motor trip by relaxing us.

I can imagine the objections to a station playing different types of music. "Can't they decide what they really like?"—"None of that stuff is my kind of music!"—"It sure isn't good car music if it doesn't shake the occupants up with a powerful, throbbing, ear-splitting beat!" No—you couldn't hear the pounding sub-woofing bass coming for blocks. All you experienced was the most delightful mix of good music you could ever wish for—if you have the ears, heart, and patience to really listen.

There's the key to the healing power of music—beautiful melodies or meaningful lyrics. There is also room for humor in music. A good chuckle produces those feel-good endorphins. You can get those chuckles from 50's rock & roll, country and western, comic operas, Broadway musicals—even some of the classics. Our Irish "Lyric Radio" played music which made us feel mellow. The next time you need a lift, put on some music with either great beauty or a sense of humor. Avoid anything which assaults your ears.

July 28

Perception

The mind is its own place and in itself can make a heaven of hell … or a hell of heaven.
John Milton

Today's quote from John Milton's *Paradise Lost* is one of my favorite quotes. The mind is where reality resides. Consider how your perception of the world is formed by the brain. Your senses receive an astonishing number of stimuli each second. Your sensory receptors convert the stimuli into electrical impulses, and transmit them to your brain, which processes them into a conscious picture of the world. This picture rapidly changes. A major league hitter has less than half a second in which to decide if a pitch is hittable. A pianist often has to read and play 64 notes in a single second. These miracles of perception require exceptional talent and years of practice. In fact, all your perceptions of the world are learned over time. We must learn how to see! To a cave-person, the core of a big city would be totally confusing. Your brain makes sense out of all the nerve impulses only when there is sufficient learning to process all the information properly.

Since each person has learned about the world from his or her perspective, each person has a unique view of the world. This view of the world is often colored by how we feel, what we expect to happen, how alert we are and especially by our previous experiences. Many people may witness the same incident yet give conflicting accounts of what occurred when questioned by the police. Court trials often leave the jurors wondering what the truth is when the memory of the events may be affected over time by the way a witness thinks. The amazing point about what is the truth is that everyone honestly believes that his or her own perception of things is the truth. We each believe in the reality of the world as we see it!

What type of world have we created for ourselves? Is our view of the world generally optimistic? Do we love and trust the people we live with? Do we believe in the fundamental goodness of human beings? Are we content and comfortable with our circumstances? Our perception is in our mind. Seeing the worst of things is a poor attitude. Good news! We can change the world simply by changing our attitude. Thank goodness that changing our mind is allowed. Heaven is reachable.

July 29

Freedom

Freedom is the open window through which pours the sunlight of the human spirit and human dignity.

Herbert Hoover

All religions, arts and sciences are branches of the same tree. All these aspirations are directed toward ennobling man's life, lifting it from the sphere of mere physical existence and leading the individual towards freedom.

Albert Einstein

Oh, say! does that star-spangled banner yet wave
O'er the land of the free and the home of the brave?

American Anthem

The True North strong and free! From far and wide, O Canada, we stand on guard for thee. God keep our land glorious and free!

Canadian Anthem

Him that I love, I wish to be free … even from me.

Anne Morrow Lindbergh

Freedom is taken for granted by people in the "free" world and longed for by people who live in oppressive regimes (or people who have been incarcerated for breaking the law.) It may surprise many North Americans to learn that freedom is denied to many people around the world. Religious persecution is more common than we care to think. Carried to extremes, persecution can result in genocide. We cringe at the memory of the mass slaughter of minorities in Africa, Serbia and Bosnia, and more recently in Chechnya. We could call this genocide an example of perverse freedom—the misconception that "free" means free to do as one pleases—quite the opposite of what "free" means. Freedom must always operate within limitations.

In the Western world, people can be slaves to traditions and to their own paradigms. I like what Anne Lindbergh implies in the quote above. I feel she means that her partner doesn't feel controlled by the ambition and action of a very strong person—namely Lindbergh herself. This may just be the reason for most divorces—the feeling of losing one's sense of freedom to a controlling partner, or in many cases, to a controlling addiction. Again, true individual freedom must always operate within limits.

July 30

Ɠaɳɗʰɪ

The future depends on what we do in the present.

You must be the change you want to see in the world.

Always aim at complete harmony of thought and word and deed. Always aim at purifying your thoughts and everything will be well.

Happiness is when what you think, what you say, and what you do are in harmony.
All from Mohandas Karamchand Gandhi (Mahatma Gandhi)

You have probably seen old advertisements for weight sets showing a man with a Herculean body kicking sand in the face of a 97 pound weakling.

Mahatma Gandhi resembled the 97 pound weakling—especially when he was on one of his fasts. Gandhi wasn't a weak man by any stretch of the imagination. He was, in fact, one of the strongest political figures of the 20th Century. He was the driving force behind India's independence as a nation.

Mohandas Karamchand Gandhi used a philosophy of non-violence to achieve his outstanding results. The name "Mahatma" was conferred on him as an honor. It means "Great Soul", and Gandhi was just that—a great spiritual leader who used pacifism to finally overcome the British colonial rule that had been dominating India since the 1800's. Gandhi was a huge thorn in the side of the great statesman Winston Churchill, and as much as we all revere Churchill as the savior of the English-speaking peoples, this is one battle the world was better off for Churchill having lost.

I love the story of Gandhi on the Indian train. You have all seen pictures of passenger trains in India, with literally thousands of Indians hanging off every square inch of the train. Apparently, Gandhi lost a sandal while hanging off one of these trains. He immediately took the other sandal off and threw it from the train. Someone asked why he had done that. Gandhi replied, "No one is going to get much use of finding one sandal!" How many of us would have the presence of mind to think of others when we ourselves had just suffered a loss?

July 31

Meditation

Half an hour's meditation each day is essential, except when you are very busy. Then a full hour is needed.

St. Francis de Sales

So I mostly only got onto real trails when we went camping. And I was always struck by the incredibly ALIVE quality of the quiet when we'd gotten away from the din of cars and campsites. Every sound that inhabited it didn't break the quiet. I haven't been anywhere with that kind of quiet in many years now, but it's in my meditation, and I float in it. There's something about pine trees, water, and a few birds, with a big blue sky overhead.

A camper commenting about the QUIET of a wilderness park

When you calm your mind and your senses, you become conscious of your always-present inner Self ... Relax your body and mind and let your Spirit soar high. Meditation is the gateway, through which you arrive to the world of freedom.

Remez Sasson

The other day we had to pick up someone at the hospital, and we were stuck sitting in the busy main waiting room for several hours. I didn't have my reading glasses, so I people-watched for an hour and then decided to close my eyes and try meditating in spite of the din. I concentrated on my breathing in and out and let myself go limp in the chair. I slipped into that gap where you are not asleep but your mind is turned off and you are suspended, aware of your surroundings but not affected by them. I could hear the din, but it was muffled and meaningless. I remained perfectly suspended and unthinking in this meditation for over an hour—awake but freely floating in the gap. That hour of meditation worked its usual miracle of making the world more meaningful and relaxed.

If you haven't tried meditating, you should Google *meditation* and follow the simple instructions. Concentrate on the slow breathing in and out. Some folks use a mantra or repeated phase. Others use a sitting yoga position while meditating. I just sit in my favorite chair. Over half the time, I fall asleep instead of into the gap. This is because I don't sleep long enough at night. When meditation is achieved, it is more valuable than sleep and leaves a feeling of calmness and clarity which can last for several days.

August 1

Quiet Reflection

Live the best possible day you can. Turn negative thoughts into positive. Forget all those past hurts, wrongs and sins. Today is a new day and a new chance to savor art and nature, human relationships and food ... as if they were all going to disappear tomorrow. Tomorrow is a desert island where today's memories are but fleeting memories. A snowflake disappears while we decide what to do with it.

From the January 1st reflection

Soon silence will have passed into legend. Man has turned his back on silence. Day after day he invents machines and devices that increase noise and distract humanity from the essence of life.

Jean Arp

Last month, we were talking about the national parks. I mentioned Yosemite, the park on the western slopes of the Sierra Nevada Mountains in California. There is a lake called Mirror Lake in which there is a spectacular stillness. The reflection is amazing. This deep quiet begs meditation, contemplation and reflection. Quiet reflection is so important to our well-being.

We began on January 1st by suggesting that a quiet reflective time at the beginning of each day would serve many purposes during the day. To live the best possible day, it is important to focus on what is beneficial and positive and to shut down the negative. Has reflecting on what is important made any difference so far this year? Are you more open-minded about the world? Are you happier and healthier? If the answer to these questions is "yes"—hooray and hallelujah! If the answer to any of these questions is "no," that's OK, but maybe we should try the following exercise over the next week.

Begin by considering the most important WORDS in your life. Two days later, write down a list of these important words. The next day, write down a list of ten. The next day, shorten the list to the five most important. Finally, put the five words in order of priority for you. In a week you have some idea of what is truly important for you personally. Consider how useful this list could be at giving you direction. (You can do this whole process in an hour if you like.)

PS   Don't be afraid to compare lists with other people.

August 2

God is a Woman

Love is patient; love is kind; love is not envious or boastful or arrogant or rude. It does not insist on its own way … It bears all things, believes all things, hopes and things, and endures all things.

1st Corinthians 13:4-8

For the aboriginal peoples of America, God was a woman. Algonquin legend says that "beneath the clouds lives the Earth-Mother from whom is derived the Water of Life, who at her bosom feeds plants, animals and men." There is archaeological evidence indicating that at one time, God was thought of as a woman. It makes sense that, since the female body is where new life develops, God must be the Great Mother who gives birth to all life in the universe. God must be the fertile spring of sexuality and creativity and should be regarded as sacred and central. There is evidence that for at least 2500 years, there were mother-centered religions in Europe, the Mediterranean, and India. These mother-worshiping cultures were stable and peaceful. Within them, women had power in government and religion. If this is true, then what happened?

Over time, men asserted their brute strength in warfare, in government and in religion. The aim of the male of the species was to use this strength to dominate. Abraham, the founder claimed by three religions, was male. All three of these religions have been dominated by men. Is it any wonder that close scrutiny of religions originating in Abraham displays sexist philosophy? When women have tried to become priests in the Catholic Church, both these woman priests and the bishops who consecrated them have been excommunicated by Rome. Men continue to exert their strength and dominate "their" religion.

It makes sense to me that God must be more female than male. Consider the statement that "God is Love" and examine the definition of "LOVE" in 1st Corinthians; these characteristics of Love are all nurturing. Make a list of all the "loving" people you know using Paul's definition found above. My list is mostly women—so for me, if God is Love, and the real Loving folks are mostly women, it simply stands to reason that God must also be a woman. Think of how much more peace there would be in this world if men would admit to this truth!

August 3

Lapses

To err is human, to forgive divine.

Alexander Pope

The essence of true friendship is to make allowance for another's little lapses.

David Storey

It is here, my daughters, that love is to be found ... not hidden away in corners but in the midst of occasions of sin. And believe me, although we may more often fail and commit small lapses, our gain will be incomparably the greater.

Saint Teresa of Avila

Have you ever noticed how some people will jump all over an unexpected lapse? A burst of temper from a normally calm soul, forgetting to acknowledge an important person or date, disagreement from someone who is always so agreeable—can all be blown out of proportion by folks who have an aversion to peccadilloes. The worst case scenario is when someone in the public eye commits the gaffe or lapse. I always feel a little sorry for politicians when the press makes the most of some error. I'm not talking here about the Nixonian "I am not a liar" or Clintonian "I did not have sex with that woman" kind of statement. These were assertions covering up huge lapses of integrity. I'm talking about slip-ups where somebody may simply fail to do what is expected of them, or someone fails to know something everyone figures they should know. Calling the Canadian head of state the "President of Canada" is a gaffe the press love to jump all over, and the peccadillo police all chime in: "How can they be so ignorant?" This is really serious stuff!

Be gentle. Be kind. Be forgiving. Be understanding. The next time someone you know and love commits an unexpected peccadillo, immediately forgive the lapse, and when things settle down talk it over—gently. It may be a simple misunderstanding or totally unintentional omission. Don't publicly jump all over a good friend for an error, but as Shakespeare and Jesus both said, "use all gently." After all, as Pope suggests, to err is human.

August 4

K.I.S.S.

To think is easy. To act is hard. But the hardest thing in the world is to act in accordance with your thinking.

Johann Wolfgang Von Goethe

Simplicity is the ultimate sophistication.

Leonardo da Vinci

Everything should be made as simple as possible, but not simpler.

Albert Einstein

Three Rules of Work: Out of clutter find simplicity; From discord find harmony; In the middle of difficulty lies opportunity.

Albert Einstein

A vocabulary of truth and simplicity will be of service throughout your life.

Winston Churchill

Simplicity is the final achievement.

Frederic Chopin

Reading the papers this morning brought home an important truth. Life seems to be too complicated at times, and it is getting more so all the time. There always seems to be some environmental disaster going on. Politicians and heads of state seem to be getting into hot water chasing after the opposite sex, or posting some outrageous statement in their blog. Normally well-behaved folks get themselves caught on video committing some nasty business. Stupidity abounds in twitters for the entire world to see. Life is sure getting complicated. Everybody seems to need a computer to tell them when and if they can scratch or even eat. What ever happened to the simple life?

We had a phrase in our department when I taught. It was: "Keep it simple stupid", or the K.I.S.S. principle. It meant that we should reduce everything down to the simplest practicable rules. We had one rule for actions in the class: "Never interfere with the right of other classmates to obtain the best possible education they deserve." We had one rule for what we expected: "Do your best!" These were easy to understand because they were simple. A long list of do's and don'ts isn't required. We have an innate sense of what we need to do to be successful. It should be a simple process. Why must we complicate things so?

August 5

Sigmund Freud

America is the most grandiose experiment the world has seen, but, I am afraid, it is not going to be a success.

Children are completely egoistic; they feel their needs intensely and strive ruthlessly to satisfy them.

Every normal person, in fact, is only normal on the average. His ego approximates to that of the psychotic in some part or other and to a greater or lesser extent.

Flowers are restful to look at. They have neither emotions nor conflicts.

Love and work ... work and love, that's all there is.

All from Sigismund Freud (May 6, 1856 – September 23, 1939)

I recall my first psychology course. There were neat words like "ego" and "super-ego" and the "id." These words were mostly inventions of the first great psychiatrist, Sigmund Freud—best known for his theories of the unconscious mind and the defense mechanism of repression, and for creating the clinical practice of psychoanalysis—dialogue between a patient and a psychoanalyst. Freud is also renowned for his redefinition of sexual desire as the primary motivational energy of human life, as well as his therapeutic techniques, including interpretation of dreams as sources of insight into unconscious desires. I especially remember Freud's three stages of childhood—the oral, anal and phallic stages. Many folks, according to Freud, would become "fixated" in one of these stages. People who love to smoke are fixated in the oral stage. Some people love "toilet" humor and have a need to work the word "toilet" into most conversations. They may be fixated in the anal stage. Obsession with sex is a fixation in the phallic stage. I wonder what you call a person who loves to smoke, tells anal jokes, and thinks of sex all the time? There are a few successful comedians who answer this description. What would Freud have labeled them?

August 6

Bear Tales

We are told the black bear is innocent, but I should not like to trust myself with him.

Samuel Johnson

When I was a kid up North, we could make really good money picking wild blueber-ries. I have to preface the incident by describing our technique. We used a bushel bas-ket as the catcher with a potato sack stapled to one side to cushion the impact of flying blueberries. Then we used our Mother's biggest sieve to hit the bushes. If it was done correctly, only the ripe blueberries came off. The down side was that it was fairly noisy. One day, I was working my way around a good size bush, and I didn't realize that a black bear was working the other side of the same bush. At one point, we came face to face, literally only a couple of feet apart. I don't know who was most startled. Luckily, we both turned around and took off like a bat out of hell. He probably had some good stories to relate to his bear buddies.

Mike Lonsdale

We were visiting some friends at their cottage up north. They informed us that a small black bear loved to wander about, so we should be on the lookout for him. I had occasion to visit the outhouse some distance behind the cottage, and I was returning through waist-high grass when a large black form suddenly jumped out of the grass at me. I almost had a heart attack but quickly realized it was only a huge, harmless dog. When I got back to the cottage and told our friend Barb, she commented, "I guess we should have told you about Zeus." Imagine naming your dog after the god of all the gods!

We were working on a construction job up north, and we lived in rail cars. The meals were prepared by a French-Canadian chef who was a short fellow with a shorter tem-per. One night there was a din outside the train cars, and we looked outside to see three large black bears going through the garbage ... and in the midst of these bears was our chef, waving a frying pan and swearing at the bears: "Maudit Tabearnac!"
The bears apparently didn't take well to the French lesson and beat a hasty retreat.

Mike Lonsdale

August 7

Driving

The one thing that unites all human beings, regardless of age, gender, religion, economic status or ethnic background, is that, deep down inside, we ALL believe that we are above average drivers.

Dave Barry

A tree never hits an automobile except in self-defense.

American Proverb

Americans are broad-minded people. They'll accept the fact that a person can be an alcoholic, a dope fiend, a wife beater, and even a newspaperman, but if a man doesn't drive, there is something wrong with him.

Art Buchwald

Never drive faster than your guardian angel can fly.

Author Unknown

Isn't it a miracle how many great drivers there are in the world? When you consider how many drivers have actually taken lessons or refresher courses, it's amazing how many good drivers there are. As Dave Barry says, "We all believe that we are above average drivers." Where are the below average drivers anyway? The roads are full of them! The next time you go for a drive, observe how many drivers appear distracted. How many tailgate, change lanes without signaling, run lights, drive aggressively or just drive without consideration for other drivers? Here's the scary fact. All these inconsiderate drivers consider themselves "above average drivers"!

Most of the drivers I know are excellent drivers. Celia is a very careful and considerate driver. Both my brothers were outstanding drivers who saved our lives several times with their remarkable skills and alertness. There is the key—alertness. To be good drivers, we must be alert to all aspects of driving and constantly hone the skills and good habits needed to properly share the road with all other vehicles. Try driving in Britain. Everything happens so fast, you will not survive unless you are a skilled driver. They drive on the "wrong" side of the road, and you have to keep saying to yourself, "Keep to the left!" All your old driving habits are changed when you drive in Europe. You cannot help but be alert!

Driving is such a great pleasure with the proper attitude and alertness. We know that many drivers act as if nobody else had any right to the road, but why let them ruin our pleasure? Avoid them—if you can.

License Plates

Vanity ... all is vanity.
Ecclesiastes

I have always liked "vanity" or personalized license plates. When they first came out, it was fun, and it still is, to try and figure out what they mean. I'm not talking about the unimaginative vanity plates with people's names on them. I'm talking about the personalized plates which have deeper meaning.

L8TR G8TR Can you figure this one out? The owner is obviously a big fan of Bill Haley and the Comets.

When they came out in Ontario, I saved my pennies and ordered two vanity plates. I gave **G CELIA** to my wife on Valentine's Day. For myself, I obtained **PAX B4U,** which is too deep for most folks. A pizza delivery man the other day said, "Peace be with you too, brother," so he obviously got it.

I know I said plates with names are unimaginative, but I thought that "G Celia" was kind of cute; if sounded out, it's "Gee Celia", which can mean a lot of things. A funny thing happened shortly after we put the plate on Celia's Accord. I was talking to a visitor from Italy, and we both admired the same Italian soprano, Cecelia Bartholdi. He had to follow our car to a party, and when we got there, he exclaimed, "You must really like Cecelia ... you put her on your license plate!"

The Ministry of Transport has now allowed eight numbers or letters on personalized plates, and for this largess, they've doubled the price. I applied to the Ministry for the plate "Psalm 100", which begins, "Make a joyful noise." Guess what? We are not allowed to put any religious stuff on our plates. So I keyed in the eight-letter word "JUBILATE", and it was accepted!

PS1   I wonder if they will ever make me give up my PAX B4U?

PS2   L8TR G8TR is probably "Later gator", which seems to mean "See You Later Alligator", from Bill Haley's song by that name.

August 9

Grass

A snake lurks in the grass.

Eclogues

The Grass is Always Greener over the Septic Tank.

Erma Bombeck

And God said, Let the earth bring forth grass, and the earth brought forth grass and the Rastafarians smoked it.

Spike Milligan

W e have a modern mindset that every house and building must be surrounded by grass. When you move into a new house with unfinished grounds, the first question you ask is, "When is my grass coming?" I cannot figure out why we are so obsessed with grass. Sure it looks decent, as long as huge amounts of labor and funds are poured into it. Grass goes brown, unless it has lots of water. A good lawn needs constant care and attention to survive. If left to itself, it soon becomes an eyesore. Why are we so in love with acres of the green stuff? Are there alternatives to pouring so much time and effort into having a weed-free green lawn?

Communities in the South where water is scarce have experimented with drought-resistant groundcovers and wildflowers. Along the sides of the road in Southern Georgia are beautiful beds of wildflowers. They require little or no maintenance and make sense in a world gone crazy with grass. Why more communities aren't catching on to this great idea is beyond me.

I watch my neighbors play the great grass game. Hire a company to put chemicals on the lawn several times each year. Pour tons of water all over the grass, sidewalks and the road at least twice each week. Get the noisy gas power mower out and cut that grass. Edge and aerate it often. The winner of the game has the perfect green lawn all summer long and everyone comments, "So-and-so has the nicest grass on the street." The kids and pets however aren't allowed on it—nor would they want to be there, when herbicides and pesticides have been poured over this lawn for years.

Does our house still have grass? Yes, but we cut our grass with a push-mower, and we seldom water. The flowerbeds have expanded so there is no grass in the backyard, and if I had my way, we would have drought-resistant ground cover and flowers in the front. I guess some people would get upset with me if I refused to play the great grass game. Who cares?

August 10

Parking

Politics ain't worrying this country one-tenth as much as where to find a parking space.

Will Rogers

One way to make sure everyone gets to work on time would be to have 95 parking spaces for every 100 employees.

Michael Iapoce

When Solomon said there was a time and a place for everything he had not encountered the problem of parking his automobile.

Bob Edwards

We have a good friend who is the luckiest person in the world when it comes to finding a parking space. It is simply amazing how often it happens. I like the joke about the old woman atheist who can't find a parking spot so she says, "Oh God ... if you will just find me a parking spot, I will even go to Church this Sunday." Just then a spot opens up, and the old gal grabs it and says, "Never mind God ... I just found one!"

The absolute best parking spot we ever got was in San Francisco at Candlestick Park. Two days before, we had parked at the Kingdome in Seattle to go to a game, and the parking was ten bucks. We parked at the Candlestick lot for five bucks, and they provided you with a grill and an electrical outlet for your tailgate party. They also allowed you to stay overnight after the game. That had to be the best parking space ever—but Candlestick Park is no longer there. Pity!

The funniest parking story I ever heard was from my friend Allan. He had driven his mother-in-law to the bank, and someone grabbed the spot in front of the bank away from Allan at the last second. Allan was so incensed by this display of rudeness that he began to have chest pains, and suspected a heart attack. He struggled into the bank and sat down. A kind customer volunteered to drive Allan to the hospital. Guess who this kindly soul turned out to be— the very person who had stolen the parking space away from Allan in the first place. It's a funny world!

August 11

A Philosophy of Living

You cannot get something for nothing.   Nothing is free in this world!

Anonymous

Most people have a philosophy of living. For some, the simple struggle for survival guides every action. Others grab everything they can while there is time. Without any guiding principles, some folks simply bounce from one situation to another, often living out comedy-tragedy every day. The reason behind this lack of direction may be the absence of a good reason to believe in a grand scheme of things. That we are part of a glorious cosmos, created and looked after by some prime mover of the universe, has been dismissed by most aimless people. Why believe in something there is no evidence for in the first place? Each religion has its own version of the initial creation of the universe. How can they all be correct? Some people use this argument to believe only in themselves and to claim a right to live life as if no one else existed in the world. This may lead to a life of selfishness in which the individual gathers as much as possible as long as they can—because if they don't "look out for number one," somebody else will.

There is a better way. We only need to examine nature to understand that everything new comes from something old. All organisms are built from the remains of previous organisms. The life force is passed on through reproduction. Energy to run the whole system is provided by the sun and is incorporated into all living organisms by the action of chlorophyll in green plant cells. Nature recycles everything over and over. Everything comes from something, and everything is interconnected in ingenious ways. All scientists and artists have marveled at the way everything interacts in nature and how life is continuously reborn from previous life. All students of nature eventually realize that the universe is no accident. This all-embracing design is an exquisite miracle accomplished by the prime mover of the universe. Does it matter who or what did this? Need we argue how or why he or she did it? Was it a he or a she? Who cares? It is done, and done well. Let us enjoy the miracle and help others to enjoy it as well. Each person on this planet has the right to enjoy this wonder we call home. Whatever your philosophy of living, it should never interfere with every other human's right to enjoy the marvel of creation.

August 12

Big Red

Any man who can drive safely while kissing a pretty girl is simply not giving the kiss the attention it deserves.

Albert Einstein

When buying a used car, punch the buttons on the radio. If all the stations are rock and roll, there's a good chance the transmission is shot.

Larry Lujack

There ain't nothin' like the sound of a well-tuned Mustang V-8 thundering along the highway.

Carroll Shelby

The first new car we bought together after we were married was a candy-apple red 1968 Ford Galaxie 500, a two door hardtop with a vinyl roof, vinyl seats and an acre of glass for a rear window. It had a "Thunderbird 302," a V-8 engine with a throaty sound and a thirst for cheap gas and highways. You could roll all the windows down and bomb along at ridiculous speeds. It would pull our tent trailers so well, you would forget the trailer was tagging along behind.

So there we were, crossing the desert in Arizona in July of 1971, pulling our Nimrod hardtop trailer. It was 110 degrees in the shade. We had all the windows rolled down. There was little traffic on this two-lane road. I was passing some lady in an Olds convertible. She didn't take kindly to being passed by "Big Red" and she sped up. It didn't matter how fast I went, she matched my speed. I put the pedal to the metal. We were bombing along over eighty, neck and neck, when up the highway a cow decided to cross the road without looking. At the speed we were going, that cow was approaching fast! I guess we both saw the cow at the same time, because we simultaneously slammed on the brakes and screeched to a stop just short of the cow, who stopped in the middle of the road and looked at us as if we were nuts. Then the cow ambled off, leaving us sitting there feeling foolish.

That silly episode ended my career as a street racer, and it's a good thing. I learned later that if you hit livestock on the free range in Arizona, it's your responsibility to pay the rancher for the loss. That cow must have known that fact before crossing the road!

August 13

Carl Jung

A ll the following quotes are from that second great "rat-man" (psychologist) *Carl Gustav Jung*, 1875 – 1961. They are so memorable, each quote deserves a sentence or two.

But what if I should discover that the enemy himself is within me, that I myself am the enemy that must be loved ... what then?
As Pogo said, "We have seen the enemy and he is us." Yes, we are often our own worst enemy, as folks are fond of saying. So let's forgive ourselves and laugh at ourselves, and get on with it.

The shoe that fits one person pinches another; there is no recipe for living that fits all cases.
The French have the expression, "Chacun a son goût!" Everyone has their own taste. We must learn is that it is alright to be different! We need to celebrate differences.

A man who has not passed through the inferno of his passions has never overcome them.
By all means be passionate. Life without passion isn't worth living. We must feel life passionately to experience living life to its fullest—yet at all times be in control of our passions and not a victim of them.

Every form of addiction is bad, no matter whether the narcotic be alcohol or morphine or idealism.
Are we in control, or is some addiction in control? You can add gambling to the above list.

Man needs difficulties; they are necessary for health.
We all have our crosses to bear. I love the story of the man who asked God to relieve him of his cross. God told him there was a special room where he could trade his cross with somebody else. The guy went to this special room and looked around at the other crosses. His cross was smaller than all the others, so he stopped complaining and bore his cross from then on with grace.

226

August 14

Sacrifice

Human progress is neither automatic nor inevitable ... Every step toward the goal of justice requires sacrifice, suffering, and struggle; the tireless exertions and passionate concern of dedicated individuals.

Dr. Martin Luther King Jr.

My major problem with the world is a problem of scarcity in the midst of plenty ... of people starving while there are unused resources ... people having skills which are not being used.

Milton Friedman

A team will always appreciate a great individual if he's willing to sacrifice for the group.

Kareem Abdul-Jabbar

A man who was completely innocent, offered himself as a sacrifice for the good of others, including his enemies, and became the ransom of the world. It was a perfect act.

Mohandas Gandhi

I am constantly amazed and envious of folks who travel to some country to do some good. When I was a kid, I remember mother telling us about the most wonderful man in the world, Albert Schweitzer. This man made the great sacrifice of running a hospital in the middle of Africa. I wanted to be a missionary and go to such a place and help people out. As it eventually developed, I became a teacher instead, and the sacrifices were of a different sort.

In the Old Testament, the word sacrifice usually meant the offering of an animal on an altar. As religions developed, most involved sacrifices of something valuable. Somebody would end up in need because of the sacrifices required. In today's world, this type of behavior would be considered as cruel and unjust and simply wouldn't be tolerated. People do still sacrifice, but it has become much more civilized. Rather than burn something up, modern folks give up their valuable time or resources. Most people seem to be quite pleased to work hard or to donate for a worthy cause. Doesn't it make more sense to end up with something that could make a definite difference—rather than a small mound of ashes?

August 15

Achievement

Great spirits have always encountered violent opposition from mediocre minds.
Albert Einstein

My subject enlarges itself, becomes methodized and defined, and the whole, though it be long, stands almost complete and finished in my mind, so that I can survey it, like a fine picture or a beautiful statue, at a glance. Nor do I hear in my imagination the parts successively, but I hear them, as it were, all at once. What a delight this is! All this inventing, this producing, takes place in a pleasing, lively dream.
Wolfgang Amadeus Mozart

Sweet Swan of Avon! He was not of an age, but for all time!
Ben Jonson

As a well spent day brings happy sleep, so life well used brings happy death.
Leonardo da Vinci

The Olympic Games put many memorable names on the tip of everyone's tongue. Will their achievements still be on the minds of folks in a hundred years? Who are the greatest achievers throughout history who will still be on our minds? Who would get gold, silver and bronze medals for the greatest lasting achievements of all time? Everyone will have a different list. Here is mine.

For lasting achievement:

GOLD: Wolfgang Amadeus Mozart

SILVER: a tie!!!   Isaac Newton and Albert Einstein

BRONZE: a tie!!!   William Shakespeare and Leonardo da Vinci

I know you question a list with no kings, queens, emperors or any political folks. So go ahead—select your own! Does your list say anything about you?

August 16

Railroads

The introduction of so powerful an agent as steam to a carriage on wheels will make a great change in the situation of man.

Thomas Jefferson

Rail travel at high speeds is not possible because passengers, unable to breathe, would die of asphyxia.

Dionysius Lardner (1842 - 1914)
US journalist, short-story writer

When I was a kid, the railroad main line ran through the front field, about a two-minute run from the house. We crossed the tracks to get to school, and we crossed at illegal places most of the time. I was fascinated by the huge steam engines. There was a grade going up from the rail yards, and the drive wheels of the locomotive would slip and do several quick turns as the steam puffed out quickly—a staccato chuff-chuff-chuff until the drive wheels gripped the track again. It was a neat thing to hear.

My mother hated the steam engines for a number of reasons. On Monday, washday, mother no sooner got her washing hung on the line when a double-header (two engines) would chuff-chuff-chuff out of the rail yard. If the wind was blowing in our direction, mom's washing would be covered with soot and have to be washed again. We loved double-headers because the first kid to see the two engines would punch the other kids and say, "Double-header ... no punch back!" This invariably started a row which mother had to break up. We also got into trouble with the railroad cops, and they visited our house several times. Mother would see them coming and say, "What have you boys done now? If it's what I think ... I'm leaving home." I remember once when we had unhitched several train cars, mom actually left, but she just stopped down the street for the after-noon at a neighbor's—and she came back in time to get supper.

Two drunks were walking upgrade between some railroad tracks. One of them said, "This is the longest stairway I have ever been on."

The other drunk replied, "It's not the stairs that bother me, it's the low banister."

229

Tolerant

The capacity for getting along with our neighbor depends to a large extent on the capacity for getting along with ourselves. The self-respecting individual will try to be as tolerant of his neighbor's shortcomings as he is of his own.

Eric Hoffer

How tolerant are we? When I read some e-mails being passed along on the internet, it would appear that tolerance went out the window when the war on terror expanded to include anyone daring to wear any type of head-dress. These e-mails do irreparable harm to the attitude of open-mindedness being nurtured in the school system. The last two schools I taught in were multicultural environments and were all the better for reflecting a variety of races and cultures from all parts of the world. Most of the students are the most racially unprejudiced generation our schools have ever seen. Generally, these young people believe racism is wrong. As a school staff, we had many strategies for maintaining an environment that encouraged and celebrated multiculturalism and acceptance of differences. These strategies are not all that different from those we can all use every day to practice tolerance of different folks. The rule is simple. Never stereotype! People are all different and will often surprise us. Give everyone the same opportunity to be successful, and be prepared for a surprise. If you already have the limitations in your mind, you anticipate disappointment before even offering a chance. That's why we always gave students the opportunity to fail. Surprise! Very few fail! Most, given equal opportunity, exceed your expectations—as long as they are realistic.

One really important learning feature of multiculturalism is the heterogeneous approach to questions and problems which can occur when the thinking is so different. When Gandhi was in London as a young man, he met Muslims, Christians and Jews in the groups he joined. He was wise enough to take the best features of each of these religions, and they served him well in his efforts to free India of colonial rule. When asked what he was, he would say mainly Hindu, but part of each of the other religions. Maybe that's what we should aim for—to adopt the best features of other cultures into our own thinking. In that way, we may truly become globally-minded people.

August 18

License Plates 2

The destiny of the world is determined less by the battles that are lost and won than by the stories it loves and believes in.

Harold Goddard

If you don't know the trees you may be lost in the forest, but if you don't know the stories you may be lost in life.

Siberian Elder

Life itself is the most wonderful fairytale of all.

Hans Christian Andersen

You may recall the personalized plate story about **PAX B4U** and **G CELIA**. (August 8 reflection) While I was ordering those plates, the gentleman at the licensing office noticed that we had three cars. He told me, "There's a really good plate coming up in a month or so, and for ten bucks I can get you a neat plate to replace the old one on your van." I said I was interested; so he told me that he would phone on the day **YOO** came up, and I would have to "get my ass" down to the office in a hurry to get the plate. Sure enough, a few weeks later he phoned, and away I went. The gentleman asked me what number I would like, and I asked him what he would suggest. "You should get the number 008," he said. "It's a favorite lucky number of Chinese folks and, along with the YOO, should look pretty good." So I paid the ten bucks and got the license plate **008 YOO**, which is easy to remember and has a nice symmetry to it.

I didn't think much more about the plate until I was filling up with gas one evening and a car full of young people said to me, "Hey mister ... where did you get the funny plate?" Then somebody at church asked me how I could drive around with such a plate. I was dumbfounded. When our son was visiting, he explained the mystery to me. "Didn't you realize that the license says, *Who ate you?*"

The man at the license bureau must still be laughing about that one.

August 19

Busy

Work expands so as to fill the time available for its completion. General recognition of this fact is shown in the proverbial phrase, "It is the busiest man who has time to spare. "

C. Northcote Parkinson

I like to work at nothing all day.

From "Taking Care of Business" by BTO

If you want to get something done, ask a busy person.

Anon

As a retired person, you find yourself as busy, or busier, than when you were employed. You just don't get paid for this busyness. Another huge difference involves choice. You can choose what you want to do—you are the boss of your retirement. The best aspect of retirement is simply this. If you don't get something done today, there's always tomorrow.

I have some friends who are always busy. If you ask the fatal question, "How are you?" the answer is always, "You would not believe how busy I am!" There was a time—about thirty years ago—when I had a full timetable—a full-time job, a family to raise, a church choir to direct, several charities to assist as a board member—etc., etc., etc. I would get up very early and go for a run or play early bird racquetball. Every evening was taken up with an activity. I rarely watched TV or had any down time. I was fortunate to feel a tremendous energy level and be surrounded by excellent family, friends and co-workers with the same energy and creativity. At school and at church we planned and put on musical shows. I also coached football in the winter and baseball during the summer. All these activities resulted in great satisfaction because the people involved had terrific talent and energy. It felt as if you could constantly feed off their energy. It never felt as if you didn't have enough time to accomplish everything. I used to tell folks, "We all have the same amount of time … 24 hours in a day!"

If you find yourself breathless from being busy, there is an easy remedy. Take some breaks and do nothing. Relax. Meditate. Catnap. Empty your mind.

You will return refreshed and reinvigorated to your tasks. Make your list and check it off—but reward yourself for its completion. Rewards and short rests are the key to accomplishing so much.

PS   Never let people know that you are busy. They feel the same way!

August 20

Comeback

Comeback is a good word, man.

Mickey Rourke

There's nothing as exciting as a comeback ... seeing someone with dreams, watching them fail, and then getting a second chance.

Rachel Griffiths

Even though large tracts of Europe and many old and famous States have fallen ... we shall not flag or fail ... we shall defend our island, whatever the cost may be. We shall fight on the beaches, we shall fight on the landing grounds, we shall fight in the fields and in the streets, we shall fight in the hills; we shall never surrender ...

Winston Churchill

Have you been in situations where the outcome seems obvious and inevitable? We prepare for the worst—like the children of Israel on the shore of the Red Sea—or the British expeditionary force at Dunkirk with the German army on their heels. All seems lost—and then—a miracle. The seas parted to allow the Israelites to escape. The British forces were evacuated by a huge flotilla of small boats which had crossed the channel from England. These wondrous rescues remind us that there is always hope. As Yogi Berra said "It ain't over until it's over."

Sports teams know the meaning of comeback. In the AFC wildcard game in 1992, the Buffalo Bills were down to the Houston Oilers by a score of 35-3. We were in a sports bar watching the Oilers pile up the touchdowns. I kept telling everyone "The Bills are going to make a huge comeback!" Hoots of derision came my way. Then it happened. Frank Reich, the reserve quarterback wouldn't give up. He drove the Bills to a tie in regulation time and they won in overtime to complete the greatest comeback in NFL history.

Speaking of comebacks, here's one of the best comebacks ever.

Nancy Astor: "If you were my husband, Winston, I should flavor your coffee with poison."
Winston Churchill: "If I were your husband, madam, I should drink it."

233

August 21

Gardens

The best place to seek God is in a garden. You can dig for him there.
George Bernard Shaw

A garden is evidence of faith. It links us with all the misty figures of the past who also planted and were nourished by the fruits of their planting.
Gladys Taber

The greatest gift of the garden is the restoration of the five senses.
Hanna Rion

God Almighty first planted a garden. And indeed it is the purest of human pleasures.
Francis Bacon

A good garden may have some weeds.

Thomas Fuller

One of the first books I remember was *The Tale of Peter Rabbit*. It was one of several Beatrix Potter books about rabbit adventures in the garden of Mr. McGregor. In her children's books, Potter extolled and power-fully illustrated the lush beauty of gardens.

Eddie Gay, our next-door neighbor when I was a little kid, had a delightful English garden with huge hollyhocks. I would have loved to pick them except for Barney, Eddie's vicious German shepherd, who patrolled the garden look-ing for little kids to eat. The beauty of gardens must have been lost on both Barney and Mr. McGregor, as they had nasty dispositions.

Sitting in a garden surrounded by a rainbow of sights and smells is simply delightful. All vacations are so much better when gardens are included. How can you remain unmoved by nature with such a sensuous smorgasbord?

One of my favorite gardens is the prayer garden at our church. Our friend, Marie Decker, designed and built the cross-shaped garden. It has several benches and a statue of Saint Fiacre, the patron saint of gardeners. I enjoy rid-ing my bike over and sitting quietly in the spiritual atmosphere while going over the prayer list.

Today is the feast of St. Fiacre. Drink a toast to the gardener's patron.

August 22

Fast Eddy

A lot of people my age are so hyper. I like hyper people.

Edward Furlong

I was a hyper kid in school and the teacher suggested to my mom she needed to do something with me.

Devon Sawa

The trouble with talking too fast is you may say something you haven't thought of yet.

Ann Landers

The last time I was in the hospital for a hip replacement, there was a very sad case in the bed beside me. The gentleman had broken his hip for the second time. He also had a series of strokes beginning when he was 52; and now at 72, he couldn't communicate what he wanted. His wonderful family visited every day, and I learned from them the sad story of this marvelous man. He had been a very successful internist in Saudi Arabia before immigrating. It was here that the series of strokes forced him to retire. His eldest son, Eddy, showed up early every morning and bounced in to reassure his father that things would be OK. Eddy often returned with his kids later in the day to love grandpa up.

Eddy was full of energy and as speedy as "Speedy Gonzales" in the Looney Tunes cartoon—the mouse who can travel at close to the speed of light and steal cheese from under the cat's nose, all the while yelling, "Ándale! ¡Ándale! ¡Arriba! ¡Arriba!" Not only did Eddy move quickly, he talked even faster, getting the most words out per unit of time of anyone I ever met. His mother said to me: "Yes ... Eddy is a wee bit hyper." That's an understatement. Don't get me wrong. I'm not complaining about Eddy. I have nothing but admiration for people with his energy. How people like Eddy can cram so much into an hour is simply amazing. Before he would leave, he would always offer to refill my water jug, and he would be back with my ice water in about 30 seconds. When I got mobile, I went to fill my own jug and discovered the ice water machine was around the block. How Eddy ever did it so fast is a mystery! Don't you just love folks who can operate at such a high level of energy?

Goldwyn

Anyone who goes to a psychiatrist ought to have his head examined.
I read part of it all the way through.
Flashbacks are a thing of the past.
If I look confused it's because I'm thinking.
Our comedies are not to be laughed at.

These "Goldisms" are all from Samuel Goldwyn, 1882 – 1974

In casual conversation, people say very funny things. Sometimes the funniest things are said by people whose language skills are poor, or even by people whose second language is English. The hilarious expressions of Yogi Berra are a prime example. (March 18) All the funny quotes today are from Shmuel Gelbfisz. While he was living with relatives in England, they Anglicized his name to Samuel Goldfish. He begged enough money for steerage across the Atlantic and eventually ended up in Gloversville, New York, the leather glove capital of the U.S.A. He became a very successful glove salesman. After moving to Manhattan and marrying the sister of Jesse L. Lasky, Goldfish convinced Lasky and Cecil B. DeMille to go into film production. The company later became the nucleus of what would develop into Paramount Pictures. His next enterprise was the Goldwyn Company, whose stars included Mabel Normand, Madge Kennedy and Will Rogers; but its most famous legacy was its "Leo the Lion" trademark, which was adopted by its successor company, Metro-Goldwyn-Mayer (MGM). Goldwyn himself was ousted from his own company before the merger. His name became part of MGM even though Goldwyn never worked a day for the company. After his firing, Goldwyn went into independent production, and for 35 years was the boss of his own production company, a mini-studio specializing in expensive "quality" films, distributed initially by United Artists and later by RKO.

Trivia: Samuel was known as a grouchy and selfish boss, and many of his biographies claim his "Goldisms" slipped out and were not even understood by Goldwyn himself. When he changed his name, he combined the first syllable of "Goldfish" with the last syllable of "Selwyn". He originally wanted to do the opposite, until someone pointed out that it would result in his new name being "Selfish".

August 24

Smartest Animal

Amongst the minds of animals that of man leads, not as a demigod from another planet, but as a king from the same race.

Human folk are as a matter of fact eager to find intelligence in animals.

Edward Thorndike

The animals were arguing about who was the smartest animal. As you can imagine, the arguments were full of nasty back-biting and rhetoric only a bunch of animals can do to claim the canny crown.

All the dogs yelped in unison that since dogs had achieved the epithet of "Man's Best Friend," the dog was surely the most intelligent. Dog shows and doggy tricks just added to the canine claim. The cats sent up a mighty meow that the dumb dogs were controlled by their masters, but cats were so clever that humans ended up being the cat's servants. Parrots and other tropical birds talked a blue streak about how the smartest title should be theirs as they could be taught language. Porpoises and chimpanzees both said that as they were the only animals to have a self-image, a definite sign of higher intelligence, there was simply no argument—they should wear the cleverness crown.

Then the pigs applied but were laughed to scorn. The pigs squealed that not only were they the brightest, they were honored by humans as the most valuable of animals. More laughter—so the pigs went on strike. No more tasty chops, ribs or bacon were forthcoming, causing the farmer to demand, "What the hell is going on?"—so they told him.

"You silly bunch," said the farmer. "You are all wrong because you have forgotten one simple thing!"

"What's that?" all the animals wailed and whined.

"You've all forgotten the most basic zoological fact—that humans are also animals! So we humans are the definitely the smartest. And now—who would like to share in a lovely cooked ham to celebrate that fact?"

August 25

Mozart

Neither a lofty degree of intelligence nor imagination nor both together go to the making of genius. Love, love, love, that is the soul of genius.

I thank my God for graciously granting me the opportunity of learning that death is the key which unlocks the door to our true happiness.

My subject enlarges itself, becomes methodized and defined, and the whole, though it be long, stands almost complete and finished in my mind, so that I can survey it, like a fine picture or a beautiful statute, at a glance.

All from Wolfgang Amadeus Mozart (1756-1791)

Music is the universal language. People all over the world can rejoice in a "catchy" tune. Most of the most elegantly catchy melodies or "tunes" ever written were written by Mozart. There is only so much you can do with the eight notes of the scale—and Mozart managed, in his short life of 35 years, to make the most of those eight notes. All composers following Bach and Mozart simply borrowed from the unbelievable amount of music these two Germanic composers wrote. Still, neither of these is my favorite. The master, Ludwig van Beethoven, is my favorite composer because of the power, glory and struggle found in his music. There is also a depth of emotion in Beethoven's music which shakes me to my very soul. I can however trace the origins of many of Ludwig's melodies back to Bach and Mozart. Without them, Beethoven's work would never have reached that power and glory. He was able to build on their work, but mainly the work of Mozart.

So if I like Beethoven more, why did I select Mozart's as the greatest lasting achievement? The answer is simply the output. In his 35 productive years Mozart composed 41 symphonies, 10 operas and 27 quality piano concertos, to list a few. His 27 piano concertos, each one a gem, equal the output of all the romantic composers who came after him. His operas continue to be the most performed and popular in the world. His compositions contained NO corrections. They flowed completely composed onto the paper.

Psychologists have shown that playing Mozart for youngsters will definitely increase their I.Q. at least 10 points. Good news! It's never too late to begin.

August 26

Clothes

*I thought I would dress in baggy pants, big shoes, a cane and a derby hat.
... Everything a contradiction: the pants baggy, the coat tight, the hat small and the shoes large.*

Charlie Chaplin

It is an interesting question how far men would retain their relative rank if they were divested of their clothes.

Henry David Thoreau

Do not trouble yourself much to get new things, whether clothes or friends. ... Sell your clothes and keep your thoughts.

Henry David Thoreau

Distrust any enterprise that requires new clothes.

Henry David Thoreau

I sometimes wonder how weddings, business meetings, galas, and awards ceremonies would go if everyone were required to attend in the nude. It's an academic question, but interesting nonetheless. We are so wrapped up in what people wear, that we risk focusing solely on fashion. The red carpet, rolled up to the venue for the Academy Awards, is one of the most watched hours in America. What each star is wearing is analyzed at great length by the commentators, who pass or fail our Academy actors on the basis of their wardrobe. What nonsense! Why do we get sucked in by this annual parade of overblown, overhyped style? Why do we equate the worth of the person with the clothes they are wearing?

I like the way teams operate, with everyone wearing the same uniform. This uniformity not only works in sports teams but in restaurants and many businesses. Our dental office has a team atmosphere due in part to the same dress worn by everyone in the office.

I love to don the robes to take part in a choral offering. When we all dress in the uniform, we are all a part of the team—unlike our individualistic celebrities who seem to relish the one-upmanship of every awards presentation.

August 27

The Great Barnyard Olympics

Pigs are ... smart, strange little creatures. They just need love.

Shelley Duvall

During the Olympics, the farm animals went largely ignored thanks to the farmer, his family and the hired hands spending so much time glued to their TV sets watching all the sportscasts from some far-off foreign land. With all the farm palaver about the games, the animals were able to absorb enough information about events to figure out a way to get more attention and perhaps more good grub from their keepers. They decided to organize their own games with races around the barn, jumping over stiles, mud-hole diving, and the usual team sports like paw-soccer and barnyard nose-ball. Many of their events stressed endurance such as marathon jumping on-the-spot. They held lots of preliminary contests when their keepers weren't watching. It soon became evident there would be one big winner and one big loser for the games the animals decided would be held for the first time the following year. The dogs dominated most events because they had better skills, sleeping quarters and the unfair attention of all the keepers. Cats on the other hand couldn't care less about wasting their energy for some small reward nobody would remember. All the other animals busted their duffs in vain trying to catch up to the dogs. It soon became clear, however, that the dogs would indeed dominate the first animal games.

Then a strange thing happened. One group of smarter animals got organized on the sly and began to train all their youngsters every day in the fine art of teamwork and endurance. They managed to make the training so much fun that all their young improved in quantum leaps.

When the great event arrived, the farmer, family and farm-hands were invited out to watch The Great Barnyard Olympics, and it was indeed a happy surprise and delight. The horses put on a magnificent show of jumping. The donkeys dominated backward kick-ass-kicking. The dogs, of course, won all the events demanding balance. The biggest surprise, however, came in all the team events and endurance contests. The most svelte, tough, and team-minded piggies prevailed, and were rewarded with extra slop for weeks after. Now we all know that getting everyone involved and having fun are the biggest pay-offs—but the cats still couldn't give a damn!

August 28

Energy 2

The energy of the mind is the essence of life.

Aristotle

Feeling sorry for yourself, and your present condition, is not only a waste of energy but the worst habit you could possibly have.

Dale Carnegie

Most people spend more time and energy going around problems than in trying to solve them.

Henry Ford

Passion is energy. Feel the power that comes from focusing on what excites you.

Oprah Winfrey

I know people who drag themselves around and use the word "tired" in any conversation. When somebody is weary all the time, we look for a physical reason. Is their blood sugar low? Do they have a condition such as hypothyroid? Is there some deeper cause of the fatigue? If none of these is the case, and the lassitude remains, what is the cause? I used to have students who were filled with weariness. Some of these same students showed a remarkable recovery when they were interested in something. Like many things, drowsiness is often a state of our mind. If we think we are tired, then we surely will be.

I always get a laugh at folks who fall asleep watching TV and then have trouble sleeping later. Sound familiar? We have all done it. Why do we do it?

When we sit there in the easy chair, our blood moves around slower and delivers less energy to all our cells. If we are inactive, our brain figures we would be better off sleeping so off we go to la-la land. It happens to me at concerts or plays. I can sleep through the loudest passages—no problem. Well, actually—there is one risk—I may wake suddenly, having committed an embarrassing social error. I recall a Mahler symphony in which I awoke with a loud snort. I swear the conductor cast a nasty glance in my direction.

The lesson to all of this is in the Oprah quote. If you are bored or inactive, there is no passion to keep you awake. You need to become excited about everything to remain charged up with energy. Again, it's our attitude which determines our state of tiredness or energy. Think energy—and you will be energetic!

August 29

Committee

A committee grows organically, flourishes and blossoms, sunlit on top and shady beneath, until it dies, scattering the seeds from which other committees will spring.

C. Northcote Parkinson

If you want to kill any idea in the world, get a committee working on it.

Charles F. Kettering

A committee is a group that keeps minutes and loses hours.

Milton Berle

Of all possible committee reactions to any given agenda item, the reaction that will occur is the one which will liberate the greatest amount of hot air.

Thomas L. Martin

I have been on hundreds of committees in my life. Some of them were eminently useful. Others were seriously devoid of use—other than to lose hours as Milton Berle suggests. The difference between the two poles depends on the folks making up the committee. If people bring their own agendas and lobby for their agenda only, the committee may go nowhere fast. You need to have a group of people willing to listen to others but also willing to add something to the mix. The ideal participant is one who espouses all the important "C" words:

Convivial & Congenial: A good sense of humor keeps the endorphins flowing and invites contribution, but a deadly serious atmosphere has a stifling effect;

Contributes & Communicates: Everyone should be made to feel they have something to add, and the chair should always be able to summarize and communicate what has been said at any point;

Cooperates & Collaborates: A team feeling should permeate. One overpowering or controlling personality is toxic to the team process.

If the chair is capable of getting all these "C" words going, committees can produce highly effective results.

August 30

The Bathroom

Oh dear, what can the matter be? Three old ladies locked in the Laverty ...
They have been there Monday to Saturday ... nobody seems to care!

Old Song

You know an odd feeling? Sitting on the toilet eating a chocolate candy bar.

George Carlin

My kids always perceived the bathroom as a place where you wait it out until all the groceries are unloaded from the car.

Erma Bombeck

So there we were stripping wallpaper off the bathroom walls. I was standing in the tub scraping old tiles off when suddenly, Celia said with a funny little grin, "Do you know what today is?"—and that's how we spent our 25th anniversary—in the bathroom!

We weren't the first members of the family to spend time in the bathroom. Celia's aunt Viola decided to paint the toilet seat, which she did—and then she forgot about it. When nature suddenly called, Vi hurried to the bathroom and sat down on her newly painted toilet seat—and there she remained—stuck fast. I don't recall exactly how Vi was rescued from that nasty position, but we all laugh every time the story is told.

What is it about bathroom or toilet humor that makes us laugh so hard? Some people just love anal jokes. Many of Jim Carrey's early movies featured some very boring toilet humor. The real truth is much funnier.

Celia had a principal who loved to tell toilet stories. He must have been fixated in the anal stage, because he worked the word "toilet" into every conversation. He even called me "Loo" instead of Lee. The word "loo" is a good old English word for bathroom. Speaking of meanings—did you know that the toilet was an invention of one Thomas Crapper? So the word "crapper" is a historically proper word to use for the toilet. Go and have a sit for a bit—and reflect on that outstanding fact.

PS Perhaps this book ends up as a permanent fixture in your bathroom library. Oh well—each 6th day story should be of a proper length for an outstanding constitutional.

August 31

Jackie Robinson

I'm not concerned with your liking or disliking me... all I ask is that you respect me as a human being.

Jackie Robinson

"In 1947, Roosevelt 'Jackie' Robinson became the first African-American major league baseball player of the modern era. His Major League debut with the Brooklyn Dodgers ended baseball segregation, also known as the color barrier. In the United States at this time, many white people believed that blacks and whites should be segregated or kept apart in many phases of life, including sports. In the late 1940s, Branch Rickey was club president and general manager of the Brooklyn Dodgers. Rickey selected Robinson from a list of promising African-American players. In 1946, the Dodgers assigned Jackie to the Montreal Royals. Jackie proceeded to lead the International League in batting average with a .349 average, and fielding percentage with a .985 percentage. Although the season was emotionally arduous for Robinson with the racist abuse he faced during the team's away games, he also deeply appreciated the enthusiastic support by the Montreal fans that followed his performance with intense interest. Because of Jackie's play in 1946, the Dodgers called him up to play for the major league club in 1947. Robinson became the first player in fifty-seven years to break the Baseball color line. Rickey reminded Robinson that he would face tremendous racial animus, and insisted that he not take the bait and react angrily. Robinson was aghast: "Do you want a player afraid to fight back?" Rickey replied that he needed a Negro player 'with the guts not to fight back.' Robinson agreed to abide by Rickey's terms for his first year."

The above paragraph is a condensation of a small section of the entry in Wikipedia for Jackie Robinson. Would we be able to endure taunts and "bite our tongue" as Jackie gamely did? He was a great baseball player, but a greater man; and thanks to his endurance and "guts," the game of baseball is now a true showcase of talent. Jackie died at the age of 53 from the complications of diabetes. His number 42 was retired from all of baseball in 1997 but was grandfathered for players wearing the number. The last player currently wearing the number is New York Yankees closer Mariano Rivera.

September 1

Labor Day

Without labor, nothing prospers.

Sophocles

The man who doesn't relax and hoot a few hoots voluntarily, now and then, is in great danger of hooting hoots and standing on his head for the edification of the pathologist and trained nurse, a little later on.

Elbert Hubbard

A mind always employed is always happy. This is the true secret, the grand recipe, for felicity.

Thomas Jefferson

Labor Day is a glorious holiday because your child will be going back to school the next day. It would have been called Independence Day, but that name was already taken.

Bill Dodds

Labor Day weekend had several significant meanings for those of us who taught. It was the last big fling before you needed to get serious again. Most of us had already been going in to school to get ready, because this weekend you had to "relax and hoot a few hoots" as Elbert suggests. The BBQ would get a good workout, and there were lots of games to play and attend. The greatest game was always the preseason Buffalo Bills at Orchard Park. The weekend parties were all just a giant tailgate party in preparation for this game. If you couldn't get tickets to this bash, you would have some friends into your house to cheer on the big boys. There is something about the game of football which reflects labor better than any other game. When those 300-pound behemoth linemen face off and bash away at each other over and over again, that is real sweaty toil. Sure the apparent heroes are the fleet backs and receivers but the game is won, as they say, in the trenches—by the big bash boys.

That is what real honest labor is all about—grunting and sweating and suffering a little pain now and then for your effort. Anyone who hasn't been a laboring grunt hasn't really lived life!

September 2

First Day

All glory comes from daring to begin.

Eugene F. Ware

All great deeds and all great thoughts have a ridiculous beginning. Great works are often born on a street corner or in a restaurant's revolving door.

Albert Camus

Be willing to be a beginner every single morning.

Meister Eckhart

The beginnings and endings of all undertakings are untidy.

John Galsworthy

Do you remember your first day of school? What was it like? How did you feel? Maybe yours is lost in a pothole down memory lane. I remember my first day. Mother walked me to school. Boys and girls had to line up at different doors. The whole experience didn't leave me with a pleasant impression. I got the strap several times. I was first to sit down in spelling bees. I felt the lady teachers there favored the girls. I failed grade two, but thank goodness, they promoted me to a new School.

The first day in this new school, a smiley lady began to read a story. I love stories, so I was really into this story when the most dreadful thing occurred. The principal showed up at our classroom door. I was somehow in the wrong class, and he took me out in the middle of that story to go to a class where we were made to work quietly. I never did find out what the story was. We were kept very busy in this new class. It was a new beginning; it took me a while to shine there, but eventually I did.

All new beginnings can be traumatic. I figure that the best beginnings are ones where we have a friendly face to encourage us. To be completely alone and face the unknown is so frightening. A little TLC goes a long way to a beginner. The extending of a helping hand is often the difference between failure and success. Remember that any time you are there at the beginning of something new.

PS Both school buildings have long disappeared—but not the memories—not too many potholes yet down memory lane.

September 3

Getting Lost

We are poor little lambs who have lost our way. Baa! Baa! Baa!
"The Wiffenpoof Song"   lyrics by Meade Minnigerode

Man is lost and is wandering in a jungle where real values have no meaning. Real values can have meaning to man only when he steps on to the spiritual path, a path where negative emotions have no use.

Sai Baba

If you have built castles in the air, your work need not be lost; that is where they should be. Now put the foundations under them.

Henry David Thoreau

Not until we are lost do we begin to understand ourselves.

Henry David Thoreau

Have you ever had that terrible feeling that you are completely lost? I remember being lost in the woods as a kid and wandering around until a familiar landmark suddenly appeared. What a relief that was. I remember *The Adventures of Tom Sawyer* where Tom and Becky are lost in the cave. *"Tom, Tom, we're lost! we're lost! We never can get out of this awful place! Oh, why did we ever leave the others!"   She sank to the ground and burst into such a frenzy of crying that Tom was appalled with the idea that she might die, or lose her reason.* Mark Twain's prose beautifully captures the sensation of hopelessness.

We were in Waikiki, Hawaii a few years back and I discovered, early one morning, a good place to have breakfast. I headed back to the hotel to get the rest of the group, but I couldn't find the damned hotel. Since it was a 20-story building, how on earth could I ever lose it? I gimped around in circles and ended up back at the good eatery, and hooray—there was my buddy Wayne, asking, "Where have you been?"

I very happily went inside and greeted the group with, "Forgive my tardiness—I was out and about exploring Waikiki." Never admit to being lost if you can avoid it.

September 4

Eating Animals

About 15 years ago, I read *Diet for a New America* by the heir to the Baskin-Robbins ice-cream empire, John Robbins. It was a fascinating book about how intelligent animals are, how poorly they are treated by humankind, and how unhealthy our meat-eating diets have become. Although I didn't become a vegetarian, the book made me change my eating habits. I have tremendous respect for people who are vegetarians on moralistic grounds. Although our family eats less meat than before, I just love the taste of a good steak washed down with a bottle of red wine. It's simply one of the great glories of the table, and I will admit to being selfish, immoral and weak when I chow down on animal protein. Perhaps one of my vegetarian friends will cook me a meatless dinner which will finally convince me to give up meat-eating for good. It hasn't happened yet—not even close! On the other hand, if we all gave up eating dead piggy, that would probably be the end of pigs on the planet. Would that be a good or a bad thing? Hmmm?

Hey—maybe piggies can replace Rover as "man's best friend." Hmmm-mmm?

September 5

Gilbert and Sullivan

It's love that makes the world go round!

I see no objection to stoutness … in moderation.

Life is a joke that's just begun.

When every blessed thing you hold is made of silver, or of gold,
You long for simple pewter.

All from W.S. Gilbert & Sir Arthur Sullivan (G&S)

Ifirst fell in love with the operettas of William Gilbert and Sir Arthur Sullivan in 1958, when our secondary school put on *H.M.S. Pinafore*, and the music director encouraged me to try out for a lead. I became the Captain of the *Pinafore*, the first role of many I was to enjoy in G&S operettas. At University, my favorite role was the Pirate King, and *The Pirates of Penzance* remains my favorite G&S. The pussy pirates and the even sillier flat-footed police have their own theme songs—at one point these songs are sung together, although neither group is aware the other is there. It's an amazing and unforgettable effect of grand theatre.

When we got married and moved into our present house, the G&S experience faded into the background, until one day when I was playing *Gondoliers* on my stereo and singing along out in the backyard. Our new neighbor, Sheldon, leaned over the fence and began to sing along with me. It turned out Shel was a G&S aficionado, and we began going to productions together. There are few to be found, but we discovered a wonderful group in the G&S Society. They put on an operetta at the end of January each year. We have enjoyed their fine productions for over 15 years.

The unbelievable fact about the operettas is that they were composed by two Englishmen who refused to speak to each other for long periods of time. Gilbert would draft the lyrics and send them to Sullivan, who would write the accompanying music. Back and forth the score would go, until the theatre manager, Richard D'oyly Carte, deemed it satisfactory. It certainly can be a "Topsy-Turvy" world at times.

September 6

Tennis 2

The primary conception of tennis is to get the ball over the net and at the same time to keep it within bounds of the court; failing this, within the borders of the neighborhood.
Elliot Chaze

Tennis is not a gentle game. Psychologically, it is vicious. That people are only just beginning to come to terms with this fact illustrates just how big a con trick has been perpetrated on the non-playing tennis public ... and even a few players, usually losing players ... for decades.
Richard Evans

It's difficult for most people to imagine the creative process in tennis. Seemingly it's just an athletic matter of hitting the ball consistently well within the boundaries of the court. That analysis is just as specious as thinking that the difficulty in portraying King Lear on stage is learning all the lines.
Virginia Wade

We were in a bridge club with four couples, and we would get together each month to have a go at the game. I really enjoyed going to the beautiful country home of one couple, Tom and Jan. They had lots of land and owned their own tennis court. We would go up early and the boys would play doubles. Tom and Terry were excellent players, and Norm and I had our moments. The games were never that serious, and we would have lots of laughs, particularly when Norm would uncork a powerful serve—right into the backside of his doubles partner. We would all laugh like hell about that—particularly Norm and I, since it would bring back the memory of an outstanding smash years before—the greatest serve I have ever had the pleasure of witnessing.

Norm and I were sitting on the bench at the tennis club, when along came the beautiful Helen and a local politician. Norm was lucky enough to get this fellow as his partner and although the chap was pleasant enough, he gave Norm some pointers. This had the effect of making Norm a little wild, and the great smash came early in that set—a mighty serve from Norm right off the backside of his partner—the good politician, who thenceforth didn't say much, but stood well off to the side when Norm was serving.

September 7

Laughter in Paradise

Life does not cease to be funny when people die any more than it ceases to be serious when people laugh.

George Bernard Shaw

Men show their character in nothing more clearly than by what they think laughable.

Johann Wolfgang von Goethe

We were privileged to attend three funerals in the past month. In all of these there was far more laughter than tears. We came home feeling good and continued to celebrate the lives of these friends for days after. The laughter at their antics while they were on this earth continues. Isn't it a blessing to believe that our time on earth should be enough fun that when we eventually depart, people can smile and say, "Today there is laughter in paradise."

I remember a very funny British movie, *Laughter in Paradise*, starring Alastair Sim. It begins at the death bed of an old man. A matronly nurse sits next to the geezer, ignoring him while she reads her newspaper. He awakes and manages somehow to light the paper on fire. While the nurse is having a fit putting out the fire, the old guy laughs so hard he dies. When the will is read, the relatives learn that to receive their inheritance, each has to perform some task that goes totally against the grain. Alastair's character has to spend exactly 28 days in jail. The movie is hilariously funny in a way only the British filmmakers seem to be able to do. When the relatives all gather for the second reading of the will, after they have jumped through hoops to perform their designated tasks, the barrister tells them, "You have all done exactly what was asked—a good thing—and now I hate to tell you that your benefactor died broke. He didn't have a single cent." After the initial shock, they all look at each other and begin to laugh uproariously. There is indeed laughter in paradise!

PS This was the first movie for Audrey Hepburn. She makes a brief appearance in a very sexy outfit—playing a cigarette girl.

September 8

Arthritis

I don't deserve this award, but I have arthritis and I don't deserve that either.

Jack Benny

The Doctor called Mrs. Cohen saying, "Mrs. Cohen, your check came back." Mrs. Cohen answered, "So did my arthritis!"

Henny Youngman

Just about everybody I know suffers arthritic pain, especially when it's cold and rainy. Most of us have injured or abused some joint, and eventually the arthritis creeps in. It's a difficult ailment to avoid. Our dear mother suffered from severe rheumatoid arthritis, an auto-immune disorder which can victimize anyone at any age. Fran's hands were especially painful, and she had difficulty holding anything in her gnarled hands. In spite of the pain she suffered with the rheumatism, I never heard mother complain about it.

The type of arthritis most of us have is called osteoarthritis. As joints get older, cartilage gets thinner and bone can rub against bone. Joints become inflamed, stiff and painful, especially in the morning. Knees seem to be particularly prone to osteoarthritis, and mine give me heck all the time from the stress of running and racquetball. I'm not alone in having bad knees. It seems to be a universal complaint from folks our age. The best remedy seems to be, "Keep moving!" Bike riding, power walking and swimming allow movement without the jarring of jogging. The stronger the muscles surrounding the joint, the less likely the joint will become inflamed.

After church one Sunday, I jokingly asked the priest what causes arthritis. He responded very seriously, "It's simple … high living is the main cause … drinking and womanizing … why do you ask?"

"Well Father," I responded, "I was reading in the paper this morning that the Pope has arthritis."

September 9

Routes

It is remarkable how easily and insensibly we fall into a particular route, and make a beaten track for ourselves.

Henry David Thoreau

We plan our lives according to a dream that came to us in our childhood, and we find that life alters our plans. And yet, at the end, from a rare height, we also see that our dream was our fate. It's just that providence had other ideas as to how we would get there. Destiny plans a different route, or turns the dream around, as if it were a riddle, and fulfills the dream in ways we couldn't have expected.

Ben Okri

How many times do we take the same route to where we are going? I used to drive the same route from our house to the church. Then one day, many years ago, we had to move a bunch of stuff over to the church; my buddy Ted had a load in his van and I had a load in mine. We left my house at the same time. I went up the street and Ted went down the street. I took my usual route over to the church—a route I had been driving for years. When I got to the church, Ted was already there and had unloaded. "How the hell did you get here so much faster?" I demanded.

Ted asked how I had driven over, and I told him. He revealed his great secret. "Well Lee ... I drove a little further but had mostly right turns and one traffic light. You had left turns and three lights, so it took you an extra five minutes! Always take right turns and few lights when you plan your route. The best route isn't necessarily the shortest!"

That simple but brilliant revelation, which I'm going to call *Ted's Terrific Tenet*, changed the way I plan—not only driving routes, but planning any endeavor. Always try and simplify your plans. I have seen folks needlessly complicate everything they do. They seem to "easily and insensibly fall into a particular route," as Thoreau suggests. Maybe it's time to wake up and take some right turns.

If you do not have brains, you follow the same route twice.
Greek Proverb

September 10

Agenda

I spend a good portion of my dinner-party conversation defending America because no matter what the political agenda, it's still a fantastic, amazing place.
Gwyneth Paltrow

As a reporter, I approach every situation knowing that everyone has his or her own agenda. It's not a bad thing; it's just a fact.
Maria Bartiromo

The Law of Triviality... briefly stated, it means that the time spent on any item of the agenda will be in inverse proportion to the sum involved.
C. Northcote Parkinson

War should belong to the tragic past, to history: it should find no place on humanity's agenda for the future.
Pope John Paul II

W hy is it so damned difficult to get folks to adjust their agendas? We meet people every day who are rolling on down their track—automatically achieving an agenda—single-mindedly blazing along, no matter what happens or who they happen to meet. If a lion or alligator suddenly confronted them, the agenda would disappear. As an interesting experiment, see how many people suddenly alter an agenda today when you find them in the middle of a task. I would be willing to bet—very few!

Opps! I lost that bet. My pants are on fire! The dogs interrupted my mull with an agenda of their own—a walk around the block with a hidden agenda—which must be removed as it doesn't remain hidden. I met three folks in the middle of tasks and guess what? They all proved me a liar by pausing to chat. The mailman stopped long enough for a couple of good chuckles. Two neighbors were cutting their grass, and they shut off their mowers when they saw us coming. We had great conversations, and they seemed in no hurry to resume their tasks.

Doesn't it make you feel great when people, by their actions, prove you wrong in your cynicism? Will we interrupt our agendas today to allow for some friendly interaction?

September 11

Reading Mysteries

The things I want to know are in books; my best friend is the man who'll get me a book I ain't read.

Abraham Lincoln

All the best stories in the world are but one story in reality ... the story of escape. It is the only thing which interests us all and at all times, how to escape.

Authur Christopher Benson

Books are the quietest and most constant of friends; they are the most accessible and wisest of counselors, and the most patient of teachers.

Charles W. Eliot

I find television to be very educating. Every time somebody turns on the set, I go in the other room and read a book.

Groucho Marx

Quite a few of the folks I know are collectors of mystery novels. One collector has the complete Agatha Christie—another, the Earl Stanley Gardner series on Perry Mason. I figure I have read all those, but the mystery stories I read over and over again are the complete Sherlock Holmes. I must have read *Hound of the Baskervilles* at least a dozen times. All the Dean Koontz and Stephen King tales have also been read as they rolled off the presses. I feel, however, that I am a mere amateur in the mystery collection business. I have two in-laws who make my collections look meager.

My brother-in-law, Father Phil, has a collection of pocket mysteries that makes my bookshelves look bare. The amazing thing about Phil's collection of British mysteries is that they are pristine. They look as if they haven't been touched by human hands. How do you read a pocket novel without getting some beer or pizza stains on the book? It's a mystery to me how Phil manages that miracle.

My sister-in-law, Dale, also loves to read mysteries and is an avid collector. Dale had such a huge collection, she opened a used book store and enjoyed trading stories with folks who were also mystery collectors. By the way, if you like to read mysteries, and if you've read this far—thank a teacher!

September 12

New Toy

We don't stop playing because we grow old; we grow old because we stop playing.
George Bernard Shaw

The true object of all human life is play. Earth is a task garden; heaven is a playground.
G.K. Chesterton

You can discover more about a person in an hour of play than in a year of conversation.
Plato

I always enjoy shopping for toys. How would you like to go on a toy-shopping spree without spending a nickel of your own money? I was able to do that when I opened the science department in a new secondary school. Pouring through science catalogues and visiting science suppliers was as much fun as being a rich kid in Toys-R-Us. The physics equipment was especially fun to order. Christmas came each day the new stuff arrived and we got to play.

I remember the day our new 250-thousand-volt Van de Graaff generator arrived. This machine consisted of a large, silvery ball on top of a stand through which a moving belt delivered static electricity to the metal ball. (You may have seen someone hold the ball with their hands as their hair gradually stands on end. All the charged hairs repel each other. It is a fun toy for any age.) We unpacked this darling after the students were gone and set it up in a vacant lab. I held a smaller ball with an insulated handle. Rick charged up the Van de Graaff, and Gord came to enjoy the flying sparks. As I moved the smaller ball close to the large one, a loud "snap" would occur as a miniature lightning bolt jumped between the balls. Suddenly, the three of us received an unexpected but juicy shock treatment which lifted us off the floor. We quickly recovered, laughing at our silly conduct. I figure we got the big shock because Gord talked animatedly with his hands and touched the ball and Rick and me at the same time. It's too bad the kids had all left. They would have gotten a real charge out of our antics that afternoon.

September 13

Memory

If computers get too powerful, we can organize them into committees. That'll do them in.

Author Unknown

After growing wildly for years, the field of computing appears to be reaching its infancy.

John Pierce

Computer memory is growing by quantum leaps at the same time the physical space taken up by computers shrinks. Back in the 60's, my brother Bert was working in the SAGE (Semi-Automatic Ground Environment) installation in North Bay, Ontario. This was a building inside a mountain, and it was a command center for NORAD, the North American Aerospace Defense Command. The whole second floor was a huge computer, the *AN/FSQ-7* model developed in the 1950s by IBM. It was and still is the world's largest computer. *AN/FSQ-7* contained 55,000 vacuum tubes, occupied about half an acre (20,000 square feet) of floor space, and weighed 275 tons. Today, there are home computers that will outperform this monster.

One of the first home computers was the Commodore 64, the C-64, with 64 kilobytes of memory. It was the bestselling computer of all time, and over 30 million C-64's were sold. My 80 gig iPod has as much memory as over a million C-64's which were so popular a mere 25 years ago. If you were to tell somebody in 1985 that a cordless devise that fit into your hand could have as much memory as a million C-64's—you would have been called a dreamer, or "nuts!"

PS There are two memories I have of the SAGE installation. We were there on a Sunday, and hardly anyone was working. I wonder what would have happened if the U.S.S.R. had decided to attack us on a Sunday? Back in the 50's, Sunday was a "day of rest." Now, it is just another day. The other memory is the computer programmers proudly showing us their best creation—a dancing Hawaiian girl graphic whose skirt fell off after her dance. Some things never change.

September 14

Reckless Abandon

Reckless abandon   synonyms: without inhibitions ... with gay abandon

Approach love and cooking with reckless abandon.
                    Unknown ... (attributed to the Dalai Lama in an e-mail)

We, the unwilling, led by the unknowing, are doing the impossible for the ungrateful.
We have done so much, for so long, with so little, we are now qualified to do anything
with nothing.
                                                                    Mother Teresa

What we can or cannot do, what we consider possible or impossible, is rarely a function
of our true capability. It is more likely a function of our beliefs about who we are.
                                                                    Tony Robbins

I have my doubts that the Dalai Lama ever said, "Approach love and cooking with reckless abandon." What does he know about cooking or love? He is one of those people who is actually in control of his life. He is a Tibetan monk after all, and as such, he is filled with peace, calm and quiet. Reckless or gay abandon—without inhibitions—would seem foreign to such a controlled person. Besides, monks are known to eat bland stuff. The whole notion of a Tibetan monk without inhibitions is hard to swallow.

When I played football, our head coach would say, "I expect you to play with reckless abandon ... as if this were your last game ... your last chance to hit anybody. Now get out there and do it!" Some guys could shift into those higher gears—like the Tasmanian devil in the Warner Brothers' cartoon. The coach's eyes would light up as a few players actually went bananas and won the game for us.

Back in the 1970's, the Philadelphia Flyers were known as the Broad Street Bullies. Their coach, Fred Shiro, was a master at controlling the pace of the game. If things were getting dull, Fred would send out "Mad Dog" Kelly. Kelly hurled his body with reckless abandon at every player on the opposing team. His antics inspired his teammates to throw caution to the wind and turn it up several notches. The Flyers won two Stanley Cups with their tough, spirited style of play.

If we wish to excel, we need to let go at times. A big heart, formidable spirit, élan, or fire can replace give-up with giddy-up.

September 15

Myth

Myths which are believed in tend to become true.

George Orwell

Without an understanding of myth or religion, without an understanding of the relationship between destruction and creation, death and rebirth, the individual suffers the mysteries of life as meaningless mayhem alone.

Marion Woodman

There is a wonderful mythical law of nature that the three things we crave most in life ... happiness, freedom, and peace of mind ... are always attained by giving them to someone else.

Peyton C. March

Some of the most popular movies in the past ten years have been about myths or fantasies. A tale like *The Lord of the Rings* takes us to places we can only visit in our minds or in the movies. These escapes from reality invariably involve struggle for survival. All good fantasy flicks revolve around the battle between the forces of good and evil. There always seems to be love and the giving of oneself to others. In *The Lord of the Rings*, the hero Frodo is challenged to destroy the ring by throwing it into the lava of Mount Doom. He will thus defeat the evil forces of the Dark Lord Sauron who forged the ring.

The challenge seems impossible and is only doable with the help of Frodo's good friend Samwise. Sam displays all the qualities we could ever ask for in a friend. He is always ready to sacrifice himself for the cause. Samwise gives everything and more—constant encouragement, commitment, and strength of purpose which sometimes lapses in Frodo. Sam is the ultimate friend—willing to sacrifice his very life for the success of Frodo's mission.

The sense of wonder and freedom shared at the conclusion of the fantasy is that feeling described by Peyton March above. We identify with Sam. By giving his all to his good friend, he obtains the happiness, freedom and peace craved by every person. It involves a choice we all must make through life. To be a Frodo—in control—on a mission—in charge: OR to be a Samwise—in support—making sacrifices—always giving. This is myth after all. Reality is more complex. Maybe we should be trying to simplify the way we live our lives.

Facts

To treat your facts with imagination is one thing, but to imagine your facts is another.
John Burroughs

What is laid down, ordered, factual is never enough to embrace the whole truth: life always spills over the rim of every cup.
Boris Pasternak

The possession of facts is knowledge; the use of them is wisdom.
Thomas Jefferson

Science is facts; just as houses are made of stones, so is science made of facts; but a pile of stones is not a house and a collection of facts is not necessarily science.
Jules Henri Poincaré

Facts can be turned into art if one is artful enough.
Paul Simon

Aunt Dorothy had a wonderful expression she used when she figured you were embellishing things, or holding forth too long on some story. Dot would look you in the eye and say emphatically, "Is that a fact?" You knew right away that Dot saw through your nonsense—or as my barber Claudio calls it, through the "boolsheet."

How can we be certain that some statement is factual, real or truthful when we enjoy fantasy so much more? We love fantastic stories, and you can imagine how much of the news would be mundane if the media didn't add their own slant to all the accounts. The inclusion of a picture—cartoon or photo—is often what wins us over to a particular point of view. As Paul Simon suggests, newspapers, radio and television are closer to art forms than dispensers of fact. We need to sift through the artful nonsense and boolsheet to get to the truth—and then we can never be absolutely certain that we have the facts—the truth—the real story. The past is just a story, and films and photos can be doctored to prove a point.

I love the story in which aliens arrive on earth long after life here has disappeared. They find a garbage dump and discover a DVD. They manage somehow to play the DVD, and they are astounded at the mannerisms of humans depicted on the movie. At the finish of the movie are the credits: *A Looney Tunes Production*. That about sums up the times we live in.

September 17

Evolution

The first half of our lives is ruined by our parents and the second half by our children.

I never wanted to see anybody die, but there are a few obituary notices I have read with pleasure.

If you lose the power to laugh, you lose the power to think.

Just think of the tragedy of teaching children not to doubt.

All from Clarence Darrow ... a witty agnostic American lawyer

Charles Darwin's *Origin of the Species* created a controversy which still rages in the minds of many people. All children eventually ask the question: "Where do we come from?" The stories of creation in the Bible were easily understood by children, and made for a simple yet elegant answer to this age-old question. The notion that God created us in his image made us feel rather special. Then along came Darwin with his scientific theory that simpler organisms changed into more complex organisms over long periods of time. In Darwin's explanation, our earliest ancestors may have been single-celled beasties in some primordial soup. Oh the horror! Evolution removed the special status granted humans in the Biblical versions of creation. Is it any wonder that many folks objected?

The most famous objection was in what many consider the trial of the twentieth century. The *Scopes Monkey Trial* pitted Clarence Darrow against William Jennings Brian, a noted orator. The trial was the basis for *Inherit the Wind*, a play which was made into a movie starring Spencer Tracy as Henry Drummond, a fictionalized Clarence Darrow. If this all sounds convoluted, it's appropriately so, since the question about where we come from is no easy answer.

Many folks divide into the "creationist" camp or the "evolution" camp. There seems to be no room for compromise. May I suggest that there is a middle ground? Perhaps evolution was the tool the Creator used to invent the world. God is said to work in mysterious ways, and maybe the seven days of creation were much longer than in the original story.

September 18

Explosions

His study was a total mess, like the results of an explosion in a public library.
Douglas Adams

As in an explosion, I would erupt with all the wonderful things I saw and understood in this world.
Boris Pasternak

Every morning I jump out of bed and step on a landmine. The landmine is me. After the explosion, I spent the rest of the day putting the pieces together.
Ray Bradbury

The safe that night looked like a soft one ... the explosion made no more noise than a pig's grunt.
Herbert Emerson Wilson

My brothers and I always had a fondness for big bangs—explosions of one sort or another. Maybe it's just a guy kind of thing. I remember my brothers putting a glass jug of water on a grate over a fire and telling me to watch it very carefully as they went to get more wood. My father saw what was going on, and took me away before the glass blew up into a million pieces.

The first year I taught, our science club was building a steam turbine in my room after school. The glass boiler blew up with a loud bang, but nobody was hit by the glass. A couple of days later, I was putting something up on the back bulletin board and found a large piece of the boiler glass embedded in the bulletin board. I damn near fainted!

In another neat science demonstration, we heated some chemicals in a large test tube. The lights were turned off, and after about 30 seconds there would be a lovely big colorful explosion out of the end of the test tube. One time, I told the students not to stand over behind the test tube. Then I turned off the lights and began to heat up the tube. BANG! The explosion was great, but the test tube shot backwards out of the stand and hit somebody! There was a large "ouch," and when I turned the lights back on, there was a student standing right where I told him not to stand. "Hey Jeff," yelled another kid, "Teach told you not to stand over there." "Is that what he said?" replied Jeff. "I thought he said, 'stand over there,' and I always do what I'm told!" Lucky for me again—no broken glass embedded in anybody from another Steeleeman explosion.

September 19

Collecting

Collecting has been my great extravagance. It's a way of being. I collect for the same reason that I eat too much … I'm one of nature's shoppers.

Howard Hodgkin

I did tests on small stones before collecting and committing myself to the larger ones.

Andy Goldsworthy

I didn't play at collecting. No cigar anywhere was safe from me.

Edward G. Robinson

I'm touched by the idea that when we do things that are useful and helpful … collecting these shards of spirituality … that we may be helping to bring about a healing.

Leonard Nimoy

W e were in several "collector" shops this week. We have never seen so many bear and moose collectibles. I was disappointed there were no pigs. Collecting anything is fun if you don't mind having to manage your collection.

Here are a few ideas for collecting which have one thing in common. They are all FREE!!! (I am certain you can generate a much longer list.)

Words: My workout buddy Mike collects words through crosswords, books, magazines and the internet.

Facts: Any sports fan knows the statistics. Music nuts know their songs. My friend Ted knows a ton of 50's pop music facts.

Books: You can place holds on line or just browse the library shelves for books. A good conversation piece is, "What are you reading lately?"

Quotes: There are lots of great quote books, but instant quotes on almost any topic are available on the internet at BrainyQuote.com, ThinkExist.com, Quotegarden.com and Quotes of the Day (qotd.org)

Folks for the Prayer List: We can all use some prayer. I keep one list near my stationary bike and beam prayer energy to lots of folks as I ride—and at other times during the day.

September 20

The Family

Family life is the normal context in which we can learn that a life filled with thinking about others instead of ourselves is the sure road to the most fulfilling joys and satisfactions.

Alan Keyes

A family is a unit composed not only of children but of men, women, an occasional animal, and the common cold.

Ogden Nash

Blood's thicker than water!

Author Unknown

It is not flesh and blood but the heart which makes us fathers and sons.

Johann Schiller

Cain said to his brother Abel, "Let us go out to the field." And when they were in the field, Cain rose up against his brother Abel, and killed him.

Genesis 4:8

Have you ever thought that perhaps your family is dysfunctional? You are not alone. The first family member in the Bible murdered the second family member. According to the story in Genesis, Adam and Eve were God's creations, and the firstborn humans on the Earth were Cain and Able. Jealousy, dissatisfaction and greed triumphed, and Cain's brother Abel became history. Thus began a whole host of dysfunctional families. A mere three pages later in the story, God became so fed up with all the wickedness, he decided to drown them all—except for Noah—who had the only non-dysfunctional family left on the Earth. Thank heavens for Noah, or we wouldn't be here.

Seriously, you have perhaps been tempted to lash out at a family member—and many families seem to thrive on the machinations resulting from the selfish "me first" attitude. Does it have to be this way? Can rancor ever be set aside in a family? Yes! We can choose to forgive past hurts, and help each other. It sounds simple but requires huge ongoing effort.

We had our share of dissatisfaction in our family, but, as the years passed, we decided to put old wrongs aside and do more for each other. We eventually drew closer together with love in our hearts. Otherwise the old expression would have been true: "Too soon olt ... too late shmartz!"

September 21

Eternal Youth

There is a fountain of youth: It is your mind, your talents, the creativity you bring to your life and the lives of people you love. When you learn to tap this source, you will have truly defeated age.

Sophia Loren

Another belief of mine: That everyone else my age is an adult, whereas I am merely in disguise.

Margaret Atwood

Life's challenges are not supposed to paralyze you, they're supposed to help you discover who you are.

Bernice Johnson Reagon

Just don't give up trying to do what you really want to do. Where there is love and inspiration, I don't think you can go wrong.

Ella Fitzgerald

The great thing about getting older is that you don't lose all the other ages you've been.

Madeleine L'Engle

A newspaper article: "86-year-old man gets master's degree", tells of how Ken Wilde obtained straight A's in working on his Master's in History. Three years previously, he earned his bachelor's degree and decided to continue with his master's. He isn't the oldest person to earn a college degree. That honor goes to Nola Ochs, who earned her bachelor's degree at the age of 95. These accomplishments are not unusual for the "elderly."

Richard Strauss wrote his "Four Last Songs" when he was 84.

Leopold Stokowski made recordings into his 90's.

Alice Monroe, b 1931, has another best-selling collection of stories.

Regis Philbin, b 1931, set the Guinness record for most hours in front of TV cameras ... 15, 188 hours ... in his 73rd year.

George Burns was still making movies in his 90's.

One key to eternal youth seems to be this. Get a vocation you love, and keep doing it for as long as you enjoy it. Good genes may also help.

September 22

Ecstasy

ecstasy (emotion),   a trance or trance-like state in which an individual transcends normal consciousness
Religious ecstasy,   a changed state of consciousness characterized   by expanded spiritual awareness, visions or absolute euphoria
Ecstasy (philosophy),   a term used to mean "outside-of-itself"

The moment you have in your heart this extraordinary thing called love and feel the depth, the delight, the ecstasy of it, you will discover that for you the world is transformed.

Jiddu Krishnamurti

The world can be transformed into a continuously joyful experience by LOVE. This experience of ecstasy is more the result of attitude than anything. Picture the happiest dog you know—tail wagging with great enthusiasm for everything—walks, food, visitors and other dogs. Depression, anxiety and whining aren't in the vocabulary of most happy dogs. There is an e-mail which circulates: *Everything I learned … I learned from the family dog!* Yes—most family dogs are totally happy—and why shouldn't they be? Everything is provided, and they are allowed to give and receive unconditional love. There's that key word again—LOVE. So if we can learn to reduce stress and enjoy food, friends, and relations—we can come closer to the ecstasy achieved by those family dogs. The key is LOVE!

This ecstasy doth unperplex
(We said) and tell us what we love ;
We see by this, it was not sex ;
We see, we saw not, what did move :

But as all several souls contain
Mixture of things they know not what,
Love these mix'd souls doth mix again,
And makes both one, each this, and that.
John Donne   from "The Ecstasy"

September 23

Photography

I think a photography class should be a requirement in all educational programs because it makes you see the world rather than just look at it.

Author Unknown

Photography records the gamut of feelings written on the human face, the beauty of the earth and skies that man has inherited, and the wealth and confusion man has created.

Edward Steichen

Today everything exists to end in a photograph.

Susan Sontag

I really believe there are things nobody would see if I didn't photograph them.

Diane Arbus

I remember my first camera. It was a Kodak "Brownie" and it took 127 film with eight black-and-white pictures. I would arrange my Dinky toys and plastic animals in the sand box, and take pictures of tableaux in sand. Often, only half the pictures were any good, but it was still exciting to go down to the drug store four days later to pick up your pictures—even if they were blurry B&W. It would have knocked your sox off back then to know how the art of photography has changed.

We showed our ninth grade science students a National Geographic video called *The Invisible World*. The pictures and film were made using high-speed cameras with very high magnification. There were unbelievable worlds within worlds in this fascinating video—which can be viewed on the internet. Just Google *Invisible World* and prepare to be amazed. The critters living on your skin and eyebrows are enough to make anyone exclaim, "Oooo … gross!" It is amazing what photography can reveal about the world.

Today, with the advent of inexpensive digital cameras, we can instantly capture any moment, and look at that moment in high definition. We can delete what we don't want to keep, and blow up scenes over and over to give us the world in all its glory. Our Aunt Dorothy didn't have much use for photography. "You are so into recording what is going on around you that you are missing what is really going on—and wasting a lot of time doing it!" I suppose Dot had a good point—but I still love taking photos.

September 24

Higher Gears

Life is like a ten speed bike. Most of us have higher gears we never use.

Charles Schultz

Super-human events stick in our minds. Many of my old friends recall Roger Bannister breaking the 4 minute mile. I can replay the race in my mind—those long strides—the announcer getting more excited—and then the magic moment when a human accomplished something that "couldn't be done." As a skinny 16 year-old, I once ran a mile in less than 6 minutes. I couldn't believe how tough it was. The pain in the last 100 yards was awful. How can athletes bear such pain? There are many examples of athletes shifting into some higher gear to overcome pain. Jack Youngblood, of the Los Angeles Rams, played in Super Bowl XIV on a broken leg. Incredible performances occur quite often in sports, but what examples of higher gears to we have in other fields?

Prolific writers:
Isaac Asimov wrote or edited over 500 books in 42 years—a rate of over one book each month. Asimov's *Foundation Trilogy* is regarded by many as the greatest science fiction series ever written.
Ryoki Inoue is a Brazilian writer, acknowledged by the Guinness World Records, as world's most prolific writer: since he began his career in 1986, he had 1075 books published—under his own name or 39 pseudonyms. It is claimed that he wrote over 900 pulp fiction books in six years—a rate of over ten books a month! (Wikipedia)

Amazing composers:
Handle claims he wrote his *Messiah* in 16 days;
Joseph Haydn, Father of the Symphony, wrote 104 symphonies;
Rossini would leave his opera overtures to the last minute, often composing them in a single day;
Bach wins the Higher Gear Prize: over 3000 compositions and 22 children—what could be more prolific than that?

September 25

Numbers

To emphasize only the beautiful seems to me to be like a mathematical system that only concerns itself with positive numbers.

Paul Klee

The intelligence of any discussion diminishes with the square of the number of participants.

Adam Walinsky

Throw away nonessential numbers. This includes age, weight and height. Let the doctors worry about them. That is why you pay them.

Internet e-mail message

Perfect numbers, like perfect men, are very rare.

Rene Descartes

Why are our days numbered and not, say, lettered?

Woody Allen

Mathematicians love numbers. Sportscasters love numbers more. We were watching a baseball game, and the most obscure stats kept rolling off the commentator's tongue. "He hit his nineteenth home run last year on August 13." How do they do that? Hitting home runs is damn near impossible, but you can easily find any statistic you want almost instantly on the web. In fact, the internet has expanded the love of numbers in exponential fashion. A buddy with a 4G iPhone loves to find the answer to any question by punching the little icons on his screen and then displaying the answer for all to admire. I must admit, high-tech instant info is addictive. I wonder how many people have become chained to these miraculous phones. Are they another tool that will eventually enslave huge numbers of us?

We have memorized quite an array of numbers—address, zip code, phone numbers—and the phone numbers of a large number of friends and relatives. I know folks who can recite large numbers of seemingly useless data. An obvious one is passages in the Bible. Ah yes, a friend tells me, "You'll find the answer in 1 Corinthians 13." I must admit to amazement when I meet someone who can dazzle everyone with their knowledge of the numbers associated with some body of knowledge. Then again—that's their interest or hobby. Given sufficient motivation, the mind can file huge amounts of information. Wouldn't it be nice if we could just forget a few of these numbers—like age, weight and our bank balance?

September 26

Value

That which costs little is less valued.

Miguel De Cervantes

We can tell our values by looking at our checkbook stubs.

Gloria Steinem

We were at the Symphony last night. We have been supporters for over 40 years, and we were pleased to see that this concert was a sell-out, and the orchestra and its guest soloist were accorded a standing ovation. When 80 or so musicians are all together, playing their hearts out for a piece they truly love, it is a spiritual experience which cannot be valued too highly. Sometimes, as in the previous week's performance of Mahler's third symphony, I feel transported to a timeless heaven—as if in a symphonic meditation. There is a wonderful feeling of awe and bliss as great music washes over you. Last night's concert was enjoyable, but I didn't feel transported. Rather, my mind wandered to other things, as occasionally happens.

I thought of a performance going on in the nearby baseball game. A pitcher was trying to win the magic number—20 games in a season. I love to do funny calculations. I wondered how much he was getting to pitch this game compared with the 80 musicians in front of me. Here's what I figured:

Baseball pitcher: $ 12 000 000, divided by 40 starts, equals **$ 300 000.**

Symphony musicians: average $ 80 000 salary per year, times 80 musicians, divided by 90 performances, equals **$ 71, 111** (for the whole orchestra).

There's something not quite right in our value system when that baseball pitcher is getting over four times as much as an entire professional symphony orchestra for one performance!

September 27

Unexpected Surprise

For it was not into my ear you whispered, but into my heart. It was not my lips you kissed, but my soul.

Judy Garland

A Scout is never taken by surprise; he knows exactly what to do when anything unexpected happens.

Robert Baden-Powell

A sudden bold and unexpected question doth many times surprise a man and lay him open.

Francis Bacon

All creative people want to do the unexpected.

Hedy Lamarr

My wife and I were unexpected surprises. Our siblings were seven years older than us, and if the pill had been available back then—we wouldn't have known it—and you wouldn't be reading this silly stuff! I know quite a number of other folks who came along when least expected. Some parents are at a loss for dealing with such surprises. According to my dear mom, I wasn't in dad's plan; he ignored me—which turned out to be a good thing. I became the spoiled doll of my teenaged sister, who read to me at every opportunity and protected me from the machinations of my older brothers. Sometimes there are definite advantages to being unexpected.

How many times in our lives do surprises happen? Unless your life is severely over-controlled, there should be some unexpected events today. Wonders wait around each corner. We need to look and listen for them, welcome them with open arms, and seize them as opportunities—*carpe diem!*

The obvious surprise is when unexpected guests come to call. If that happens, every effort should be made to include them in your plans.

I love the story of the prodigal son. The younger son demands his inheritance and wastes it. Down and out, he returns to his father, who could easily say: "You've had it all ... and that's all you are getting!" Instead, the old man—much to the chagrin of the older, controlled son—welcomes the prodigal back and puts on a huge feast in his honor. The father tells the older son: "He was dead to us ... but now he is alive!" This father knows exactly what to do with the unexpected. Being a good "Scout" means being prepared for surprises.

September 28

Medication

The least costly treatment for any illness is lethal medication.

Walter Dellinger

I will remember to take my medication.

Nancy Cartwright

Marijuana is the finest anti-nausea medication known to science, and our leaders have lied about this consistently. Arresting people for medical marijuana is the most hideous example of government interference in the private lives of individuals. It's an outrage within an outrage within an outrage.

Peter McWilliams

I was under medication when I made the decision not to burn the tapes.

Richard M. Nixon

My mother, Francis, suffered from a triple-whammy. Fran had a weak heart from rheumatic fever that she had as a child. To this, add severe rheumatoid arthritis and Parkinson's disease. Mother took these trials with grace and courage. She also took a load of medications. Every once in a while, Fran refused to take her medications. There must have been side effects to all those pills, and Fran figured the cure was worse than the disease.

I was in the hospital as a follow-up to my hip replacement, and I met a chap whose hip had been dislocated for almost a year. Instead of fixing his hip, the unfortunate man was kept on a pain reliever containing narcotic. I asked him how he felt about that. "I just feel 'dumb' all the time," was his response. I felt the same way about narcotic pain relievers after my surgery. I found that simple acetaminophen was almost as effective and didn't dumb me down.

Another example of medication gone wrong involved a diabetic friend. She had been ill all summer with some unknown affliction. After three months, she discovered that the pharmacy had changed the supplier of her diabetes medication. There had been complaints of sick people, but the pharmacy and doctors didn't make connections. It was the same drug, but different "filler", and that had probably upset many of the folks who were never initially informed of the change.

September 29

Stress Busters

Take rest; a field that has rested gives a bountiful crop.

Ovid

For fast-acting relief, try slowing down.

Lily Tomlin

We were playing bridge one evening, and someone commented on my hair—all on the top of my head where hair should be. "Lee has so much hair because he has NO STRESS!" I guess this person supposed, as many folks do, that a teacher's job is a piece of cake. Actually, I have always been lucky enough to have some stress-busting routines. (And bountiful hair genes.)

1. Start the day with quiet thanks. Don't get the paper right away! I begin with a short reading and reflection and some quiet prayer. It only takes a few minutes to get into a good frame of mind, and reading a positive reflection gives you something to fall back on during the day.

2. Do something during the day to produce some endorphins—walk, run, ride, dance, sing, laugh—anything to produce those happy endorphin molecules. "Hoot a few hoots!"

3. Plan ahead. Make some little lists and tick them off. Multitask whenever you can to give yourself more time. Turn them into FUN if you can!
    (If you are like me, this is a tough habit to perform with regularity.)

4. Do something new each day—new route—new anything! Don't let yourself go on autopilot! Life is an adventure to be lived anew each day.

5. Escape from those high-tech devices for some uninterrupted time by yourself—turn off the phone, computer, T.V. and car and *RELAX*.

September 30

Lightning

Since I was man,
Such sheets of fire, such bursts of horrid thunder,
Such groans of roaring wind and rain, I never
Remember to have heard. Man's nature cannot carry
Th'affliction nor the fear.

William Shakespeare (From *King Lear*)

We had an unusual number of thunderstorms this summer. It's always an adventure in our house. Our dogs are afraid of thunder and other loud noises, and they try to get under the covers in a storm.

Thunder is the result of lightning, which is a huge pile of electrons frying the air as they zoom down from the clouds to the ground—or more often, from the ground UP to the clouds. The air is superheated. The air molecules all rush out, making a partial vacuum. Then they rush back together with a loud crash—the thunder. Some people think that "lightning never strikes twice." Wrong! Tall structures like the Empire State Building can be struck many times during a single storm. The lightning rod on top of the tower is connected to the ground, allowing the excess electrons to go in and out of the ground with no damage being done to the tower.

The funniest story we heard about lightning was from "To Tell the Truth" on television. A park ranger had been struck seven times and lived. The host asked him to describe the last time he had been struck. "Well," he replied in a southern drawl, "I was sittin' in mah truck when the lightnin' struck the truck, and it arched across the roof … thus relieving me of mah eyebrows!" After the audience had stopped laughing, the host asked the park ranger where one should go during a thunderstorm. The ranger replied: "Well … ah wouldn't recommend that you stand anywhere near me!"

I ran out of gas one night on the highway. Luckily, I found a service station nearby. They were out of gas containers, so I filled two used oil cans with gas and headed back to the car. It began to storm, and there was a tremendous lightning flash and instant thunder. It scared the hell out of me for sure—and I thought after—I guess I would have gone up like a torch if it had struck me. The Lord looks after fools and his own.

October 1

Dyslexia

I was, on the whole, considerably discouraged by my school days. It was not pleasant to feel oneself so completely outclassed and left behind at the beginning of the race.

Winston Churchill (famous dyslexic)

He told me that his teachers reported that . . . he was mentally slow, unsociable, and adrift forever in his foolish dreams.

Hans Albert Einstein, on his father, Albert Einstein (famous dyslexic)

My teachers say I'm addled . . . my father thought I was stupid, and I almost decided I must be a dunce.

Thomas Edison (famous dyslexic)

The students have been in school a month now, and many teachers have already sorted out the "bright" and "dim" lights. The poor kids with some learning disability may have already been labeled as "dim", as had the three famous folks above. When Winston Churchill's relatives came to visit his school, the school placed the students in order of how well they were doing. His aunt quickly remarked, "Oh my, look at that ... poor Winnie is the last one of all." The savior of the English-speaking peoples had a terrible time in school. So did two great scientific geniuses, Albert Einstein and Thomas Edison. They all had trouble with reversing numbers and letters. Arithmetic and spelling gave these dyslexics fits in school. As teachers and parents, we need to be aware of learning disabilities like dyslexia and Attention Deficit Disorder (ADD), so we don't label such students as weak or dim.

I used to lay lots of subtle funny stuff on students in the first couple of weeks. Then I would watch carefully to see who really understood the subtleties. I was often quite pleasantly surprised to find some real gems among previously-labeled students. Many of them simply needed a different learning style to shine! Not all brilliant people like to sit quietly and listen!

Did you hear about the dyslexic, agnostic insomniac?
He would lie awake all night wondering if there really was a dog!

Have you heard about the new group, DAM? It's "Mothers against dyslexia."

The Last Act

When we are born we cry that we are come to this great stage of fools.

All the world's a stage, and all the men and women merely players: they have their exits and their entrances; and one man in his time plays many parts, his acts being seven ages.

Life's but a walking shadow, a poor player that struts and frets his hour upon the stage and then is heard no more.

All from William Shakespeare

The last act is bloody, however pleasant all the rest of the play is: a little earth is thrown at last upon our head, and that is the end forever.

Blaise Pascal

Applaud friends, the comedy is over.

Ludwig van Beethoven
(On his deathbed)

Do you ever get the feeling that you are merely a player in a humongous play—and it's the last act? Sometimes it seems as if all the dialogue comes out prefabricated, without anybody having to think about it. I find myself replying, "Yes ... of course ..." and then suddenly—oops—it could very well be *my* last act as other players discover I haven't heard a single word. I might be thinking it's a comedy, but others see my inattention in a much darker light—and so it goes. Our lifelong play could be comedy or tragedy—or perhaps both. Do we look at the last act and laugh or cry? Do we *strut and fret* our hour on a tiny wee stage, or has our play encompassed the world? Are we mere puppets being played upon by perverse puppeteers, or can we modify our play to our personal predilection?

There is a pat answer that comes at least once each week in an e-mail: "Live each day as if it's your last." Sounds great, doesn't it—but what the hell does it mean? Should we go out and purchase a bull-whip and flog all the bastards that have tried to make our lives miserable? Should we indulge ourselves in one last sex orgy? Should we have a giant happy hour and feast on everything we enjoy—and end up getting dead drunk as well? Just what would you do if you knew it were the finale of your last act?

October 3

Barber Ramblings

No matter how bad things are … they can quickly get a whole lot worse! It's just a matter of LUCK!

Claudio, my Barber

I was having my ears lowered this morning and my barber, Claudio, was rambling on about how things can very quickly go from bad to worse, or the reverse, and how it's just a matter of luck. He was recounting a story about how he and another kid were walking down a shallow stream when the water suddenly got deeper and he was in over his head. He and his friend couldn't swim, but an adult spotted them and pulled them out. Claudio survived, but his friend drowned. Claudio wonders why luck favored him and not his friend. Claudio asked, "Have you had an experience where you were 'lucky' like that?"

He went on to say how he figures the main objective in life is to remain healthy—if you can. He says this is a result of good genes and good luck. You have to have been lucky enough to receive a healthy body and mind in the first place, and then to keep it that way by avoiding toxic stuff every day. Then, Claudio figures, you can do all the right things and still be wiped out by a drunk driver, as several innocent people have in the past couple of weeks. If you are lucky enough to avoid all these pitfalls, you then may spend the last years of your life in pain, wishing you had exited earlier. This is certainly a dark musing from Claudio, but it was true in my dear Aunt Dorothy's case.

When Dot moved into a nursing home at the age of 92, she was suffering the pain of arthritis. She told me that she had "had enough" and that she would "like to exit!" She mentioned a dear old friend who would know "what to do" and told me to find out. What I found out was that this old friend had already exited 25 years previously—so I told Dorothy.

"How did he die?" Dot asked me.

"He drank and smoked himself to death." I told her.

"Hmmmmmmmm …" mused Dot, "maybe I should try that!"

I said, "They don't allow smoking in here Dot… what kind of booze would you like me to smuggle in tomorrow?"

October 4

Farm Tales

Definition: FARMER   *a man out standing in his field*   (Anon)

The poor old farmer ... what a fix he's in ... the crows get fat and he gets thin. He shoos them all off with his gun, but they come right back ... every doggone one!

The Farm Relief Song

The fight to save family farms isn't just about farmers. It's about making sure that there is a safe and healthy food supply for all of us. It's about jobs, from Main Street to Wall Street. It's about a better America.

As long as there are a few farmers out there, we'll keep fighting for them.

Both from Willie Nelson

Real farmers are a rare breed these days. The factory farm has replaced the good old mixed farming enterprise which my grandfather, Andrew Joseph Knight, ran almost a hundred years ago. Farms have become more like business enterprises. A true 100 acre farm with vegetable gardens, horses, cows and pigs seems to be a rarity today.

When we drive up through the farm country of this region, there are huge farms with much bigger buildings on them. My cousin, who lives on the family farm, informs me that the old style 100 acre mixed farm has disappeared. Owners of smaller farms lease out their land to a conglomerate. The whole agribusiness has changed to the factory model. Large seems to be the only way to survive. A 100 acre mixed farm simply cannot make enough money to survive. Such a farm owner would need another job or business to be able to keep the farm. This means that a chicken or pig farm has huge buildings full of animals kept in tight quarters. The treatment of these animals is simply inhumane. The free range chicken or pig is a very rare animal. Big agribusiness has changed everything.

Who would have ever thought that our image of a farmer, working dawn to sunset to produce a variety of foods for the survival of us city folks, would be all wrong?

October 5

Proverbs

Give every man thine ear, but few thy voice….
Excerpt from Polonius' advice to Laertes in *Hamlet* by William Shakespeare

You may recall studying Shakespeare's *Hamlet* in school. I thought this speech from Polonius was very interesting. The advice is great, and one would do well to live by it—yet there are two big problems with these words of wisdom. They come out of the mouth of a silly, interfering man who is portrayed as an old fool in the rest of the play. The second problem is that, as with most good advice, we often learn these wise lessons the hard way—on the street. Maybe that is the point Shakespeare is making by giving the speech to a busybody. We don't heed advice very well. Rather, we seem to have to learn wisdom by making mistakes. It is a damn fine speech, however.

The largest body of advice I know of, other than Ann Landers' columns, resides in Proverbs, in the Bible. These wise sayings are attributed to Solomon, the son of David. After watching political debates and the almost slanderous attack ads on television, I figure everyone running for political office would be wise to take a few of these sayings of Solomon to heart.

"When words are many, transgression is not lacking."

"Whoever belittles another lacks sense ."

"One who forgives an affront fosters friendship, but one who dwells on disputes will alienate a friend."

"Whoever walks in integrity walks securely!"

With all the political backbiting, one wonders if there is such a thing as integrity in politicians. A resounding "YES" goes to two perennial favorites—Franklin and Eleanor Roosevelt. Each year in the Gallup Poll of America's most admired people, the Roosevelts finish in the top ten.

In 1999, the Gallup Organization produced a list of the most admired for the 20th century. In first place was a politician! Guess who? This politician with such huge integrity and universal admiration is found in the July 30 reflection.

October 6

Smells

Life expectancy would grow by leaps and bounds if green vegetables smelled as good as bacon.
Doug Larson

Dogs see the world with their noses. I know this for a fact because every time I take our dogs for a walk around the block, it becomes a tug of war—a yank and pull session where I often lose. They have to smell everything, and some smells are attractive and powerful. One day, Chewy became infatuated with a bird dropping in the middle of the road. He stood, frozen to the pavement, his nose forever glued to this social error.

The worst moment occurs when you meet a lady, with a cute wee doggie, and our male dogs are truly tacky—sniffing rear ends ad nauseum. The reason why they do this is found in the following poem, which my dear sister Noni used to recite at family gatherings—and our uncle Bobs would sing.

The Doggie Party

The dogs, they had a party, they came from near and far.
Some dogs came by taxi, and some dogs came by car.

Each dog signed his name upon a special book,
And each dog hung his asshole upon a special hook.

One dog was not invited, and this aroused his ire.
He stormed into the party and loudly shouted FIRE!

The dogs got so excited, they all forgot to look,
And grabbed the nearest asshole, from off the nearest hook.

This is a sad, sad story, for it is very sore,
to wear another's asshole, you've never worn before.

So this is why when dogs roam, o'ver land or sea or foam,
they sniff each other's asshole, in hope they find their own.

Many versions of this poem can be found on the internet. It may be an old British song since the word "arsehole" is often used. No source is named.

October 7

Warts

I had plenty of pimples as a kid. One day I fell asleep in the library. When I woke up, a blind man was reading my face.

Rodney Dangerfield

A man in love mistakes a pimple for a dimple.

Japanese Proverb

Mike and I were having our usual morning workout, and we were talking about our frustration with writing. We both experienced compositional failure when we used imaginative spelling and poor grammar. A teacher in Mike's school entered one of Mike's essays in an essay contest for the whole province, and it came in third. Mike then handed in his copy of the essay to be marked by his English composition teacher, and it came back with a mark of 47! Mike figured that the first teacher thought the essay was brilliant and had corrected the spelling and grammar errors before entering it. The rule was that three major grammar errors would produce a failing mark. The thought and argument could be outstanding and still produce a failure.

I find the same frustration with the evaluation of writing. I'll hand somebody a reflection, and they will hand it back with a circle around a typo or spelling error. Many folks instantly discount substance when the delivery has an error. It's rather like a beautiful woman with a wart on her nose. We look at the wart. The spelling and grammar errors stick out like warts ruining the beauty that lies beneath. It's frustrating, but it happens with most judgmental evaluation.

The same process occurs in our judgments of public speaking. I once won a public speaking contest with what could be considered as frivolous substance. Another contestant had a much deeper and more scholarly topic—argued in an incredibly fine fashion. I figure the reason I won was a smooth delivery—with a good voice—and NO warts! It's exactly this evaluation that wins elections. A charismatic speaker with a weak platform will always win over an average speaker with the greatest platform in the world, particularly if this person has some wart. We need to get beyond the delivery and into the real substance before we put our "X" on the ballot. We must overlook warts to find the inner substance—and rest assured—God will accept our best effort—warts and all!

October 8

Profit

All told, these profit levels have put the world's five largest publicly traded oil companies on track to earn more than $100 billion before year's end. Yet, at the same time that Big Oil's bottom line is going up, so are Americans' energy costs.

Allyson Schwartz

The big pharmaceutical companies are set up to handle blockbusters with their massive sales forces, and I don't think they have done anything to really address this future in any useful way.

Regina Herzkinger

Pharmaceutical companies are enjoying unprecedented profits and access with this Administration. Yet the Republicans' prescription drug plan for seniors has been a colossal failure, and over 43 million Americans wake up every morning without health insurance.

Jim Clyburn

In the barbershop the other day, we were hashing over what everyone needs—like a good haircut naturally—but clean air, water and good soil rate right up there. Without these three, we don't last very long! All the folks discussing the question of need were seniors, and pretty soon the topic of gas prices came up, and you should have heard the moaning and groaning. "I filled up the other day and it was over a hundred bucks for the first time," one of the boys said.

Another said, "Everybody is hurting ... even the folks who produce the gasoline ... because their stock has been going down!" I suggested that just because the stocks are lower doesn't mean they are hurting. In fact, the oil companies are making unprecedented profits, as is the pharmaceutical industry. Everybody needs gasoline and drugs, and these companies are making huge profits even as economies go into recession. The big three car companies used to determine the economy of America. Much of the control has switched to two conglomerates—oil and pharmaceuticals.

The average person has no control over the rocketing price of petroleum. As this person ages, health care expenses are going through the roof. The government has set up the tax structure in such a way that all the costs are borne by the taxpayers, and all the profits are made by the conglomerates. I wonder just how long this can go on before the whole damned structure collapses. Maybe it is collapsing already?

October 9

Markets

October: This is one of the peculiarly dangerous months to speculate in stocks. The others are July, January, September, April, November, May, March, June, December, August and February.

The safe way to double your money is to fold it over once and put it in your pocket.

Frank Hubbard

Have you ridden a toboggan or skied down a gentle hill, when suddenly the hill becomes steeper and you lose control? A huge panic sets in. When that happens, it pays to have some insulation. Investors in the stock markets must feel a similar panic when the stocks begin to tumble. How far will they go? Where is the bottom? Should we sell and take a huge loss? Should we be buying excellent companies whose stocks have become a bargain? No one has a market crystal ball, or we would all be rich. I suggest that it is imprudent to sell the stock of good companies when the markets go for a "dump." If you need the money, don't invest in stocks, but if you are in, go for long-term growth and stay the course, as Warren Buffet has shown. (There are exceptions. See March 7.) In the long term, the markets have always gone up. Market decline, to my mind, is mostly psychological. It's a vicious circle—an overreaction to the credit crunch. It may take time, but the downward slope will end and we will recover. Just don't give in to panic. It pays to have some insulation!

I was racing my bicycle on a paved country road one summer. I came over the top of a slight rise when suddenly, I found myself on a very steep downhill. The smooth pavement had been replaced by fist-sized rocks. The thin tires of a touring bike are not made for loose stone, but if I fell on this surface, I would be cut to pieces by the jagged rocks. My heart was in my mouth as I slid and bounced down that hill on my bike. Somehow, I managed to keep my balance by standing up and just steering. After another miraculous escape, we celebrated with fine food and wine.

If the global economy suffers, we all share in the suffering. I pray that you escape the market carnage, and when these markets eventually recover, remember to give thanks and celebrate!

October 10

Black Boxes

Black box is a technical term for a device or system or object when it is viewed primarily in terms of its input and output characteristics. Almost anything might occasionally be referred to as a black box: a transistor, an algorithm, humans, the Internet.

In aviation, the term Black Box refers to the flight data recorder and cockpit voice recorder responsible for recording all communications in the cockpit of an aircraft in flight. The phrase has become popularized by modern media while reporting aircraft crashes, despite the fact that the devices are usually not black.

Wikipedia

We did an experiment with black boxes in grade 9. The students were given a box with probes sticking out which they could withdraw from the box. They could NOT look in the box and needed indirect evidence to guess what might be inside. The whole exercise was to eventually develop an understanding of how scientists developed MODELS of atoms without actually being able to see directly inside the atom.

Many of the items we depend on each day are black boxes to most of us—cars, TV, computers, telephones and most kitchen appliances, to name a few. We cannot see what's happening inside, nor do we care—until the device stops working.

My workout partner, Mike, was an engineer who could get the workers in the nuclear plants to figure out what was going on inside a reactor by asking the appropriate questions. Sometimes by examining the "input and output characteristics" mentioned above, Mike could direct the technicians to the solution for a problem in the nuclear reactor black box.

By asking the right questions, black boxes such as atoms, car engines and even nuclear reactors can be persuaded to give up their secrets. I suppose the same principle applies to the complex inner workings of humans as well? It's true—to a degree—but there's always seems to be some new twist coming forth from the black box known as the human psyche.

October 11

Thought Experiments

Much of modern physics is built not upon measurement but on thought experimentation.

Martin Cohen

Scientists tend to use thought experiments (Gedankenexperimente in German) in the form of imaginary, 'proxy' experiments which they conduct prior to a real, 'physical' experiment. In these cases, the result of the 'proxy' experiment will often be so clear that there will be no need to conduct a physical experiment at all.

Wikipedia

Many modern theories in science are based on pure thought rather than the results of actual experiments. Physics is an interesting field these days because of the huge machine, the *Large Hadron Collider* in Switzerland. Physicists using this 8 billion dollar toy will be able to find the "Big Bang" particle from which the universe is constructed (the GOD particle.) Paradoxically, the biggest ideas in physics in the last century involved no expensive experiments whatsoever. Albert Einstein, sitting in the Swiss patent office as a clerk, had loads of time on his hands; by imagining himself riding light beams, he was able to formulate his famous Theory of Relativity. Einstein also came up with his equally famous $E = mc^2$ by rearranging existing mathematics equations. The equivalence of energy and matter, and the idea that enormous amounts of energy could be released by conversion of a small quantity of matter, were hypothetical until the atomic bombs were built and tested.

The best thought experiment I recall was performed by the head of science at my first school. Jack had spent at least an hour setting up an elaborate physics demonstration on the front desk of his downstairs classroom. He left a *DO NOT DISTURB* sign on the equipment and went upstairs to his first class. When he came down later for his physics class, the first period teacher had missed his sign and had taken the equipment apart and put it out in the preparation room. To add to Jack's panic, an inspector was sitting at the back of the classroom to observe the class. Thinking quickly, Jack did the whole demo without equipment as a thought experiment, and gave the students sample data to work out a result. To Jack's great relief, the inspector loved the lesson, and Jack had a great story to tell us later in the day. Jack's "invisible demo" saved the day.

October 12

Staying Youthful

I read an article the other day with a recipe for staying "young." The recipe contained dozens of cosmetics and supplements and very little free stuff. You may not remain young forever, but here's a list of free POINTERS for staying youthful—all beginning with the letter "P" to aid your memory:

Pachyderm NOT: If you stay active and limit your food and drink, you'll be slim and trim, look healthier and have more energy;

Pharmaceuticals: Avoid alcohol, tobacco and other addictive drugs—take your vitamins and other useful supplements—and know the side effects of your medications;

Play: Produce those endorphins—be happy and stress-free—dance, sing, laugh and lots of aerobic exercise —have a sense of FUN about living;

Pliable skin: Keep good olive oil or other quality oil in your diet and get some sun for vitamin D. Stay active—endorphins give you a "space cadet glow";

Poisonous people NOT: Avoid the cynics, whiners, losers and users— allow too many of them around you, and you become like them;

Posture: Pretend there is a strong rope attached to the top of your head, pulling you up straight. Walk like a president;

Pray: And get lots of others to include you in their prayer. Prayer works to heal and gives you the spiritual energy to overcome difficult times;

Proactive: Plan for enjoyment, relaxation, learning and discovery;

Protein: Get enough at every meal—but not too much animal protein, which slows everything down while it's being digested;

Purpose: Have a sense of being productive.

If you are retired, VOLUNTEER!

October 13

GOD Outside the Box

All gods are homemade, and it is we who pull their strings, and so, give them the power to pull ours.

Aldous Huxley

My religion consists of a humble admiration of the illimitable superior spirit who reveals himself in the slight details we are able to perceive with our frail and feeble mind.

Albert Einstein

We were listing examples of Black Boxes in an earlier reflection. God is the prime example. No matter how we probe and experiment, we can never fully know God. Many would take exception to this notion. Some folks would say, "He is there in the Bible for all who have eyes to see." There are certainly very different Biblical images, from "wrath" to "love", depending on where you are reading. May I suggest that we need not form human images of God through human thought experiments? Some astute individual asked a perceptive question about an earlier reflection, where I suggested that God is a woman. This reflection reader asked, "Does it really matter whether God is male or female?" The answer is a definite "no." I repeat: God remains unknowable. All our attempts to define God are a result of our desire to get our hands on a concrete God, a God "in a box" where we can examine God and understand what God is really like.

I like to think of God as being outside the box, everywhere, in everything and everybody. This is sometimes called the "immanence" of God, which usually means that God pervades all things, and that you can find God wherever you look. Many early inhabitants were quite comfortable with the notion that the force of creation could be seen in everything. Celtic and Aboriginal spirituality saw God's presence in all of nature, and the interconnectedness of all components of nature. Many scientists believe, as in Einstein's statement above, that God can be found in every aspect of the universe. Nature is far too complex to be a result of chance alone.

We are able to see God in all of creation and hear God in all the music of the great composers. We can feel God in the fur of a newborn pup and smell God after a rainfall. God is everywhere, in everything and every person—outside any box we could ever construct.

October 14

Autumn Season

Mark how fleeting and paltry is the estate of man: yesterday in embryo, tomorrow a mummy or ashes. So for the hair's breadth of time assigned to thee live rationally, and part with life cheerfully, as drops the ripe olive, extolling the season that bore it and the tree that matured it.

Marcus Aurelius, Meditations

We love to go for rides and hikes in October. The autumn colors are at their best, and it's usually warm enough for a light jacket. All the red, yellow, and orange leaves make a wondrous splash against the deep dark evergreens. It's as if these trees know the harsh weather is coming, and a huge show is called for before they die for the winter. Observing the beauty of these colorful trees in autumn demands close, leisurely enjoyment. Get your boots on and your binoculars out.

The autumn of our human journey should be viewed with the same awe and leisurely celebration. Our elders possess this same autumnal beauty as the trees. The great wisdom and inner beauty of our "ancients'" stories need savoring before the season is over—if we but take the time to savor.

Along the line of smoky hills,
the crimson forest stands,
And all the day the blue-jay calls
throughout the autumn lands.

Now by the brook the maple leans,
with all his glory spread;
And all the sumachs on the hills
have turned their green to red.

Now, by great marshes wrapt in mist,
or past some river's mouth,
Throughout the long, still autumn day
wild birds are flying south.

"Indian Summer" by William Wilfred Campbell (1860-1919)

October 15

Synergy

For we are all God's servants, WORKING TOGETHER. (senergo ... Greek)
1 Corinthians 3:19

We know that all things WORK TOGETHER for good ...
Romans 8:28

Synergy and serendipity often play a big part in medical and scientific advances.
Julie Bishop

"Politics makes strange bedfellows." Political interests can bring together people who otherwise have little in common. This saying is adapted from a line in *The Tempest*, by William Shakespeare: "Misery acquaints a man with strange bedfellows." It is spoken by a man who has been shipwrecked and finds himself seeking shelter beside a sleeping monster.

The term "SYNERGY" was originally used by the Apostle Paul to mean that the final outcome is greater than the sum of the parts. Great outcomes would be available for those who worked together in God's grace.

Synergy usually arises when two persons with different complementary skills cooperate. The fundamental example of synergy is the cooperation in a marriage. In business, people with different skills will enhance the outcome when they work together in a collaborative rather than a competitive atmosphere.

A synergistic effect may also occur in the combinations of two or more drugs which can interact in ways that magnify one or more effects, or side effects, of those drugs. Tylenol 3's contain codeine mixed with acetaminophen to enhance the action of codeine as a pain reliever.

We are living in the time of a credit crunch in America. Wouldn't it make sense for democrats and republicans to swallow their pride and work together to produce the best solution to our dilemma? Synergistic elected officials—what a novel concept!

October 16

Symbiosis

Symbiosis definition: *Two dissimilar organisms living together for their mutual benefit.*
From our 10th grade botany text

Two can live more cheaply than one.

Old Saying

The first year I taught, I had several classes of 10th grade botany. One of the topics I really enjoyed in the course was "symbiosis." There were a number of fun examples, including the rhinoceros and the tic bird. If you have seen pictures of the big old African rhino, a close look always shows at least one tiny bird, a "tic" bird, riding around on the back of the big beast. The tic bird eats the rhino's tics, and so the bird gets food (and protection and a free ride.) The rhinoceros gets comfort (freedom from biting bugs), and an early warning system. The bird will issue a shrill warning song if lions try to sneak up on the rhino. These two very different animals are mutually beneficial.

Lichens are perhaps the prime botanical example of symbiosis. Those scaly growths on rocks are actually two plants in a symbiotic relationship. Fungi and algae combine to survive in zero soil. The fungus extracts water and minerals from rock for the algae, and the algae carry out photosynthesis to produce food for both partners. Working together for mutual benefit usually has a synergistic result! In this case, rock is slowly broken down to eventually form soil.

PS1 *THE POWER OF TWO:* My brother Bert and his spouse lived on a sailboat for two summers and a winter! They loved their sailboat, appropriately named the "SYMBIOSIS."

PS2 THE POWER OF FIVE: When we were first married, my wife would issue a stern warning if I committed a social error: "Hey Lee… do you see these five fingers? Well, individually they may not be much, but rolled into a fist … they become a weapon terrible to behold!" Then if I persisted in poor behavior, a well-placed punch would land on my arm. This is one synergistic effect my poor arm really didn't appreciate—so I was generally well behaved, since there was no punch-back for social errors!

October 17

Synchronicity

I am open to the guidance of synchronicity, and do not let expectations hinder my path.

Dalai Lama

With Synchronicity, all the resources we need are made available to us at the precise moment that is appropriate. The people who come into our lives are the ones we need at that moment in time. Everything is perfect. We only need to recognize this and tune in to the flow.

Alex Chua

The intellect has little to do on the road to discovery. There comes a leap in conscious-ness, call it Intuition or what you will, the solution comes to you and you don't know how or why.

Albert Einstein

A lot o' people don't realize what's really going on. They view life as a bunch o' uncon-nected incidents 'n things. They don't realize that there's this, like, lattice o' coincidence that lays on top o' everything.

From the 1984 cult film *Repo Man*

Have you experienced the feeling that seemingly unrelated occur-rences are pointing you to towards something which is very impor-tant to you personally? It could be something someone says. Perhaps someone you don't know makes a statement which throws light on a problem you have. In other words, one or more coincidences suddenly have great meaning. The psychologist Carl Jung called such experiences SYNCHRONICITY. Some folks believe, as the Dali Lama does, that everything happens for a reason, and that we need to be tuned into our surroundings and what people are saying in order to take advantage of the "guidance of synchronicity."

Sometimes, totally unrelated events can bring you to a sudden realization, a revelation or a "leap of consciousness", as Einstein calls it. At that moment, a light bulb goes on in your head, and you feel like shouting, "Eureka—I have it!" Jung may have called this synchronicity, but I feel that such moments often happen when we let our subconscious mind direct us to the revelation. There are two things we can do to help this to happen. We need to tune into our sur-roundings and be able to recognize when synchronicity is around. We don't want to keep making the mistake of wondering, "What's happening ... if any-thing?" Awareness is everything. Synchronicity!

October 18

Animal Idol

A champion owes everybody something. He can never pay back for all the help he got, for making him an idol.

Jack Dempsey

My definition of an American Idol is someone who is a great talent and who communicates well with the audience.

Blake Lewis

The animals were suffering from lack of attention again. This wanton disregard for their well-being resulted from the farmer and his hands watching too much TV—too many reality shows, and that bothersome "American Idol" nonsense. All too often the feed came late or bedtime dragged on into the wee hours, while the keepers idled away their time watching their silly shows. After some rancor, barnyard unanimity came quickly when the animals decided to hold their own animal idol. The only problem was: who would they get to judge the best beastly vocalist? After some discussion, they achieved unanimity again with the great idea that the veterinarian and her husband, the music teacher, would be admirable animal adjudicators, as they loved all the animals equally well, and would be unbiased. So work began for the splendid secret show.

The night of the amazing animal idol arrived with an abundant audience in attendance. The attendees cheered as dogs howled in unison, pigs grunted in harmony, and whole collections of farm birds sang their hearts out. The judges conferred and came up with the surprise winner—the donkey!!! "The donkey made the 'ideal idol' with his wonderfully musical 'He-Haw' song—which happens to be a perfect interval called a fourth—absolute perfection!" was the judge's comment.

That just goes to show you that you don't need to sing in unison, harmony, or like a bird to win the idol. Just learn to bray in perfect intervals—like an ass.

October 19

Laughology

You grow up the day you have your first real laugh at yourself.

Ethel Barrymore

Against the assault of laughter, nothing can stand.

Mark Twain

We are in the world to laugh. In purgatory or in hell we shall no longer be able to do so. And in heaven it would not be proper.

Jules Renard

If you Google "Laughology", you will find a British website detailing a registered company which arranges seminars incorporating laughter into the workplace. You will also find a Canadian documentary movie which is "screamingly funny" according to one national newspaper. We don't need laughologists or movies to explain why laughing is good for us. Laughing produces endorphins, those feel-good molecules which are the natural pain-killers of the endocrine system. It has been well-established that folks who laugh a lot live longer—and have more fun in the living. Why would you bother with longevity if everything makes you grouchy?

When I was about 18, one of my cousins died of cancer. That was one sad funeral and wake. Thank goodness my uncle Bobs was able to rescue me. Bobs was an extremely funny fellow who was always joking—even at funerals. He took me aside where the others couldn't hear us, and began to tell me the funniest stories and jokes. Some of these were even musical. I remember his story of the doggy party in which the dogs have to hang their behinds on a hook before they go into the party. (See October 6 on Smells.) Someone yells "fire" and in their haste, the dogs all grab the wrong rear end. And then Bobs would sing "and that's the reason why each doggy smells the a—h—- of another doggy—he's looking for his own a—h—-." All this time I was attempting to stifle my laughter so as not to disturb the very serious wake going on. Oh well—I went home feeling better. As someone rightly observed, laughter truly is the best medicine!

October 20

Elegance

Elegance is innate. It has nothing to do with being well dressed. Elegance is refusal.
Diana Vreeland

If only for the sake of elegance, I try to remain morally pure.
Marcel Proust

His (Haydn's) was a long, sane, sound, and on the whole, fortunate existence. For many years he was poor and obscure, but if he had his time of trial ... with practical wisdom he conquered the Fates and became eminent.
From *Haydn*   J. Cuthbert Hadden

My mother and sister wrote beautiful letters. The prose was informative, loving and elegant. There were often wee drawings of cats, birds or some such interspersed with the writing. Letter writing has been replaced by e-mail, and thank heavens there are still folks who craft their messages with care. I love the warmth of a simple yet well-crafted message, a precious gem in this age of trash talk. We could laugh at nonsensical Internet posts if they weren't so pitifully written. Hooray for all the contributors who write excellent reviews on Amazon and e-music.

My workout buddy, Mike, brought over a biography of Haydn, the composer. This plain old volume was over a century old and looked all worn out. Yet when I opened it up—Surprise!— the margins were wide enough to accommodate notes, and there were useful subtitles elegantly embedded in the text. Reading this old-style book was almost as pleasurable as reading the King James Version of the Bible—a rare treat.

Some folks exude dignity and gracefulness. We had a nonagenarian guest to lunch recently. Nina seemed to be from another planet when compared to the cell-phone-addicted, trash-talking folks you often encounter these days. Nina was a polished jewel in dress and demeanor. The atmosphere was instantly elevated to a higher plane when we were introduced. I felt a sense of peacefulness and tranquility in our conversations.

When encountering genuine refinement, we wish it to continue. I suppose it's as simple as refusing to be inelegant.

October 21

Bridge

If you marry into the Steels family, you have to learn how to play bridge.
Allen Steels   (to my bride on our wedding day)

I say, let's banish bridge. Let's find some pleasant way of being miserable together.
Don Herold

Investing is not as tough as being a top-notch bridge player. All it takes is the ability to see things as they really are.
Warren Buffet

My wife made me join a bridge club. I jump off next Tuesday.
Rodney Dangerfield

Good sex is like good bridge. If you don't have a good partner, you'd better have a good hand.
Mae West

There are several items common to almost every newspaper—including the horoscope, the crossword puzzle and the bridge hand. The first gives you a good laugh, the second a mental workout and the third—frustration. Sure bridge is a complex game, but how the hell they come up with the weird conventions is beyond me. We always figure out how we would have bid and played the hands before we read the column. It's a rare day when our strategy matches what the bridge columnist reveals. The game of bridge is interesting because, like chess, there is infinite variety in the game. Many other games have far too few variables to keep your interest, but there always seems to be something to learn when you have 13 cards in your hand. (The whole deck of 52 cards is dealt out to 4 players—13 cards each.) So I say hooray for the newspapers, for providing food for thought each day.

When my father joked about having to play bridge when you married into the family, I thought to myself, "Hmm … not a good thing to say on our wedding day." But as things turned out, we play the game often—for fun of course. Life is too short to take any game seriously. How can you take a game seriously when the following are regularly said by bridge players?

"Lay down, and let's see all you've got."
"How many rubbers did you score?"
"Hey dummy, don't sit there doing nothing. Go get the drinks!"

October 22

The Cactus

I have learned the difference between a cactus and a caucus. On a cactus, the pricks are on the outside.

Morris K. Udall

I consider it the highest compliment when my employees go out and start their own companies in competition with me. I always send them a plant to wish them well. Of course, it's a cactus.

Norman Brodsky

Who wants to become a writer? And why? Because it's the answer to everything. To "Why am I here?" To uselessness. It's the streaming reason for living. To note, to pin down, to build up, to create, to be astonished at nothing, to cherish the oddities, to let nothing go down the drain, to make something, to make a great flower out of life, even if it's a cactus.

Enid Bagnold

In the middle ages, people took potions for their ailments. In the 19th century they took snake oil. Citizens of today's shiny, technological age are too modern for that. They take antioxidants and extract of cactus instead.

Charles Krauthammer

The spindly plant quietly panicked yet again. "Nobody seems to care," she thought as she was passed over at watering and feeding time.

All the rest of the plants cried in derision: "You are simply good for nothing, other than to be a prickly snob, and nobody gives a damn. They don't even water you."

"What good am I?" thought the lonely little cactus. "I'll just dry up and fade away." As if in response, a large lump began to grow on her head. "This is it," she supposed. "I must have the cancerous blight, and it's just as well because it will be over quickly!" The lump began to open and open—and out popped the most colorful and enduring flower ever seen in the household. Everyone came to admire this beautiful bloom and used words like rare, astounding, and worthwhile. Just when she was about to give up her quiet existence, a butterfly-like metamorphosis had changed the lonely little cactus into something spectacular—something the other showy plants could never attain.

"Thank you Lord," thought the wee cactus, "thank you for your power working within me … a power which did more than I could ever ask or imagine."

LaFF

We aim to bring sunshine and fun to your day ... so come on out and enjoy LaFF ... Life after Fifty-Five.

Enid Stronach

Mirth is God's medicine. Everybody ought to bathe in it.

Henry Ward Beecher

The most wasted of all days is one without laughter.

E. Cummings

Laughter is an instant vacation.

Milton Berle

I have the good fortune of knowing Enid Stronach, who organizes a monthly show for seniors. The show is called "LaFF" *Life after Fifty-Five,* and most of the performers and audience have reached that golden age. The show usually has singers, dancers, short skits and lots and lots of laughs. It is put on in the parish hall of a local church which has a retirement home next door so some folks can walk to the show. This cabaret-style performance has an excellent reputation, and folks come from all over town once a month to get a light meal and the show. It is a great privilege to be in one of Enid's LaFFs. Not only do you get a real high from performing for a delightfully appreciative audience, you get to see real talent in the dancing and singing mix so thoroughly and thoughtfully organized by Enid and her committee.

What a wonderful production this LaFF show has become, particularly when you see the smiles on the faces of both audience and performers. This is about the closest thing to a "love-in" that you can imagine, and I look forward to being a part of this smashing show as often as possible—which may not be that often since there are large numbers of terrifically talented singers, dancers and funny folks around at any age. Thank goodness for all their laffs!

October 24

50's Music and Dances

I would believe only in a God that knows how to dance.

Friedrich Nietzsche

Never trust spiritual leader who cannot dance.

Mr. Miyagi

Nobody cares if you can't dance well. Just get up and dance.

Dave Barry

Yesterday:

We remember the first 50's dance at our new church. We did everything our-selves; decorations, food and the dance itself. Ted brought his huge collection of 45's (remember those discs with the big hole in the middle.) Bob brought his tape collection (remember those little cassettes.) I brought my heavy Marantz receiver and heavier speakers. Marie made a wonderful cloth cover with the "BLT'S" (Bob, Lee and Ted) on it. Everybody danced to Elvis, Buddy Holly, Pat Boone, Connie Francis and Paul Anka etc. We danced the jive, the twist and plenty of "clutch and grab." There were spot dances and snowball dances and everybody had fun—until the toilets in the washrooms backed up—but that's another story. (We put on "Splish Splash I was Takin' a Bath" when that happened.) We kept those dances going every year until we eventually got tired of doing everything—but everybody sure had fun. Nobody ever complained about the music.

Today:

We were at a wedding last weekend, and everything was just lovely—lovely service, setting and dinner—until the DJ cranked up his modern moronic machine—so ear-splittingly loud, it hurt! Celia said that not only did the first "song" give her a headache; she actually felt pain in the rest of her body. After a couple of dances we managed to sneak away before our hearing was com-pletely shot. Not only was the "music" too loud, but about 80% of the stuff was just noise—rap and funk—and you couldn't dance to it. Why do many of today's DJ's play such trash at painfully loud levels? I must be getting old, because it sure beats the hell out of me. Unintelligible lyrics, no melody and a huge bass beat are NOT "dance" music—to my ears. I guess I'm getting old.

298

October 25

Stuff

All the stuff that you visualized that was going to work so beautifully, you discover is trashed, so you jump to something else.

F. Murray Abraham

Religion is excellent stuff for keeping common people quiet.

Napoleon Bonaparte

Buy land. They ain't making any more of the stuff.

Will Rogers

I never drink water; that is the stuff that rusts pipes.

W.C. Fields

Why don't they make the whole plane out of that black box stuff.

Stephen Wright

A woman looks at a floor and sees a surface that needs cleaning. A man looks at a floor and sees a giant shelf good for holding all his stuff. I forget who gave me that truism, but in my case it really is true. My inner sanctum—the den—holds so much stuff, it's like a giant museum crammed into one small room. I know lots of other guys who have loads of stuff. When Celia's brother, Father Phil, moved out of a temporary apartment he had, we took the seats out of our van and loaded it up with liquor-store boxes full of his apartment stuff. We took these to his locker in the basement of his apartment building and guess what? The locker already had lots of boxes stuffed with stuff! I think they are still there. (Some of them have ridden around in his car trunk for years.)

My friend Terry invented a formula for deciding how many boxes you need for your stuff:

# of boxes (liquor) = shelf length in feet ÷ 2

Terry recently moved his son, and he said he measured 174 feet of stuff on shelves—so he got 87 liquor boxes. I wonder how long some of them will remain unopened.

October 26

Time 2

The only reason for time is so that everything doesn't happen at once.

Albert Einstein

Every day has been so short, every hour so fleeting, ever minutes so filled with the life I love, that time for me has fled on too swift a wing.

Aga Khan III

Whether it's the best of times or the worst of times, it's the only time we've got.

Art Buchwald

The time you enjoy wasting is not wasted time.

Bertrand Russell

Whenever someone asks me to take on a new undertaking requiring large amounts of time, I always respond, "Let me think about that—I'll get back to you." We are talking here about requests for a long-term commitment. I remember when I was first asked to direct our church choir. The organist assured me that it would be nothing more than counting the time now and then to help out. "Just wave your hands in front of them when I need it," she said. I immediately replied, "Yes ... I'll be happy to help out when you need me." The time commitment to this volunteer task kept growing over the years, reminding me to consider carefully when somebody says, "I have a little job for you."

If you have commitments which require more time than you have available, get help. Family members will usually come to the rescue. In *Cheaper by the Dozen*, a story about a family with 12 children, the older children are organized to help out the younger kids. Everybody has a task, and each person is expected to perform his or her task without being asked. If you don't have a large family, or if they seem to be "users" or "takers," consider obtaining an extended family. We are fortunate to have large extended families in our work-colleagues, neighbors, friends and our church. Many of them have made light work—a labor of love—for lots of big jobs. Teamwork, a sense of fun, and simple strategies help accomplish practically any task. The Beatles had it right when they suggested, "All you need is LOVE ... LOVE is all you need."

October 27

Lead

It is remarkable that this metal (lead), when dissolved in an acid, has the property of imparting a saccharine taste to the fluid. Thus the common acetate of lead is always called 'sugar of lead.' It was perhaps on this account that the Greeks and Romans used sheet lead to neutralize the acidity of bad wine ... a practice which now is happily not in use since it has been found that all combinations of lead are decidedly poisonous.

Scientific American, 1857

The skin of lead workers is apt to bear the same color of the metal ... Demons and ghosts are often found to disturb the miners.

Bernardo Ramazzini, physician, 1770

The Opinion of the mischievous Effect from Lead is at least above Sixty Years old, and you will observe with Concern how long a useful Truth may be known and exist before it is generally receiv'd and practic'd on.

Benjamin Franklin, Printer, 1786

The phrase "get the lead out" usually means get more energetic—more animated—more enthusiastic—or simply, "Move it!" It has its origins back in the 30's when jobs were scarce so you had to move quickly, or get the lead out of your pants, to get there when jobs were being handed out. The expression has a ring of truth, since heavy metals such as mercury and lead can accumulate in the body and produce lethargy. Physical and mental slowness result from heavy metal poisoning, and if the metal continues to build up in the body, "demons and ghosts" can take possession as Ramazzini noted. A person with accumulated lead would definitely have little energy—and maybe even be as "mad as a hatter."

How common is lead poisoning? There is a theory that the Roman Empire fell because the populace became lethargic from the lead in lead goblets used for drinking wine. Nobody knows for sure if this is true, but it's an interesting possibility. Do we have any fear of lead today? Lead is found in old paint and is ubiquitous in the environment from tetra-ethyl lead, which was used in gasoline as an anti-knock agent for almost sixty years until it was banned. Maybe all the tiredness and lack of concentration are the result of some agent such as lead in the environment. Who knows for sure?

October 28

Tea

Strange how a teapot can represent at the same time the comforts of solitude and the pleasures of company.

Author Unknown

Is there no Latin word for Tea? Upon my soul, if I had known that I would have let the vulgar stuff alone.

Hilaire Belloc

Drinking a daily cup of tea will surely starve the apothecary.

Chinese Proverb

There is no trouble so great or grave that cannot be much diminished by a nice cup of tea.

Bernard-Paul Heroux

My father had a set method for brewing and drinking tea. He would fill the teapot with cold water and plug in the electric kettle. Then he would slowly pour the water into the spout of the kettle and leave the teapot upside down with its spout in the spout of the kettle. (This warmed the interior of the pot.) At the instant the water began to boil, he poured the water quickly into the pot over two tea bags. The cover and a large cozy were placed on the pot. After exactly five minutes of steeping, the bags were removed, and the fresh tea was poured into each cup. The milk was already in the cup. It was sacrilege to add it after. This procedure NEVER varied. I must admit, the brew was eminently drinkable.

My wife convinced me to drink tea clear, and the brew certainly has more flavor. One bag will do a whole pot if you don't use milk. Herbal teas are also excellent, especially in the evening.

In these times of "recession coming", it makes sense to drink an inexpensive beverage. May I suggest clear tea—weak and wet? You can use the bag over again. In fact, during the Depression and the 2nd World War, folks used the same tea bag for weeks at a time.

We had a kettle; we let it leak:
Our not repairing made it worse.
We haven't had any tea for a week...
The bottom is out of the Universe.
Rudyard Kipling

October 29

Consistency

Consistency is contrary to nature, contrary to life. The only completely consistent people are dead.

Aldous Leonard Huxley

Consistency is the last refuge of the unimaginative.

Oscar Wilde

A foolish consistency is the hobgoblin of little minds, adored by little statesmen and philosophers and divines. With consistency a great soul has simply nothing to do.

Ralph Waldo Emerson

If a man would register all his opinions upon love, politics, religion, learning, etc., beginning from his youth and so go on to old age, what a bundle of inconsistencies and contradictions would appear at last!

Jonathan Swift

Consistency requires you to be as ignorant today as you were a year ago.

Bernard Berenson

One would think, after reading the above quotes, that being consistent is a characteristic not to be desired. Why would all these smart folks be so down on being consistent? After all, someone who is consistent is someone you can always depend on. Where would we be if everyone were the opposite—completely inconsistent? It would seem that everything that depends on scheduling from meals to mail to mothering would all go "down the drain." Nobody and nothing would be dependable from trains and buses running on time to doctors and nurses giving the proper care for all our ailments. Chaos and anarchy would soon reign. Somehow, I figure these smart folks all meant something else with their "down with consistency" palaver.

I am sure what these bright lights meant by putting the knock on consistency was to shake us from the comfort of moving through life on autopilot. How many of us seek the comfort of old habits? How many of us like nothing better than to stay on the rails—plodding the same old path—doing the same old same old every day with little imagination. Being alive requires us to try new things and to do the old things in new ways. After all, we all love a surprise party, and shouldn't living be full of delightful surprises? All it takes is a little imagination every day.

October 30

Cleveland

Cleveland rocks!

The Drew Carey Show

...a deadly, dull, dead place.

Henry Miller

I don't get no respect.

Rodney Dangerfield

There are some cities which "get no respect." We live close to two of these cities, both near the shores of Lake Erie—which often suffers from the same lack of respect. These cities are Niagara Falls, N.Y. and Cleveland, Ohio. Perhaps the famous environmental disasters have something to do with the reputation. Love Canal, a toxic mélange of chemicals, ruined a whole neighborhood in Niagara Falls. Cleveland is infamous for June 22, 1969, when an oil slick and debris in the Cuyahoga River burned, drawing national attention to environmental problems in Ohio. National headlines screamed, "River catches fire … only in Cleveland."

I would like to stand up for Cleveland. There are two reasons for this. One is the Cleveland Symphony Orchestra (CSO). Under George Szell, the CSO became the orchestra with the greatest precision in the world. Their Beethoven recordings are magnificent performances. The CSO is still a marvelous instrument. My second plug for Cleveland is the experiment of Michelson and Morley. The speed of light was measured using a huge interferometer constructed in Cleveland. Michelson was the first American to win the Nobel Prize in science—and the experiment was in Cleveland, Ohio!

Besides, where else can you find a group of sports fans called "the Dog Pound?" Only in Cleveland! Cleveland rocks! Speaking of rock, the Rock and Roll Hall of Fame is at 1100 Rock and Roll Blvd. Cleveland Ohio!

October 31

Text Messaging (T.M.)

A collection of T.M. for Halloween: (found on the web)

What does a vampire never order at a restaurant?

A stake sandwich...

What is a skeleton's favorite musical instrument?

A trombone...

What's a vampire's favorite fast food?

A guy with high blood pressure...

Why did the Vampire subscribe to the Wall Street Journal?

He heard it had great circulation...

There was an article in the paper about drivers who text message while they drive. Apparently, it's getting to be another amazing asinine aspect of modern living. Folks think they can multitask while driving. According to this article, one young lady was observed using her knees to steer, since her hands were busy sending text messages. I have never driven with anyone who is talented enough to be able to multitask in this way, but I have observed such strange driving. This irresponsible tiny typing is just another way to make motor trips even more of a hazard.

I simply don't understand folks who use cell phones and Blackberries in public places as if no one else exists. Loud talking and text messaging without regard for people around is rude and seems to be getting worse. We were at a vocal recital recently where the soprano had a lovely soft voice. Concentrated listening was required. In the middle of one of her songs, a cellphone idiot behind us began to tap out a text message. He pinged along for the rest of the song, ruining it for all of us. When the song ended and the audience began to clap, one of the incensed fellows in our row turned around and said to this T.M. fool, "Turn that f—-ing thing off ... NOW!" The inconsiderate clod got up and departed! This received a huge round of applause from all of us.

November 1

Conversion

God is not glorified in any transaction upon earth so much as in the conversion of a sinner.
Archibald Alexander

One day I'm a prostitute and the next day I'm a nun. Where else could you get instant conversion like that?
Lois Bootsin

I do not believe in telling people of one's faith, especially with a view to conversion. Faith must be lived, and when it is, it becomes self-propagating.
Mahatma Gandhi

I love the scene in the movie *O Brother, Where Art Thou* where the zealots—all dressed in white — are singing "Down to the River to Pray" and baptizing new members by full immersion in the river. Our three escaped criminals see this, and one of them is so taken with the process that he rushes in and gets baptized. He excitedly hurries back and tells the other two escapees that he is saved and all his sins are forgiven. The pseudo-brainy but warped leader (played by George Clooney) tells him, "Well, Delmar ... that may be true in the eyes of the Lord but not in the eyes of the great state of Mississippi." This is true about conversion. It doesn't automatically make you better—especially in the eyes of the law. So why are zealots always trying to convert folks?

We go down to the mall to palaver every Saturday morning with our friends Letty and Bill. On a number of occasions, a well-dressed and pleasant gentleman comes along and distracts Bill away from the table conversation. Bill is too polite to be dismissive, so he listens to what the gentleman has to say. I have overheard snippets of the spiel, and this man is trying his best to convince Bill to convert to his system of belief. After an extensive mini-sermon, the chap finally moves on. I ask Bill, "What was that all about? What is that fellow trying to sell you, Bill?"

Bill tells me, "The gentleman was an electrician ... as I was once ... and he knew me then, and he now believes that by telling me all the wonders of his faith, I may see the 'Light'. I just don't have the heart to tell him that I am just as strong in my own beliefs, but these beliefs are not the same as his."

Perhaps we should put Mahatma Gandhi's quote above on some cards and silently give them out to any conversion zealots who come our way.

November 2

Día de los Muertos

To live in hearts we leave behind is not to die.

Thomas Campbell

He spake well who said that graves are the footprints of angels.

Henry Wadsworth Longfellow

He who has gone, so we but cherish his memory, abides with us, more potent, nay, more present than the living man.

Antoine de Saint-Exupery

Oh, may I join the choir invisible
Of those immortal dead who live again.

George Eliot, The Choir Invisible

Yesterday, November 1, is known as "All Saints' Day." November 2 is known as "All Souls' Day." These two days together are a major celebration known in Mexico as *Dia de los Muertos*, or "Day of the Dead". Mexicans really get fired up on this national holiday: firecrackers, carnivals, parades, promenades in cemeteries, Ferris wheels, altars with skulls, and of course, huge parties with lots of tamales. The belief is that on these days, the souls of the departed will come and visit; so families go to great lengths to make these departed souls feel welcome. Elaborate altars are built, with favorite foods, flowers, keepsakes and photos. Although these offerings (ofrendas) are meant to attract the departed, they are often enjoyed afterward by all members of the family. Many believe, however, that the food's nutritional value has been taken away by the departed souls.

Those with writing talent sometimes create short poems, called *calaveras*, "skulls," mocking epitaphs of friends, sometimes describing interesting habits and attitudes or some funny anecdotes.

Calavera   (*Skull*)
Por aquí pasa la muerte   *Here pass the souls of the dead*
Con su aguja y su dedal   *with needle and thimble*
Remendando sus naguas   *mending their skirts*
Para el día del carnaval.   *for the day of the dead.*

This *Dia de los Muertos* makes our celebration of Halloween look very tame. Brazil, Spain and the Philippines also celebrate the days of the dead.

November 3

Conservation

Thank God men cannot fly, and lay waste the sky as well as the earth.
Henry David Thoreau

There is a sufficiency in the world for man's need but not for man's greed.
Mohandas K. Gandhi

We do not inherit the earth from our ancestors; we borrow it from our children.
Native American Proverb

I remember little books of coupons from the Second World War. They were "ration" books, and the coupons could be exchanged for a pound of butter or whatever. You still had to pay for it, but what was happening was rationing. The government was making sure you conserved everyday staples. Of course, greedy folks could still be wasteful by paying extra for somebody's coupons. There were also black market ration books. When governments try to do the right thing, there are always plenty of folks who will make a dishonest living circumventing any regulation, including rationing. The idea was good, however, in that conservation was mandated, even if some shysters cheated.

The opposite of conservation by rationing is to control the price and make a commodity so cheap that everyone feels they have to take advantage of the terrific bargain. The government did that with cigarettes for the armed services. I recall my brother bringing home cartons of them when he was in the air force. He got them at the BX on the base for less than a dollar a carton. What a great time we would have smoking up a huge storm with those cheap cancer-sticks. This was wasteful excess, but it was close to being free. In the long run, this excess turned out to be a painfully expensive health hazard.

Most of the earth's resources are finite. With the number of folks now living on the planet, we need to conserve valuable planetary resources. The commodity in greatest need of conservation is fresh water. Apparently, 90% of the folks living on the planet do NOT have access to clean fresh water, and 75% of all ills can be traced to contaminated water. Fluid for thought!

November 4

Keep Moving

To me, if life boils down to one thing, it's movement. To live is to keep moving.
Jerry Seinfeld

Never confuse movement with action.
Ernest Hemingway

In the midst of movement and chaos, keep stillness inside of you.
Deepak Chopra

Life is like riding a bicycle. To keep your balance you must keep moving.
Albert Einstein

When someone asks me for my philosophy of living, I look them in the eye and very seriously say, "Never stand when you can sit—never sit when you can lie down—and never, ever pass up the opportunity for a good nap!" After we have our little laugh, I usually answer that my real philosophy is to keep moving—because the opposite is deadly. I am now at an age when moving is more important than ever. Getting up in the morning, everything is stiff and hurting. Knees hurt. The back is stiff. Hands are painful. Chances are these complaints won't improve over the day—without some nice easy movement to keep things going. It's not just the joints that need movement to silence their complaints. Both the brain and the body benefit from working out as often as possible. If we don't keep the blood flowing and the neurons firing, we eventually seize up. Without movement, death is inevitable.

In an interview, the world's oldest man was asked for his secret. He suggested: "Each day I get up and gently stretch. Then I lift some easy weights. I make sure to walk every day ... and above all ... I keep moving ... as gently as I can." Pretty good for 114 years ... or any age!

We were at a visitation of a departed loved one, and the casket was open—a rare occurrence these days. I could hear people's comments and heard the line, "What would you like them to say about you when it's your turn to lie there in your casket?"

The second person chuckled and replied: "I would like them to look at me lying there and say ... 'Oh look ... he moved!'"

November 5

Confusion

If you can't convince 'em, confuse 'em.
Harry Truman

Be not careless in deeds, nor confused in words, nor rambling in thought.
Marcus Aurelius

Confusion is a word we have invented for an order which is not understood.
Henry Miller

Boys, if you ever pray, pray for me now. I don't know if you fellas ever had a load of hay fall on you, but when they told me what happened yesterday, I felt like the moon, the stars, and all the planets had fallen on me.
Harry Truman after FDR died in April 1945 and Harry assumed the Presidency

Don't you just love Harry Truman? America is a great place when people with names like Harry, Ronny and Obama can win the presidency. There used to be a phrase associated with Truman: "Give 'em hell Harry!" And he did just that—many times. Some folks think that it was President Roosevelt who made the decision to drop the atomic bomb. Actually, it was Harry Truman. FDR died in April of 1945 and the Vice-President, Harry Truman, became president. They were very different men. FDR was patrician and larger than life. Harry was folksy and considered himself a hard-working grunt. When it came to tough decisions, however, there was no confusion in Harry's decisions. This was perhaps a result of his life-long love affair with books, particularly history books. Everything he read suggested there was no "quit" in the Japanese. In Harry's opinion, the A-bombs were needed to save lives on both sides. Whether you agree or not with Harry's decision, the second bomb ended the war.

Harry Truman certainly polarized Americans. They either loved him or hated him, and he achieved at times the highest and lowest ratings of any president. The only other president to have received such confused ratings is none other than George Bush. Time tells all and historians now rate Harry as one of the greatest American presidents.

PS: The second atomic bomb, dropped on Nagasaki, was a totally different design that the first. It was also the first one of this new design and was dropped without a test. What would have happened if it had been a dud?

November 6

Fishing

Fishing is the sport of drowning worms.

Author Unknown

A bad day of fishing is better than a good day of work.

Author Unknown

The fishing was good; it was the catching that was bad.

A.K. Best

Follow me and I will make you fish for people.

Matthew 4:19

I am the world's worst fisherman. I get a rod in my hands, and everyone near me is in trouble. My pole turns into a lethal weapon—but not for the fish. They all gather beneath my spot to laugh themselves silly. People around me, however, should move very far away; hooks, lines and sinkers will soon come at them from my uncontrollable hands as fish-o-phobia overtakes me. I avoid the lure of the rod like the plague.

Still, every once in a decade, someone convinces me to try again; so when Wayne suggested that our friend Cliff would like to go out on the Gulf for a day, I thought to myself, how could I possibly muck up a charter boat with about 20 fisher folk, out for a few hours of fun? I would come prepared with my iPod and paperback novel, and fall back on these aids after the usual initial failure. Well, things didn't quite work out.

I got up late when the alarm failed to go off. That should have been my warning. I was out of the trailer in five minutes—with a cooler of liquid—but without my fall-back aids. In spite of the fog, (another bad omen), we arrived at the boat in time, and paid our 60 bucks each, along with 20 other enthusiastic folks. The boat shoved off and churned through the choppy water into the Gulf of Mexico—at least I think it was the Gulf, as the fog hid everything. After two hours of deafening diesel, blasting horn and rocking motion, we stopped and let out our lines. My reel immediately became a mess of line. "Oh ho," said the mate, "you have made a 'nest' because you didn't keep your thumb on the line like I told you."

"Here we go again," I thought, as the mate made it right again. "What could possibly happen next to the world's worst fisherman?"

November 7

Élan

Élan - noun   *they performed with uncommon élan*
flair, style, panache, confidence, dash, éclat, energy, vigor, vitality, liveli-
ness, brio, esprit, animation, vivacity, zest, verve, spirit, pep, sparkle,
enthusiasm, gusto, eagerness, feeling, fire; informal: pizzazz, zing, zip, vim,
oomph

Barry Tuckwell spoke of the élan Kertész could coax out of the London Symphony, many of whom Tuckwell regarded as 'old codgers not bloody likely to dance to any youngster's tune.'

From an entry in Wikipedia about István Kertész

In our workout this morning, Mike and I were wowed by a recording of Dvorák's Seventh Symphony, conducted by István Kertész. The reading has a freshness and sparkle, and at one point, Mike said the horn playing made the hair stand up on the back of his neck. After the workout, I looked up István Kertész, and his life story brought tears to my eyes.

Kertész recorded all the Dvorák symphonies when he was in his mid-thirties—a very young age for a major conductor. (These London Symphony recordings have remained the benchmark recordings for Dvorák symphonies.) Kertész then applied for the conducting job of the Cleveland orchestra. The Cleveland players voted 96 to 2 in favor of Kertész, but the board turned him down—probably because they considered him too young to conduct their beloved orchestra. Sadly, István Kertész drowned a few years after this at the age of 42. His recordings of Dvorák symphonies remain a magnificent tribute to his conducting skills.

Age discrimination can affect the young as well as the old. The paradigm that "age brings wisdom" may mean the exclusion of the exuberance, enthusiasm and élan of youth. The salesmanship to convince folks to try something in a different way isn't age-dependent. In my teaching career, I often found young people who were so gifted in an area, they could accomplish surprises in that area—given the chance. There's the catch. We need to be open enough to allow the vitality of youth to have its fling. (And there's certainly nothing wrong with a good performance—at any age!)

November 8

Frugality

In recessions we smoke less, drink less, and exercise more. U.K. divorce lawyers even say couples are sticking it out.

MacLean's Magazine

The new frugal could help the green movement. Big-car sales are down; industrial emissions will likely drop.

MacLean's Magazine

The donations to the food bank have dropped off. At the same time the number of people using us has nearly doubled in the past 4 months. What can we do?

A food bank worker quoted in the Toronto Star

A few years back, a banker friend was whining to us about how her Christmas bonus was only 50 thousand, and that she might be forced to move next year because of this. At the time, neither of us came close to that wage for the whole year. I read an article on the Christmas bonuses of Wall Street brokers in 2006. (See March 19.) The average bonus was 450 thousand, and few didn't receive a substantial bonus. I wonder how many bankers and brokers will get bonuses this year, as their business has managed to remove trillions from the pockets of retirees' pensions and mutual funds. During the hard times many are facing this winter, frugality is back in fashion, and most people will be learning to live on less, much less!

Unless we end up on the street, frugal living is often healthier living. We learn how to eat leaner with less meat. The fat North American was a rare beast in the Depression, and maybe the collective continent can become "the greatest loser" with a slimmer, healthier populace. The "bigger is better" mind set may just become "small is beautiful", as our paradigm changes from extravagance to survival.

One of the senseless changes I have observed in houses built in our area in the past few years is the requirement for TWO master bedrooms, both with full bathrooms and walk-in closets. Young couples love this extravagance, since both partners work at different times and have different tastes. When I think about how 99% of the world lives, I feel that building houses with huge wasted space is simply immoral.

Perhaps the planet is teaching us a good lesson in this return to frugality.

November 9

Jubilate

Weeping may linger for the night, but JOY comes with the morning.

Psalm 30 verse 5b

The Psalms are universally used and loved by many religions. There are also folks who don't claim formal religion but still know and love these hymns of praise. Many can recite the famous 23rd Psalm, and do so, especially in times of trouble. Although the collected works are often called "The Psalms of David", they were used as hymns and chants for at least 500 years after David's death before they were written down. Most Hebrew scholars attribute fewer than half of the Psalms to King David; they suggest that there were numerous authors. When you read the collection over, it becomes clear that the Psalms cannot be the work of one person. Although there are many upbeat and uplifting Psalms, there are almost as many full of lamentation and questioning of God's ways.

The poetry and rhythm of the Psalms makes them ideal to set to music and there are many musical settings for them. For me, the shorter psalms, such as the 23rd, the 84th and the 100th are compact but powerful, illustrating that the greatest prayers often have the fewest words.

I suggest that Psalm 100 (Jubilate) is the ideal of a song for every religion.

Make a joyful noise to the LORD, all the earth.
Worship the LORD with gladness; come into his presence with singing.
Know that the LORD is God.
It is he that made us, and we are his; we are his people,
and the sheep his pasture.
Enter his gates with thanksgiving and his courts with praise.
Give thanks to him, bless his name.
For the LORD is good;
his steadfast love endures forever and his faithfulness to all generations.

We should all be celebrating—singing an Ode to Joy—since we have the Lord to thank for our being here together. Where could you find a better reason for celebration than this universally uplifting message?

November 10

Treed

I frequently tramped eight or ten miles through the deepest snow to keep an appointment with a beech-tree, or a yellow birch, or an old acquaintance among the pines.
Henry David Thoreau

I met an old school chum recently for dinner and a concert. I hadn't seen Jeff Heath in 47 years since we graduated from high school. He went on to become a professor of English literature. We had a great evening talking about the old stomping grounds and the fun we had in the back field. Jeff told the following story about a huge willow tree in that field.

"The tree was a great old willow that stood in 'the field' ... we could see it rising up magnificently, in the distance, from our house. It must have been 40 or 50 years old, was surrounded by bushes and grass, and by its own debris, which had fallen off over the years. I never knew whose land it was and nobody ever looked after it. One of the limbs that had fallen was a big one, likely two feet in diameter and 25 feet long. It was gnarled and wrinkled and bumpy with knotholes, just as an old willow branch should be, and was overgrown by weeds and ivy. It was partially rotted at certain points. One day I decided to shimmy up the big willow's trunk ... not a new feat but this time I was alone. Where the first bunch of branches diverged there was one fine old inviting limb that looked secure, with good natural hand-holds, so out I crept until I was half-sitting about 20 feet in the air; aloft in my unaccustomed perch I could see all around and was glorying in the view I commanded when I suddenly found myself on the ground looking up ... I had fallen 20 feet straight down, right across the old limb on the ground, but luckily not on any of the little knots and stubby branches. They could have done me real harm. I lay quietly for a bit, in a state of what later I would recognize as shock (I was then only ten or eleven). My arms and legs seemed to work, my head would swivel, so I picked myself up and made my way home quite slowly, reflecting on just how amazingly sudden the change in perspective had been. The same sort of thoughts came over me later in life, usually prompting memories of my fall from the grand old willow ... almost as if it had shrugged me off for so arrogantly surveying its territory from above."

A wonderful story isn't it—and all the more amazing because I had the same 20 foot fall from a tree in those woods—just not from the same tree nor with the same sense of poetry as Jeff.

November 11

Soldier

War may sometimes be a necessary evil. But no matter how necessary, it is always an evil, never a good. We will not learn how to live together in peace by killing each other's children.

Jimmy Carter

The soldier was rough and tough and physically ready. All that training had put on muscle and developed stamina. All the training in the world, however, couldn't prepare the soldier for what happened on the first day in that forbidding foreign place. Carrying a powerful gun, and armed to the teeth, the soldier sat in the armored carrier as the rookies made their way from the landing strip to the base. Suddenly there was a loud bang—and then—blackness. The next thing the soldier knew was a sense of peace and quiet. The cool white hospital ward on the ship contrasted sharply with the previous stifling heat and darkness. Finally, some kind person came and told the soldier about luck. A bomb buried in the road had detonated just as the carrier passed by. The soldier was the lucky one and would fully recover, to fight those terrorists who had killed the other soldiers in the carrier. They had been her friends—and now they were gone. WAR IS HELL!

The FINAL Inspection: an excerpt

> *I know I don't deserve a place among the people here.*
> *They never wanted me around, except to calm their fear.*
> *If you've a place for me here, Lord, It needn't be so grand.*
> *I never expected or had too much, but if you don't, I'll understand.*
> *There was a silence all around the throne, where the saints had often trod,*
> *As the soldier waited quietly for the judgment of his God.*
> *"Step forward now, you soldier, you've borne your burdens well.*
> *Walk peacefully on Heaven's streets; you've done your time in HELL."*

Author Unknown

November 12

Fishing 2

May the holes in your net be no larger than the fish in it.

Irish Blessing

Give a man a fish and he will eat for a day. Teach a man to fish and he will eat for a lifetime.

Confucius?

I am the world's worst fisherman—and there I was, stuck on a tub with 20 avid anglers. The mate had just cured my bird's nest line, so I dipped it down again into the Gulf of Mexico. All around me, fish were being reeled up. To my left, my buddy Ted caught one in less than five minutes. The two ladies to my right caught fish equally fast. Wayne had soon caught three. I had a nibble and reeled up a beauty. The mate grabbed him and threw him back before I had a chance to admire him or her, or whatever. All the fish were getting thrown back in, as they failed to measure up. The mate kept telling us to "throw him back in, and catch his older brother," whatever that meant. I caught another baby and took the squirming, slippery wee fellow off the hook—but not before he managed to stab me with his spiny fins. He didn't appreciate the fact that I was trying to save his life.

Cliff, whose idea it was to join this expedition, caught one fish, but soon disappeared inside the small cabin of the tub. Ted went to see what was up and came back to report that Cliff was "looking a little green around the gills." The boat shifted to a new area, and the rain began. I was beginning to lose what little enthusiasm I'd had for this endeavor, but it didn't seem to dampen anyone else's spirits, other that Cliff's. The wet, and an aching back, finally drove me to join Cliff inside the cabin. He was sitting there with his eyes closed and a baggy in his hands. Seeing his barf-bag, I remembered that the captain had been adamant about being sick.

"Don't mess up the cabin—go over the side," he'd told us at the start. I felt badly for Cliff, but as I sat yawning away, I began to feel woozy myself. I have been on many boats and have never felt ill—but here, between yawns, my stomach felt every up and down—so I quickly went back outside to my spot. One look at the bait bucket was the last straw for my poor stomach. I complied with the captain's order, much to my embarrassment. It might have been my imagination, the sniggering all around the boat—waves, fish and folk all echoing: "world's worst fisherman."

November 13

Big Bob

The secret of this game ... girls ... is to move your ass!
Big Bob ... enthusiastically instructing a boys' class of tennis players

One of the fellows I played racquetball with was an easygoing bear of a man. We called him "Big Bob". Bob was a business teacher and the tennis coach at the school. He was muscular but had never lifted weights in his life. He was one of the strongest yet quietest men I've ever met. Bob could crush your hand with his handshake, but he didn't. He was gentle in many ways and a very enthusiastic coach, always cheering on his players with cute expressions.

We played cutthroat racquetball early in the morning. The third chap and I were both runners and about 15 years younger than Bob. That huge man moved like a cat around the court, and he possessed a wicked kill shot. We were hard-pressed to beat Bob, and we were very vigilant during the fast games. You never wanted to get run over by Big Bob.

Bob wasn't home much. He played early-bird cutthroat most days, taught his business classes, coached tennis, and taught both high school and college night classes. During our staff meetings he would try to keep awake, but they were often tedious, and one day he fell fast asleep. The principal—also a great strongman, jock and coach, woke Bob up. After the meeting, they had it out in the prince's office. I would have hated to see them come to blows. They were both big, powerful men.

I knew that Bob had been in a couple of bad car accidents, but he insisted on driving me to school one morning after racquetball. He drove fast and went right through a stop sign without slowing down.

"You drove right through that stop sign, Bob. Didn't you see it?"

"It's O.K. Lee," Bob said, "don't worry. I'll stop twice at the next one!"

November 14

Plantar Fasciitis

Heaven is under our feet as well as over our heads.

Henry David Thoreau

The civilized man has built a coach, but has lost the use of his feet.

Ralph Waldo Emerson

About 25 years ago, my feet began to complain. I was running and playing racquetball almost every day, but soon I was forced to stop. Even getting out of bed was painful. The doctor sent me to a podiatrist, and he ordered up $400 orthotics. My feet kept on hurting. They eventually settled down, but after I resumed playing, the pain returned—only worse. After a number of remedies, none of which worked, a gal in the school physical education department recommended an athletic injury specialist. This specialist told me: "You have plantar fasciitis, or heel spurs; when you put your foot on the floor each morning, you re-injure the inflamed area." She gave me a card which told me what to do. The strategies worked.

A number of friends complain about their feet with the same symptoms. I have told them what worked for me. A few of them still complain, so I'm not certain if they tried the treatment.

Here's the three-part cure; your feet will love you for this, even if you don't have plantar fasciitis. It works for me.

1.   Roll your feet with a grooved foot-roller before taking your first step of the day. You can often buy foot-rollers at flea markets or craft sales.
2.   Keep a two-liter soft drink bottle 95% filled with water in the freezer, and roll your feet with this while you watch T.V. or play on your computer.
     (Put the bottle back in the freezer. Fill the bottle to 95% as ice has more volume than liquid water and will break the bottle when it expands.)
3.   Soak your feet in ice water and/or warm water with Epsom salts.

Quality Verses Quantity

It is better to be happy for a moment and be burned up with beauty than to live a long time and be bored all the while.

Don Marquis

W.A. Mozart	Prolific Composer	1756–1791	35 years
George Gershwin	Composer	1898–1937	39
Franz Schubert	Composer (over 600 songs)	1797-1828	31
Felix Mendelssohn	Composer	1809-1847	38
Fredric Chopin	Composer	1810-1849	39
Buddy Holly	Singer-songwriter	1936-1959	23
Elvis Presley	Pop Singer	1935-1977	42
John Lennon	Singer-songwriter	1940-1980	40
John F. Kennedy	35th U.S. President	1917-1963	46
Martin Luther King	Civil Rights Activist	1929-1968	39

How long do you expect to live? Life expectancy has increased over time. If you are a woman in Japan, you can expect to live 86 years on the average. North Americans can expect around 80 years. Examine the above list of famous folks. The first five, all composers, never made it halfway to the magic fourscore years. They all died young. In spite of an early demise, they each left a legacy of masterpieces that will endure as long as humans enjoy good music. In their short lives, they penned unbelievable numbers of compositions. How did Mozart write 41 symphonies and over 30 concertos in his brief 35 years? How did Schubert write over 600 songs in his 31 years? They certainly didn't sit around watching TV. The word boredom was never in their vocabulary. To accomplish these writing miracles, they had to pack more into an hour than most of us pack into a day—and into a year what we might pack into a lifetime. They had an intense zeal for music, and like a fast-burning candle, their lives ended all too quickly.

The second group of five also displayed a great passion in their lives. These famous people all left legacies of celebrated accomplishments before their lives were snuffed out prematurely.

What the short lives of all these famous folks shows us is this. We need to live every moment with a zest for life. A year of passion and love is surely better than 80 years of autopilot.

November 16

Freed

Slavery was established by decree of Almighty God...it is sanctioned in the Bible, in both Testaments, from Genesis to Revelation...it has existed in all ages, has been found among the people of the highest civilization, and in nations of the highest proficiency in the arts.

Jefferson Davis, President of the Confederate States of America

When an owner strikes slave ... and the slave dies immediately, the owner shall be punished. But if the slave survives a day or two, there is no punishment; for the slave is the owner's property.

Exodus 21:32

Slaves, obey your earthly masters with fear and trembling, in singleness of heart, as you obey Christ.

Paul's letter to the Ephesians 6:5

Slavery is truly an abominable practice. It goes against the moral absolutes any normal sane human seems to have been born with. Mistreating others is not something we normally do, unless we are forced into insensitive actions as young children. Most of the folks on the planet today know that slavery is immoral and illegal. However, the disgusting practice persists, and many humanitarian organizations state that there are tens of millions of slaves all over the world. The number of girls sold as slaves in the sex trade is a disgrace found in every country. Whole groups of people in Africa, India and China are forced to work as slaves, even if it is against the law. In Haiti, families are so poor that they sell their oldest daughters to rich folks, who use the girls as servants with no pay. Authorities ignore the problem as impossible to prevent. So this ugly practice continues to rob millions of people of their freedom.

For much of human history, slavery was an accepted practice. The Bible contains many passages about how to treat slaves. These Biblical excerpts were used to condone slavery in the Southern States before the civil war. Internationally, the United Nations General Assembly passed a historic resolution on December 2, 1949 to suppress the Trafficking and Exploitation of people as slaves. Each December 2 recalls this International Day for the Abolition of Slavery; we need to celebrate our freedom and perhaps spend some time before December 2 learning how we can truly eliminate this immoral curse from our modern world.

Routines and the "H" words

Earlier we had a bunch of "P" words to help us stay youthful. Today we look at a bunch of "H" words to help us with our routines—not that we should keep strictly to routines. Rather, we should have routines which help us live better but allow for exploration at any time.

Healthy: Eat lots of raw veggies and fruit and drink ice water instead of "pop." Have a brisk walk every day.

Happy: Laugh at every chance—especially at yourself. Here's a good question to get the laughter going: "What's the silliest thing I did today?"

Harmony: Do chores together. Remember doing the dishes together: "You wash and I'll dry."

Habits: Brush those teeth and floss every day. Mouthwash is good. If you turn it on, turn it off. If you open it, close it. If you take it out, put it away. (I have real trouble with this one! Just ask my frustrated wife!)

Helpful: If you see somebody who needs help, offer to help!

Healing: Lavish good care and prayer on somebody who is hurting. Avoid lecturing. (I am guilty as charged!)

Hopeful: Never give up. There is always a fairy Godmother around.

Homage: Have a system of belief and give the Creator homage and lots of "THANKS." (I believe I'll have some single malt. Thank God for the Scots!)

Holiday: Take a holiday from work and routine—do something different.

Humble: No narcissism—do you really need all those clothes? Learn to live simply and with humble "Thanks." Spend your money. Why save it all up? You never see a hearse pulling a U-Haul trailer!

Fishing 3

Time is but the stream I go fishing in. I drink at it, but while I drink I see the sandy bottom and detect how shallow it is. Its thin current slides away, but eternity remains. Many men go fishing all of their lives without knowing it is not fish they are after.

Henry David Thoreau

Fishing seems to be the favorite form of loafing.

Edgar Watson Howe

Fishing is boring, unless you catch an actual fish, and then it is disgusting.

Dave Berry

I am the world's worst fisherman. Here I was in a tub on the Gulf, soaked from the rain. I had been sick on a boat for the first time. I could take some solace in the fact that I had complied with the captain's order to lean overboard. After a second bout, I felt somewhat better, and I went back into the cabin where Cliff sat quietly. We were soon joined by several others who weren't having much fun. I just wanted to get back to land as quickly as possible. I kept myself positive by imagining what it would be like to be in the water without a life jacket. There we sat and nodded off—leaning at various angles—sometimes up against a total stranger. The tub finally turned around and began heading back to its berth, and we were happy the expedition would finally be over. I moved over to the other side of the cabin to console Cliff.

"Not much fun!" I grossly understated. "What are you thinking about?"

Cliff replied, "I'm sitting here figuring—I fished for a grand total of three minutes for 60 bucks. That works out to 20 dollars per minute—not very good entertainment value!" We both had a chuckle about that one.

"Oh well," I said, "It will soon be over. No one seems to have caught much. I probably jinxed the whole trip—being the world's worst fisherman."

Cliff thought for a minute, and then he said something that is so typical of somebody with a great, positive outlook on life. "You realize that when this is all over—when we have recovered from our silly seasickness—we sure will have fun relating today's stories ... and we'll be telling those stories and laughing for a long time." He was right! The ladies had a wonderful evening laughing at the antics of the world's worst fishermen.

November 19

Hate

Love your neighbor as yourself.

Leviticus 19:18   Mark 12:31

In this cry of pain the inner consciousness of the people seems to lay itself bare for an instant, and to reveal the mood of beings who feel their isolation in the face of a universe that wars on them with winds and seas.

John Millington Synge

In great cities men are brought together by the desire of gain. They are not in a state of co-operation, but of isolation, as to the making of fortunes; and for all the rest they are careless of neighbors. Christianity teaches us to love our neighbor as ourselves; modern society acknowledges no neighbor.

Benjamin Disraeli

I Shall Not Hate.

... the title of a new book by Abuelaish Izzeldin

Hate is a self-defeating emotion. We have all felt it at times. Being victimized by someone who has a wanton disregard for human life can engender feelings of hate, which literally eat up the victim. Drunk driving, terrorist bombings and indiscriminate shooting with guns or artillery result in the death or injury of many innocent people every year. Many victims spend the remainder of their days focusing their thoughts on why this happened to them and blaming those who allowed this to happen. People can become more victimized by their hateful feelings, as healing and recovery are impossible in a totally negative atmosphere.

If anyone has a reason to hate, it is Abuelaish Izzeldin, a doctor working at a hospital in Israel and living with his family in Gaza. Izzeldin has always worked for peace between the Israelis and the Palestinians. His wife recently died of cancer, and Izzeldin was at home with his eight daughters and a niece, when shells from Israel rained down on his building, killing three of his daughters and his niece. Since overcoming his anguish, Abuelaish Izzeldin has written a book, *I Shall Not Hate*, in which he continues his work for a peaceful resolution to the conflict between the Israelis and Palestinians. We can only hope and pray that his message reaches major political players on both sides—changes their hearts—and helps bring a lasting peace to the region.

November 20

Commitment

The difference between 'involvement' and 'commitment' is like an eggs-and-ham breakfast: the chicken was 'involved' ... the pig was 'committed'.

Anon

An ounce of performance is worth pounds of promises.

Mae West

The quality of a person's life is in direct proportion to their commitment to excellence, regardless of their chosen field of endeavor.

Individual commitment to a group effort ... that is what makes a team work, a company work, a society work, a civilization work..

Both from Vince Lombardi

What are you committed to today? I imagine some of you might respond that after what you are expected to accomplish today, you may need to be committed to an institution. Others might say, "I'm committed to demolishing a few beers and some pizza." Most of us, however, have responsibilities to others—spouses, children, siblings, students, patients, customers, bosses and clients. All of them have definite expectations of us, and we need to deliver or they might be disappointed—or worse. We can't have one of those days like Alfred E. Newman, where we clasp our hands behind our head and sing: "I like to work at nothing all day." Heaven forbid!

The whole world might collapse if we decided to forget our commitments for a day. Right?

Wrong! Consider this. If you died this very minute, would the world suddenly end? If you didn't show up for work, would the enterprise collapse? If you had an accident and couldn't arrive somewhere, would somebody be left in dire straits? If the answer to any of these questions is "yes"—then perhaps you are overcommitted, and you need to scale down. You might try and arrange a day where everything you do is for you! Take a day off!

November 21

Quartets

We used to play the underground clubs like the UFO, and Middle Earth, and they were great because they would have on things like a poet, string quartets, and then a rock band! It was kinda cool!

Alvin Lee

The Detroit String Quartet played Brahms last night. Brahms lost.

Bennett Cerf

Our Saturday coffee klatch friends returned from a Mediterranean Cruise and related their experience with the music on the ship. The cruise ship theater played loads of high-tech music and dancing, with little substance but high volume. Our friends discovered a string quartet, playing in a lounge where folks mostly ignored their playing. Letty and Bill loved the sound of the quartet. The harmonies and interplay were entirely new and quite exciting to discover for the first time.

Much of the music written by the great composers is based on the quartet, in having four parts or sections:

Choral music: soprano, alto, tenor bass;

String quartets: 1st violin, second violin, viola, cello;

Orchestra: strings, woodwinds, brass, percussion

Sure there are tons of solos, duets, trios and more complicated stuff, but the huge canon of music has four voices involved in the harmony. It's almost as if there is an unwritten understanding that the human brain seems very pleased to follow the interaction of four parts. I know that I love to listen to string quartets with headphones. The reason for this is that you can place the four instruments spatially in four corners and follow the interplay and harmony easily. Try it. It's a blast!

November 22

Saints

It is not so essential to think much as to love much.

St Teresa

How happy I am to see myself imperfect and be in need of God's mercy.

St Therese

To be taken with love for a soul, God does not look on its greatness, but the greatness of its humility.

St John

Saint: A dead sinner revised and edited.

Ambrose Bierce

Sainthood emerges when you can listen to someone's tale of woe and not respond with a description of your own.

Andrew V. Mason

I am fortunate to have several friends who are saints. They have to be, to put up with me. I can be very contrary at times, and I am often that way just to get a reaction from those around me. Saints are those folks who dispense help to others but never draw attention to the delivery of their kindness. It isn't that they are free of transgressions themselves. Quite the contrary! They often get themselves into hot water with those who have some kind of political agenda and who like to do everything the right way, even if it isn't necessarily the right thing. This is where saints shine. They want to do the greatest good, even if it lands them in trouble. Then they often become martyrs for a great cause that just happens to be contrary to the rules and regulations of the day.

I love the story of Saint Cecilia, whose family members were early second century Christians. Cecilia's husband and his brother were both killed by the Roman prefect Almachis about the year 175 AD. The officers then went after Cecilia, but she showed remarkable resilience. Almachis' officers attempted to scald Cecilia to death and then execute her by decapitation. After three botched attempts, the executioner fled. Cecilia survived another three days before succumbing. According to legend, Cecilia praised God by singing to His name as she lay at death's door. For this musical martyring, she was eventually given the title of the Patron Saint of Music, and her day is celebrated every year on the 22nd of November.

November 23

Sublime Moments

We will have these moments to remember.
Words & Music by Al Stillman & Robert Allen   Recorded by The Four Lads, 1955

Memories are made of this.
Words & Music by Terry Gilkeyson, Richard Dehr & Frank Miller
Recorded by Dean Martin, 1955

How many sublime moments have you had in your life? These are moments of elation which are etched into your memory forever. For some it may be the moment of proposal and acceptance, of the wedding ceremony, or the birth of a child. Some may have an achievement such as the moment you received congratulations upon being accepted for an important job or position, of winning an election, or setting some record. How can we forget the elation of Joe Carter as he rounded the bases after hitting his famous home run, or Donovan Bailey when he won the gold with a new Olympic record? Many of these special moments occur in sporting events but they can also occur in a variety of situations. How many come instantly to your mind?

Here are two I can play back in my mind, like a movie or video playback. They both have to do with music performances.

In my second year at university, we performed *The Pirates of Penzance* by Gilbert and Sullivan. On opening night, we pirates wait on the stage behind the curtain as the orchestra plays the overture. A timpani roll: the curtain goes up to reveal the orchestra and audience, and we sing "Pour Oh pour the pirate sherry ... Fill Oh fill the pirate glass!" Wow! The moment that curtain goes up, and we begin to sing accompanied by a marvelous orchestra—a sublime moment I can replay in my mind whenever I feel like it. Another enduring scene for me was sitting behind the Toronto Symphony, singing with the chorus, all conducted by the renowned Eric Kunzel. The panorama of symphony, conductor and huge audience before me, and feeling the close sound of the orchestra and chorus, is for me a sublime moment. I imagine yours are quite different. Enjoy your replays!

November 24

Open Fire Cooking

There is something fundamental about cooking over an open fire. I love the flames, I love the smells, and of course, I love the taste.
Alice Waters, chef and owner, Chez Panisse

We don't know if camping food tastes better because it is cooked outside, or because you are so hungry from all your hard work. But we DO know that anything cooked outside on either a camping stove or over a fire is the best food around!
Campfish.net

Mono meal: We were on a fishing trip about 25 years ago. We were a party of three big kids and five little kids. John Tutty was the leader of our expedition, and he told us that we would "remember today." We got into our three canoes, and off we went down a shallow but rapid stream. It was hard work keeping upright, but the stream opened into a lagoon. John told us to get out our gear and use worms. Within 20 minutes, we had caught over a dozen rainbow trout. We pulled onto shore, and John moved fast. He got a fire going and prepared the trout. He fried them all in a large iron pan with plenty of butter. They tasted unbelievable.

Variety: We were camped in Robert Treman State Park in Ithaca, New York with our camping buddies, Jane and Ted. We had a variety of grub—corn on the cob, potatoes, strip loin, marinated chicken breast, and shrimp. The fire pits had grates, so we built a fire; when the coals were just right, we grilled all this great grub. We set a new world record for the number of "mmmmmmm-mmm's" that meal—all cooked over an open fire!
PS Have you eaten with Japanese folks? If the food is good, they put great energy into hearty and frequent "mmmmmmmmm's." Enjoy your food and drink!

Dessert: Our introduction to Family Campers and RVers (F.C.R.V.) came at the invitation of Jack and Sonya Smye. At this enjoyable weekend, we learned plenty of new games and discovered a new fire tool—the PIE-IRON. Two pieces of bread and any filling are sandwiched in the iron and held in the fire. Some folks used cherry pie filling. It made a hot dessert—but be careful not to eat too many. They are that tasty!

November 25

Green

The human brain now holds the key to our future. We have to recall the image of the planet from outer space: a single entity in which air, water, and continents are interconnected. That is our home.

In the environmental movement ... every time you lose a battle it's for good, but our victories always seem to be temporary and we keep fighting them over and over again.

Both from David Suzuki

Global warming is the slow but gradual increase in the average temperature of the atmosphere due to the increase in "greenhouse gases." The two primary heat-holding gases are carbon dioxide, CO_2, and methane, CH_4. Although there is much less methane than carbon dioxide, methane is 17 times as effective an insulator as carbon dioxide! What can each of us do to lower the concentration of these two greenhouse gases in the atmosphere?

Drive less and bicycle and walk more: On a trip to the West Coast and back, the average vehicle puts over 6 tons of CO_2 into the atmosphere—and that is driving less than 8000 km!

Eat less meat: Ruminants like cattle, sheep and pigs produce large quantities of methane gas and require more energy to grow than grains. Eating vegetarian is far less harmful to the atmosphere.

Plant a tree: Trees are the most environmentally friendly organisms on the planet. They remove carbon dioxide and produce oxygen. If you can't plant a tree, reduce your use of paper products which come from trees.

Get educated: There are large numbers of internet sites explaining global warming and what we can all do to reverse this disaster. If you only have a little time to learn about it, obtain *An Inconvenient Truth* from the library or video store and watch it carefully. It's a shocker we all need to take to heart.

November 26

A Burning Candle

Just as a candle cannot burn without fire, men cannot live without a spiritual life.
Buddha

Last week the candle factory burned down. Everyone just stood around and sang Happy Birthday.
Steven Wright

Jesus bids us shine with a pure clear light ...
like a little candle burning in the night.
Susan Bogert Warner

How far that little candle throws its beams! So shines a good deed in a naughty world.
William Shakespeare

When I was teaching chemistry in the 1960's, a new program, *Chem Study*, came out. The first experiment in the manual was *The Study of a Burning Candle*. I figured, at first, that this experiment was just too simple for pseudo-sophisticated teens, and that looking at a lit candle would be laughed away in derision. Surprise! The students loved the exercise and exceeded every expectation. How many observations can you make about a burning candle? Try it yourself. The answer is at the end of today's reflection. No peeking until you have at least given the question some thought.

The ritual of burning candles is central to every religion. In the Festival of Light, the candles of the Menorah are lit on successive nights, each one signifying an increase in the good a person does in this world. This is only one of many rites in which burning candles take on great significance.

And the answer to the number of observations made? The average student would come up with 20 observations in 15 minutes. Some, however, would fill a page. The grand champ is Michael Faraday, a famous chemist from the 1800's. If you Google *The Chemical History of A Candle, 1860*, you will get a site with the six lectures Faraday delivered about candles. The burning candle exercise is excellent for improving observation skills, and we eventually used it in grade nine as the first exercise of a series of experiments designed to improve observation skills. Everyone, at every age, needs a daily reminder not only to observe our world—but to keep our light shining in it.

November 27

Choir

I love to hear a choir. I love the humanity to see the faces of real people devoting them-selves to a piece of music. I like the teamwork. It makes me feel optimistic about the human race when I see them cooperating like that.

Paul McCartney

It is my belief that everything you need to know about the world can be learned in a church choir.

Connie Willis

The first time I sang in the church choir; two hundred people changed their religion.

Fred Allen

The moment was sublime. The Mendelssohn Choir made a triple pianissimo entrance in the final movement of Mahler's "Resurrection Symphony." The German words, *Aufersteh'n, ja aufersteh'n Wirst du, Mein Staub, Nach kurzer Ruh'* —so soft and caressing, they could be felt rather than heard—an ecstatic moment, sending shivers up and down your spine.

It is a miracle when a choir sounds good. A stirring or touching perfor-mance is not an accident. So many details go into the performance. So many things can go wrong. The notes and pitch must be perfect. The rhythms must have unanimity. The words must be delivered properly, or no one understands what is being sung. Even if these three aspects of choral singing are perfect, the piece may be boring if the dynamics or emotion are lacking. In order to deliver all this, the singers must sing as one singer and subdue their egos to produce a blended sound. I remember the first time we sang for Eric Kunzel, a conductor of "pops" recordings. Very early in the rehearsal, Kunzel stopped the orchestra and chorus and looked sternly at a member of the chorus. "You are never to hold notes too long or too loud … and I expect you won't do it again … thank you." There is the very essence of singing in a choir—the teamwork and cooperation mentioned by Paul McCartney.

In the illustrious choir of humanity, great moments result once we learn to subdue the self and work together.

November 28

Immortality

Do not try to live forever. You will not succeed.

George Bernard Shaw

I don't believe in an afterlife, so I don't have to spend my whole life fearing hell, or fearing heaven even more. For whatever the tortures of hell, I think the boredom of heaven would be even worse.

Isaac Asimov

I shall tell you a great secret my friend. Do not wait for the last judgment, it takes place every day.

Albert Camus

I do not believe in the immortality of the individual.

Albert Einstein

I don't want to achieve immortality through my work. I want to achieve immortality through not dying.

Woody Allen

Much has been written about what happens after we "shuffle off this mortal coil," as Shakespeare so poetically described the end of our earthly life. Great rewards or greater punishment await us, according to different beliefs. Some figure we come back in another form or another life, and we keep recycling into these future "lives." Others put us into limbo—but with no definition of limbo. For most religions, there remains a promise of eternal life as a reward for being good. Most of the folks I know believe in life after death, and that we will indeed go to a "reward."

However, as Shakespeare so rightly noted, no one has ever returned to tell us about this reward of the afterlife. Folks who have had a near-death experience describe a very pure light that they were moving toward when they were so rudely snatched back to this earthly life.

Why worry about what we cannot possibly know for sure? At least, our bodies will all eventually be recycled into new life. The Earth's ecosystems renew themselves—by recycling, and in this way grant all life immortality.

November 29

Meditation vs. Medication

My workout partner, Mike, had his yearly physical recently, and the doctor was pleased with Mike's overall health. He asked what medications Mike was taking and was doubly pleased that Mike was only taking preventive pills, such as vitamins and some natural supplements recommended by a holistic practitioner. The doctor finished the consultation by recommending to Mike that he consider "meditation." Mike found this interesting, coming from a medical doctor who usually prescribes medications. Preventive medicine makes great sense to our overall health, and I wonder why we don't hear more about it from our general practitioners. One of the best pieces of advice I ever received from our family doctor was to add more bran to my diet. This was given to me about 25 years ago. I've followed this wise advice, and the bowels have been working well ever since.

In the past few years, several of my friends have developed type 2 diabetes. This form of diabetes often develops in individuals over the age of fifty. Although there are genetic factors, two factors thought to contribute to the onset are diet and weight. Does this sound familiar? These two factors contribute to the development of a whole host of health issues. Although my osteoarthritis probably resulted from wear and tear, being overweight certainly aggravates the condition. Good news! Meditation can help reduce the pain and the desire to fill up on snack foods. In fact, meditation has been found to have many health benefits and is a helpful way of avoiding the need for medications as we age. Meditation can be considered as the ultimate preventive medicine. Beginning and ending the day with stillness and quiet may just be the best way to give you a timeless mind and ageless body.

Frederic Premji has come up with 100 benefits of meditation. Here are a few from his list of 100, which can be found on the Internet. Meditation:

14- Enhances energy, strength and vigor
44- Increases feelings of vitality and rejuvenation
67- Reduces need and dependency on drugs, pills & pharmaceuticals
87- Brings body, mind, spirit in harmony
96- Creates a widening, deepening capacity for love

November 30

Early Bird Champ

I could have a roomful of awards and it wouldn't mean beans.

Bobby Darin

The Nobel awards should be regarded as giving recognition to this general scientific progress as well as to the individuals involved.

John Bardeen

When I was a kid, the school had an awards day, and everybody seemed to get something for attendance, or whatever. I never even came close, but I didn't much care. Like Bobby Darin, awards didn't mean much to me. When I graduated from high school and then college, I received some awards but didn't get very excited about them. I remember a singer, Michael Fletcher, who was truly talented. When we both received a Performing Arts Award, he said to me, "Why are you so blasé about this? It's a real big deal, you know!" It may have been for him, but I often wondered why awards and trophies were doled out for having talent. The award to me was in the huge lift you received from the actual performance.

I never received any awards for athletics. They didn't have the LEAD prize for motor-morons, or I would have gotten several. I had two left feet, and hands that were totally unaware of their location. Then all of that changed when I hit 40. I was in an early-bird league at the local racquetball club, and I became decent at racquetball for some unknown reason. In the league championships, I managed to get by guys in their 20's. It felt great to beat somebody half my age. In the final, I had to play the Doc. This guy was good and he was left-handed, so he had cleaned up on all the righties. (He didn't know that I played 3 hours every Saturday with one of the better lefties in the club.) It was best two out of three. The Doc cleaned my clock in the first game. I managed to sneak by him to win the second. The third was no contest. I had better stamina and I repaid him with a good beating to win. And that's how I won my second jock award. Hooray!

Today, I could no more play racquetball than fly to the moon—but I still have that trophy, and I am prouder of the "Early-bird Champ" than all the others. To overcome a lack of ability really meant something to me.

December 1

Prayer Position

Please stand and join in as we say the Lord's Prayer…
an invitation to the flock in some churches

I prayed for twenty years but received no answer until I prayed with my legs.
Frederick Douglass … escaped slave

Practical prayer is harder on the soles of your shoes than on the knees of your trousers.
Austin O'Malley

When you are unwell, you must cough, sneeze, and ache prayer.
Carrie Latet

There is a picture commonly seen in many churches and homes. It's a picture of a kneeling, bearded Jesus. His hands are folded as if he is about to pray. As kids, we were taught to say our prayers in the same prayerful kneeling position, with bowed head and folded hands, before we went to bed. Then for years, we all put our poor knees on hard kneelers in the Episcopal Church. Many folks still do. Must we be in a supplicant position to offer prayers?

When I attended a Cursillo weekend—a short course in Christianity, which ran from Thursday evening to Sunday afternoon—we were encouraged to pray anywhere, at any time, in any position. A circular prayer chain is the arrangement we use in the choir. We all join hands, and a different person prays each time. This quiet time before performing helps calm the nerves and reminds us why we are performing. Again, before I sing any solo, I make a quiet petition to allow me to do my best for the music and the listeners. It never fails to put me at ease in the music.

So—the next time you are stuck in a line-up in the food market with no one to talk to, you can say your prayers. If you're lying awake with a dismal headache, say your prayers. We can pray anytime—anywhere—in any position. Well—almost any time. It may not be prudent to be saying prayers as you hurtle on down the highway at some ridiculous speed (or maybe you should!)

December 2

The Universe

There is a theory which states that if ever for any reason anyone discovers what exactly the Universe is for and why it is here it will instantly disappear and be replaced by something even more bizarre and inexplicable. There is another that states that this has already happened.

Douglas Adams

How many planets are there in the universe with living organisms, as on planet Earth? The answer is simple. We don't know.

All we can do is estimate, since we cannot see many planets. Our telescopes are not yet good enough to see planets around distant stars. An estimate of the number of planets which may have living organisms goes something like the following calculation. (This boggles the mind!)

Conservative estimate of the total number of galaxies in the known universe = 200 billion = 2×10^{11}

The average number of stars in a galaxy = 50 billion = 5×10^{10}

Total number of stars in the known universe = $2 \times 10^{11} \times 5 \times 10^{10}$

= 10^{22} **stars** (ten thousand trillion trillion)

Now suppose one in a thousand of these stars has planets, and one in a thousand of these planets is in the same position as planet Earth, and one in a thousand has the same conditions as Earth, and one in a thousand has developed life. We multiply by 0.001, or 10^{-3}, four times.

10^{22} **stars** $\times 10^{-3} \times 10^{-3} \times 10^{-3} \times 10^{-3} = 10^{10}$ **PLANETS**

This conservative calculation simply means:

There could be at least ten billion planets in the known universe with living organisms!

December 3

Yoga

Blessed are the flexible, for they shall not be bent out of shape.

Author Unknown

Yoga is the fountain of youth. You're only as young as your spine is flexible.

Bob Harper

Yoga teaches us to cure what need not be endured and endure what cannot be cured.

B.K.S. Iyengar

The yoga mat is a good place to turn when talk therapy and antidepressants aren't enough.

Amy Weintraub

Yoga is the practice of quieting the mind.

Patanjali, translated from Sanskrit

When the breath wanders the mind also is unsteady. But when the breath is calmed the mind too will be still, and the yogi achieves long life. Therefore, one should learn to control the breath.

Hatha Yoga Pradipika

I have a friend who practices yoga—at least she assumes the postures and stretches that are part of the yoga fitness system. Yoga itself is an ancient practice which is intended to advance body, mind and spirit. By quieting the mind and stretching the still body, a state of peaceful meditation can be obtained; when repeated, this state has remarkable benefits with regard to breath, flexibility and self-awareness. Currently the most popular form here in North America is "hatha" yoga, a system of bodily exercises and positions initially intended to prepare the body for meditation. Most people practice yoga and tai chi as fitness exercises mainly intended for flexibility and stress reduction.

The wonderful aspect of both yoga and tai chi is that they focus on technique and can be done at any age. Older adults may find tai chi appealing because the gentle movements are low impact and put minimal stress on muscles and joints. Stretch until it feels good!

December 4

The Truth

Heresies are experiments in man's unsatisfied search for truth.

Human history is in essence a history of ideas.

The forceps of our minds are clumsy forceps, and crush the truth a little in taking hold of it.

No passion in the world is equal to the passion to alter someone else's draft.

All from H. G. Wells

Giordano Bruno was a Dominican monk with muddy ideas. He thought that folks should respect the ideas found in different religions. He also praised the new Copernican model of the universe with the sun at the center. These thoughts were anathema to the Church in the late 16th century. Bruno was charged with heresy, found guilty and burned at the stake in 1600. His search for the truth ended in a morbidly painful death. Having ideas contrary to the thinking of theocrats and politicians can ruin the lives of those daring individuals willing to seek the truth and speak out when they think they have found it. I use the word "muddy" to describe Bruno's ideas, since speaking out against those who wield power in any society often results in your name being changed to "mud." Today, you wouldn't be burned at the stake, but you might end up being blackballed—or worse.

Folks who find their superiors are committing crimes face a quandary. If they tell the truth, they could end up in a battle with powerful people. Many such whistleblowers have been subjected to punishment and in extreme cases, feared for their lives. To expose the truth about misbehavior by people in positions of trust is often a battle lost before it is begun. If you find yourself in this position, you need the largest possible support group you can muster, the strength to confront nasty people, and the realization that sacrifices may accompany a search for the truth.

December 5

Poets

But an old age serene and bright, and lovely as a Lapland night, shall lead thee to thy grave.

Golf is a day spent in a round of strenuous idleness.

Not without hope we suffer and we mourn.

The best portion of a good man's life is his little, nameless, unremembered acts of kindness and of love.

The Child is the father of the Man.

All from William Wordsworth   1770-1850   English Romantic Poet

When I was convalescing after a hip replacement, my workout buddy, Mike, loaned me an old book with the poems of Robert Service, a famous Canadian poet. These poems were perfect for just dropping in for a few minutes—or a few hours. You have to take a concentrated dip in order to appreciate the poetry. These poems, like a good symphony, demand to be savored repeatedly to reveal all their pleasures. I still have Mike's book, and I am still enjoying a great wordsmith.

Some poets seem to find just the proper words to beautifully express profound thoughts. I loved the British sitcom, *Rumpole of the Old Bailey*. Rumpole's wife Hilda was "she who must be obeyed," and Rumpole would often respond to Hilda's didactic nature (as well as to judges behind the bench) by quoting Wordsworth. The quotes were lost on those around Rumpole but often summed up the situation as only a poet can. Great stuff!

...my voice proclaims
How exquisitely the individual Mind
(And the progressive powers perhaps no less
Of the whole species) to the external World
Is fitted: ... and how exquisitely, too,
Theme this but little heard of among Men,
The external World is fitted to the Mind ...
William Wordsworth

December 6

Friday

Only Robinson Crusoe had everything done by Friday.

Anon

There will be a rain dance Friday night, weather permitting.

George Carlin

It's bad luck to fall out of a thirteenth story window on Friday.

American Proverb

Mondays are good. Tuesdays are terrific—and the rest of the week is also outstanding, especially Friday, which anticipates the weekend. Everybody loves to get in a celebratory mood early, so Friday is often lived with the energy of anticipation.

We had lots of rituals for Friday. The most fun at the high school where I taught was usually on Fridays. Henry, our biology teacher, would put in an announcement for Beatrice Bones, which was the name of our skeleton in the science department. Then we would all laugh like hell when the announcement was read seriously over the PA system. Whoever had a spare would make popcorn, and we would munch it down as we told each other what we had in store for the weekend.

The one Friday black mark had to do with the drive home. I was run off the road several times by crazy drivers—on Friday. I noticed that the drive home could be adventuresome because of drivers who were thinking of their weekend—or perhaps those who had begun around noon and were already three sheets to the wind. I learned to be extra vigilant when driving on Fridays!

Now, remember always to give 100 % at work:

20% on Monday	(The week has to begin somewhere)
25 % on Tuesday	(OK ... we're getting on a roll)
40 % on Wednesday	Over the Hump day)
10 % on Thursday	(Shout Hooray ... It's Thursday)
And 5 % on Friday	(Thank God It's Friday)

December 7

Heart

The Christian life is about a new heart, an open heart … a heart of compassion.

Being part of a church creates opportunities for the collective practice of compassion …

The Bible is not about saving individuals for heaven, but about a new social and personal reality in the midst of this life.

When Jesus is seen as the incarnation of a path universally spoken about elsewhere, the path we see in him has great credibility.

All from Marcus J. Borg   *The Heart of Christianity*

We have been fortunate enough to read Marcus Borg's *Heart of Christianity* several times. This is a book that every person who professes to be Christian should read. There are changes at work in religious practice today—many resulting in the hardening of hearts, with a reduction of reason and compassion. There are some who seriously believe that theirs is the only true path, and that they hold the only key to "heaven." There is a return by some to the fundamentalist cry, that "if you're not with us, you're against us!" Into this bewildering trend comes a book that illuminates exactly the kind of transformations we really need today. Borg inspires readers to think deeply what they believe about the Christian journey. We cannot recommend this book too highly, and we have no higher praise than that of Peter C. Gomes of the Harvard Divinity School:

> *"We have no better guide to the recovery of an authentic Christian faith for these difficult times than this book … we are reminded that the heart of Christianity speaks directly to the human heart as a lived, living, and loving faith: now more than ever, we need this authentic affirmation."*

December 8

Working Out

Things turn out the best for the people who make the best of the way things turn out.

Art Linkletter

Things have a funny way of working out.

Anon

The technology of lasers had an auspicious beginning. The first lasers appeared in the early 1960's, and although they were a scientific curiosity, they couldn't be used for much more than burning holes in bricks. The intense light beam produced by the laser made them a natural for science fiction writers and for movies. H.G. Wells foresaw the laser in his novel, *War of the Worlds*. The Martian invaders use a very intense ray to incinerate everything. James Bond in the movie *Goldfinger* somehow manages to keep his cool as a laser burns its way up the bench to which he is strapped. Most of us envisioned the laser as an ultimate weapon. Laser guns might radically change the way wars would be fought. Things haven't worked out that way, though; who would have thought that lasers would be used in so many different fields—but NOT as weapons!

Many of today's technologies make use of lasers. In medicine, lasers are bloodless scalpels, to operate on the retina of the eye, to blast kidney stones and to perform microsurgery on blood vessels—to name a few applications. In manufacturing, lasers make for very accurate measurements. The close fit of today's automobiles is accomplished this way. From the checkout counter in stores to computer hard drives, to the CDs and DVDs we play, lasers are an indispensable part of modern living. The surprising point of all of this is that nobody predicted that this marvel of science would have so many applications. The first idea to use lasers as weapons never came about. Things did not work out as first envisioned.

There is an important lesson for us in all of this. We shouldn't be too eager to find a quick fix or to make things happen. If there is the luxury of time, we should relax, and refuse to get excited. Let things develop; situations have a way of working themselves out, and an unforeseen solution is often the result. Things often work out for the best—if we let them.

December 9

Paying Attention

I think the one lesson I have learned is that there is no substitute for paying attention.
Diane Sawyer

If you want your spouse to pay attention and really listen to every word, talk in your sleep.
Anon

I love the scene in the movie *Midnight Run* where the comical bad guys are arguing over how they are going to locate another truly bad guy who has sent them a photograph of their hostage he has stolen, and is restraining in a motel room. (Yes—the movie is that convoluted!)

The conversation goes something like this:

Dumb bad guy: *How are we ever gonna find them? If we fail … the boss is gonna kill us!*

Smarter bad guy: *You bozo! The answer is right in front of your face. Take another look at the photo!*

Dumb bad guy: *I don't see nuttin'!*

Smarter bad guy: *Turn the photo sideways, you dummy. Take a look at the towels. When are you gonna learn how to pay attention?*

At this point the dumb bad guy takes a close look at the photo and spots the name of the motel on the towels hanging on a rack. He gives the smarter bad guy a big smooch.

Paying attention can be hard work, especially if we are not accustomed to take in the detail of what is continually going on around us. Our brains actually take in an uninterrupted barrage of stimuli and filter out the unimportant stuff. This is a good mechanism, and when the brain fails to perform this screening, the world ceases to make sense—as when someone is autistic. An autistic person can often make out amazing details but cannot comprehend the overall picture. The rest of us often go in the opposite direction and habitually over-filter, causing us to miss some detail which should have been evident to us. This happens for a variety of reasons, but very often it's our poor habits of perception. We can be lazy or simply lack concentration. We just don't pay attention. Try driving a car in England, Ireland or Italy. You will quickly learn how to pay attention!

344

December 10

Symphony Orchestra

An orchestra full of stars can be a disaster.
Kurt Masur

For better or worse, you must play your own little instrument in the orchestra of life.
Dale Carnegie

Have you experienced listening to music played by a symphony orchestra? Of course you have. Almost every famous Hollywood movie has a soundtrack played by a symphony orchestra. There are movies with pop music soundtracks, but many of the famous Academy Award winners are by composers such as John Williams, who wrote the *Superman, Star Wars, Jurassic Park* and *Indiana Jones* scores. Do a search for John Williams, and you will find over a hundred movies for which he composed the soundtracks—all played by symphony orchestras.

Have you been to a concert with a large symphony orchestra? We are talking here of sixty to a hundred musicians, playing their hearts out with some Beethoven, Brahms or Tchaikovsky. The first large orchestra I heard was the Cleveland Orchestra. The conductor, George Szell, had molded the Clevelanders into the top ensemble in North America. The precision was so exact that Beethoven's 8th Symphony seemed to flow out of Szell's baton. Each member of the orchestra had subjected his or her ego to the control of the conductor. For an inspired performance, these musicians must look, listen, and play as if they were one instrument; and that instrument represented Beethoven in the concert we heard. With Szell in control, we could hear the symphony as Beethoven must have imagined it in his head. Such is the performance of a symphony orchestra when all the musicians give up their individuality to the vision of the composer, as interpreted by the conductor.

So it is with life itself. We are together in our journey on the planet. We have a choice—to live life as if we alone were uppermost in the great scheme of things—OR—to "play our own little instrument in the orchestra of life," as Carnegie suggests. To play individually or in concert with others—it's our choice.

December 11

Birds

Did you ever see an unhappy horse? Did you ever see a bird that had the blues? One reason why birds and horses are not unhappy is because they are not trying to impress other birds and horses.

Dale Carnegie

You must not know too much or be too precise or scientific about birds and trees and flowers and watercraft; a certain free-margin, and even vagueness ... ignorance, credulity ... helps your enjoyment of these things.

Henry David Thoreau

Use what talents you possess; the woods would be very silent if no birds sang there except those that sang best.

Henry Van Dyke

Here in Florida, the signal lights at intersections are often placed above the intersection on long horizontal bars. This morning we went out for breakfast and at the intersection near the restaurant, there must have been fifty black birds sitting side by each on the bar on the north side of the road. After breakfast, the same birds were all sitting on the bar on the south side. Strange—but maybe they can bombard the largest number of cars by moving back and forth. On the way back to the RV Park, the "Florida Department of Highways" had gathered around a large road kill near the entrance to the park. That's what the locals call the turkey vultures that clean up the roads around here.

Humans have always been fascinated by birds because birds fly. There is a strong desire to take to the air, and there is no end of stories of how inventive humans have emulated birds by trying to become airborne, often resulting in ignominious crashes.

Birds are actually quite intelligent. Most of them avoid the cold by flying south for the winter. We have emulated this pain-reduction strategy—and for this, we are now known as "snowbirds."

346

December 12

Hustle

Good things happen to those who hustle.

Anais Nin

Things may come to those who wait, but only the things left by those who hustle.

Abraham Lincoln

I played the game one way. I gave it everything I had. It doesn't take any ability to hustle.

Wade Boggs

We hustle at both work and play, and consequently enjoy neither to the utmost.

William Feather

I was watching baseball the other day, and a slow-footed player hit a double-play ball. This hitter felt sure he was going to be called "out", so he didn't run hard to first base. The second baseman dropped the ball. Then he recovered in time to throw it to first to complete the double play. The hitter was out because he failed to hustle. He probably heard about it from both players and the manager. If Pete Rose had been the manager, everybody would have heard him admonish the lack of hustle. Pete was known as "Charlie Hustle", and it was high praise. In a game where it's easy to take it easy, the players need constant reminders to play with some reckless abandon.

Most of the enterprises we attempt can be done better when we show enthusiasm and hustle. One person with some drive can raise everyone's energy level. Working and playing with some heart often gets good results. Teams with hustlers like Rose never let up. They can overcome teams of superior talent, simply by out-hustling them!

Sometimes of course, it may be wise NOT to hustle. As William Feather suggests, there are times when we need to slow down and savor some pleasure.

A young bull and an old bull are looking down a hill at a herd of lovely heifers.

Young Bull: "Let's run down and romance a cow."

Old Bull: "No ... Let's walk down and romance the herd."

December 13

Fartlek Prayer Circuit

fart·lek (färt | k) Origin: Swedish for *speed play*
An athletic training technique, used especially in running, in which periods of intense effort alternate with periods of less strenuous effort in a continuous workout.

A hunter who chases two rabbits will catch neither.

Buddha

The dog and I just finished a fartlek prayer circuit. This mile around the park has several "stations" where we take advantage of a pooch leash-free area. While Mozart races around smelling a cornucopia of delights and accomplishing other tasks, I perform a variety of calisthenics—arm circles, knee bends, leg raises—whatever comes into my head. Instead of counting repetitions, I use people's names and say prayers for them. I also have my iPod on. This is multitasking at its best—walking the dog, listening to music, getting exercise and saying prayers—all at the same time. During the fartlek prayer circuit, I feel a terrific endorphin rush. It is especially good when it is over!

Many folks tell me that you can't concentrate on more than one task at the same time. Nonsense! I remember our son Craig coming home from his first week of music school, and telling us of a cool demonstration done by one of his professors. The fellow asked for any newspaper, and placed the paper opened randomly to a page on his piano stand. The teacher then proceeded to sing a song while playing his own accompaniment on the piano. When he finished the song, he gave the paper back to the student and said, "Ask me any question you want on any article." To the amazement of the class, this multitasking marvel knew the content of the newspaper. His explanation was simple: different areas of the brain can perform different tasks simultaneously. His amazing demonstration proved that multitasking is definitely possible.

PS Our mother must have known all about fartlek multitasking. Managing a home and raising us made it a requirement—along with lots of prayers!

December 14

Respect

I don't get no respect!

Rodney Dangerfield

There is no respect for others without humility in one's self.

Henri Frederic Amiel

The final test of a person is his respect for those who can be of no possible service to him.

Anonymous

In our warm-up room at last night's concert, there was a collection of colorful bulletin board displays. The room was a classroom for music and drama students during the day, so I was interested to see what the teachers had posted up on the boards. In among applications and advertisements for drama and music schools, I found the anonymous quote on respect above. It brought back plenty of memories of times when respect for others seemed forgotten by folks who mistakenly thought that their haughty handling of fellow travelers was acceptable. They were, in effect, ignoring the marvelous advice in this "final test" found on the classroom bulletin board.

Some people expect everyone to respect their position as most authoritative, because of a series of letters after their name or the position they have attained. One of my golfing buddies is gimping around with a sore knee. Having been there several times, I can certainly sympathize. I asked Don, "What did the doctor say about it?"

Don replied, "He didn't even look at it. He said it was arthritis, and he gave me an anti-inflammatory. He said if it didn't improve we could try to scope the knee—and if that didn't improve it, there was always replacement."

Guess what. My first knee doctor scoped both my knees, and they got worse. After a two minute "consultation" six months after surgery, I was put on an anti-inflammatory which gave me acid reflux. My poor knees got worse so I changed knee doctors. The new orthopedic surgeon is empathetic, thorough and gentle. He listens, shows respect for the situation, and explains the alternatives. I can be of no possible use to this doctor. He simply respects each person's worth and gives the best possible treatment in the most effective way.

December 15

Shape

The race is not always to the swift but to those who keep running.

Anonymous

That body is strongest and fittest that can relax between efforts.

Frank Crane

I watch in awe as many folks walk with purpose around the RV Park here in Florida each morning. Just like our friends Nan and Mike, they walk quickly for over half an hour. They are all in terrific shape and look and act much younger than their chronological age.

How many times has any one of us said, "I'm going to get in shape … even if it kills me"? All of us desire to improve our shape. We know that keeping active is a key to a long and healthy life. Many of our efforts, however, come to naught for the same reason cramming in school didn't work. The brain and body cannot respond overnight, no matter how hard we work. In fact, we often end up worse off when we overdo it. I don't know how many times I begin to see results and then try to make a quantum leap—and end up injured. Why does this have to happen?

When we use muscles, toxins are produced, and they must be excreted by the body. If they build up too quickly, the body signals us to stop. Try flexing your index finger quickly for one minute. The resulting pain is telling you to quit before you damage the joint. The same principle applies to self-improvement. Science is discovering that spaced-out workouts are better than intense training every day. Some endurance workouts can actually depress the immune system and bring on illness. It's the intelligence of the body avoiding injury. It's as if the body is saying, "If you don't stop getting carried away, I'll make sure you do!"

Joints are particularly susceptible to overexertion, and if pain is ignored, the whole fitness plan goes down the drain in what becomes a vicious circle. I haven't quite learned how to gradually build up to greater levels. One of these days I'll smarten up enough to quit going whole hog and instead, just ease into a good routine—like Mike and Nan, who get out there for a good walk twice each day. The "trick" obviously is to get a good routine and make it a habit.

December 16

The Look of Love

I have three daughters and I find as a result I played King Lear almost without rehearsal.

I was irrevocably betrothed to laughter, the sound of which has always seemed to me the most civilized music in the world.

Intelligent or not, we all make mistakes and perhaps the intelligent mistakes are the worst, because so much careful thought has gone into them.

It is our responsibilities, not ourselves, that we should take seriously.

Love is an act of endless forgiveness, a tender look which becomes a habit.

All from Peter Ustinov

I loved watching Peter Ustinov narrate documentaries. His voice was wonderful, but what made him so outstanding was the manner and "look of love" he had for everything he did. It was the sincerest look and voice you could imagine. He seemed so laid back as well—as if nothing could or would ever get him riled. He just seemed to ooze politeness and sincerity from every pore. What a fabulous role model and mentor to emulate!

I have tried to follow that laid back way and to treat problems with humor the way Ustinov seemed to—but I find myself getting riled when dealing with the frustrations our modern technology of computers and telephones continually seem to throw our way. My dear wife wonders why I talk "the look of love" and then lose it so fast when things don't work. I keep saying, "I just cannot deal with design stupidity." Well I guess that's me. We all can't be Peter Ustinov—but wouldn't it be nice next time something doesn't work to calmly put it aside and forget about it for a while, and smile with a look of serenity and even—dare we say it—*the look of love?*

The look of love is in your eyes.

Hal David added lyrics to the instrumental written by Burt Bacharach in 1967 for the James Bond movie, *Casino Royal.* According to Bacharach, the melody was inspired by watching Ursula Andress in an early cut of the film.

December 17

Composers

Bach almost persuades me to be a Christian.
Roger Fry … quoted in Virginia Woolf

Without craftsmanship, inspiration is a mere reed shaken in the wind.
Johannes Brahms

Handel understands effect better than any of us … when he chooses, he strikes like a thunderbolt.
Wolfgang Amadeus Mozart

Neither a lofty degree of intelligence nor imagination nor both together go to the making of genius. Love, love, love, that is the soul of genius.
Wolfgang Amadeus Mozart

There are several questions about the great composers. The first question deals with their longevity. Why did so many of them die so young? Mozart, Chopin, Schubert, Mendelssohn, and George Gershwin all died before the age of 40. Having burned very brightly, it seems as if their lives were snuffed out far too early. However, all of these geniuses produced huge amounts of glorious music that is still loved by anyone willing to listen. I love all their music, and yet I have only scratched the surface of much of their production. Mozart and Schubert wrote so much music, they must have never slept. Perhaps that explains why they exited early. Exhaustion!

The second question is simply this. Why are there no really noted women composers? There are some very good lady composers. Felix Mendelssohn's sister Fanny was reputed to be a more accomplished musician than her famous brother. Yet, people rarely listen to any of her compositions. I discovered a French composer a few years back, Lili Boulanger, who wrote powerful music for chorus and orchestra. When I tried to find out more, I was overcome with a huge sadness. Lili died when she was 25! She had written some of the greatest French choral music in her teens, but an intestinal disorder led to her early death. Her sister Nadia lived to the age of 92 and taught musical composition to Lennox Berkeley, Elliott Carter, Aaron Copland, Jean Francais, Thea Musgrave and Walter Piston. Nadia, however, never left a legacy of her own—just that of these modern composers. The mystery of musical composition continues!

December 18

Shopping

When women are depressed, they eat or go shopping. Men invade another country. It's a whole different way of thinking.

Elayne Booster

Shopping is better than sex. If you're not satisfied after shopping you can make an exchange for something you really like.

Adrienne Gusoff

I always say shopping is cheaper than a psychiatrist.

Tammy Faye Bakker

I am not a good shopper. My idea of shopping is to find a good website and order my stuff on the internet. My two favorite websites are Amazon.com and Tower records—both located in the good old U.S.A. Apple's iTunes is also right up there with 99-cent tunes, including karaoke. All this great music can be ordered without leaving home. That's my idea of shopping. There is one store here in Florida that we really like—ACE hardware. It's like an old-fashioned hardware store where they have everything, and they also know where it is. When you enter the store and begin to look around, somebody quickly asks, "How can we help you today?" It's like an old family-owned business, where they make you feel you are somebody. They actually want to help you!

Here's a shopping experience from last week at the food market. As our shopping carts collided in the store, a poor soul looked at me as if about to expire or worse. "Why so glum?" I gently inquired.

"It is just not a happy day," came the sad reply, "and now I've mashed your cart, and it's my fault. Sorry!"

"Hey, no damage done. But why so glum … what's the trouble?"

"It's nothing … just family problems! You wouldn't understand!"

"Hey … everybody has them," I suggested, "but pray for them, and maybe things will improve."

"Hmm … I never thought of that," was spoken as we went our ways to finish shopping. Later in the parking lot, I met this weary woman again—and received a wee smile and a mouthed "Thanks."

December 19

Autopilot

Give me odorous at sunrise a garden of beautiful flowers where I can walk undisturbed.

Walt Whitman

If you wait to do everything until you're sure it's right, you'll probably never do much of anything.

Win Borden

Don't let what you cannot do interfere with what you can do.

John Wooten

Lots of folks go through life on autopilot, accomplishing very little. How many times have you heard the excuse, "What's the use ... I just have bad luck!" Remaining in a state of operating the same way every day is a poor way to exist. Why do people continue to relive the same old day every day? Do you recall the movie *Groundhog Day*, where our hero the weatherman, played by Bill Murray, gets to live the same day repeatedly? Actually, the screenplay of this comedy was well written and makes you wonder how differently you would behave if you could indeed live the same day over again. Guess what? Folks on autopilot are doing just that—only they just keep making the same errors repeatedly.

When we forget to actually live as if every day could be our last day on earth, we may be inviting a self-fulfilling prophecy of failure. Autopilot just guarantees that we'll have the same old day, with the same old nonsense. We let what we cannot do interfere with what could happen, as coach Wooten so aptly puts it. Try to begin the day in a more proactive fashion. If you read the paper, listen to the news or watch morning news on T.V., the bad news or a passive activity won't fire you up. Begin with a routine which gives you some direction. Pray, meditate or do some activity which produces endorphins. Once you get a sense that you have already accomplished something, you feel like getting some more results out of your day, and you have the energy to do just that. Banish that autopilot!

December 20

Immortality

Everything will pass, and the world will perish, but the 9th Symphony will remain.

Michael Bakunin

Music is a higher revelation than all wisdom and philosophy: it is the wine of a new procreation, and I am Bacchus who presses out this glorious wine for men and makes them drunk with the spirit.

Ludwig van Beethoven

O Mozart, immortal Mozart, how many, how infinitely many inspiring suggestions of a finer, better life have you left in our souls!

Franz Schubert, Diary, 1816

The immortal god of harmony!

Ludwig van Beethoven ... on J.S. Bach

Shakespeare has been around for 400 years. It has been well over 200 years since Bach and Mozart wrote their masterpieces. It was 195 years ago, in early December, when Beethoven's 7th Symphony was first played. It was an immediate "hit" and still is to my mind the greatest symphony ever written—powerful and rhythmic. The question arises: WILL BEETHOVEN'S MUSIC BE AROUND IN ANOTHER 200 years?

Silly question! Of course it will—along with Elvis and the Beatles! Great music never grows old. Musical masterpieces, great poetry, prose and paintings are timeless. Works of celebrated art bestow immortality on their creators. Shakespeare will live forever!

This artistic immortality begs another question. Do great artists have a self-awareness of their immortality through their work? After all, many of the greatest composers, playwrights and painters faced scornful criticism during their lives. Many of Beethoven's middle works, such as the "Eroica" Symphony, met with outright negativity. Mahler's symphonies were received with stunned silence, as if listeners wondered, "What the hell is he trying to say?" Before he died in his 50's, Mahler knew the public couldn't understand his huge complex symphonies. Mahler believed in their worth, and he said before he died, "My time will come." He was correct. These magnificent, monolithic masterpieces are greatly loved by music devotees. Mahler's time has come, even if it took the better part of 100 years. Indeed, great art is timeless and grants immortality to its creator.

December 21

Messiah

Whether I was in my body or out of my body as I wrote it I know not. God knows.

George Frideric Handel

He is the greatest composer that ever lived. I would uncover my head and kneel before his tomb.

Ludwig van Beethoven

Handel is so great and so simple that no one but a professional musician is unable to understand him.

Samuel Butler

There is one piece of music that is too often sung before Christmas—Handel's *Messiah*. You can choose among a number of differing performances including a sing-along *Messiah*, in which the audience sits in four sections according to voice. Many people love the long oratorio, and everybody knows the "Hallelujah" chorus. I have sung the *Messiah*, whole and in pieces, in a number of different choirs. I'm afraid I disagree with Beethoven's above assessment of Handel. While some of Handel's writing is melodic and interesting, I find much of it incredibly tedious. Hearing the same lyrics sung repeatedly, with runs up and down the scales, actually irritates me. I have the same difficulty with some repetitious pop, like "If I had a million dollars." I would like to choke the sound right out of "artists" when I'm forced to listen to monotonous nonsense. That's how I feel about much of Handel's boring Baroque bombast. I suppose that's just too bad for me.

I love the story about the *Messiah* performance in an old English cathedral, which had a push-bellows organ. The bellows were located in the basement. The performance had always been conducted by the same choir director. A new guest conductor led a performance much more slowly than usual. Halfway through the "Hallelujah" chorus, the organ suddenly quit playing, forcing the whole performance to shut down. After a minute, a small door opened at the side of the chancel, and out stepped the grizzled old custodian (and organ bellows pusher.) He took one look at the shocked faces of the conductor, organist and choir, and announced in a loud voice, "*Messiah* takes exactly 5120 bellows pushes ... and you've had them all."

December 22

Road Rage

Insult is powerful. Insult begets both rage and humor and often at the same time.
Suzanne Fields

When you see someone who shows some aspect of road rage, separate yourself from them as quickly and safely as possible.
Automobile Insurance Flyer

As this busy time of the year, the roads become clogged with folks cramming in last-minute shopping trips just before Christmas. Folks should be in a decent frame of mind, but often it's just the reverse. It's best to avoid aggressive drivers and never become provoked with their "I own the road" attitude.

I was driving to a convention during morning rush hour when a driver in the lane beside me made lewd gestures at me and mouthed obscenities, including commentary on both my intelligence and driving. I had no idea what driving sin I had committed, but it must have been a dandy because she wasn't giving up until I responded. When traffic stopped at the next light, a torrent of obscenities came at us. My passenger friends were very embarrassed at the language. I left my window up and didn't respond. This driver then cut us off and proceeded to cut in and out of traffic, yelling at other drivers in front of us. She should have been on a racetrack. Maybe she thought she was, and my sin was just being in her way.

One of my passengers said to me, "I can't figure you out. You were driving well, and yet you sat there and took all that unfair abuse in front of your friends. How can you do that?" The explanation is simple. To lapse is human. If we responded to every person's lapse with the same rage they display, our days would be full of confrontation and not much fun. I try to ignore drivers who seem to welcome confrontation. That way, you can avoid getting upset while driving and have a more relaxing trip.

The same approach can be used in any situation—even in a crowded store of shoppers trying to get their last minute shopping done. If you relax and insist on excusing all perceived rudeness, you are the recipient of a better day. Courtesy is contagious. Try it today—use that *"look of love"* from the laid back champion of courtesy—Sir Peter U.

December 23

Thin Places

SKLEROKARDIA … a Greek word meaning 'sclerosis of the heart' where a person's heart is 'hard-hearted' or 'proud, puffed up and enlarged' or 'made of stone' rather than made of flesh.

A thin place is anywhere our hearts are opened … a mediator of the sacred … a place where we feel God … a means of grace …

Both from Marcus Borg *The Heart of Christianity*

Have you had experiences where the presence of a divine spirit seemed tangible? You could also describe these experiences as a feeling that God seemed to be very close to you. Marcus Borg calls these experiences "thin places", when the layers of our humanity seem to be stripped away to reveal the divine. In his book, before he discusses thin places, Borg spends time explaining why many people never experience spirituality. Borg suggests that the reason may be "sklerokardia." As we experience the challenges of life, we may find that we survive better by putting on a layer of protective armor. If we see the world as threatening, a good tough layer may seem just the answer for many people. Folks who are used to keeping a big buffer zone of protection around them may perceive spirituality as something for "softies" who just can't "cut the mustard" in a competitive world. Unfortunately, this armor or buffer zone may result in sklerokardia, a hardened heart.

How do we escape this condition? We can try to open our hearts to the thin places available to us. A thin place may be geographical—a holy place—or in nature itself where we can see the glory of God. It could be in the arts—in music, poetry, literature or visual arts and dance. People can become thin places.

Perhaps the most astounding thin place is pure meditative silence itself— "Be still and know that I am God."

December 24

Greatest Gift

Give what you have; to some it may be better than what you dare to think.
Henry Wadsworth Longfellow

Christmas Eve is a time for joyous anticipation. My favorite story of anticipation is the story of the miracle of the bells. As I recall, it goes something like this. (Please pardon the embellishments.)

Once upon a time in a small town, the people lived in various conditions, just as they do today. There were rich, poor and middle-class folk, just as there are today. It was a small town like most small towns, except for one thing. This town had the largest church in the country. In this church, there was a huge belfry with the most magnificent bells. The problem was that these bells were so many and so large that nobody had ever been found to ring them to their full potential. There was, however, a rumor that the greatest gift given on Christmas Eve mass would please God so much that God would ring the bells. Although the event had never happened, each year the people lived in great anticipation that this would be the year the miracle would occur, and the bells would ring out.

Now this particular year had been tough. The economy was in recession. Many people were out of work. The weather had been poor. The crops had failed. People were living on the edge. They needed a miracle like never before. At the traditional Christmas Eve service, the church was packed. At the offertory, many gifts were stacked on the altar. Rich people gave large amounts of money, jewels and other riches. Fortunes were offered, but no bells rang. After everyone had made their offering, an old woman hobbled up and quietly placed something very small on the altar. People paid her little heed. She was the local bag lady. Folks avoided her. The priest was about to continue with the mass when suddenly the bells began to ring. The miracle had happened—and what a wonder it was. The tolling of the bells was the most beautiful sound people had ever heard. The people strained to see what the old lady had given. What was her great gift that had given them the miracle? Only the priest was close enough to see what it was—a dirty old penny! How could this be? How could this penny bring the miracle when all the riches had failed? Simple! The woman had given a penny—but it was all she had. (See Mark 12:41-44 and Luke 21:1-4 for *The Widow's Offering*.)

December 25

Christmas

Christmas waves a magic wand over this world, and behold, everything is softer and more beautiful.

Norman Vincent Peale

He who has not Christmas in his heart will never find it under a tree.

Roy L. Smith

Christmas, children, is not a date. It is a state of mind.

Mary Ellen Chase

Christmas is the gentlest, loveliest festival of the revolving year - and yet, for all that, when it speaks, its voice has strong authority.

W.J. Cameron

We sang "I'm dreaming of a White Christmas" last night in our Christmas Eve show here in the trailer park. There isn't a speck of snow anywhere around here. In fact, it was 80 degrees in the shade today. Yet—everybody is in the spirit. The pavilion here has huge white snowflakes hanging from the ceiling. Giant Christmas cards adorn the walls—works of art lovingly done by park residents. Colorful Christmas trees and strings of lights are everywhere and huge parties occur all day. This mindset where everybody is loved "all to bits" is the attitude in our RV Park. Most folks are in a Christmas mood all year—without one snowfall.

I love what Dickens says about Christmas. Don't you wish we could have this "kind, forgiving, charitable time" all year long?

"I have always thought of Christmas time, when it has come round, as a good time; a kind, forgiving, charitable time; the only time I know of, in the long calendar of the year, when men and women seem by one consent to open their shut-up hearts freely, and to think of people below them as if they really were fellow passengers to the grave, and not another race of creatures bound on journeys."

Charles Dickens

December 26

Paradise

The mind is its own place and in itself can make a heaven of hell ... or a hell of heaven.
John Milton, Paradise Lost (See July 28.)

People are about as happy as they make up the minds to be.
Abraham Lincoln

I love the Christmas story about the twins. One was an optimist and the other a pessimist. The parents were always at a loss as to what to get them. After much deliberation, they thought they had the answer. On Christmas morning the twins were instructed to go to different rooms. The little pessimist entered a room with a huge tree decorated as befits the royal family. In this room were mountains of gifts which were torn into and opened in no time at all. After he finished with the last gift, he lamented, "Is this all there is?"

Meanwhile, our little optimist entered a room where there was a tiny tree with a tiny box under the tree. Our optimist was delighted by the cute wee stuff, and after looking at them for a while she carefully opened the box. The little optimist was taken aback for a moment at the contents of the box—a tiny pile of frightfully fresh dung! Then she looked around the room with wide eyes and proclaimed, "Ho, ho, ho ... they can't fool me ... where there is manure, there has to be a pony!"

We said yesterday that folks down here are generally happy all the time—and why not? The weather is mostly sunny and warm. There are plenty of activities and no really competitive folks to spoil the play. Everybody seems to as happy as a pig in pooh! There are lots of dogs, bicycles, golf clubs and kayaks in the park, and lots of time to play and socialize. There also seems to be an unwritten law: "NO WHINERS ALLOWED AT RIVERSIDE!" It begins in the office and is contagious. The word "paradise" is heard every day. As Lincoln suggests, the folks who live here have made up their minds that they live in a heaven—and so they do!

361

December 27

Engineers

Scientists dream about doing great things. Engineers do them.

James A. Michener

One has to look out for engineers ... they begin with sewing machines and end up with the atomic bomb.

Marcel Pagnol

To define it rudely ... engineering is the art of doing that well with one dollar, which any bungler can do with two after a fashion.

Arthur Wellesley

Have you ever heard somebody say, "Engineers and accountants are boring people," or "Teachers can't really do anything and that's why they teach," or "Lawyers are all shysters"? I have heard these statements from folks who are making the same mistake kids make. They are stereotyping—tarring a whole group with the same brush. I used to tell my students, "Never stereotype people." Yet some adults do it all the time. Sure, there may be boring engineers, or teachers who can't do much, or dishonest lawyers—but I've never met many. All the engineers I know are funny folks who are knowledgeable and a delight to talk to. Most of the teachers I know volunteer at a variety of things and are terrific organizers. If you hear someone stereotype a group of people, let them know about a terrific person who happens to be a member of that group—and remember, "NO STEREOTYPING!"

An engineer was crossing a road one day, when a frog called out to him and said, "If you kiss me, I'll turn into a beautiful princess."

He bent over, picked up the frog and put it in his pocket. The frog spoke up again and said, "If you kiss me and turn me back into a beautiful princess, I will stay with you for one week ... and do ANYTHING you want."

The engineer took the frog out of his pocket, smiled at it and put it back into his pocket. Finally, the frog asked, "What is the matter? I've told you I'm a beautiful princess and that I'll stay with you for one week and do anything you want. Why won't you kiss me?"

The engineer said, "Look, I'm an engineer. I don't have time for a girlfriend ... but a talking frog ... now that's cool."

December 28

Self-reliance

Happiness is not the absence of problems; but the ability to deal with them.
Author Unknown

Self-reliance is like a flashlight; no matter how dark it gets, it will help you find your way.
Author Unknown

Self-reliance is the only road to true freedom, and being one's own person is its ultimate reward.
Patricia Sampson

The dogs in the pound were fit to be tied. For some unexplained reason, the keeper hadn't shown up on that particular day, and water was running low. "Where is he?" All the dogs whined in unison. "We can't last another night without water." Then the Golden Labrador got lucky. His cage door was loose and he frantically pushed on it. Suddenly it flew open. "Three woofs for the Lab," all the dogs howled ... "Now find our food, and quickly!"

But the poor Lab whined, "How am I supposed to know where the chow comes from? It simply appears." The dogs all began to howl at their hopeless situation—until the keeper finally showed up, having been delayed by the worst snowstorm in a decade. The mutts were saved at last. Hooray!

Domesticated animals and small children are totally dependent on their "keepers." Left to their own devices, they wouldn't last long in the real world. The human baby is the most helpless of all earth's creatures. It takes a couple of decades for most humans to become self-reliant. (Some never make it.) The greatest accomplishment a person can have is to finally achieve true independence. There is a long list of learning which must occur for this to really happen. As a teacher, my number one objective was to show students how to learn how to learn so they wouldn't need me. That sounds like double talk, but what it means is that instilling the tool for life-long learning—self-reliance—is the greatest gift we can ever give our children.

December 29

A Banquet

Life's a banquet and most poor suckers are starving to death!
... Auntie Mame

Patrick Dennis

Someone gave a great dinner and invited many ... but they all alike began to make excuses ... please accept my regrets ... I cannot come.
From Luke 14   The Parable of the Great Dinner

The kingdom of God is not coming with things that can be observed ... for, in fact, the kingdom of God is among you.
Luke: 20-21

I love the story of the great banquet. A fellow threw a lavish party, but all his friends made excuses why they couldn't come. In the story, one fellow had just bought some land. Another had just bought a team of oxen. A third had just gotten married. How often have we used those excuses? Hardly ever—probably never! We do, however, have a plethora of our own excuses for refusing invitations:

"Somebody has to look after the dog/cat/fish/birds."

"I've got more important fish to fry ... I've no time for frivolity!"

"I'm up to my armpits in alligators."

"I would but I'm sick ... I can barely keep my head above water."

... and everybody's favorite all-time excuse: "I'm too busy!"

Isn't it a shame that in filling up our lives with business and busyness, we miss out so many invitations to enjoy the banquet which surrounds us. The world is a huge ongoing invitation—beckoning us in a multitude of ways. We are called every minute to the feast of nature, friendship and fantasy. It's akin to being in toy-land—and choosing not to play. Must we always choose not to enter into the kingdom?

Today I will accept every invitation into the kingdom. Today, I will stop and smell the roses.

December 30

The Number Game

One is the loneliest number worse than two.

From the Three Dog Night song "One"

John saw duh numbah dat no man could numbuh

From a Negro Spiritual

If you think dogs can't count, try putting three dog biscuits in your pocket and then giving Fido only two of them.

Phil Pastoret

The single digit numbers were arguing over which of them deserved the greatest respect. ZERO claimed that he was greatest since "anything divided by zero is huge … infinitely so."

ONE retorted, "Humans are always chanting 'We're number one!' Everything can be represented digitally by zero and one, including all other numbers so all other numbers are superfluous!" said ONE.

TWO claimed, "Everything comes in two … partners, couples and all the animals that originally lined up to get on board the ark."

THREE began to speak but the rest of the numbers showed no respect; shouting, "Two is company but three is a crowd!"

… "But, but, but" cried poor THREE, "think of the Trinity!"

FOUR harmoniously sang, "There are four parts in choirs and in quartets!"

FIVE chimed, "Five fingers on each hand and five toes on each foot!"

SIX was shouted down as being twice as bad as three. "Six sides to a cube … and I'm the biggest number on a die … and everybody knows a half dozen!"

SEVEN chortled, "I'm the luckiest number … and remember … seven candles on a Temple menorah!"

EIGHT claimed to be the most stable since "Eight electrons in the outer shell is the most stable configuration … a stable octet."

Before NINE could stake the claim, the other numbers shouted in derision, "Nine is the worse number of all … being just three times three."

"OK then," replied NINE, "why did Beethoven, Schubert, Bruckner, Dvorak and Mahler each write nine symphonies? Because nine is the perfect number, and everybody has heard Beethoven's Ninth!"

Sing an "ODE to JOY" for the greatest number of all, the number NINE.

December 31

Writing

Writing is making sense of life. You work your whole life and perhaps you've made sense of one small area.

Nadine Gordimer

Be yourself. Above all, let who you are, what you are, what you believe, shine through every sentence you write, every piece you finish.

John Jakes

The difficulty of literature is not to write, but to write what you mean.

Robert Louis Stevenson

I love talking about nothing. It is the only thing I know anything about.

Oscar Wilde

And so we come to the last day of the year. Why did we begin the journey together in the first place? I suppose it began with the same idea in mind as any journey begins. We need a sense of purpose, a sense of accomplishment, a way of identifying ourselves so others may have some idea of who we are. As one of our earlier quotes suggested, we must let out whatever is stored up inside us. Each of us has that desire of expression. It may be one of an enormous variety of human expressions—playing games, dancing, working, inventing, caring for others, nurturing—the list goes on forever. Writing is only one way of expressing how we feel—but in one way, it may be the most private of all forms of expression. After all, if you can write volumes but without readers, what does it mean? What is the use of a private diary? May I suggest that the introspective process of diary or journal writing is a wonderful way of reliving those sublime moments and of relieving any hostile feelings? We can put it all down and then have a good laugh or maybe a good cry—but now it's out there, instead of just being inside us. Let it all out—on paper. Include the baggage—especially the baggage and the trash. I have discovered through this process that it comes out more often in a way which allows you to have a real good laugh—at yourself.

It is my hope that along the way, you have also been able to laugh or cry at some of my notions, stories, ramblings and reflections. Perhaps you have recognized along with me that life is something to be continually celebrated.

Hooray and Hallelujah—and especially—Jubilate!

CPSIA information can be obtained at www.ICGtesting.com
Printed in the USA
LVOW122311231012

304179LV00001B/6/P